Water for All

Water for All

Community, Property, and Revolution in Modern Bolivia

Sarah T. Hines

UNIVERSITY OF CALIFORNIA PRESS

University of California Press
Oakland, California

Library of Congress Cataloging-in-Publication Data
    Names: author. Hines, Sarah T., author.
 Title: Water for all : community, property, and revolution in modern
Bolivia / Sarah T. Hines.
    Description: Oakland, California : University of California Press, [2021]
| Includes bibliographical references and index.
    Identifiers: LCCN 2021018749 (print) | LCCN 2021018750 (ebook) |
ISBN 9780520381636 (hardback) | ISBN 9780520381643 (paperback) |
ISBN 9780520381650 (ebook)
    Subjects: LCSH: Water-supply—Bolivia—Cochabamba—History. |
Social movements—Bolivia.
    Classification: LCC HD1696.B54 C6333 2021 (print) | LCC HD1696.B54
(ebook) | DDC 333.91009864/23—dc23
    LC record available at https://lccn.loc.gov/2021018749
    LC ebook record available at https://lccn.loc.gov/2021018750

Manufactured in the United States of America

25   24   23   22   21
10   9   8   7   6   5   4   3   2   1

To my parents, Sheldon Hines and Virginia Bradley Hines

CONTENTS

List of Illustrations   ix

Acknowledgments   xi

A Note on Terminology   xvii

   Introduction   1

1. Water for Those Who Own It: Drought, Dispossession, and
    Modernization in the Liberal Era   19

2. Engineering Water Reform: Military Socialism and Hydraulic
    Development   48

3. Water for Those Who Use It: Agrarian Reform and Hydraulic
    Revolution   81

4. Popular Engineering: Hydraulic Governance and Expertise under
    Dictatorship   121

5. The Water Is Ours: Water Privatization and War in Neoliberal Bolivia   151

6. After the War: Water and the Making of Plurinational Bolivia   195

   Conclusion: Water for All   225

Appendix: Maximum Holdings under the 1953 Agrarian Reform Decree Law   229

Abbreviations   231

Notes   233

References   277

Index   301

ILLUSTRATIONS

FIGURES

1. Topography of Bolivia 6
2. Cochabamba haciendas and water sources in the early twentieth century 33
3. The city of Cochabamba looking northeast from San Sebastián Hill, circa 1920 41
4. The Angostura dam under construction, circa 1945 56
5. Peasants and President Victor Paz Estenssoro celebrate the Agrarian Reform Decree Law in Ucureña, 2 August 1953 88
6. Lake Wara Wara in the 1920s 101
7. Cover of *Bolivia: 10 años de revolución (1952–62)* 119
8. Cochabamba mayor Francisco Baldi inspecting a water project, 1967 129
9. March from Vinto and Sipe Sipe to Cochabamba, October 1994 170
10. Crowd gathered in Cochabamba's 14 de Septiembre Plaza during the last battles of the Water War in April 2000 192
11. Banner reading "¡El agua es nuestra, carajo!" ("The water is ours, damn it!") hangs from the balcony of the Central Obrera Departmental (COD) building in Cochabamba's 14 de Septiembre Plaza during the final mobilizations of the Water War, April 2000 194
12. March against the Sacaba water service's plan to "municipalize" neighborhood cooperatives and irrigators' water sources, Cochabamba, September 2011 213
13. Lake Wara Wara and its dam, May 2011 214
14. El Paso residents protest efforts by Cochabamba's municipal water service SEMAPA and Quillacollo's municipal water service EMAPAQ to take over wells drilled for El Paso in the 1990s, August 2011 215
15. Lake Wara Wara overlooking Cochabamba's Central Valley, May 2011 217

MAPS

1. Bolivia   *xix*
2. The Cochabamba region   *9*
3. Distribution of lands by Inca emperor Huayna Capac   *22*
4. Cochabamba's colonial-era *pueblos reales de indios*   *23*
5. Plano de la ciudad de Cochabamba, 1899   *37*
6. Urban expansion and municipal water coverage, 1940   *63*
7. Cochabamba's Central Valley and the Tunari Mountains   *67*
8. City of Cochabamba neighborhoods and zones   *93*
9. Tiquipaya haciendas and irrigation systems   *103*
10. The Misicuni project   *138*
11. Cochabamba metropolitan area water coverage, 1994   *154*

ACKNOWLEDGMENTS

Researching, writing, and revising this book was a labor of love that took a decade. At one point along the way, someone asked me, what's the rush? While I can by no means claim to have hurried, it felt urgent to finish and publish this book, for it represents the work and experience of many communities: an academic community of researchers, archivists, colleagues, and mentors. A personal community of family and friends. And a community of water activists, policy makers, and users who made the history recounted here. This is their story and history. I hope that my version of it does them justice. My most important debt is to them.

Research and writing were made possible by generous financial support from the Social Science Research Council, the Inter-American Foundation, the University of California, Berkeley Institute for International Studies, the UC Berkeley Graduate Division, Barnard College's Alumnae Association, the Conference on Latin American History, the American Historical Association, the Fulbright Program, the US Department of Education, the Mellon Foundation, the American Council of Learned Societies, and the University of Oklahoma's College of Arts and Sciences. The OU History Department provided me with an indispensable semester of leave to finish revisions. I am grateful to the people behind the scenes at each of these institutions.

Archivists, librarians, engineers, and water users facilitated document collection and oral historical research in Bolivia, the Netherlands, and the United States. Special thanks to Iviça Tadic at the Biblioteca Arturo Costa de la Torre, Luis Oporto of the Bolivian Congressional Archive, Rossana Barragán at the Archivo de La Paz, Cecelia Illanes Iriarte at the Centro de Documentación e Información Bolivia (CEDIB), and Cristina, Guido, Guy, and Estefanía at Cochabamba's Municipal Archive. Thanks also goes to staff at the International Institute for Social History in

Amsterdam, Bolivia's National Archive and Library, the Bolivian National Meteorological and Hydrological Service, the German Technical Cooperation Agency (GTZ), Cochabamba's Colegio de Arquitectos, the Cochabamba Irrigators' Union FEDECOR (Federación Departamental Cochabambina de Organizaciones Regantes), Fundación Simón Patiño, and the Universidad Mayor de San Simón (UMSS), Universidad Mayor de San Andrés (UMSA), UC Berkeley, Smith College, the University of Maine at Machias, and the University of Oklahoma Libraries.

Research took me to the archives of the institutions I was studying, including those of the World Bank, the Inter-American Development Bank (IDB), the Empresa Misicuni, Cochabamba's municipal water company SEMAPA (Servicio Municipal de Agua Potable y Alcantarillado), the Cochabamba department planning office, and the Cochabamba branch of the agrarian reform service INRA (Instituto Nacional de la Reforma Agraria). I am grateful to Sherrine Thompson at the World Bank, Jean Paul Velez at the IDB, Guadalupe Escalante Lunario at the Empresa Misicuni, and Edmundo Arce and Magda Thames at Cochabamba's departmental archive. Antonio Camacho at INRA-Cochabamba graciously shared a corner of his busy desk with me, trusted me to search the shelves for what became some of my most cherished sources, and let me work through lunch. A special thank you to Samuel Gareca at SEMAPA. Justina Arispe led me to her neighbors and relatives' homes in the folds of Tirani's foothills, where she translated between Quechua and Spanish. I am grateful to Tirani community members and other water users across the valley for opening their homes and offices to me and sharing their stories and documents. Thanks to Zenobio Siles Sainz, who assisted me with research in the Misicuni Valley.

I have benefited from the guidance and instruction of talented and dedicated teachers from my early years. Judy Judson, the late James Patty, Doc Miller, Steve Mancini, Elliot Lilien, Andrei Joseph, Kevin Harding, William Ireland, Denis Cleary, Victoria Moskowitz, and Maura Roberts helped kindle passions for history and literature. At Barnard College and Columbia University, Pablo Piccato, Ben Vinson, Herbert Klein, and Jaime Rodriguez were wonderful teachers of Latin American history and the historical method. At the City College of New York (CCNY), Amon Diggs was an inspiring teacher and example. At UC Berkeley, Robin Einhorn, David Henkin, and Michael Watts opened up new worlds. Richard Candida-Smith provided incisive comments on my work, and Gill Hart encouraged me to develop the spatial aspect of the project.

Three mentors deserve special recognition. I first discussed the idea for this book with Mark Healey, who has shepherded its author and provided wise council ever since. Both he and Margaret Chowning encouraged me to question my assumptions, let myself be surprised, and take people seriously on their own terms. Brooke Larson encouraged me to go back to Cochabamba and provided invaluable advice and feedback at multiple stages. All three are model mentors, historians, colleagues, and friends.

In Berkeley I found a supportive community of fellow graduate students and friends who worked intensely by day and cooked and communed by night. Thanks to Celso Castilho and Camilo Trumper for the warm welcome and *fútbol* and to my fellow *latinoamericanistas*, especially Lynsay Skiba, Germán Vergara, Javier Cikota, Becca Herman Weber, Alberto García, and Andra Brosy Chastain. Leigh Johnson, Rachel Chodorow-Reich, Nick Kardajhi, Charles Shaw, Gabe Hetland, Alisa Sánchez, Dmitri Seals, Brian Palmer-Rubin, Emily Hamilton, and Xochitl Marsilli were wonderful officemates, roommates, running partners, and friends. Most of all, I am grateful to the camaraderie of my fellow "Sarahs"—Sarah Selvidge and Pablo Palomino—for their steadfast friendship, humor, and wit. Thank you to Barbara and the late Bob Selvidge for meals and conversations, and to Sarah and Greg, Eleni, and Felix Leventis for being like family.

A transnational community of Bolivianistas helped me steer this project forward. The late Tom Lewis encouraged me to embark on this journey. Sinclair Thomson gave ongoing guidance. Matt Gildner, Hernán Pruden, and Jeff Webber helped me get started. Carwil Bjork-James, Cristina Cielo, Ben Dangl, Jorge Delpic, Susan Ellison, Nate Freiburger, Lesli Hoey, April Howard, Alder Keleman, Andrea Marston, Julia McDowell, Pablo Quisbert, Huaskar Rodriguez, Mariela Rodriguez, Raul Rodriguez, Miriam Seefrau, Sara Shahriari, Susan Spronk, Chuck Sturtevant, Jason Tockman, Simon Tu, Anna Walnycki, Bridgette Werner, and Mareike Winchell were collaborators and friends during research and since. Karl Swinehart put me up in at least three cities. Nancy Egan, Elena McGrath, Ben Nobbs-Thiessen, Nicole Pacino, and Liz Shesko gave helpful comments on drafts. Kevin Young read more versions of the manuscript than almost anyone. Carmen Soliz read drafts, provided boundless counsel, and gave me a home away from home in La Paz, where Silvia Urrutia and the late Andrés Soliz Rada welcomed me to meals and conversation at their bright kitchen table. Thanks also to Pamela Calla, Steve Cote, Linda Farthing, Thomas Grisaffi, Laura Gotkowitz, and Gabi Kuenzli.

A community of researchers, mentors, and friends in Cochabamba made this project possible. Janine and Joaquin Hinojosa collected me at the bus station when I visited Cochabamba for the first time in 2004 and were generous guides thereafter. Gustavo Rodríguez Cáceres was a mentor across projects. Rocio Bustamante offered leads and feedback, and she and Alfredo Durán provided vital assistance in obtaining a residency visa. Carlos Crespo invited me to work at the Centro de Estudios Superiores Universitarios (CESU), where a corner desk became a refuge where much of this book was written. His door was always open, and his belief in this project and his friendship helped me soldier on. Thanks to Manuel de la Fuente, Alejandra Ramirez, Vicky Salamanca, Alba Rojas, and Don Victor for folding me in. Members of CESU's Misicuni Project Working Group (including Carlos, Rocio, Pablo Regalsky, Julián Pérez, and Gonzalo Maldonado) shared their knowledge and gave useful feedback. Marina Sturich offered wise council, Marcelo Delgadillo always answered my questions, and Oscar Olivera encouraged me from the start. Meals at Marcela Olivera's home gave much-needed respites from research and writing, and her feedback and assistance later on were invaluable. Thanks also to Aliya Ellenby, Chelo Arias, Julianne Chandler, Pedro Rodriguez, Ida Peñaranda, Lenny Peñaranda, Fernando Machicao, Michael Shanks, Kathryn Lederbur, Jessie Robinson, Heidi Baer-Postigo, Jim Schultz, Lynn Nesslebush, and Lee Cridland. Words cannot express my appreciation for Magena Badani.

I finished writing and revising this book at Smith College, the University of Maine at Machias, and the University of Oklahoma. I am grateful to my students at Smith, UMM, and OU for reminding me who we write for and why. At Smith, Jeff Ahlman, Josh Birk, Sergey Glebov, and Liz Pryor provided insightful comments on early drafts. At OU, I am fortunate to have found supportive communities within the History Department and the Center for the Americas. I am especially grateful to Jim Cane, David Chappell, Jennifer Davis, Fabio De Sa e Silva, Lauren Duval, Elyssa Faison, Raphie Folsom, Jamie Hart, Sandie Holguín, Jenn Holland, Anne Hyde, Charlie Kenney, Adam Malka, Mandy Minks, Michelle Morais, Rhona Seidelman, Janet Ward, and the members of Committee G for their support, guidance, and camaraderie. Special thanks to Mabel Lee, Lyn Minnich, Christine Alexander, Janie Adkins, and Christa Seedorf for their support, and to Taylor Cozzens for his assistance.

Several people read the full manuscript in its final stages. I would like to thank Sinclair Thomson, Mikael Wolfe, and Kevin Young who reviewed the book for the University of California Press. I am also grateful to Gil Joseph, Chris Boyer, Kathy Brosnan, and Dan Mains for participating in a manuscript workshop sponsored by the OU Humanities Forum and to members of the Oklahoma Latin American History Workshop for doing the same. Brooke Larson, Jose Gordillo, Sarah Foss, and an anonymous member of the University of California Press editorial committee also commented on the full manuscript. Sarah Selvidge edited the final manuscript with care and grace. All of these readers' insightful questions, comments, and suggestions were tremendously helpful as I made revisions. I have tried to respond to them all, but any remaining errors or shortcomings are my responsibility alone.

I am also grateful to the individuals and institutions that granted permission to use the maps, photographs, and illustrations included in this book, especially Roberto Mamani Mamani whose painting graces the cover. Stacy Eisenstark at UC Press has guided this project to completion. Thanks go to her, Naja Pulliam Collins, David Peattie, Amy Smith Bell, PJ Heim, and the rest of the production team who delivered this book into the world despite a pandemic, wildfires, and other challenges.

A community of friends has sustained me over the years. Katherine Haver, Molly Greene, and Bethany Cagen have been like sisters for more than two decades, as have my Barnard crew, Brittany Retherford, Ori Scherr, Caroline Whalen, Margaret Woollatt, and Jessie Kindig. Andrew Decker, who passed away far too early, will always be in my heart. In Norman, Elyse Singer, Leslie Kraus, Brandin Steffensen, Erin Duncan-O'Neill, Robbie Craig, Tess Elliot, Amy Clark, Matt Pailes, Traci Voyles, Jennifer Saltzstein, Brian Chance, Joan Hamory, and all their littles have made this place home. Many more friends have been there along the way than I can name here; you know who you are—thank you.

I am thankful to my daughters' caretakers and teachers—from Cochabamba to Northampton to East Machias to Norman. They made research and writing possible.

Finally, I could not have written this book without the love and support of my family. My grandmother, the late Betty Anne Matchette Adams, always believed in me, even when she didn't quite understand what I was up to. Thanks to my siblings, Andrew and Anna, my nephew Ananda, and my aunt and cousins. My mother and father, Virginia Bradley Hines and Sheldon Hines, taught me to value truth, act with integrity, and seek justice by their example.

This book would not be the same without the contributions of Jorge Camacho Saavedra, who created the book's maps and illustrations, conducted follow-up interviews, tracked down image permissions, and talked this project through with me from the beginning.

Over the course of this project two little munchkins arrived who mean the world to me. Maia was born as I was finishing dissertation research. Nina was born days after I accepted a new job as my dissertation deadline loomed. They have been a joy at every step ever since. *Les amo tanto.* So much.

A NOTE ON TERMINOLOGY

Studying the history of social struggle over water involves understanding the relationship of different social groups to land and water. As land bounded and held water sources, legal rights to land and obligations of workers to landowners defined the terms of struggle. Haciendas were large landed estates first established in the colonial period. *Hacendados* owned hacienda land with associated water rights. *Colonos* were estate workers who provided *hacendados* with labor and personal service in exchange for usufruct rights to small plots of hacienda land and irrigation water. *Arrimantes*, landless rural laborers who worked for *colonos*, were often referred to as "the colonos of the colonos." *Piqueros* were independent smallholders who owned plots of land, with or without corresponding irrigation rights. *Comunarios* are members of a rural community. *Campesino*, "peasant" in English, refers to people who cultivated small or medium-sized parcels of land, whether they owned them or not, even if they did not call themselves *campesinos*. I study the development of *campesino* as a class category and a political identity as historical processes. *Campesino* usually refers to subsistence-oriented agricultural producers, but agricultural wage laborers and farmers who grow cash crops for sale on the market on a small scale sometimes consider themselves *campesinos* as well.

The terms "Indian," "indigenous," and "native" refer to individuals or groups identifying or being identified by others as having ancestral and/or cultural ties to peoples who lived in the Americas before the arrival of Europeans. "Mestizo" refers to people of mixed ancestry and/or cultural traditions. "Creole" refers to people of Spanish descent born and raised in the Americas. Although popular usage in the United States is changing, I follow the standard approach in the field of Latin American history, which is not to capitalize terms such as "indigenous," "native," and "mestizo." I use lowercase so as not to reify these categories, to signal that they are constantly in flux, and because their equivalents are not capitalized in Spanish. The exception is the term "Indian," which is conventionally capitalized in English. These are loose definitions of terms whose uses and meanings have changed over time and been fiercely contested. I employ these terms differently depending on the context and explore their evolving uses and meanings in relationship to social struggles over water.

MAP 1. Bolivia. Created by the Central Intelligence Agency, 2006. Map in public domain, accessed via University of Texas Libraries, Perry-Castañeda Library Map Collection, https://legacy.lib.utexas.edu/maps/americas/bolivia_pol-2006.pdf.

Introduction

"Our lakes are not natural," Javier Molina told me as we sat by a soccer field perched in the foothills above the city of Cochabamba, Bolivia on a sparkling day in the austral winter of 2011. "They were built," he explained, "in the time of *pongueaje* by *colono* labor."[1] Molina was an elected leader of the peasant union of Tirani, a rapidly urbanizing agricultural community nestled in the foothills of the Tunari Mountains that crown the northern rim of Cochabamba's Central Valley. The community holds rights to two mountain lakes, San Juan and San Pablito, which provide irrigation water to its corn, bean, alfalfa, and flower fields and drinking water to its residents. A legacy of Bolivia's coercive unpaid labor on estates (*pongueaje*), the lakes also exemplify water users' ongoing efforts to defend and establish autonomous collective control over the Cochabamba region's water sources. Tirani splits rights to the lakes with Cochabamba's municipal water company SEMAPA (Servicio Municipal de Agua Potable y Alcantarillado), but Tirani's share is hard-won community property.

Every year for more than a century, Tirani community members have climbed the steep mountainside, laden with tools, supplies, and provisions, to maintain the dams and canals that capture and channel lake water to their fields. Hacienda *colonos*, estate workers with usufruct rights to small plots of land, built the lakes' dams and canals at the turn of the twentieth century. Over the next five decades, *colonos* maintained and expanded this hydraulic infrastructure on behalf of, and mostly for the benefit of, a series of *patrones*, the owners of large estates called haciendas. After the 1952 Bolivian revolution, Tirani *colonos* were among the tens of thousands of Bolivian estate workers who won hacienda land, water sources, and irrigation infrastructure through unauthorized seizures and government-

1

sponsored agrarian reform.[2] From that time forward, Tirani community members have claimed the San Juan Lakes and accompanying irrigation infrastructure as community property, even as they share rights to the lakes with the city. On their annual pilgrimage up the mountain, ex-*colono* communities like Tirani not only make necessary repairs, they also assert their right to own, control, and use water sources and systems they inherited from their ancestors. Their treks and labor make their property claims visible to state officials and their neighbors and constitute the basis for these claims.

The shift from hacienda ownership to community and municipal ownership of the San Juan Lakes was part of a broader democratization of water access and governance in Cochabamba in the twentieth century. At the beginning of the century, rural estate owners hoarded water sources that the growing urban population, independent smallholders, and hacienda *colonos* needed for irrigation and drinking water. By the turn of the twenty-first century, in contrast, a plethora of public water utilities and water-using communities owned and controlled water sources like the San Juan Lakes that had been hacienda property a century before. This book tells the story of the struggle for the democratization of water in Cochabamba over more than a century that brought about that sea change. It argues that democratization owed to the efforts of communities of water users who transformed Cochabamba's water tenure regime in the twentieth century through their labor, planning, protest, purchases, and seizures of previously hoarded water sources.

The watershed moment in this process came after the 1952 revolution, when hacienda *colonos* like Javier Molina's grandparents won land and water rights away from hacienda owners. These new land and water owners joined independent smallholder (*piquero*) communities who already held water rights and the municipal water company as water owners. Over the seven decades after the revolution, the constellation of water owners grew to include peripheral neighborhood residents who built independent water systems and acquired rights to mountain lakes and mountainside springs. Piquero communities, ex-*colono* peasant unions, and neighborhood water cooperatives all performed collective labor in the mountains to maintain their access and rights to water sources like the San Juan Lakes in these years. But in early 2000, instead of traveling up the mountainside to sustain their flows, they headed down into the core of the valley to do battle in what became known as the Cochabamba Water War.

A CENTURY OF STRUGGLE

In April 2000, Molina and other Tirani *comunarios* joined a massive popular uprising against water privatization that shut down the city of Cochabamba. Local groups had been organizing for several months against the national government's decision to privatize water in the Cochabamba Valley. In late 1999 the government granted a contract to Aguas del Tunari, a consortium of companies that included the US construction giant Bechtel, to administer water sources and provision in the department capital and surrounding valleys. The new company dramatically increased water rates for municipal customers and took over independent drinking water systems in periurban neighborhoods and irrigation networks in agricultural communities. In response, protestors from across the region occupied city streets, erected barricades, and held assemblies to make proposals and decisions. Rather than negotiate, the government dispatched soldiers and police who unleashed tear gas, clubs, and bullets, leaving a seventeen-year-old bystander dead and more than one hundred wounded. Undeterred, the protestors regrouped and their numbers grew.[3]

Remarkably, the protestors won. In response to the uprising, the Bolivian Congress modified a November 1999 water law that permitted the state to grant exclusive water rights to private firms, and Hugo Banzer, the former dictator turned democratically elected president, canceled the government's contract with Aguas del Tunari. News of the Cochabamba Water War quickly spread around the globe. Global justice activists celebrated Cochabamba's victory against neoliberal privatization policies, and within days the movement's principal spokesperson, factory union leader Oscar Olivera, traveled to Washington, DC, to join protests against the World Bank and the International Monetary Fund. Water privatization had sparked protests from Atlanta to Johannesburg to Delhi to Jakarta, but Cochabambinos were the first to overturn it.[4] Anti-privatization activists and pro-privatization international financial institutions the world over took notice, whether to invigorate their own anti-privatization movements or to retool privatization strategies.

Until the Water War, international financial institutions like the World Bank had held Bolivia up as a neoliberal success story. Although countries like Chile and Argentina had begun neoliberal economic restructuring under dictatorships, Bolivia was the first to do so under a democratically elected government.[5] In the 1990s the Bolivian government had partially privatized a series of state-owned enterprises (SOEs), including the national oil and gas, telecommunications, airline, smelting, power generation, and railroad companies, the country's six largest.[6] Proponents of this economic model promised that privatization would attract private and foreign capital to improve and expand services like water provision. Instead, privatization repeatedly led to mass layoffs and rate and fare hikes. The earlier SOE privatizations had sparked protests, especially from the companies' unionized workforces, but water privatization was the first to inspire a militant mass uprising that changed the course of national (and international) politics.

The Water War set off five years of what political scientist Jeffery Webber has called a "left-indigenous insurrectionary cycle" against neoliberal economic policies, parties, and politicians. Mexican social theorist Raquel Gutiérrez called these years of rebellion, from 2000 to 2005, a "community-popular" *pachakuti*, a Quechua term meaning an upheaval of time and space. Cochabamba water activists' call for a constituent assembly to refound Bolivia as a more just and democratic nation, which echoed an earlier proposal by lowland indigenous groups, became a rallying cry of social movements across the country as protests spread and intensified. Five years of rallies, strikes, blockades, and marches toppled two presidents and paved the way for the election of Evo Morales Ayma, the country's first indigenous president, in December 2005.[7] Morales and his Movimiento al Socialismo (MAS) party government joined Latin America's so-called Pink Tide, a wave of left-leaning vaguely socialist governments elected in Venezuela (1998), Brazil (2002), Argentina (2003), Uruguay (2004), Chile (2006), Ecuador (2006), Paraguay (2008), and beyond on surges of popular mobilization.

In his inauguration speech, Morales vowed to end five hundred years of foreign plunder of the nation's resources and to guarantee a form of autonomy for indigenous peoples. He blasted his predecessors for privatizing basic services like water, avowing that "water is a natural resource that we cannot live without and so cannot be a private business."[8] Morales's opposition to privatization was clear. But the sincerity of his commitment to autonomy would be tested over the almost fourteen years of his presidency. The Water War directly contributed to Morales's election. But whether the MAS-led state would respect indigenous communities, peasant and irrigator unions, and urban peripheral neighborhoods' control over water sources and systems remained to be seen.

The outcome of Cochabamba's Water War is at first glance surprising. After all, at the start of the conflict in 1999, Cochabambinos were up against a former dictator, the national army and police forces, the World Bank and the Inter-American Development Bank, and a neoliberal orthodoxy that had taken hold across Latin America and around the world. To explain their success, many participants and observers highlighted the broad cross-class and inter-regional makeup of the Coordinadora de Defensa del Agua y de la Vida (Coordinating Committee for the Defense of Water and Life) that organized the protests. Raquel Gutiérrez, who helped found the Tupac Katari Guerilla Army in the 1980s and later participated in the 2000 Water War, credited the Coordinadora's "noninstitutionality," its loose organizational structure, and its decentralized decision-making practices.[9] Coordinadora leader Oscar Olivera pointed to the urgency of access to water, a resource vital for survival, and to water's sacred cultural significance.[10] Others attributed the birth of Bolivia's new social movements, including indigenous movements in the highlands and tropics, to economic stagnation, aggressive coca eradication, and the decline of state economic revenue from the privatized oil and gas sectors.[11] Indeed, when massive numbers of Cochabambinos flooded into the streets, they found allies across the country because water privatization was a flash point in broader disputes over foreign influence, neoliberalism, resource governance, and state power. But water warriors' power—and conflicts over water access and ownership—had deeper roots.

This book contends that during the 1999–2000 Cochabamba Water War, Cochabambinos fought to defend something that peasants, urban periphery dwellers, and city-center residents had already won over the course of more than a century of social struggle: democratization and popular control of the region's water sources and infrastructure. Water monopoly, scarcity, and protest were more intense in the Cochabamba Valley than anywhere else in Bolivia, and water tenure transformation there from the 1870s to the 1990s was more dramatic. As Javier Molina and so many other water users who appear in the following pages emphasize, Cochabambinos' water property rights today are based on their historic labor to build and maintain water infrastructure and long-term struggles to gain water access. Estate workers, independent peasants, migrants on the urban periphery, and city-center residents constructed and paid for the region's water sources and systems with little to no assistance from the national government. Their power in the 2000 Water War flowed from their physical control over water sources and infrastructure, and from their knowledge about water systems that they had built, maintained, and defended over generations. Historian Richard White has written that "humans have known nature by digging in the earth, planting seeds, and harvesting plants."[12] In Cochabamba such labor produced knowledge as well as community, property, and revolution. The 2000 Water War was just the latest battle in a century-long war.

ANDEAN WATERSCAPES

The Andes Mountains cut down the western side of the otherwise lush, green South American continent. At the Nudo de Vilcanota, in southern Peru, the mountains split into two ranges. Between them lies the Altiplano, the highland plateau that widens to 129 miles across in Bolivia before the ranges converge again at Llullaillaco on the Chile-Argentina border south of Bolivia.[13] The central Andean region boasts dramatic geographical diversity. Heading east from the Pacific coast, sand dunes quickly give way to the Cordillera Occidental's steep and arid western flank that ascends to the Altiplano. From the Altiplano the Cordillera Oriental descends more moderately through semiarid inter-Andean valleys before yielding to the vast tropical lowlands that roll out to the east.

The great "water tower of South America," as geographers Axel Borsdorf and Christoph Stadel have called the majestic mountain chain, is generous with its surplus.[14] Abundant rainfall at higher elevations collects in mountain glaciers, lakes, and rivers that supply water to mines, fields, taps, and hydroelectric plants in the highlands, valleys, and lowlands below. In the tropical central Andes, gla-

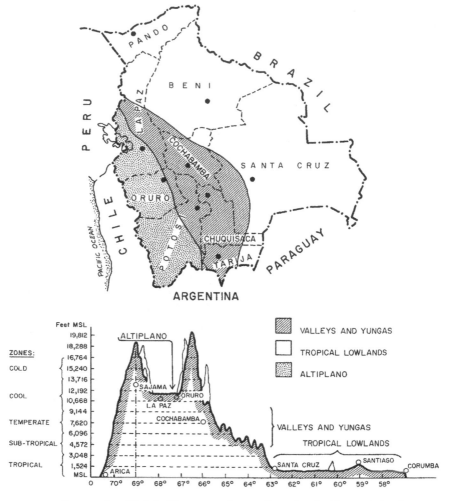

FIGURE 1. Topography of Bolivia. Illustrator unknown. Reproduced with permission from Cambridge University Press through PLSclear.

ciers formed as long ago as the Pleistocene provide meltwater for irrigation and drinking water.[15]

The central Andes have been the site of intense human settlement and movement for centuries as Andean people have taken advantage of different "ecological niches" at different heights. Precolonial Aymara extended kin groups, or ayllus, were centered in altiplano punas, where they grazed llamas and alpacas and cultivated potatoes and other tubers. Ayllus sent groups of settlers, or mitimaes, to sites dispersed along what came to resemble "vertical archipelagos," as anthropologist John Murra found, establishing "vertical control" over extended areas. Some mitimaes went west to the coast to harvest seafood and collect guano to fertilize their highland fields. Others journeyed east to the valleys and lush tropical slopes to cultivate maize, squash, chili peppers, coca, and cacao and gather palm fruits.[16]

Even before the rise of the Inca empire (ca. 1400–1533), water linked sites scattered along vertical archipelagos, connecting ayllus' dispersed settlements. Since ancient times, Andean peoples have revered water sources such as springs, lakes, and glaciated peaks and treated them as sacred places (huacas).[17] Ayllus traced their origins to their lands and the water sources they shared with other communities. Over time, as anthropologist Jeannette Sherbondy has shown, "connections between bodies of water" created "local regions."[18] Because various communities drew on interconnected water sources, allocation and dispute settlement required administration beyond the village level.[19] Increasing coordination around water and the belief that bodies of water were "hierarchically ordered by size and interconnected component parts of a great hydraulic circulatory system," in anthropologist Tamara Bray's words, helped give rise to nested political organization in the Andes.[20] As the Incas built their empire, they appealed to the cosmological unity of water sources to claim a common origin of all Andean peoples and thereby justify their reign.[21] Just as water was central spiritually and politically to the vertical organization of Andean society, community water worship was also deeply connected to labor. As Sherbondy has written, "People made offerings and prayers to [water] sources to ensure their goodwill and supply.... Often group labor projects were linked to those rituals."[22] As this book shows, water users have employed collective labor and ritual practices to gain water access and defend it ever since.

Over the six centuries since the Incas established their empire, trade, conquest, imperial labor drafts, and other forced and voluntary migrations have shuffled people across and around the central Andes. Since at least the fifteenth century, the Cochabamba region has been, to use historian Ben Nobbs-Thiessen's phrase, a "landscape of migration."[23] Around the turn of the sixteenth century, the Incas moved some natives out of the region to defend and expand their borders further east and moved highland mitimae settlers into the region to work as agricultural laborers. The Spanish wars of conquest in the 1530s and 1540s pushed many mitimaes back to the Altiplano to seek refuge in their home communities. In the 1570s, Spanish viceroy Toledo resettled the motley mix of indigenous peoples who remained in Cochabamba after these decades of upheaval in Spanish-style towns called reducciones or pueblos reales de indios.

In the face of onerous labor and tribute requirements in new resettled communities, many community members fled. Runaways found sanctuary in other communities or on haciendas where they took on new burdens as hacienda laborers. In time, many moved from haciendas to Cochabamba's growing urban center or migrated to Bolivian silver mines, Chilean copper mines and nitrate fields, or sugar fields in northern Argentina and back again. Many were able to purchase plots of land and join the ranks of the region's powerful smallholding peasantry in the late colonial period and early republic.[24] In the twentieth century, severe droughts led many Bolivians to leave rural communities for its cities, including Cochabamba. Rural-to-urban migration intensified after the Chaco War (1932–1935) and again during the droughts and economic restructuring that devastated livelihoods in the countryside and mining centers in the 1980s. It has continued apace since.

The department of Cochabamba is home to Bolivia's largest and most productive agricultural valleys and its third largest city, the eponymous department capital.[25] Its large semiarid valleys, set in the heart of the tropical southern Andes, possess fertile lands that have attracted cultivators despite near desert-level rainfall levels. Cochabamba's average annual rainfall is just 485 millimeters per year.[26] For most of the year, mountains to the north block rain clouds from crossing into the valley. But when the long dry season gives way to summer rains, intense winds sweep heavy rainclouds over the mountains into the valleys. During the rainy season from November to March, rainwater collects in lakes in the Tunari Mountains north of the valleys, in mountainside springs that continue to flow after the yearly rains have ceased, and in the soil and deep reaches of the fractured rock layers below the valley floor.

This geography distributes mountain flows to the four valleys surrounding the department capital but does so unevenly (Map 2). The Valle Bajo and the Central Valley are the most fortunate, due to their close proximity to the Tunari Mountains that capture and channel annual rains. The Central Valley receives runoff from the higher Sacaba Valley and Valle Alto as well.[27] The Valle Alto, in contrast, suffers from chronic water shortages due to lower rainfall and due to the water subsidy it has provided to the Valle Bajo by way of the Angostura reservoir since the 1940s. In fact, many areas have depended on other regions for water, which has sometimes caused conflict. Already in the late eighteenth century, Cochabamba intendent Francisco de Viedma classified different subregions' waters as ranging from "regular," "regular and abundant," "good," "excellent," or even "exquisite" to "not good," "little and poor quality," "bad," "very bad," or "temperamental."[28] Water has been such a prized resource in the region that fights over irrigation water have been as if not more important than fights over land.

For more than three thousand years, Cochabamba farmers have used floodwater and canal irrigation to guide mountain flows to their fields.[29] For the past five hundred years, distant rulers and local farmers alike have designed extensive irrigation projects aimed at making Cochabamba the region's breadbasket, first of the Inca and Spanish empires and later of the Bolivian nation. To direct water to fields and fountains, farmers, imperial and state officials, and contractors dammed lakes, dug and lined canals, tapped mountainside springs, drove water up from aquifers,

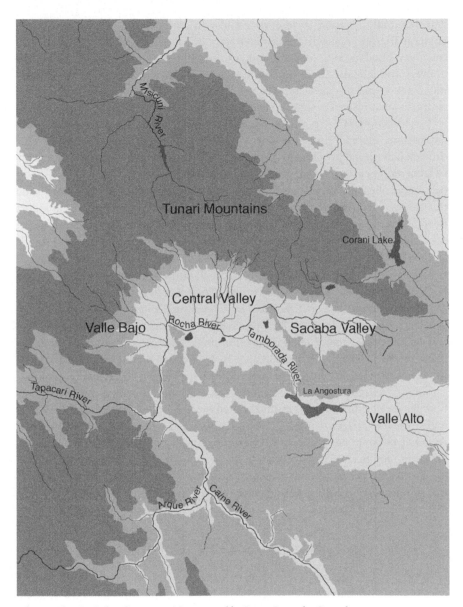

MAP 2. The Cochabamba region. Map created by Jorge Camacho Saavedra.

and stored all this water in reservoirs and tanks large and small. Techniques to engineer irrigation and drinking water sources have changed over the centuries (open-air canals were joined by underground pipes, artesian wells gave way to pumps), and climatic conditions have evolved, but these basic means of capturing, moving, and storing water—dams, wells, canals, reservoirs, and tanks—have endured. So too have struggles to gain access to adequate water.

Periodic drought has posed an ongoing challenge to accessing water in Cochabamba since colonial times. In 1805, Viedma wrote his superiors that a five-year drought had turned people into "wandering corpses" who were forced to "eat roots of withered grass to survive," if they survived at all.[30] But while droughts used to occur episodically, a warming climate along with inept national and local state policy have produced a long-term drought that has turned the region into a dust bowl. In La Paz, glaciers like the one that crowns the majestic mountain Illimani are melting rapidly, leaving communities that depend on them vulnerable to floods and avalanches, and hotter, drier, and dustier than before. Others, like eighteen-thousand-year-old Chacaltaya in La Paz and all of the Tunari Mountains' glaciers in Cochabamba, have disappeared entirely. Cochabamba's río Rocha runs dry except during rainstorms, onetime lakes have been supplanted by city streets, buildings, and a soccer stadium, and riverbeds and watersheds have been paved over.

Glacial retreat, higher temperatures, unpredictable weather, and extreme climatic events wrought by climate change have upended life for small farmers and urban residents alike. Peasant communities have adapted by drawing on long-standing practices of verticality, food storage, and communal land and work rotation. But faced with land scarcity and limited markets, many peasants have increasingly turned to cash crop production and migration to cities and mining centers.[31] As water became more scarce, Cochabamba's urban population grew from just 21,900 in 1900 to close to 1.3 million in the metropolitan area in 2020.[32] The growing population put increasing pressure on existing water supply, setting the stage for intense social struggles over irrigation and drinking water in the twentieth and early twenty-first centuries.

COCHABAMBA'S POPULAR HYDRAULIC SOCIETY

How to provide adequate water to all in the city and countryside was a central question in Cochabamba in the twentieth century. Addressing it involved political negotiation, social mobilization, and hydraulic engineering that transformed the region's waterscape and, at times, national and global politics. A range of different individuals, groups, and institutions, from Cochabamba to La Paz to Washington and beyond, took up this challenge and claimed that their proposals could achieve this goal. Water for all was thus a key challenge and an ambitious claim in Bolivia and Cochabamba in the twentieth century.

This book is a social, political, and environmental history of water access and hydraulic engineering in Cochabamba over more than a century, from the 1870s to the 2010s. It explores the relationship between people and water, examining how humans altered the waterscape, how nature conditioned those interventions, how political power shaped the ongoing production of Cochabamba's waterscape, how people's ideas about water tenure changed over time, and how political, economic, and social power was forged through contests over water. This history bears out the central premise of environmental history that humans are part of nature and also shows that people exercise disproportionate control over the rest of nature.[33] The process of transforming nature to meet our needs and fulfill our desires shapes the character of human society, which in turn molds our relationship to other life, a process that Karl Marx called metabolic interaction.[34] Emphasizing humans' role in producing nature highlights the dynamic relationship between humans and nonhuman nature and foregrounds the role of politics—internal differences of power within human society—in creating physical waterscapes and the social geography of water access and governance.[35] In short, who produces what kind of nature in what conditions, and who benefits from these processes, are questions of power.[36]

Forces beyond human control have always played a role in human history.[37] Wind currents bring rain, mountain ranges store rainwater in lakes and channel it to mountainside springs and valley aquifers, rocky terrain lets runoff seep in, and aquifers organize and store water. In choosing how and where to build structures, roads, dams, and canals, people both respond to natural realities like the geography of watersheds and influence those dynamics. To riff on Marx, people help produce an ever-changing nature, but not by themselves, and not in conditions of their own choosing.[38] The outcomes of ongoing contests over water have had significant consequences for water users and the hydraulic environment alike.

Historical studies of hydraulic engineering tend to take a top-down approach. Many portray water users and environments as either victims or passive beneficiaries of powerful states and private capital and assume that water engineering and management have been the exclusive domains of state and professional engineers. This perspective, rooted in the "hydraulic empire" or "hydraulic society" theory advanced by sinologist Karl Wittfogel and further developed by historian Donald Worster ignores the active participation of water users who often shape the waterscape in important ways. Both Wittfogel and Worster analyzed arid environments. Wittfogel argued that agricultural societies' irrigation systems required centralized bureaucratic structures to build and maintain them, which in turn demanded the development of despotic political regimes, what he called "hydraulic empires."[39] Worster applied Wittfogel's thesis about ancient empires to power relations in the modern, capitalist US West where, he argued, a "coercive, monolithic, and hierarchical" alliance of capitalist agribusiness and government bureaucrats dominate people and the environment by controlling irrigation infrastructure.[40] While Worster acknowledged that decentralization was possible, like Wittfogel he argued that undemocratic state institutions and wealthy elites controlled populations by controlling water sources.[41] Historians have since challenged this view by demonstrating the intimate relationship between farmers and water systems, emphasizing the ways farmers have used this connection to pressure engineers and empires.[42] But victim narratives persist in studies of hydraulic engineering and water access, especially those dealing with the urbanizing Global South.

Scholars who write about what they call the "urbanization of water," for example, have emphasized the costs of expanding municipal water utilities: unequal distribution to wealthy versus poor neighborhoods and extraction of water from cities' hinterlands. These authors rightly focus on the importance of water to urban metabolism and the potentially harmful impacts of urban hydraulic expansion on rural water users and environments. Indeed, in cities across Latin America and the Global South, including Cochabamba, municipal customers pay far less for their water than households on the excluded periphery forced to rely on private water vendors.[43] But these studies too often portray rural people and resources and poor city-dwellers as hapless victims of professional engineers whose unsustainable projects to increase urban water supply dominate the story. Their portrayal of cities as starkly divided between privileged municipal customers with little idea where their water comes from and powerless excluded periurban neighborhoods is similarly misleading.[44] By focusing on the power of state institutions, even while criticizing their ineptitude and failures, these scholars unwittingly extend a Wittfogelian analysis to what they call the "urban hydraulic frontier."[45]

Scholarship on hydraulic development more generally often focuses on invasive, costly, and unsustainable projects imposed from the outside. In *Seeing Like a State*, scholar James Scott has tracked the history of modern states' efforts to make society "legible" in order to organize and standardize social practice and the natural world through authoritarian high modernist development projects like megadams. In his account states pursue these projects against the will of a "prostrate civil society that lack[ed] the capacity to resist these plans."[46] Scott does not consider sites where civil society was not "prostrate," however. Nor does he investigate projects that beneficiaries embraced. Despite recognizing a more complex history in his study of the New Deal–era Tennessee Valley Authority (TVA) planners, whom he credits with involving local subjects, Scott nevertheless concludes that TVA planners' "democratic faith" was impossible to reconcile with technocratic planning, concluding that efforts to involve beneficiaries resulted in "participatory autocracy."[47] Historical sociologist Jess Gilbert has more generously dubbed TVA planners' efforts to pursue modernization through citizen participation "low modernism," which, he suggests, succeeded in "narrowing the gap between expert and citizen."[48] But even these more fine-grained accounts of the TVA share the assumption that the initiative for modernist projects like dams has come exclusively from above and outside local communities. So too, critical development literature tends to focus on outside improvement initiatives that usually end up empowering the state, elites, or both.[49]

The history of Cochabamba's waterscape offers an alternative history of hydraulic development, governance, and expertise that departs from the paradigm of destructive projects imposed from the outside and instead highlights the power and knowledge of water users. *Water for All* contends that, in Cochabamba, watering a semiarid environment did not produce authoritarianism but rather served as a major channel for democratic imagination. Rather than falling victim to state builders and experts, Cochabambinos built a *popular* hydraulic society in the twentieth century, with the high point in the years following the 1952 Bolivian revolution. Cochabamba water users, including hacienda tenants, independent peasants, urban peripheral neighborhood residents, and municipal water service customers, democratized water access, engineering, and governance in the twentieth century. Over these decades, rural, periurban, and urban communities gained control over regional water sources and infrastructure and became hydraulic experts in their own right. In defending, regaining, and engineering new water sources and infrastructure, Cochabambinos built a diverse network of coexisting water systems with differing (and at times competing) claims to water rights and community control. Rather than merely reacting to projects introduced from the outside, Cochabambinos demanded and crafted their own improvement schemes, including plans for state action and underwriting from international development agencies.[50]

What has unified Cochabamba's popular hydraulic society is, first and foremost, a common claim to collective control over water sources, infrastructure, planning, and provision in the region's myriad water systems. As Javier Molina's remark at the outset of this introduction suggests, Cochabamba water users claim not only use rights but also ownership of water sources and infrastructure on the basis of their historic labor and struggle. Andean communities have a long history of creating hydraulic property through the investment of labor and materials.[51] Starting in the mid-twentieth century, Cochabamba water users extended collective practices developed in the countryside to build and manage irrigation systems to periurban and municipal water systems. Members of Cochabamba's rural and periurban community-run irrigation and drinking-water systems manage sources and distribution systems that community members built and have since maintained, in periurban areas for several decades, in rural areas for generations. Municipal customers constructed neighborhood systems and have influenced water policy through their labor and protest.

These collective water management practices are a form of what I call "vernacular environmental governance," meaning community management of natural resources.[52] As other Andean water scholars have argued, environmental governance involves "not only 'governance of nature'" but also "'governance *through* nature."[53] Community governance relies on groups of people bound to a particular place and each other, often through their common need to access shared resources like water. Governance is not merely the exercise of power by elites.[54] It is also the work of collectivities who manage resources like water with varying degrees of autonomy from the state.[55] As political economist Elinor Ostrom has written, "communities of individuals have relied on institutions resembling neither the state nor the market to govern some resource systems with reasonable degrees of success over long periods of time."[56] The communal labor to build and manage water infrastructure, organize distribution, and influence state policy has required forming disciplined organizations to manage, defend, and vie for water access. Their labor has involved not only physical work but also planning, engineering, and social struggle, both for and against major water development projects.

State-led urban water development in Cochabamba *has* threatened rural people and environments and excluded large numbers of the urban poor. But when urban officials have attempted to reach deeper into their hinterlands to commandeer more water sources, rural water owners have forced them to negotiate. Peasants gained tremendous power through their conquest of water during the 1952 Bolivian revolution. Nor were the urban poor merely victims. As anthropologists of urban citizenship have shown, poor residents of self-built urban peripheries across the Global South have fought for urban citizenship rights like access to housing, electricity, transportation, sanitation, and water. While their gains have been partial, they have crafted a form of belonging that anthropologist James Holston has called "insurgent citizenship."[57] So too in Cochabamba, peripheral neighborhoods outside the municipal water network have negotiated the terms of their inclusion and exclusion. The municipal system has grown in part by incorporating independent neighborhoods' water sources and systems. Some neighborhood systems that remain outside the municipal system have water sources of their own, while others purchase water from the municipal water company. All of Cochabamba's water users, including municipal customers, are highly aware of where their water comes from, and where it goes. This is because water supply expansion for all of the region's systems has required water users to contribute funds and labor, increasing supply has involved intense social conflict, and distribution is unequal within and among the region's systems and therefore highly contested.

Through their labor and efforts to defend and improve water access, Cochabambino water users developed what I term "vernacular hydraulic expertise."[58] Peasant communities engineered irrigation systems, residents of the growing urban periphery built new neighborhood water systems, municipal water service customers critiqued and defied rate hikes, and residents from across the valley rallied behind dam projects in the Tunari Mountains that promised to improve water access for all. These vernacular hydraulic experts borrowed from the expertise of salaried professionals, and formal experts drew on vernacular expertise.[59]

Cochabambino water users drew on their hydraulic experience and knowledge to vie for control of the region's water infrastructure, especially in the decades after the 1952 revolution, fortifying their power to shape regional policy.[60] State officials and formal experts often deemed popular groups incapable of understanding technical problems and blamed them for environmental degradation. But time and again, ordinary water users flipped the script, chastising officials and engineers for their failures and putting forward alternative proposals—including plans and demands for state-led hydraulic development.[61]

Through these efforts, Cochabambino water users developed an alternative vision of modernity. Modernity is not the exclusive domain of the rich, the white, the powerful, or the North. Nor is it necessarily a capitalist project. As alternative modernities literature rightly insists, a diversity of groups and individuals have embraced modernity's promises and demanded that state and financial institutions fulfill their promises to deliver the real and perceived benefits of modernity.[62] As anthropologist Ashley Carse has argued, those lacking infrastructure like roads often fervently desire it.[63] In Cochabamba the decisive impulse for modernist hydraulic development came not from state planners but rather from Cochabambino water users who felt neglected by a national state that had not bothered to make them legible. Cochabambino support for state-led hydraulic development was an instance of what I call "vernacular modernism"—creative appropriation and adaption of modernist development paradigms from below on practitioners' own terms. While high modernism requires ignoring local history, knowledge, people, and ecology, vernacular modernists draw on their knowledge of history and ecology to advocate for fulfillment of modernity's promises.[64] Unlike authoritarian high modernism, vernacular modernism aims to democratize modernism and indeed modernity itself.[65]

For more than a century, Cochabambinos have demanded that state institutions provide them with water.[66] And they have gone further by claiming—and winning—the right to own, control, and manage water sources and systems, and to oversee and direct state institutions, planning, and projects. Cochabamba's community-run water systems have not been victims of the state, nor have they operated completely outside state view, regulation, or intervention. They have self-governed with degrees of independence from state institutions (and more recently international financial institutions). As the late anthropologist William Roseberry wrote, "subordinate populations" are not "deluded and passive captives of the state," but nor are "their activities and organizations ... autonomous expressions of a subaltern politics and culture." Rather, subaltern culture is forged in relationship with the world of which it is part.[67] Instead of attempting to achieve full autonomy,

Cochabambino water users have worked to define when, where, and how the state intervenes, and on whose terms.

More than national politics, even under dictatorship, the power to access water and shape regional water policy has depended on grassroots mobilization and collective control of water sources and infrastructure. Cochabamba's subaltern communities often won control over and access to water by obstructing or disrupting the operations of their opponents, what anthropologist Carwil Bjork-James has called "disruptive space claiming."[68] By withholding labor and payment and physically disrupting water expansion projects through land and water seizures, project site occupations, road blockades, and city occupations, Cochabambino water users time and again thwarted the aims of state and financial institutions. Even the mere threat of such action, or elites' own fear of the masses taking things into their own hands, often aided peasants, urban workers, and the poor. At times, the actions of water users have been defensive, aimed at safeguarding the measure of control and access they already had. In other moments, water-using communities have gone on the offensive to expand their water access and control over water provision and policy. In 1952 and again in 2000, Cochabamba water users' efforts to defend and democratize water access converged with broader mobilizations to transform Bolivian society. While many institutions, groups, and individuals worked to improve water access in Cochabamba, the most fervent "will to improve" has consistently come from below.[69] Ongoing defense of and demands for water access and vernacular governance have strengthened local communities, transformed regional property relations, and helped revolutionize Bolivian society.

ORGANIZATION

Water for All weaves together urban, rural, national, and transnational history over a period of 140 years. It begins in the late 1870s, when a severe drought, national policy, and landlord greed coalesced to produce famine, community dispossession, and extremely unequal water ownership. After outlining water tenure relations under the Incas, the Spanish, and the early Bolivian republic, chapter 1 examines the drought, the dissolution of Cochabamba's indigenous communities, the rise of a new constellation of hacienda water monopolists, and the ways smallholders, hacienda tenants, and city residents and officials dealt with the water monopoly from the 1880s to the 1920s. Chapter 2 investigates state-sponsored efforts to make more water available to farmers and urban residents after the Chaco War (1932–1935), focusing on two major hydraulic infrastructure projects—one for irrigation, the other for urban supply—in Cochabamba in the 1940s.

Chapter 3 explores social struggle over national and local water policy after the 1952 revolution, mapping the reach and limits of revolutionary-era water reform. Chapter 4 follows water users' efforts, in negotiation with national and interna-

tional actors, to realize the revolutionary promise of water for all under dictatorship from the mid-1960s to the early 1980s. Chapter 5 examines water users'
efforts to defend and expand Cochabamba's popular hydraulic society under neoliberal democracy that culminated in the 2000 Water War. Chapter 6 discusses
the Water War's aftermath and water politics during Evo Morales's presidency
from 2006 to 2019. The conclusion reflects on the legacies of Bolivia's long history
of social struggle over water and the lessons this history holds for the present and
future.

A NOTE ON SOURCES

A wide range of people with different visions of hydraulic justice produced the
sources that made this book possible.[70] It is based on two years of interviews and
archival research in Bolivia and the United States for my doctoral dissertation
(2010–2012) as well as earlier interviews I conducted as a Fulbright scholar in Bolivia (2006–2007). I carried out follow-up research as I was writing my dissertation while still living in Cochabamba (2013–2015) and additional research in Bolivia and the United States as I transformed it into this book (2015–2020). In total, I
interviewed around 112 people, 45 of whom are quoted in this book. Along the way
I consulted, shared research findings with, and solicited feedback from Bolivian
scholars, activists, officials, and other interlocutors.

I drew documentary evidence from more than twenty archives, including official national, state, and municipal archives and the informal archives of various institutions, unions, communities, and individuals. Documents in these collections
reveal how estate owners, peasants, estate workers, peripheral neighborhoods, and
the municipal water service gained control over water sources and infrastructure.
Some of the most illuminating sources include purchase agreements and expropriation records resulting from state officials' negotiations with hacienda owners over
water sources that I uncovered in Cochabamba's state (prefecture) archive. The
archive of the Cochabamba office of the Instituto Nacional de la Reforma Agraria
(INRA) is a busy place where peasants from around the department come seeking
evidence to document their land claims. Its agrarian reform case records reveal
that agrarian reform involved distribution of water as well as land.

Water-sharing agreements in legal department files at the municipal water company SEMAPA show that the municipal system grew by incorporating periurban
neighborhoods. They also disclose how SEMAPA gained access to water sources in
rural communities. SEMAPA staff very generously allowed me to borrow binders
containing these agreements. Hydraulic studies and project plans uncovered in
SEMAPA's archive and in the regional planning department's archive document
decades of efforts to alleviate Cochabamba's shortage of drinking water. SEMAPA
officials at first told me that its records had been lost. But one day, my closest con-

tact there took me to a building in the middle of the complex that turned out to be the company archive. When we found a locked glass cabinet containing what appeared to be the oldest and most relevant documents, we went to the main office where a manager handed us a bucket full of keys. When none of them worked, my friend pressed the cabinet's doors apart to free its cylindrical lock and slid its doors open, releasing some of this book's most important sources.

Newspapers were crucial sources as well. Articles from more than a dozen different local and national newspapers from the 1870s to the 2010s provided information about key moments in urban water development and day-to-day water management. They also offered insight into local and national debates about hydraulic development. Bolivian newspapers were usually affiliated, either officially or unofficially, with particular political parties; Cochabamba's were often owned by wealthy and powerful creole (European-descended) families. I carefully considered their slant when using newspaper coverage and editorials to reconstruct events or to discern protagonists' perspectives.

I interviewed, observed, corresponded with, and established friendships with Cochabambino water users and managers over the roughly six years I lived in Cochabamba between 2006 and 2016. Interviews with water-service managers and engineers, national authorities, foreign engineers, and other officials provided essential perspectives. I also interviewed urban residents with widely ranging forms of access to water, and members of agricultural communities with rights to regional water sources. Observation at key sites across the waterscape gave me useful insight into the construction of Cochabamba's waterscape. Most rewardingly, community and neighborhood residents shared personal and community stories as well as historical documents that testify to their water rights claims. Following historian Daniel James's wise suggestion, I pay attention to the ways that testimonies are "mediated ... by existing narratives and dominant ideologies," but also take what he calls "the leap of faith that direct historical experience will break through and find expression in an individual's testimony."[71] I cross-referenced all of my sources as every historical source bears the marks of its author's biases and omissions. The names of public figures I interviewed (including government officials, most water service general managers, and prominent union and activist organization leaders) remain unchanged. I assigned pseudonyms to all other informants.

These rich sources facilitated a deep historical study, a multiscalar approach, and attention to the power of a range of different groups in the construction of Cochabamba's waterscape. The stories of the people who produced these sources are the subject of the chapters that follow.

Water for Those Who Own It

*Drought, Dispossession, and Modernization
in the Liberal Era*

Cochabamba's 1877–1878 rainy season began as most did, with rains in September and October that encouraged farmers to plant early. But in December, after the first crop had been planted, rain all but ceased for the next three months.[1] Crops withered, disease festered, and thousands of people perished.[2] Residents of Cochabamba's semiarid agricultural valleys, which had long drawn settlers to farm their fields, were no strangers to drought. But while the 1878–1879 famine might seem like the inevitable result of dense human settlement in semiarid valleys prone to periodic drought, this was no natural disaster.

The immediate source of Cochabamba's predicament was a major El Niño event, which began in 1876 and peaked in the 1877–1878 austral summer, causing climate disruption around the world. An El Niño/Southern Oscillation episode occurs when sea surface temperatures rise and trade winds wane in the equatorial Pacific, producing floods in some areas and drought in others. Drought-induced famine killed an estimated 20 million to 30 million people across Asia, Africa, and South America during what Brazilians still call the "Grande Seca" of 1877–1878, the most intense El Niño event of the nineteenth century.[3] While floods ravaged coastal Ecuador and northern Peru, drought swept the Central Andes of Peru and Bolivia, hitting hardest in Bolivia's inter-Andean valleys. From Cochabamba to Chuquisaca, drought gave rise to devastating famine, epidemic disease, and social unrest.

Famine was not inevitable. As historian Mike Davis has written, "although crop failures and water shortages were of epic proportion" during late nineteenth-century drought waves, "absolute scarcity was never the issue."[4] And as economist Amartya Sen, historian Eve Buckley, and others have argued, marginalized populations are more vulnerable to disasters like droughts. "Overemphasizing the 'natural' causes of their suffering," Buckley writes, "deflects attention from the social dynamics that perpetuate the insecurity of the poor."[5] In Cochabamba, famine owed to land and water accumulation in the hands of a privileged few who consciously took advantage of the drought to profit off of the misery of their neighbors. More than three hundred years of land and water dispossession had left indigenous and peasant communities vulnerable to the vicissitudes of the region's volatile climate—and to landlords who used their disproportionate control over land and irrigation water to speculate on grain during the drought.

The 1877–1878 drought and famine reshaped the social and hydraulic geography of the Cochabamba. First and foremost, it left Cochabamba's already frail indigenous communities much more vulnerable to state efforts to dismantle them. Three centuries of land and water dispossession and attrition had already weakened their ability and even willingness to oppose dissolution in the 1870s and 1880s. Although historians have documented the role of land dispossession in this process, they have paid less attention to how water dispossession weakened communities and strengthened landlords.[6] I contend that the drought gave state officials an opportunity to put earlier disentailment laws into practice. A long-term process of land, water, and irrigation infrastructure dispossession weakened communities and allowed *hacendados* to speculate in deadly ways during the drought. Community closure along with a new water regulation introducing a riparian system of water rights that conferred water rights to landed property owners allowed a new constellation of landed elites to consolidate a near monopoly over the Cochabamba region's water sources in the late nineteenth century. Water dispossession was thus a "hidden violence," in sociologist Silvia Rivera Cusicanqui's words, wrought by the colonial structure of elite domination that endured after independence.[7]

Because officials concluded that the spread of disease could have been averted with improved water distribution and hygienic practices, the drought also spurred modernization of the department capital's drinking water system. Improvements entailed expanding urban water supply through a series of projects in the Arocagua area in the Tunari foothills northeast of the city and distribution infrastructure in the city itself. But water access in the city remained highly unequal. While rural elites tried to preserve and expand their near monopoly over the region's water sources, popular groups worked to make urban water access more equitable. Increasingly urban officials joined them, challenging rural elites and the national government. Due to a shared experience of unequal and insufficient water access, independent smallholders (*piqueros*), estate tenants (*colonos*), and city residents forged a regional mestizo culture where collective access to water was central in the decades after the drought and community closure.

This chapter first reconstructs the history of competition over limited water resources from the time of the Incas to the early republican period. It then examines how Cochabambinos experienced the 1877–1878 drought, how national officials took advantage of the drought and famine to dismantle the region's indigenous communities and establish a riparian water property rights regime, and how regional hacienda owners capitalized on all of this to construct a near monopoly of the region's water sources. Finally, the chapter traces the creation of a modern drinking water supply and distribution system in the department capital and early challenges to the rural water monopoly. This history reveals that elites mobilized natural disaster to implement liberal policies and that water users and urban officials mobilized to oppose them.

COLONIAL DISPOSSESSION AND PROTECTION

Drawn by its potential to feed the imperial army, the Incas colonized Cochabamba's Central Valley and Valle Bajo in the late fifteenth century under Emperor Yupanqui (1471–1493). Imperial officials drafted Cochabamba's peoples to serve the empire's agroimperial aims, sending the Cotas and Chuyes to the frontier to guard its border and retaining the Soras of Sipe Sipe as herdsmen.[8] Yupanqui's successor, Huayna Capac (1493–1527), oversaw a major state-directed agricultural project in Cochabamba's valleys that transformed the region into the empire's premier southern food supplier.[9] Integrating existing irrigation techniques, Inca officials drafted roughly fourteen thousand laborers from a vast array of highland nations to build a vast irrigation system to direct water to state-operated farms.[10] A rotation system was established that granted particular land parcels a share of water from a specific water source according to a schedule. For instance, a land parcel might receive its turn when water is released from a mountainside lake during the dry season every thirteen days for one hour. These turns or shares are called mitas.

In the rainy season teaming rivers swelled and cut down the mountainside, providing mitas to long, narrow strips of agricultural land the Incas called *suyus*. In the dry season a rotational distribution system supplied water from irrigation canals to the suyus whose borders were defined by deep mountain ravines (Map 3).[11] As anthropologist Jeannette Sherbondy has explained, *suyu* organization "also implied a division of tasks, a division of group labor."[12] The Incas adopted a dual system of water management, distributing it equitably in times of scarcity and hierarchically in the rare times when it was abundant.[13] Starting then, water rights in Cochabamba became attached to land ownership as well as to collective labor necessary to capture and channel irrigation and drinking water. Land dispossession thus entailed the less visible appropriation of water sources, infrastructure, and labor invested to engineer water infrastructure.

After defeating the Incas, Spaniards built imperial control over Cochabamba's valleys by appropriating valley land, water sources, and irrigation infrastructure through a combination of purchase, theft, and royal grants. In the first few decades

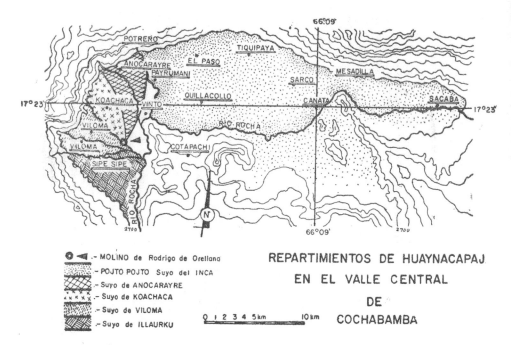

**REPARTIMIENTOS DE HUAYNACAPAJ
EN EL VALLE CENTRAL
DE
COCHABAMBA**

○◀ .- MOLINO de Rodrigo de Orellana
.- POJTO POJTO Suyo del INCA
.- Suyo de ANOCARAYRE
.- Suyo de KOACHACA
.- Suyo de VILOMA
.- Suyo de ILLAURKU

MAP 3. Distribution of lands by Inca emperor Huayna Capac. Map created by Ricardo Cespedes. *Source: Repartimiento de tierras del Inca Huayna Capac (Testimonio de un documento de 1556)* (Cochabamba: Universidad Boliviana Mayor de San Simón, Departamento de Arqueología, 1977), 7.

of Spanish rule, colonial officials granted Spanish settlers called *encomenderos* authority over Indian communities, diverse and fragmented groups of highland migrants who stayed through and survived the Spanish-Inca battles only to find themselves cut off from their home communities and required to supply labor and tribute to their new overlords. In the 1570s, Viceroy Francisco de Toledo's forced resettlement program concentrated Cochabamba's multiethnic indigenous population into Spanish-style towns called *pueblos reales de indios*. As Silvia Rivera Cusicanqui has explained, this "forced unification…homogenized and degraded a diversity of peoples and identities into an anonymous collective expressed in the condition of *indio*, that is to say, of the colonized."[14] Toledo's General Resettlement yielded three resettled indigenous communities in the Cochabamba heartland: Sipe Sipe, Santiago del Passo (or El Paso), and San Miguel de Tiquipaya (Map 4). The crown required community members called *originarios* to pay tribute and to work as draft laborers every seventh year in the Potosí mines. While the *reducción* process was incredibly disruptive, especially in areas like Cochabamba that provided draft laborers to the Potosí mines, it also built on and preserved the

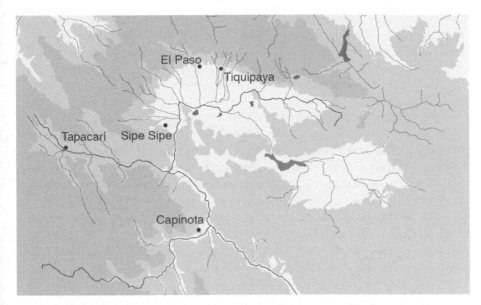

MAP 4. Cochabamba's colonial-era *pueblos reales de indios*. Map created by Jorge Camacho Saavedra.

vertical archipelago and existing communal land and irrigation water allocation. Remarkably, when Cochabamba mitimaes asked to be liberated from highland communities' claims to their labor and tribute, Toledo sided with the highland communities.[15]

In the decades after the General Resettlement, three kinds of agricultural settlements emerged in Cochabamba's Central Valley and Valle Bajo: the three *pueblos reales de indios*, large landed estates called haciendas, and small and medium-sized estates called *chácaras*. While the indigenous communities and haciendas were situated in the valley's northern foothills, the *chácaras* were located further down in the valley. Their location downstream put *chacareros* at the mercy of upstream hacienda owners and community leaders that controlled—and fought over—water from lakes, rivers, and springs. This tripartite division of land and water allocation endured over the next two hundred years, as the number of small properties slowly grew and *hacendados* gradually encroached on community land and water sources.[16]

Over time, Spanish and creole *hacendados* used various tactics, including purchase, force, and fraud, to appropriate community land and water rights. As historians Robert Jackson and Jose Gordillo have written, "the first conflicts between the hacendados and the communities were over control of water provision, not land."[17] After resettlement, Spanish and creole haciendas, *chácaras*, and urban towns attracted pueblo members willing to forsake their land, water rights, and community ties to escape tribute levies and labor drafts.[18] One way that communities acquired cash for tribute was by leasing or selling community land, along with these parcels' irrigation rights, to neighboring hacienda owners. As they lost members to haciendas, communities sold or rented even more land and water to cover lost tributary dues, and *hacendados* gained still greater water access by forcibly inserting themselves into the irrigation rotation system.[19] As a result, community plots received water less frequently and hacienda landholdings came to possess disproportionate water rights. *Hacendados'* dispossession of communities' water sources was less visible than land appropriation but more extreme. As Jackson and Gordillo write, haciendas "obtained rights to all of the important water sources."[20]

Water dispossession was offset somewhat by protections that Spanish water law offered indigenous communities, small farmers, and townspeople. When the Spanish Crown proclaimed ownership over all land and water in "the Indies," it empowered colonial officials to grant colonists land, water, woodlands, and pastures. All remaining Crown land, water, woodlands, and pastures were supposed to be available for common use by settlers and natives alike. But while the public could freely use crown water sources for drinking, bathing, recreation, and watering animals, use for irrigation required specific allocation to a native community or privately owned land parcel. Landed property generally fell into one of two categories: "tierras de riego" that possessed irrigation water rights or "tierras de temporal" that lacked them. Owners of nonirrigated parcels could purchase water from a neighbor with "excess" water rights (*sobras*), buy irrigated land with water rights included in the purchase, or rent common water from the town council (*cabildo*). While at first officials gave generous land and water grants to Spaniards, in the late sixteenth century, the Crown ordered officials to protect native communities from abuse by colonists, specifically requiring colonial officials to ensure that concessions occur "sin agravio de los indios."[21] If there was a dispute, a colonial water judge or other official might conduct a "repartimiento de agua," dividing available water among Spanish and Indian users or simply ordering them to share it.

Spanish law required officials to consider not only who could claim prior use and who held legal title, but also need, equity, and the common good. This was not a riparian system that granted water to owners of the land the water was found on unless the water source originated on the landowners' land (such as in the case of a well or a spring). Even then, "the owner could not maliciously deny it to others."[22] Therefore, although private landowners and native communities possessed water rights, these allocations were subject to change. There was no guarantee that officials would carry out a redistribution to make access more just, however, and Spaniards and creoles were able to acquire disproportionate water rights. Spanish law allowed landowners to pass water rights down to children, sell land with corresponding water rights to their neighbors, and rent excess irrigation water to them, practices that locked unequal access into place over time. In Upper Peru, Spanish officials recognized *pueblos reales'* communal land and water holdings in exchange for tribute and labor payment (what anthropologist Tristan Platt has called the colonial "pact of reciprocity") to a degree. But they also allowed Spanish and creole *hacendados* to usurp land and water.[23]

When Cochabamba *pueblos reales* sued hacienda owners in colonial courts for illegal land and water appropriation, colonial authorities seem to have offered little remedy.[24] Geographer Karl Zimmerer has found that when faced with legal challenges to water appropriation by native communities claiming to have been granted *suyu* units by the Incas, Spaniards successfully countered that their property "descended directly from holdings of the vanquished Inca state rather than... through usurpation of other Indian holdings."[25] Nevertheless, in the colonial period there was always the possibility that officials could redistribute available water sources according to need. After independence, these protections and commitments, feeble as they were, disappeared.

Spanish and creole dispossession of native communities' agricultural land and water sources drove the process of *mestizaje* in the valley. In both the Altiplano and the valleys, colonial rulers folded multiple ethnic identities into the single generic category *indio*. But whereas altiplano communities remained in their ayllu (extended kin group) centers, most valley *pueblos reales* were ethnically diverse and all were under great pressure to produce tribute and draft laborers and therefore prone to dispersion.[26] Both the resulting weakness of the valley's indigenous communities and the attractiveness of their land and water sources for agricultural production led to greater encroachment on their territory than in the highlands. This in turn entailed gradual dissolution of indigenous identity as communities lost members. To avoid tribute payment on haciendas or in colonial towns, migrants attempted to cast off their status as *indios* and pass as mestizos, defined in the colonial period as persons with one European-descended parent, as opposed to tribute-paying Indians and *cholos*, persons with one European-descended grandparent.[27] Pueblo-to-hacienda migration, land and water appropriation by Spaniards and creoles, and the weakening of indigenous communities fueled the emergence of a mestizo cultural identity among the region's rural toilers and urban artisans and laborers.

The regional hacienda economy grew in the early colonial period by exporting grain to the booming Potosí silver mines. But by the late colonial era, Cochabamba haciendas had begun to lose out to highland grain producers, a problem that became a crisis after independence. Their predicament opened space for the growth of an independent smallholding peasantry that gained control over local markets and purchased parcels of hacienda land. One way that landlords tried to mitigate these difficulties in the colonial and early national periods was to accumulate excess irrigation rights (*sobras*). This allowed them to exploit periodic droughts by using their still vast landholdings and disproportionate irrigation water rights to produce surplus grain for storage during plentiful harvest years to sell dear when drought hit and prices soared.[28] Smallholders and *pueblo* members with less favorable irrigation water rights or nonirrigated holdings could lose entire crops during a drought and thus be forced to purchase grain from landlords. City residents were completely at their mercy. Landlords' wager that drought would shield them from the threat posed by their smallholding neighbors and foreign grain producers was a risky gamble with devastating consequences for Cochabamba's peasantry and urban poor when drought hit in 1877.

DROUGHT, DISPOSSESSION, AND PRIVATIZATION

At what should have been the height of the rainy season in February 1878, the local Conservative Party–allied newspaper *El Heraldo* reported that the wheat crop had failed and warned that if relief measures were not taken quickly, the population would "be forced to witness...the most tragic misery and disorder." By disorder, the paper meant the likelihood of speculation by large landowners and the probable fury of the people in response. No one should think, the paper editorialized, that "the great, well-provisioned property owners of Trojes will be the most fortunate in this disgraceful situation, because the hungry masses are more destructive than the floods caused by the most violent storms." The editors called for requisitioning estates' grain stocks from previous years and whatever could be salvaged from the current season to feed the population during the famine that was sure to come. Predicting that "the liberty of industry and the right to property" would be invoked against such measures, they argued that "in the face of such a danger, these individual rights should be silent in favor of common salvation through just redistribution."[29] This position contrasted sharply with the emerging liberal economic orthodoxy that the two major political parties, the Conservative and Liberal Parties, shared.[30] Rain resumed in March, but it was too late.

Sure enough, famine and disease soon hit hard in the departmental capital and surrounding provinces. The drought destroyed half of the corn and wheat crops and left pools of stagnant water in riverbeds where disease-carrying mosquitos multiplied, causing outbreaks of typhoid, malaria, and dysentery.[31] At the end of 1878, the Municipal Council reported that rural people, "beaten down by disease, have seen their meager resources, their families, and their livestock disappear, and are not even capable of harvesting their pathetic crop." Sick and starving *piqueros*, *colonos*, and *pueblo* members fled the countryside where hacienda owners (and provincial authorities) failed to offer assistance to their starving and disease-stricken workers and neighbors, instead selling hoarded grain at exorbitant prices.[32] In the capital, local hospitals overflowed, dead bodies littered the streets, and the sick and starving "swarmed the streets," begging for assistance. President Hilarion Daza's administration, which had come to power in an 1876 coup, offered no aid, leaving the municipal government, affluent citizens, and local ecclesiastical institutions to organize relief efforts.[33]

The growing influence of economic liberalism, with its celebration of private property rights and the free market, was evident in municipal officials' response to the crisis. While they willingly organized relief efforts and encouraged charity, authorities shied at imposing price controls or grain requisitions that would infringe on private property rights and free market exchange. The municipality enlarged existing hospitals, created ten new clinics in the provinces, prohibited *chicha* (corn beer) production to save water, closed schools to redirect their budgets to relief efforts, and channeled funds to private and ecclesiastical relief centers.[34] Although the spread of infectious disease threatened rich and poor alike, price hikes did not.[35] Officials' efforts to challenge speculators were timid and met with fierce criticism. In April 1878 the municipality tried to purchase large stocks of grain to sell to the population at cost, but the plan fizzled when the National Bank failed to provide a loan. Within a month grain prices tripled.[36]

Protests broke out across the region denouncing hoarding and speculation and demanding price caps on basic foodstuffs. In response, Cochabamba's municipal council congratulated "the majority of our people" for their "respect for property and the rights of others." But the council reprimanded "the lower classes" for "not understanding the consequences that the violation of economic laws would produce." While protestors' position was "excusable" given the seemingly limitless price hikes by some "speculators on the people's misery," their "violent" and "exaggerated" methods of making their demands were not.[37] The hungry rose up in the Valle Alto towns of Cliza, Tarata, Punata and Arani, and in Sucre as well. In Arani protestors threatened grain-hoarding landowners with death, leading *hacendados* to charge that they were trying to establish a "Commune" and were "following Communist ideas." In Sucre a crowd demanding price caps lynched hoarders.[38] As historians Michela Pentimalli de Navarro and Gustavo Rodríguez Ostria have argued, these protests were rooted in popular groups' belief that basic needs and survival, what James Scott calls the "subsistence ethic," trumped rights to private property and market freedom.[39]

By the second year of the crisis, it looked like the Municipal Council would cede to popular demands. The council at first decreed a compensated expropriation of one-fifth of the corn harvest and 10 percent of the wheat and barley crops to feed the population. It also prohibited bulk sales of grain "in order to prevent speculators from exploiting the anguish of the proletariat." But the council quickly backtracked, arguing improving agricultural conditions made "the application of these measures unnecessary." While rains returned in 1879, speculators purchased haciendas' entire harvests and pushed prices up even higher than during the drought.[40] Many Cochabambino drought survivors fled the region for Chile, just as war broke out between the two nations.

The drought-induced crisis may have helped to ignite the War of the Pacific (1879–1884) and almost certainly influenced its course and outcome. The war over Bolivia and Peru's nitrate- and guano-rich coastal provinces, one of the Americas' longest and most deadly wars, was fought between an alliance of those nations and Chile.[41] The war broke out after Bolivia imposed a new minimum tax on the Anglo-Chilean Nitrate and Railway Company that, according to historian and former Bolivian president Carlos Mesa (2003–2005), owed to the economic crisis wrought by the drought.[42] As historian Jorge Basadre has written, "Bolivia intervened in the war...under terrible conditions." Drought and disease killed thousands across Cochabamba, Sucre, and Potosí, crippling Bolivia's war machine.[43] Chile won the war and, with it, Bolivia's Litoral province and Peru's Tarapacá.[44] Bolivia's loss sparked uprisings in La Paz and among troops on the Peruvian coast that drove Hilarion Daza from the presidency. His fall ended an era of rule by military strongmen, opening a new period of a modern parliamentary system of government as elections became contests among civilian leaders of contending political parties. The Conservative, Liberal, and Republican Parties that ruled the country in turn from 1884 to 1935 in the service of the country's mine- and estate-owning aristocracy oversaw a silver boom followed by a tin boom while haciendas expanded in the Altiplano.[45]

At a moment when the perils of private land and water ownership were appallingly clear, the national government launched a sustained attack on *pueblos'* communal land and water holdings. The previous two decades had seen a series of national administrations, alternating between military and civilian presidents, committed to free trade and the dismantling of Bolivia's indigenous communities.[46] A series of laws passed in the 1860s and 1870s attacked community land tenure, including the 1874 Ley de Exvinculación that abolished indigenous communities as legally sanctioned collectivities and instructed the national state to distribute individual titles to land, forests, water sources, and animals held in common and to sell off additional lands considered vacant or unused.[47] Cochabamba liberal intellectuals and politicians such as Nataniel Aguirre and José María Santiváñez supported this effort in hope of demonstrating the superiority of a smallholding model over that of the corporate Indian community and the hacienda, which they considered backward and inefficient. But, as Gustavo Rodríguez Ostria has pointed out, they were "timid liberals," eager to apply their logic to community lands but unwilling to challenge hacienda owners' private property rights.

The crusade against indigenous communities was rooted in both economic liberalism's opposition to corporate property and positivist anti-Indian racism. Proponents of privatizing community land called for transferring land from the "dead hands" of ignorant, unskilled, and poor indigenous community members to the "industrious hands" of national and foreign private landowners. One such text forecast that, in the transition to a hacienda *colono*, the former Indian community member would improve his condition by becoming "like the landlord's son"—in other words a propertyless estate laborer.[48] Bolivian positivists like Daniel Sánchez Bustamante believed that economic modernization would naturally entail the disappearance of "the uncivilized races."[49] Even the 1900 census forecast that "the indigenous race" would soon, "if it has not been completely wiped off the face of the planet,...be reduced to a minimal expression."[50] But like famine, the decline in the indigenous population was neither natural nor inevitable. Rather, it resulted from dispossession of indigenous communities' land, water, and right to exist. By 1900 the national state had carried out one of the most aggressive efforts to dismantle indigenous communities in Latin America.[51]

While at first the state could rarely enforce disentailment laws, the drought provided an opportunity to put them into practice in Cochabamba. In 1878, at the height of the drought and famine, government commissioners circulated in the Central Valley and Valle Bajo, distributing land titles to community members who could document their usufruct rights and "returning" "excess" land to the state for sale. As historian Laura Gotkowitz has explained, late-nineteenth-century *revisitas* "authorized an army of bureaucrats—whose earnings were tied to the number of land titles sold—to penetrate, interrogate, and literally divide up the land of Indian communities."[52] In the highlands Indian communities rebelled violently against these laws and prevented their full implementation.[53] In Cochabamba, in contrast, the transition seems to have been swift and complete due to an already advanced process of population loss and individualization of land ownership—and irrigation water access—within communities.[54] More prosperous members of Cochabamba's *pueblos* who acquired titles to their large holdings may have welcomed the reform as they could now sell or purchase even more land. But land-poor and water-starved community members reeling from drought, disease, and famine who would have likely opposed it could not stop the state from titling preexisting inequalities.[55]

The breakup of indigenous communities in the late nineteenth century spelled the end of formal indigenous self-identification in Cochabamba's central valleys. In the late nineteenth century *indio* was a fiscal category that denoted an individual's membership in a tribute-paying indigenous community. Before community closure, *indio* status at least afforded access to land and irrigation water despite tributary and labor obligations to the state attached to it.[56] When community members received title to their lands, they ceased being *indios* and joined the ranks of the region's mestizo *piqueros*. In Bolivia, and particularly in Cochabamba, *mestizaje* was a process of biological and cultural mixture such that mestizo identity implied not only mixed Spanish and indigenous ancestry but also a mixed cultural identity. This identity shift did not shield mestizos from anti-indigenous racism, however.

Cochabamba remained a creole-dominated society that disparaged and exploited people creoles continued to call Indians and demonized mestizos and urban *cholos* (urbanized Indians) in order to divide and dominate them.[57] In this heyday of scientific racism and community dispossession, a new racial order emerged.[58] With tribute abolished, *indio* ceased to be a fiscal category and instead became, in anthropologist Olivia Harris's words, "more like a class position."[59] As historian Rossana Barragán has explained, late nineteenth-century Bolivian elites conceived of Indian as synonymous with rural laborer.[60]

As Cochabamba's population reeled from famine and disease and authorities dismantled the region's indigenous communities, the executive introduced a new water regulation that granted water rights to landowners. Under Spanish colonial law, private ownership of water was neither based on riparian right nor absolute. An extensive new water regulation introduced in 1879 and elevated to law in 1906 established a riparian water property regime that considered water an accessory to land. In contrast to colonial water law that proscribed allocation of water according to a combination of prior use and need, the new riparian system granted ownership over water sources that were found within, that were located under, or that flowed through a property to the land's owner, including non-navigable rivers and streams, ponds and lakes, aquifer sources, and rainwater. The regulation allowed the prefecture to carry out compensated expropriations of private water sources to supply the public during droughts, but the overwhelming thrust of the law was to establish and protect private water ownership.[61] The new water regulation, the natural counterpart of the Ley de Exvinculación, helped a new group of landowners consolidate extensive control over the region's water sources.

Cochabamba's traditional landlord class emerged from this moment of drought, community closure, war, and water privatization in crisis. After Bolivia's loss to Chile in the War of the Pacific, new free trade policies and railroads gave altiplano markets access to cheap Chilean grain imports that undercut Cochabamba estates. The same free market logic that led to the destruction of indigenous communities and speculation on grain during the famine devastated the region's estates as cheap Chilean wheat flooded altiplano markets.[62] As a result, according to historians Jackson and Gordillo, community closure did not lead to expansion of haciendas in Cochabamba, as it did in the Altiplano. Indebted owners of large estates were mostly unable to purchase pueblo land; those who did likely rented it out as in small parcels to *arrendatarios* (renters).[63] Instead, *piqueros*, landless peasants, hacienda *colonos*, and artisans purchased much of the community land that the state put up for sale. These groups were unencumbered by debt or dependence on far-off markets and amassed capital trading their products in the region's vibrant peasant markets, performing seasonal labor on haciendas, or working in altiplano mines, Chilean nitrate fields, or Argentine sugar plantations.[64]

In El Paso, for instance, *hacendados* purchased around one-quarter of community land, new or existing smallholders bought around 30 percent, and community members kept around 34 percent, now as smallholders with land titles.[65] As *hacendados* descended further into debt, they sold off parcels of their estates to colonos, *arrendatarios*, and *piqueros* whose misery had sustained them during the drought. Sales of both community and hacienda land allowed many *piqueros* to grow their holdings, many *colonos* to escape the confines of hacienda tenancy, and many landless peasants to become smallholders just as community members joined the ranks of the region's *piqueros*. Approximately ten thousand *colonos* became smallholders by purchasing hacienda or community land between 1882 and 1912.[66] The breakup of the Central Valley's indigenous communities and hacienda fragmentation thus helped further consolidate a formidable independent mestizo peasantry in the Cochabamba Valley at the turn of the twentieth century.

Smallholders were not the only beneficiaries of community and hacienda land sales. Newly wealthy elites also bought community and hacienda property, displacing those traditional elites who lost all or most of their land. The most important of these new landholders was the Salamanca family. José Domingo Salamanca, who previously owned little land, began buying up large holdings in the Valle Bajo in the 1860s.[67] By his death in the 1890s, Salamanca's estates included the haciendas Sumunpaya, Collpapampa, Molle Molle, Bella Vista, Montesillo, Chapisirca, and Chacnacollo. Among Salamanca's heirs was his son Daniel, who would go on to found the Republican Party, which split from the Liberal Party in 1914, and to serve as the nation's president from 1931 until he was ousted in 1934 during the Chaco War.[68]

While smallholders increased their ownership of land in these final decades of the century, this new constellation of large estate owners controlled the region's most important sources of water. *Piqueros* purchased plots primarily in the valleys and foothills. Most lacked water sources within their properties and were left with the usually insufficient irrigation turn rights they purchased with their plots, if they had water rights at all. Available records indicate that hacienda owners reduced the duration and frequency of the turns that corresponded to the plots they sold, adding the extra water turn portions to those of their remaining land. In one case, the buyer of a lot in Cala Cala sued the seller, claiming that the seller was allocating the property just two and a half days of water every nine days instead of "the three days and their nights distributed by custom."[69] Those without mita rights had to make do with unpredictable seasonal rains—or buy water from *hacendados*. The property of many haciendas, many of which now had new owners, encompassed mountain lakes in the high reaches of their properties. The 1879 water regulation made these water sources *hacendados'* property. Thus, while the customary mita rights regime still mostly reigned in practice, landlords began to peel water rights away from land by sometimes selling land parcels without all of their customary water rights.

As the owners of a series of haciendas along the Tunari foothills with territory extending up into the mountains, the Salamancas were the region's biggest water owners. Thanks to both the water rights they purchased along with their estates and the 1879 water regulation, the Salamancas owned several large lakes in the mountains and held rights to significant portions of the river water that flowed down the ravines alongside their haciendas. Water owners like the Salamancas possessed more water than they needed to irrigate their own land, a surplus they "rented" to their water-poor *piquero* neighbors and soon marketed to the growing city. While Spanish water law had discouraged such a state of affairs, the new water regulation encouraged and facilitated it.

Hacendados compelled *colonos* and *arrendatarios* to maintain existing irrigation infrastructure and build new dams and canals to tap mountain lakes and rivers in the high reaches of hacienda properties. These irrigation systems provided larger amounts of water at more convenient times to estate fields and less water less often at inconvenient times to *colonos* and *arrendatarios*' plots. This was the case with Saytukocha, a lake dammed at the behest of four *hacendados* in these years, and the San Juan Lakes. In 1880 a group of *hacendados* formed the Sociedad de Explotación de las Aguas de las Lagunas de San Juan (San Juan Lakes Water Users Society) to dam and channel waters from the San Juan Lakes (the lakes San Juan and San Pablito). Their heirs sold their shares and rights to the lakes' waters to the Bolivian tin mining magnate Simón Patiño in 1934 when he purchased several area haciendas, including the hacienda Tirani.[70]

Yet *piqueros* and *colonos* retained and gained control over water sources and infrastructure in various ways in the late 1800s and early 1900s. Groups of *piqueros* built irrigation systems in these years, at times in conjunction with *hacendados*, in other cases independently, thereby expanding their irrigation water access. A group of *piqueros* along with the *hacendados* Vicente Gumucio and José Salamanca improved the Lagunmayu irrigation system, for instance, building a rudimentary sod-and-rock dam to increase the lake's capacity and new canals to channel water from the lake to their fields in the valley below.[71] The Lagunmayu system likely has precolonial origins.[72] The second directorate of lake users, headed by Daniel Gamucio and Daniel Salamanca, oversaw improvements in the 1920s.[73] Hacienda *colonos* and *arrendatarios*, not the *hacendados* themselves, carried out the *hacendados*' share of the labor required. Most *hacendados* were quite removed from the physical labor of transforming the regional waterscape.

In 2011, I spoke with many of the oldest residents of Tirani, now an ex-*colono* community on the northern edge of the city of Cochabamba that was one of the Salamanca family's estates at the turn of the twentieth century. The elders, who were born in the late 1920s and early 1930s, recounted that every year after the dams were built, *colonos* trekked up the mountainside laden with tools, materials, and provisions to spend several days repairing and improving dams and

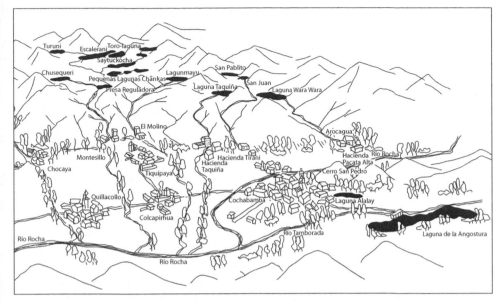

FIGURE 2. Cochabamba haciendas and water sources in the early twentieth century. Drawing by Jorge Camacho Saavedra.

canals.[74] Their accounts offer a window into generations of collective hydraulic labor by hacienda *colonos* and ex-*colono* communities. For these former hacienda *colonos* and their descendants, this historical labor makes them owners of the San Juan Lakes and irrigation infrastructure that their ancestors engineered. Indeed, Cochabamba's waterscape is the product of water users' ongoing work, what anthropologist Hugh Raffles has called "the work of place-making" and "nature-making."[75]

Neither the eclipse of indigenous communities by haciendas and smallholdings nor water privatization eradicated collective water management. In continuing to use collective knowledge and labor to build and maintain irrigation systems, even after the state had privatized water and abolished communal landholdings, *colonos* and *piqueros* retained a connection to the region's multiethnic past that gave them power.[76] *Colonos* and *piqueros* refashioned Andean traditions of communal labor, distribution, and control over water to repurpose existing irrigation systems and build new ones. Collective labor required group discipline, precise organization and coordination, and hydraulic expertise—for instance, creation and knowledge of and adherence to irrigation turn arrangements. On estates this labor built irrigation systems owned by the *patrón*, but it also cohered *colono* communities that built unions starting in the 1930s and seized land and water sources *hacendados* had appropriated from their forbearers in the 1950s. To borrow historian Sonia Lipsett-Rivera's term, a mestizo "culture of water" emerged that was deeply rooted in the region's multiethnic past.[77] Before and during Inca rule, as anthropologist Tamara Bray has written, "it was participation in the communal labor parties and rituals associated with the upkeep of local irrigation canals that confirmed one's members in the corporate body and ensured access to water for the coming agricultural cycle."[78] The same could be said about the twentieth and early twenty-first centuries. Annual communal labor to clean and repair irrigation infrastructure endured among smallholders and on haciendas and persists to this day in *piquero* and ex-*colono* communities.

The drought, water privatization, and *hacendados'* control over regional water sources had significant implications for the city's efforts to increase its water supply. During the drought the springs that fed the city's taps dried up almost entirely, laying bare the vulnerability of the urban water system and generating a strong sense that the city needed to modernize its water system. The way to do this, all agreed, was to gain greater and more reliable water sources for the growing city, which would require access to an appropriate water source, significant funds, and technical expertise. After the drought abated, urban officials and residents turned their attention to this task, pursuing water sources outside the city's immediate environs, now mostly owned by large estate owners and definitively their property.

SUPPLYING THE CITY

In the late nineteenth century, national governments across Latin America and the world set about modernizing cities and integrating national territory through infrastructure such as water distribution networks, roads, and railroads.[79] This was also the case in Bolivia, where efforts to modernize urban water infrastructure and increase water supply to growing cities benefited from a new period of stable civilian oligarchic rule. All three parties in power during this period—the Conservatives (1884–1899), the Liberals (1899–1920), and the Republicans (1920–1935)—were committed to a free market economy, economic modernization, and urban development and public works.[80] State-builders proposed and often carried out public works projects to diffuse political opposition, ease social tension, and modernize the country.[81] As military historian Elizabeth Shesko has shown, these governments marshalled the armed forces to build infrastructure, including water works like dams, irrigation canal, and wells.[82] Hydraulic development became increasingly central to modernity in Cochabamba and cities across the world as urban planners worked to expunge filth and disease from their cities by improving urban water supply and sewerage in this time of what historian Jean-Pierre Goubert has called "the triumph of hygiene."[83]

During Bolivia's liberal period, only literate adult men who met property and income requirements possessed citizenship rights like the right to vote. The literacy rate rose from around 7 percent in 1846 to 17 percent in 1900.[84] But as Laura Gotkowitz has noted, for late nineteenth-century statesmen, citizenship "also conjured up a more figurative sense of national development or belonging" that excluded "the indigenous and mestizo masses," rural and urban alike.[85] Rural toilers excluded from the benefits of citizenship performed poorly compensated labor for elites as estate workers, draft laborers, and conscripts.[86] Although they did not win citizenship rights until later, Cochabamba's mostly illiterate city residents demanded and worked to realize the benefits of urban citizenship—modernized urban infrastructure and public services—in the early twentieth century.[87]

Scholars have written about the divide between European-descended urban elites of the "lettered city" and popular urban and rural classes.[88] Yet, in Cochabamba, urban middle classes and elites without large rural properties were more progressive than landed elites. In the early twentieth century, urban officials and *letrados* increasingly joined urban workers and the poor in efforts to make basic services like water and sewerage more accessible and equitable. Their support owed to amalgam of conviction, pressure from vernacular modernizers, and partisan power plays. At first, local officials and engineers planned unequal access into their overhaul of the system such that the modernization of the city's water infrastructure disproportionately benefited propertied elites. But petitions and letter-writing campaigns pushed local officials to make urban distribution somewhat more equitable within the city and to increase urban water supply. The city's poorer residents were *vernacular* modernizers who pushed urban officials and *letrados* to challenge rural water monopolists and make the regional water tenure regime more public.

Before the drought Cochabamba's urban drinking water system consisted of a series of natural springs whose water flowed through open canals to a central water tank in the city's northeast corner that supplied public taps in half a dozen plazas. By the 1870s many pumps were dry or provided only intermittent supply due to insufficient sources and structural problems. After the drought the central plaza's tap was the city's only functioning water source.[89] The municipal water service was technically the responsibility of the prefecture (state government), and would remain so until 1950, but the Municipal Council spearheaded its administration and overhaul. The council had already started to make improvements before the drought and afterward made this issue its top priority, in 1891 appointing a commission headed by Boleslao Mayerski to develop a plan to "supply the city's taps and fountains with distant water by way of a costly and difficult project," something "everyone now sees as indispensable."[90]

The Mayerski Commission proposed purchasing the Aguas de Arocagua, a series of abundant natural springs located in the foothills northeast of the city owned by Ana María Terrazas. The springs were fed by Lake Wara Wara in the mountains above Terrazas's hacienda, as well as by rainfall that flowed down the Arocagua ravine and underground mountainside passageways.[91] The commission settled on the Arocagua Springs because their water was plentiful and pure, it emerged from the mountains high enough to allow for gravity-powered conduct to a tank above the city, and its owner was a single individual who happened to be a council member's close relative likely willingly to sell. The other springs they considered, in contrast, watered the fields, orchards, and vacation homes of multiple urban elite families who Mayerski argued "should not be deprived of a single drop of water."[92] With support from city residents and the press, the Municipal Council lobbied the national government for funding, citing public health concerns, funding that the national government had provided for drinking water systems in La Paz and Oruro, and "el tributo de sangre" that Cochabamba had paid by providing more than a quarter of all Bolivian troops in the War of the Pacific.[93] The national government came through with the funds, purchasing the Arocagua Springs directly from Ana María Terrazas.[94] Per the 1879 water regulation, property owners owned water and could sell it away from the land it had traditionally served.[95]

Under Conservative Party rule the national government made drinking water for the city of Cochabamba a national priority for the first time. The Aniceto Arce (1888–1892) and Mariano Baptista (1892–1896) administrations paid for most of the work, which took three years and involved laying 7,000 meters of new pipes, installing thirty new public taps, and erecting a new fountain in the center of 14 de Septiembre Plaza (Map 5).[96] The Aguas de Arocagua Committee's final report harkened back to the 1879 drought: "The need became ever more urgent as, apart from the spring water's poor quality and scant quantity, a drought year like that of 1878–1879 could reoccur at any time and threaten the people with true thirst."[97] Not even two decades later, Cochabamba boasted of one of the best urban water systems in the country. Even though the 1879 water regulation favored rural property owners over city residents, the city's needs were modest enough that meeting them did not threaten the interests of rural water owners. The city met its needs through a deal with just one water owner, who consented to expropriation and was generously compensated. But the balance between urban and rural landed interests would prove difficult to maintain as the city grew.

The Liberal Party that took national power after their victory in Bolivia's 1899 civil war left Cochabamba's newly configured landed oligarchy intact but gave rise to a new cadre of urban officials with weaker ties to *hacendado* water monopolists.[98] The war was fought between the Conservative Party that represented the interests of the traditional silver oligarchy based in the old capital Sucre and the Liberal Party that represented emergent tin mine owners based in La Paz. The Liberal Party won in large part due to its alliance with altiplano indigenous leaders who took advantage of the crisis to defend communal land ownership and advance a program of local self-rule.[99] Upon victory, however, the Liberal adminis-

MAP 5. Plano de la ciudad de Cochabamba, 1899. Note the San Pedro Tank (Ref. #28) and the Caja de Agua (Ref. #10). Map created by José Manuel Pando. *Source*: Gobierno Autónomo Municipal de Cochabamba, "Propuesta para la definición del area de regulación urbana de Cochabamba" (Cochabamba, 2014).

tration of José Manuel Pando disarmed the party's Indian supporters and executed indigenous leader Zárate Willka along with thirty-one other Indians. The Liberals then set about building a strong central state committed to private property, modernization, and ethnocidal assimilation.[100]

The Liberal Party maintained the national state's pledge to provide Cochabamba with drinking water. But as elites in the city and its rural outskirts challenged municipal control over the public water supply, Liberal officials' dual commitments to state-led economic and urban modernization on the one hand and the sanctity of private property on the other increasingly came into conflict. One challenge came from landowners in Arocagua. The urban water service received reports that hacienda owners there, including former state engineer and municipal official Juan de la Cruz Torres, who had purchased Ana María Terrazas's estate, were diverting water from the Arocagua Springs to water their fields. The water service issued a warning to Torres and denied his request to use "excess" Arocagua water, but in the years that followed he allegedly continued to use more water than the purchase-sale agreement allowed him.[101]

The water service also faced opposition from a series of urban residents with private connections to water from Arocagua who claimed to own it. In response, the Ministry of Public Works declared that "the waters of Arocagua are public property," given that the national government funded their conduction and that previously obtained titles to Arocagua water conferred use rights, not ownership.[102] In an ongoing conflict with Ambrosio Vera, who claimed to own the water that flowed through a canal the municipality was closing, the Municipal Council determined that Vera had only rented this water from the municipality.[103] This resolution was one among many municipal, prefectural, and national resolutions declaring Cochabamba's drinking water state property in this period.[104] Liberal-run state institutions thus affirmed state ownership and control over municipal water sources, but the challenge of balancing their commitments to state-led urban water development and private land and water ownership plagued municipal officials.

This contradiction was also manifest in the city's highly segregated system of water access. Like in many cities around the world at the turn of the twentieth century, Cochabamba's urban water infrastructure development was uneven and unequal.[105] While most residents drew water from unreliable outdoor public taps, the water service granted "concessions" to businesses and wealthy homeowners who paid a hefty connection fee but only a modest monthly payment thereafter for water piped directly to their homes.[106] In theory, the water service was supposed to prioritize the public over private clients, but in reality the latter had far better service and won reduced fees by collectively refusing to pay their bills.[107] The proliferation of new private artesian wells in these years added a third tier to the differentiated structure of water access.[108]

Periodic drought, infrastructural failures, and increasing demand left those dependent on public taps vulnerable to water shortages, sparking protest against unequal access. In the face of widespread water insecurity, the opposition press began to criticize private water rental and wells. In 1909, for example, the Conservative Party–affiliated newspaper El Heraldo accused private well owners of refusing to give "even a little water to the thirsty who ask them for it when public sources fail to flow," arguing that "selfishness of this sort should be severely punished" and threatening to publish the names of these greedy well owners if they did not change their ways "so that the anger of the people may fall upon them."[109] El Ferrocarril alleged that while wealthy residents with private connections could water their decorative gardens, the public taps that the poor majority, schools, and prisons relied on supplied contaminated water and often remained dry for months on end.[110] Fights sometimes broke out around public water taps whose slow and irregular flow forced residents to wait in long lines.[111] Even after the distribution system was renovated in 1917, pipes continued to break and leak water into the streets.[112] Although the political leanings of the papers reporting these complaints no doubt reflect partisan views, press reports suggest that poor residents were quite vocal about water shortages and may have been critical of private water connections as well. These complaints suggest a developing urban plebian moral economy aimed at democratizing the benefits of modernity.

While Liberal Party officials in the national Public Works Ministry and the Cochabamba prefecture saw private connections as crucial for supporting the water service financially and fomenting local industry, local officials increasingly contested inequality.[113] In 1912, in the face of severe water shortages, the Municipal Council requested that private service be suspended. National and prefecture officials refused.[114] In 1913 the Municipal Council proposed providing private connections to all city homes and eliminating troublesome public taps altogether. But with the distribution network in disrepair and supply insufficient to meet growing demand, the council put this lofty goal on hold.[115] By 1916 the water crisis was so pronounced that the Municipal Council voted unanimously to suspend private water service in order to improve flow to public taps.[116]

Newspaper reports indicate that, in addition to paying various taxes on beer, chicha, and exports that paid for water infrastructure, residents provided labor and funds to maintain and expand water distribution. Residents of the Zona Sud neighborhoods of San Antonio and San Sebastián were especially active in demanding improved service and contributing funds for new taps and labor to connect new fountains and taps to the distribution network.[117] Christina Jiménez has similarly found that the residents of Morelia, Mexico, whom she calls "popular modernizers," supplied labor and funds for urban modernization projects during the Porfiriato and after the Mexican revolution (1910–1920). Her finding that "the municipal government desperately needed and depended on popular initiative and individual investment for the creation of public services" also describes Cochabamba. In both cities the infrastructure that residents built became public property.[118]

"PRIVATE INTERESTS FADE BEFORE COLLECTIVE NEED"

The Liberals ruled unchallenged for more than a decade in large part due to their investment in massive public works projects.[119] But dependence on foreign trade for state revenue made Bolivia vulnerable to the whims of the international market. In 1914, after a decline in tin exports caused an economic depression, a faction led by Bautista Saavedra and Daniel Salamanca split from the Liberals to form the Republican Party.[120] When the Liberals tried to rig the 1920 elections, Republicans staged a coup, ending two decades of Liberal rule. In the 1920s, Republican administrations faced increasing challenges from indigenous communities, labor unions, students, soldiers, and new political parties. Bautista Saavedra, president from 1921 to 1925, was an *indigenista* who had garnered support among urban and mine workers. *Indigenismo* was an elite ideology that glorified the region's native past and defended Indians but sought to keep them in their rural and subordinate place.[121] In the 1920s *indigenistas* no longer defined Indians as tributaries but rather adopted a broad definition of *indio* synonymous with *campesino*.[122]

Saavedra's trajectory exemplified the contradictions of Bolivian *indigenismo*. A lawyer born and educated in La Paz, Saavedra published a study of pre-Columbian indigenous society, *El ayllu*, in 1903, the same year he served as the defense lawyer for Aymara Indians accused of carrying out a massacre during the 1899 Federal War. Yet Saavedra's "defense" rested on describing the violent character of this "degraded race...arriving at the final phases of its disappearance."[123] Despite his promises to protect Indians and support organized labor, as president, Saavedra sent troops to violently repress an indigenous uprising in Jesús de Machaca in 1921 and a miners strike in Uncía in 1923.[124] Saavedra also faced opposition from within his own party.[125]

In many ways the Republicans were, as historian Herbert Klein has put it, "a carbon copy of the Liberals."[126] As the Liberals had, Saavedra's Republicans promoted economic modernization, especially urban public works.[127] But in Cochabamba, Republican officials challenged the rural water monopoly more aggressively than their Liberal predecessors had. Charging the Liberals with denying water to their political opponents, Cochabamba's new Republican water authorities vowed that now "no one [would be] more privileged than the next in gaining a connection." By cutting service to defaulters, limiting private concessions to just one cubic meter per day per home, and cracking down on pilferers, they pledged that "all would equally enjoy the same rights."[128] The water service quickly added one hundred new home connections. But to fully make good on officials' promises would mean increasing water supply, which would in turn require confronting large estate owners in the city's hinterlands who aggressively defended their water property. In these fights local Republican authorities and the press proved themselves much more willing to challenge private water owners and private water ownership than national Republican officials who circumvented local authorities to placate powerful rural water owners such as Ramón Rivero.

Efforts to expand urban water supply in the 1920s exposed water access inequalities within the city and disparities between the city and the countryside. In the forty years since community closure and water privatization, hacienda owners had managed to attach even greater water rights to their landed properties than before by damming lakes in the high mountain reaches of their properties, as discussed earlier in this chapter. In Arocagua, the site of the city's main water source since the 1890s, estate owners such as the Rivero Torres family had attempted to direct water from the publicly owned springs to their own fields.

In the early 1920s the prefecture secured Bs. 100,000 from the national government to increase the city's supply and once again looked to Arocagua to do so.[129]

FIGURE 3. The city of Cochabamba looking northeast from San Sebastian Hill, circa 1920. Photo by Rodolfo Torrico Zamudio. Courtesy of the Fundación Cultural Torrico Zumudio.

Ramón Rivero, owner of Arocagua's Pacata property, offered his water sources for sale to the city. As Municipal Council president in the 1910s, Rivero had called for greater investment in public works like bridges, water supply, and sewer systems.[130] To this day, he is remembered as a dedicated urban booster; a central city avenue named after him honors his legacy. Yet when asked to choose between his commitment to urban public works and his personal interests, he opted for the latter. When Rivera offered to sell his water to the city, he professed deep concern for the "pressing need that exists in the city of Cochabamba for water" and claimed to own "various sources that could provide abundant quantities of this desired liquid."[131] Whether he truly owned these water sources, however, was questionable. The Rivero Torres family, who had purchased the Pacata property from Ana María Terrazas in 1897, undoubtedly held rights to the 2.5 liters per second that had been designated for Doña Ana's personal use in the 1891 purchase-sale agreement. But whether the family owned the more extensive sources Rivero was now offering for sale provoked a heated controversy involving Rivero, the local press, the Municipal Council, and the national government.

At first the case focused on how much water Rivero truly owned, a debate that hinged on how much water the state had actually purchased from Ana María Terrazas back in 1891. Prefect Alejandro Soruco and head water service engineer Federico Rocha held that Rivero owned only the Fuente de Doña Ana's 2.5 liters per second while all other water on the Pacata property and in the Arocagua ravine "belonged exclusively to the state." In response to Rivero's charge that state capture of subterranean flows was hurting his fields' productivity, Soruco retorted in a long and scathing essay in *El Heraldo* that the 2.5 liters per second reserved for the property were meant not for irrigation but rather for use in Doña Ana María's bathroom. In other words, the Pacata property had given up the right to be a productive farm back in 1891.[132] In an attempt to put the matter to rest, the prefecture passed a resolution affirming that all Arocagua water apart from the Fuente de Doña Ana was state property.[133]

In his appeal Rivero contended that the 1891 agreement had reserved not only the Arocagua ravine's surface water for the property's owners but also the ravine's underground flows. Indeed, Rivero had hit on a loophole in the contract. Whether national officials understood the term "springs" ("manantiales") to refer strictly to surface water or to also include underground flows could only be answered by those officials themselves. Rivero cited them to bolster his case, quoting Julio Pinkas, who as director general of the Public Works Department in 1894 had stated, "we did not buy underground water, only springs." Rivero also cited testimony from the *juez de aguas* at the time, who later recalled that "in his official role he had only received custody of 18 springs and their conduction works and not underground water." For Rivero this evidence "ended all discussion."[134]

The controversy became even more heated when Rivero abandoned his negotiations with the prefecture and appealed directly to the national government. In May 1921 he had offered to sell the Chullpakaka Springs (reserving an unspecified portion of them so that its owners "could enjoy the benefit of having their own water in their property in perpetuity") to the prefecture's water service for Bs. 60,000, estimating the work to transport them to the Arocagua collector would cost another Bs. 60,000. At Rivero's suggestion the water service sent former national engineer Alberto Cornejo to measure Rivero's water flow, which Cornejo determined could provide the city with an additional 16.75 liters per second. A month later, Rivero submitted a proposal to the prefecture to carry out the capture project himself. But the next day he abandoned his offers to the prefecture, and together with Cornejo, the supposedly independent evaluator, presented a proposal directly to the Public Works Ministry to sell the Chullpakaka Springs for Bs. 60,000 and carry out the capture project for Bs. 40,000. Then, the day after that, Rivero withdrew all previous proposals that he claimed had been presented "without sufficient study" and submitted a new offer to the Public Works Ministry to sell his water for Bs. 120,000, now claiming that they could provide Cochabamba with an additional 60 liters per second and to carry out the project for Bs. 100,000 instead of the Bs. 40,000 he had quoted a day earlier. Cochabamba authorities and the press were outraged. Clearly, Rivero had not carried out new studies overnight. According to both the prefect and *El Republicano*, the Republican Party–affiliated paper, Rivero was offering to sell water that the municipal water service already owned and used.[135]

The Rivero controversy opened up a broader public debate about the legitimacy of private water ownership at a time when more city residents than ever before lacked sufficient water access. While Rivero claimed that his offer represented a contribution to the city, many local observers felt he was attempting to profit off the city's water crisis. As soon as Rivero offered the water for sale, El Heraldo's editors criticized what they called his "mercantilist attitude," charging that Rivero was trying to "steal the people's money."[136] After witnessing negotiations, the paper argued that given city residents' needs, Rivero should cede the water for free, calling Cochabamba and Arocagua "two inseparable concepts."[137] More generally, this Conservative Party–allied paper contended that private water owners should not be allowed to profit off of urban thirst. "For the good of social harmony and the general interests of the community," the editors boldly argued, "private interests should be sacrificed" and private water property should be abolished to make water access a universal right.[138] In the editors' words, "The water that flows above and below ground is essential for life; wanting to take possession of it is equivalent to trying to gain ownership over the air we breathe. With this criteria of a universal right, the private interests of one or two individuals fade before collective need."[139] The daily's critique of private water ownership and call for universal access would have been unimaginable forty or even twenty years earlier and reflected broader political radicalization.

Despite intense protest, the national government negotiated a deal directly with Rivero that was highly favorable to him. Rivero had shown no intention of backing down. In January 1925, he and his neighbors contracted 150 laborers to construct a 200-meter-long stone wall in just two days that threatened to cut off water to the city. Water service technicians warned that the wall threatened the Arocagua guardhouse and collector with destruction, an eventuality that would deprive the city of water "for a long time, leaving the population thirsty and vulnerable to disease with incalculable consequences."[140] National officials' decision to generously compensate Rivero ended the impasse and once again smoothed over the contradiction between the private rural water monopoly and the city's water needs. In addition to the Fuente de Doña Ana's 2.5 liters per second, the government purchased additional water that officials concluded "had not left the domain of the owners of the Pacata property in the sale realized by former owner Doña Ana María Terrazas." In line with Rivero's view that the 1891 agreement excluded subterranean flows, national officials determined that the earlier sale had "included the springs situated to the left and right to the ravine" but "not those that flow in its bed." The state paid Rivero Bs. 60,000 for the Fuente de Doña Ana and an additional Bs. 80,000 for the ravine's underground flows, the damages the water loss would cause his property, and 18 hectares of land.[141] Regardless of whether Rivero was the rightful owner of these other sources, the state compensated him doubly, for the water itself and for the damage its loss would cause to the value of his land that, according to water service director Rocha, had given up its irrigation water rights thirty years earlier.

While the national government defended private water owners, local officials and other local elites, including members of the ruling Republican Party, increasingly opposed private water owners when the urban public interest was at stake. When the state water service officially took possession of Rivero's land and water in Arocagua a year later, *El Heraldo* declared the transfer illegal due to overpayment and sale of land that the paper charged already belonged to the state.[142] Members of the newly formed Comité Pro-Captación de Aguas and former prefect Soruco boycotted the event to protest the terms of the deal and the national government's decision to override their authority.[143] While power struggles between national and local authorities continued to plague the effort to bring additional Arocagua water to the city, the capture-conduction project concluded in 1929. City residents often attended authorities' inspections and along with the press expected the project to finally put an end to water shortages.[144] So when it only yielded 28 liters per second of the 40 to 45 liters per second promised, they declared it a failure and a swindle.

El Comercio, edited at the time by future Chaco War correspondent and Movimiento Nacionalista Revolucionario (MNR) Party founder Augusto Céspedes, charged that Cochabamba was now "in a worse situation than before" and that the project "had not increased water supply in the slightest."[145] Water renters connected to the new distribution network reported that they received barely enough water for a drink.[146] A Cochabambino engineer accused the project's promoters of offering a "false and fantastical poem" that got authorities and the public excited only to leave them "without enough water once again."[147] Even *El Republicano* lamented, "The trusting inhabitants of this valley thought, full of happiness, that they would have enough water to drown in. But the reality has been bitter: we have beautiful tanks and an extensive network of pipes. The only thing we lack is water."[148]

Regardless of who was to blame, all agreed that the city needed yet another water-capture project.[149] One possibility was bringing water from Lagunmayu, the mountain lake owned by a group of *hacendados* and *piqueros* discussed earlier in the chapter. A congressional commission appointed to inspect the lake and the press painted a mesmerizing picture, raising people's expectations.[150] The water service could not afford the project, however, so opted to purchase an additional 10 liters per second in Quintanilla to direct to the nearby Arocagua collector instead.[151] The Aguas de Quintanilla project was inaugurated in October 1931, just before the country entered a devastating war with Paraguay over control of the Gran Chaco.[152] The Chaco War (1932–1935) was the longest and bloodiest international war in Latin America in the twentieth century. While the border dispute between Bolivia and Paraguay in the Chaco was long-standing, in 1931 Bolivian president Daniel Salamanca (1931–1934) shifted from a defensive to an offensive position, aggressively confronting Paraguay in a bid to distract the country from economic crisis and social unrest.[153] Recent scholarship has shown that while oil companies did not instigate the conflict, "fossil fuel capitalism," to use anthropologist Bret Gustafson's term, fueled the militarist nationalism that undergirded it. Foreign oil companies benefited from Latin American nations' dependence on fossil fuels, and many Bolivians initially supported the war to defend petroleum reserves and win an export outlet to the sea.[154] Bolivia lost the war, ceding rather than gaining territory in the Chaco. As Herbert Klein has noted, while Bolivia had lost more valuable territory to Chile in the War of the Pacific, "the impact on the population itself [was] slight."[155] The Chaco War, in contrast, led to a huge loss of Bolivian—and Paraguayan—lives. The military ousted Salamanca in November 1934, elevating his vice president and Liberal politician José Luis Tejada Sorzano to the presidency.[156]

The combined effects of war and the Great Depression, which led to the collapse of tin prices and bankruptcy, meant that residents' complaints about drinking water shortages and resulting health problems found little response in the early 1930s.[157] Wartime austerity and mobilization left the city without funds or labor for water projects such that by the war's end the city's population was surviving on minimal water rations. As the country emerged from the war, there was a growing consensus in Cochabamba that a new water-capture project was urgent, and that it could not come from the already overstretched springs around Arocagua. Increasingly, public officials and observers turned their attention to lakes in the Tunari Mountains. In a moment of particular enthusiasm, the new local newspaper *El Imparcial* imagined that "as the lakes of the Tunari Mountains are many, with some determination we could collect all of this water for the city."[158]

Between the War of the Pacific and the Chaco War, the department capital had grown from a village to a major city. In 1935 it was Bolivia's second largest city with 52,000 people, more than double the population of 21,900 in 1900.[159] The development of the municipal water system was a measure of the change that had taken place. The water service had procured new sources in Arocagua and its surroundings, built conveyance and distribution infrastructure, and increased the number of outdoor public taps and in-home connections in the growing city. Yet throughout this period, residents constantly complained of deficient service and unequal access. By its end, the water service had yet to obtain water sources sufficient to meet current let alone future demand. Whether more ambitious water-capture schemes would be possible in the new period of recovery and reform that was opening remained to be seen.

CONCLUSION

Due to long-term processes of land and water dispossession and resulting internal inequalities, Cochabamba indigenous communities were weaker than in other areas of the country, and private land and water ownership rights were stronger. Nevertheless, Cochabamba's indigenous communities, resettled in the late sixteenth century, survived this onslaught through the late 1870s. It was only then, when the most severe drought in nearly a century allowed national officials to completely privatize remaining community landholdings and water sources, that indigenous communities juridically organized as such disappeared from the Cochabamba Valley. Along with land, haciendas (and community elites) had appropriated irrigation rights, leaving most community members almost entirely dependent on fickle seasonal rains. Thus, when severe drought struck in the late 1870s, *hacendados* were poised to take advantage of it, while those without the grain stores that irrigation access facilitated went hungry. When national officials arrived to title community lands in 1878, those who might have otherwise opposed them were either starving or dead.[160]

Liberal economic and political reform had contradictory impacts on land and water property relations that owed to the contradictions of classical liberalism itself. Breaking apart indigenous communities and privatizing their land and corresponding water rights favored inefficient and unproductive haciendas that liberal reformers theoretically opposed as much as *pueblos de indios*. In the Altiplano, communities more successfully resisted disentailment and haciendas benefited from community land sales. In Cochabamba, in contrast, disentailment destroyed the vestiges of indigenous communal land and water ownership in the valley, strengthening private land and water ownership rights more than in the Altiplano. But free trade policies also eroded Cochabamba *hacendados*' grip on traditional highland markets, damaging the traditional hacienda-dominated local economy. Community closure and hacienda crisis opened up indigenous community and hacienda land for sale, giving smallholders the opportunity to buy land as community members also became *colonos* and title-bearing *piqueros*.

Newly wealthy elites also purchased community and hacienda land along with much of region's water supply. The 1879 water regulation legalized what had until then been an informal system of private water ownership, allowing large landholders to extend their control over the region's water sources still further. While water had long been in private hands in the Cochabamba region and across the country, establishing a riparian system that granted formal property rights to water sources found within landowners' properties gave them new power in a drought-prone, semiarid region where smallholders, industrialists, and residents of the growing city all craved greater water access. *Hacendados* mobilized estate workers and *piqueros*' knowledge and labor to expand their access to the region's water sources and used their disproportionate control over regional water sources to battle *piqueros* in markets and to extort the growing city. But *piqueros* and *colonos* also developed hydraulic knowledge as they engineered new irrigation infrastructure in these years.

Privatization policies divested the state of its power to organize and regulate water use, undermining officials' ability to improve and expand urban infrastructure and services after the drought ended. Once water was legally the private property of rural landowners, and an overwhelming concentration of water sources came under their control, authorities had no choice but to bargain with them to increase water flow to the growing urban population. So long as urban water needs were modest and the national government was willing pay inflated prices, local officials could smooth over the contradiction between water hoarding and growing urban demand—and deal with the state's self-imposed weakness—by purchasing water from *hacendado* water monopolists. But when private water ownership began to threaten the future of the department's capital city, local officials and the press broke with the national government and challenged rural water owners' monopoly and price gouging. Under pressure from urban residents in the 1920s, a period of radical ferment across the Andes and Latin America, local officials tried to expand water supply. Resulting conflicts between urban officials and hacienda water owners sparked heated public debates about private water ownership that began to challenge its legitimacy. Popular pressure also pushed officials to challenge unequal distribution within the city.

The devastating Chaco War temporarily halted these efforts and discussions but ultimately fueled demands for more radical change. After the war popular groups began to take a more active role in protesting water scarcity and pressing for hydraulic development. With migrants streaming in from the countryside and the front, the city's population swelled and the region's social composition began to change. Migrants returning from highland tin mines and Chilean nitrate fields in the 1910s and 1920s brought back traditions of militant class conflict and union organization while soldiers arriving from the front in the 1930s carried strong claims to the promises of national belonging. In the post-Chaco reform era, local authorities and urban and rural water users debated how to supply greater water to fields and urban neighborhoods, where it should come from, and who should get to decide.

Engineering Water Reform

Military Socialism and Hydraulic Development

When the Cochabamba prefecture expropriated mountain lake flows that irrigated perhaps a dozen haciendas along with hundreds of small farms to increase water supply to the department capital in 1940, affected *hacendados* and small farmers (*piqueros*) protested. But while the *hacendados* offered no concrete alternative, the *piqueros* proposed expropriating the Chapisirca Lakes, owned by the children of Daniel Salamanca, the late president who had led Bolivia to war in the Chaco in 1932. Remarkably, the prefecture withdrew its original plan and expropriated the Salamanca family's Chapisirca Lakes instead. This episode was at once a measure of how much and how little national politics and local water tenure relations had changed in the aftermath of the Chaco War (1932–1935).

The horror of the war and Bolivia's loss to Paraguay produced a political crisis that ended the rule of the liberal oligarchic parties that had lasted for more than half a century. In addition to a large swath of its southeastern territory, the war cost Bolivia somewhere between 2 and 3 percent of its population, around fifty thousand to sixty thousand lives.[1] By so callously sacrificing Bolivian lives, President Salamanca inadvertently sped up a process of political radicalization already under way in the country's mines, universities, factories, and fields. This crisis gave rise to what political theorist René Zavaleta Mercado has called a "national-popular consciousness" opposed to the mineowner-landlord oligarchy and its state.[2] The war ended the old order once and for all, ushering in a period of reform in which new political leaders and parties, social movements, and organized labor contended to erect a new one.

After the war, miners, urban workers, peasants, and indigenous communities mobilized, left-leaning political parties grew and exerted influence, and junior military officers known as "military socialists" assumed the presidency. Among the demands of peasants, indigenous communities, and residents of growing cities was improved water access. The post-Chaco period saw protests against urban and rural water inequality and water scarcity across the country, most of all in Cochabamba, where after centuries of dispossession and a half century of liberal economic policies, landlords controlled water even more than land. Drought and urban migration after the war made an already difficult situation desperate.

After the Chaco War the presidency passed back and forth between conservative high-ranking military officers who represented the discredited aristocracy and reformist junior military officers who aligned themselves with the masses. The military socialist period began when Army chief of staff, lieutenant colonel, and Chaco War hero Germán Busch seized the opportunity presented by a general strike in La Paz to overthrow President José Tejada Sorzano in 1936. Busch ceded power to his superior, Colonel David Toro (1936–1937), whom he then succeeded as president from 1937 to 1939. This was the first time that the military had directly intervened in politics in more than fifty years.[3] As historian Kevin Young has explained, "military socialism combined resource nationalism"—leveraging natural resources to serve the population—"and mildly progressive labor policies with an authoritarian corporatist vision intended to bring society's conflicting groups under state direction."[4] The military socialist administrations put state-led economic and infrastructural development, which they believed could reconcile conflicting classes, at the center of their agenda.[5]

The Toro and Busch administrations were unwilling to challenge the unequal land tenure regime, but they made water more accessible to the poorer classes in the city and countryside, most decisively in Cochabamba. This chapter examines two major hydraulic infrastructure projects that involved redistribution of water sources in Cochabamba: the Angostura irrigation project and the expropriation of the Chapisirca Lakes to increase drinking water supply for the department capital. These two projects were the most important efforts to increase water access in Cochabamba since the Arocagua Springs expropriation in the 1890s. They expanded water access and challenged private property more than earlier projects. Cochabamba was the ideal site for engineering water reform: smallholdings were prominent, the importance of haciendas in the regional economy had declined, the water tenure regime was much more unequal than the land tenure regime, Cochabamba remained the country's most important agricultural center, and the urban population was growing quickly.

Water reform was possible politically and preceded land reform precisely because its architects meant for it to prevent the latter. The military socialists, other reform-minded intellectuals and politicians, and the governments that followed Busch—conservative and reform-minded alike—saw hydraulic infrastructure as a technical fix to expand irrigation water access, increase agricultural production, and improve urban water access without significantly challenging large landed interests. These projects promised to increase irrigation water for *hacendados* and smallholders alike as well as city dwellers without expropriating much water or land from landowners. Like the technocratic projects meant to alleviate drought in the Brazilian *sertão* studied by historian Eve Buckley, hydraulic infrastructure seemed to promise "an apolitical means to end poverty" that would "reduce elites' monopoly over natural resources and wealth without provoking violent confrontation."[6] The military socialists sought to engineer water reform not by redistributing *existing* privately owned water sources but by building new hydraulic infrastructure that would produce and distribute *new* irrigation water sources and by purchasing water sources rural estates were willing to sell to supply to the city. Yet Bolivia's water reform program was more radical than it appeared. By expropriating private land to create the Angostura dam and reservoir and expropriating hacienda water sources to supply the city, reform-era hydraulic engineering helped pave the way for more extensive redistribution of water and land in the revolutionary decade that followed.

CARDENISMO IN BOLIVIA

In April 1938, Bolivia's new ambassador to Mexico, Alfredo Sanjinés, undertook a twenty-day tour of Mexican irrigation systems and dam projects in several northeastern states guided by the director of Mexico's new Comisión Nacional de Irrigación (CNI), Francisco Vázquez del Mercado. The ambassador was struck by Mexico's similarities to Bolivia and became convinced that a similar national irrigation program would allow Bolivia's military-socialist-led state to build its presence in the countryside and improve agricultural productivity and peasant living conditions. He vowed to see that Bolivia follow Mexico's example and soon proposed that the CNI send a mission to Cochabamba.[7] Mexico's irrigation program was appealing to Bolivia's military socialists, intent as they were on spurring agricultural production without confronting unequal land and water ownership.

Organized labor, the left, and military socialists alike agreed that to end the economy's dependence on mining and foreign food imports would require jumpstarting agricultural production. This raised the question of how to address the unequal landed property regime, especially in the Altiplano where large, often unproductive estates dominated. As recent scholarship has emphasized, military socialist presidents and new left parties were timid in their approach to agrarian reform in this period.[8] Intense popular mobilization by peasants and indigenous community members in the countryside in the 1930s and 1940s led to important reforms, most importantly the abolition of *pongueaje*, the system of uncompensated, obligatory, and humiliating labor on estates and public infrastructure, tentatively in the 1938 Constitution and more definitively after the first National Indigenous Congress held in 1945. The 1938 Constitution also expanded the electorate by eliminating property and income requirements but maintained the literacy requirement that barred a majority of Bolivians from the franchise. In 1950, 69 percent of the population was illiterate.[9]

But although all of the 1940s-era reform parties discussed ways to increase agricultural production, they mostly balked at expropriation and redistribution of land to the peasantry. This hesitancy on the agrarian question owed to the significant political and economic power of large estate owners even after the rise of the military socialists. Despite the political crisis for the traditional oligarchy and its political parties, few were willing to take on the property rights of the *hacendado* class or the landowners associations that represented them. Military socialist governments thus sought other ways to build and leverage state power to diversify the economy and uplift the rural indigenous peasantry, looking to Mexico as a model. President Busch oversaw the drafting of a new constitution in 1938 that followed the example of Mexico's 1917 Constitution by making the state responsible for guaranteeing social welfare and making private property rights conditional on social utility.[10] Bolivia also took Mexico's lead on water tenure reform and hydraulic development by launching a national irrigation program. The military socialists modeled their national irrigation program on the Mexican example and invited Mexican engineers to Bolivia to design and build a major irrigation project, the nation's first, in Cochabamba. While the military socialists were unwilling to extend the logic of social utility to agricultural land, they did apply it to the water tenure regime and hydraulic development, in the constitution and in practice, and drew on Mexico's example and Mexican expertise to do so.[11]

The question was what water reform would look like in a country that had not undergone land reform. In Mexico the 1917 Constitution was the product of a bloody, decade-long social revolution. The revolutionary charter nationalized all water sources and revolutionary polices promised to make them available to small farmers and cities. These measures built on prerevolutionary laws that had expanded state control of water and responded to urban and rural demands. Renewed protest in the 1920s and 1930s pushed the national government to fulfill this commitment to a significant though limited degree.[12] Under President Lázaro Cárdenas (1934–1940), the Mexican government carried out a massive land transfer and undertook projects across the country to improve irrigation water access for peasants newly endowed with land.[13] Bolivia, of course, had not redistributed land, let alone undergone a major social revolution. But starting in 1938 under President Busch, the Bolivian government began to make water more accessible in the country's agricultural valleys and cities, inaugurating a period of hydraulic reform that involved unprecedented large-scale hydraulic engineering projects.

First, the military socialists nationalized a range of water sources. As part of its mission to condition property rights on social utility, the 1938 Bolivian Constitution federalized rivers, marshes, and medicinal waters as well as "all of the physical forces able to be used for economic purposes."[14] The "physical forces" in question were not specified and it was therefore unclear if privately owned water sources that could be used for irrigation, hydroelectric production, industry, or human consumption qualified. But the constitution's bold declaration of state ownership of at least some if not all water sources upset the 1906 water law (based on the 1879 regulation) that had privatized water ownership. This partial nationalization together with the assertion of the state's right and obligation to infringe on private property and industry in the interest of "public security and needs" quietly established the state's right to expropriate privately owned water sources and redirect them to needy farmers and consumers. While Herbert Klein has argued that the 1938 Constitutional Convention's "active reformism left Busch rather bewildered," President Busch enthusiastically took up the opportunity to pursue an irrigation project that promised to increase agricultural production and improve food security.[15] While the Constitutional Convention was under way, Bolivia's ambassador to Mexico was laying the groundwork to offer Busch's government an opportunity to put its vision of state-led economic and hydraulic development into practice.

Alfredo Sanjinés, the prominent Paceño lawyer, journalist, and writer who served as ambassador to Mexico under Busch, was the period's most vocal advocate of water reform and one of Bolivia's earliest and most unequivocal promotors of land expropriation and redistribution. In his 1932 book *La reforma agraria en Bolivia*, Sanjinés had called for "better distribution and use of land."[16] Clearly referring to the Mexican Constitution's Article 27 in a moment when the oligarchy still ruled the country, Sanjinés asked, "Does land in Bolivia meet social needs, and is the property exercised in the collective interest? Does private capital even modestly meet one of its most basic purposes, which is to lower the cost of living in order to contribute to the general wellbeing?"[17] While Sanjinés stopped short of calling for complete expropriation of hacienda land, and supported indemnification, these were radical questions in Bolivia in 1932. His proposal was the first articulation of the program ultimately adopted after the 1952 revolution: expropriation of unproductive estate land—and water sources—and their redistribution to estates' tenant laborers. Already in 1932, Sanjinés proposed that the national government carry out irrigation works.[18] After the war military socialists took up Sanjinés's call for the state to build irrigation works, a mission he found the opportunity to advance personally.

As ambassador to Cárdenas's Mexico in the late 1930s, Sanjinés became enthralled with the achievements of land reform and hydraulic development. During Cárdenas's presidency the Mexican state redistributed forty-five million acres of land and the Comisión Nacional de Irrigación, established in 1926 under President Plutarco Calles (1924–1928), built a series of dams to increase the productivity of *ejido* land.[19] The Mexican example was equally compelling to Bolivian president Busch and his new minister of agriculture, Carlos Salinas Aramayo. Busch and Salinas agreed with the Mexicans and Sanjinés that increased peasant access to irrigated land was crucial for rejuvenating agricultural production. Bolivian military socialists were drawn to the *cardenista* model of state-led reform aimed at economic diversification, greater agricultural productivity, and uplift of the rural poor. Military socialists' commitment to indigenous and peasant communities reflected the prevailing *indigenista* ideas of the reformist intellectuals and elites in the 1920s and 1930s.

Like in other Latin American countries at the time, *indigenistas* generally took one of two approaches to the "Indian problem" in the prerevolutionary period, prescribing either education and social uplift or access to land. The first outlook was based on the explicitly racist idea that Indian culture and perhaps biology was backward but evinced some "hope" that education and other cultural projects could redeem, uplift, and civilize Indians. The second position blamed indigenous peasants' poverty on land dispossession and advocated returning land to indigenous communities. These visions were not mutually exclusive, but peasant and indigenous community organizing began to push creole and mestizo reformists toward the land and labor reform approach. The reformist state's effort to provide peasant and indigenous communities with water recognized the material basis of rural poverty but, like irrigation projects in Brazil's semiarid *sertão* and *zona da mata*, skirted the contentious issue of unequal land ownership.[20]

As ambassador, Sanjinés played a key role in bringing Mexican engineers to Bolivia to design and build the Angostura irrigation dam. After six months of negotiations between the two governments facilitated by Sanjinés, President Busch invited CNI director Francisco Vázquez del Mercado to bring an irrigation mission to Bolivia in December 1938.[21] Busch and the Mexican engineers settled on the Angostura project in Cochabamba, the country's historic breadbasket, for Bolivia's inaugural state-led irrigation project. Cochabambino Carlos Saavedra Antezana, one of the Angostura project's lead engineers and later a prominent national irrigation department official, explained why. In an article in the CNI publication *Irrigación en México*, Saavedra reported that while Cochabamba enjoyed "all of the favorable essentials for large-scale development: land, water, and climate," just 40,000 of the Central Valley's approximately 100,000 hectares of agricultural land were irrigated.[22] The CNI engineers proposed a 22-meter-high dam to detain and store water from the Sulti River (now the Tamborada River) in Cochabamba's Valle Alto to irrigate 10,000 hectares of underused land in Cochabamba's Central Valley.[23] The dam was to sit at a narrow opening in the mountains where the Tamborada flows from the Valle Alto down into the Central Valley (see Map 2). The beauty of this plan was that it would not require expropriating water already in use but would instead utilize water that would have otherwise followed its natural course into the Central Valley's Río Rocha and then out of the region. Both *hacendados* and *piqueros* stood to benefit.[24]

By the time construction was set to begin in 1940, President Busch had died by suicide and the conservative oligarchy had regained power. Although, as Herbert Klein has written, "the traditional parties were to discover that a return to prewar conditions was impossible," they certainly tried to go back. Conservative military presidents Carlos Quintanilla (1939–1940) and Enrique Peñaranda (1940–1943) tried to dismantle reforms enacted by the military socialists, especially peasant unionization and *colono* purchases of hacienda land in Cochabamba's Valle Alto. But these conservative military regimes continued to pursue the Angostura project and a broader national irrigation program.[25] Both the military socialist and conservative regimes agreed with Saavedra that irrigation works like the Angostura project were necessary to overcome overdependence on the mining sector.[26] They were also facing pressure from indigenous communities and peasants to make land and water more accessible. When indigenous Quechua communities convened for regional indigenous congresses in Sucre in 1942 and 1943, for example, they implored the government to construct "irrigation works that reach all communities."[27] Military socialist and conservative governments' mutual commitment to improving irrigation flowed from their shared desire to diversify the economy and quell unrest in the countryside without confronting the landed oligarchy.[28]

Efforts to diversify the economy by stimulating agricultural production soon found another foreign advocate: the 1942 US economic mission to Bolivia, led by Merwin L. Bohan. The mission's influential report recommended economic diversification to reduce dependence on tin exports and bolster domestic production of consumer goods. Like Bolivian reformers, Bohan concluded that change should begin with increasing agricultural production, which required expanding irrigation access. This first formal US economic planning counsel in Bolivia, which took place during World War II as part of US president Franklin Roosevelt's Good Neighbor Policy, is best remembered for its call to expand agricultural production in Santa Cruz, which was its recommendation for immediate action.[29] But its authors also endorsed a national irrigation program to increase agricultural production across the country's varied geographic regions, from the Altiplano to the valleys to the tropics to the lowlands. As the report recognized, such a program was already under way in Cochabamba. Once the Angostura project was complete, Bohan predicted that Cochabamba, already the country's "most productive area," would be able to "satisfy a large part of Bolivia's large demand for fresh produce."[30]

It fell to conservative governments to expropriate Valle Alto land parcels slated to be flooded under the Angostura reservoir. Just days after he assumed the presidency, Quintanilla decreed land expropriations for the Angostura reservoir on the basis of "public need and use."[31] Peñaranda, Quintanilla's successor, cited the military-socialist-era 1938 Constitution's Article 107 to justify expropriations.[32] Nearly all affected landowners were peasant smallholders. These eighty-five farmers, who owned parcels ranging from just 0.3 hectares to 20 hectares, skillfully negotiated an agreement with the government that allowed them to benefit from the project. While Peñaranda's decree established that the state would indemnify landowners, many of the affected smallholders offered to cede their land for free in exchange for freedom from taxation as well as rights to farm the ceded portions when reservoir water levels receded during the dry season, to draw on the reservoir's water to irrigate their remaining parcels, and to reclaim their lands if the state canceled the project.[33] These proposals demonstrate smallholders' close acquaintance with the hydraulic environment, infrastructure, and the law, as well as their growing confidence and ability to advocate for greater irrigation access. Peñaranda accepted their proposal.[34]

The farmers explained their motivations in both practical and political terms, expressing willingness to sacrifice for the general welfare. One smallholder, León Rocha, indirectly referring to the 1938 Constitution, explained, "Because the works being constructed in Angostura are for the public good, aimed at storing water for the irrigation of the valley, and most of all in order to obtain the benefits in accordance with the Supreme Decrees of July 31 and December 15, 1942, I am pleased to cede [my] parcel for free."[35] The language in these agreements is quite similar, suggesting that the smallholders made a collective agreement with the government and that the documents were drafted by a notary or lawyer.[36] Fifty-nine of the eighty-five smallholders affected made this deal, including the owner of the biggest (20-hectare) property, Isabel Reyes. It is unclear how much of this land was irrigated before, but the terms of the deal suggest it was only partially irrigated at best. It is hard to know if these smallholders were connected to Valle Alto *colonos* who were organizing unions and trying to rent estate land in the 1930s and 1940s.[37] But the fact that those who should have been most negatively affected by the project became its beneficiaries helps explain why the project was successful and testifies to peasant smallholders' growing negotiating power in this period of hydraulic reform.

The government forcibly expropriated portions of just two large estates. Antonio Zapkovic had purchased a 488-hectare property for Bs. 160,000 thousand in 1939, and Esteban Yankovic 494 hectares for Bs. 300,000 in 1940. When the state attempted to expropriate 56 hectares of Zapkovic's land and 61 hectares of Yankovic's, the two men demanded more for these portions than they had paid for the entire properties, nearly Bs. 600,000 total, on the basis of the properties' wealth of irrigation resources. The state assessor countered that they should be paid Bs. 100,000 each. The prefecture then hired a mediator who assessed the parcels' worth at Bs. 500,000 each—a sum he, like the owners, based on the properties' significant irrigation water rights.[38] The case dragged on for three years and

FIGURE 4. The Angostura dam under construction, circa 1945. Photographer unknown. Courtesy of the Viceministerio de Recursos Hídricos y Riego, Ministerio de Medio Ambiente y Agua.

was ultimately decided under reformist military president Gualberto Villarroel (1943–1946).[39] The decision in the Zapkovic-Yankovic case is revealing. It was determined that the men had purchased the land speculatively, with knowledge of the coming dam construction project, intending to resell it to the state at an inflated price. The official overseeing the case berated the men for attempting to defraud the state, citing the 1938 Constitution, which, anticipating such schemes, established that indemnification costs be determined according to previously assessed values. The Ministry of Agriculture paid the men just over Bs. 100,000 each and revoked the apparently corrupt mediator's agronomist engineer's license.

This case and the Angostura project more generally reveal the contradictory dynamics at work in military-socialist governments' approaches to water reform. The state expropriated the property of two newly rich large landowners (and a few dozen smallholders) in the interest of the public good, economic modernization, and agricultural productivity. The landowners were compensated, but on the state's terms, preventing them from profiting (too much) off of the public interest. For now, the national government was able to use projects like Angostura to satisfy multiple interests—those of small peasant farmers, hacienda owners, and economic development—while maintaining the illusion that hydraulic development would reconcile the conflicts among them. State leaders and professional engineers supported the Angostura dam because, as historian Matthew Vitz has written about similar efforts in postrevolutionary Mexico, the project "fused scientific claims, modern engineering's transformative potential to spur agricultural productivity, and the imperative to build the new state."[40] Like in the Brazilian *sertão*, the project seemed to offer a technical fix to the problem of unequal water access.[41]

But the Angostura project's benefits were distributed unevenly. All of the water went to Central Valley properties where haciendas benefited more than small farms, and small farms closer to distribution canals in the Tunari foothills benefited more than those further down in the valley. As Jose Gordillo has explained, "Piqueros in the northern foothills of the Tunari Mountains were the main beneficiaries of the free water project, for it placed them in a powerful position in contrast to piqueros in the south. The former group would probably profit from free water, selling their water surplus to the latter group."[42] Later, with redistribution of hacienda land and water rights in the 1950s, former hacienda *colonos* became Angostura beneficiaries as well. But in the 1940s, Angostura mostly benefited haciendas and smallholdings that already held rights to irrigation sources flowing from the Tunari Mountains.

Despite its benefits for haciendas, Cochabamba's Federación Rural (FRC), which represented *hacendados* and spent the 1940s attacking land reform proposals, opposed the project. Sanjinés reported that the FRC accused him of bringing "communist elements" to Bolivia and demanded to know why he had not asked their permission before inviting the Mexican engineers. He also recounted that an ex-minister and congressman advised him to tell the Mexicans "not to talk too much about irrigation problems since we don't have those problems here."[43] So too, in Mexico's fertile Laguna region, many large landowners opposed irrigation dams because they threatened to allow collective indigenous peasant landholdings called *ejidos* to become more productive and therefore more competitive.[44] Likewise in the Brazilian *sertão*, landowners opposed plans to create irrigated smallholdings that they feared would attract laborers away from their estates.[45] On the one hand, the Angostura project was the perfect test case for a technocratic approach to hydraulic development: it did not require expropriating land or water from established Valle Alto haciendas and Central Valley estates stood to benefit from the project. Even if it had threatened Central Valley haciendas, their owners were more urban based than in the past and less dependent on income from agricultural production. On the other hand, Federación Rural members were right to worry. After all, in Mexico under Cárdenas, land and water redistribution were the closely linked products of a violent social revolution that overthrew the reigning elite.

The CNI mission to Cochabamba inaugurated and became a model for a broader Mexican effort to spearhead irrigation projects and water tenure reform across Latin America in the final years of Cardenás's presidency. Cárdenas and other Mexican political leaders at the time were eager for the Mexican revolution and its institutionalization to become an international model for development.[46] Sanjinés reported that Cárdenas "wanted to demonstrate that the Mexican Revolution had not only been built in that country but could also serve as a model and guide beyond its borders."[47] Cárdenas met personally with Sanjinés and expressed particular interest in spreading Mexico's hydraulic program to Bolivia due to both countries' large and disadvantaged indigenous peasant populations. Cárdenas thanked Sanjinés for his role in the project, and for the interest he showed in Mexico's problems, "especially" his interest "in the indigenous, who you are studying with a truly scientific approach."[48]

While CNI engineers were still at work in Cochabamba, Cárdenas promoted a Latin America–wide irrigation program, one of his last acts as president, at the First Inter-American Indigenista Congress. The congress was first planned to be held in La Paz in 1939 but ultimately took place in Pátzcuaro, Mexico, in 1940. The Mexican delegation proposed extending land, water, credit, and technical assistance to indigenous groups across the Americas in a proposal titled "La política de irrigación en beneficio del indio" ("Irrigation Policy to Benefit the Indian"). Complete with a cover featuring little red men dotting a map of the Americas on the US Bureau of Indian Affairs edition, the congress's final act recommended that countries with significant Indian populations and extreme land concentration "correct any abuse in this situation" "in accordance with equity and justice" and help Indian populations "improv[e] their economy" by providing them with "land, water, credit and technical services." While the congress did not explicitly call for land expropriation, it recommended that American governments protect "small individual holdings and the collective holdings of the Indians" by making them "inalienable" and that they "give every consideration to the development of irrigation projects, particularly small ones in regions inhabited by natives" to "elevat[e] the material and moral standards of living of the Indians."[49] Despite its paternalistic tone, the congress's calls for governments to provide land to indigenous peasants, protect peasant and indigenous communal land holdings, and extend water access, credit, and technology to native peasants had radical implications, especially for the countries that had not experienced social revolution and land reform to date—all except Mexico. After Cochabamba, Vázquez del Mercado visited other Latin American nations, including Chile and Colombia, where he promoted expanding irrigation access.[50] Bolivia's hydraulic reform was distinctive for coming so early in this regional process and for preceding land reform.

The Angostura project was the first of a series of irrigation projects across Bolivia in the 1940s. The new national irrigation authority, the Dirección General de Riegos, headed by a Mexican engineer who had worked on the Angostura project, built dams across the country, from the Altiplano to the inter-Andean valleys to the tropical lowlands. The irrigation service also laid plans for additional large dams as well as medium- and small-scale irrigation projects to benefit *hacendados*, smallholders, and indigenous communities.[51] National officials considered Cochabamba's La Angostura, also known as "Irrigation System No. 1," to be the nation's most important due to both the challenges and opportunities for increasing agricultural production in Bolivia's breadbasket where smallholders needed water more than land.

Yet unity around hydraulic infrastructure belied deep differences about what modernizing agriculture, rural life, and the nation's economy would require. While Carlos Saavedra and Alfredo Sanjinés's views of the project at first glance seem complementary, they had radically different visions for rural modernization. Writing in 1946, Saavedra was optimistic that completing the Angostura project and others like it would increase agricultural production, thereby uplifting rural Bolivians. He was vague, however, about whom he hoped irrigation projects would benefit, referring to "propietarios" and "comunidades indigenales" without differentiating between large estate owners and smallholders. There are hints that Saavedra wanted to see hydraulic development benefit the indigenous-peasant majority, as when he wrote that "planning exploitation of [Bolivia's] natural resources like land and water will allow us to make agricultural production prosperous and vigorous, which will naturally lead to improved economic and social wellbeing for the country's majority class.[52] But as one of Cochabamba's largest estate owners, he was hardly about to call for land redistribution. Rather, Saavedra saw irrigation works as a means to increase agricultural production and improve indigenous and peasant communities' livelihoods *without* redistributing land, a position he shared with the military socialists who were unwilling to confront large landowners like him.[53]

Sanjinés, in contrast, offered a more radical vision of hydraulic development's potential. For him, the Angostura project was "preparing the Cochabamba valleys for a generous agrarian reform through agriculture irrigated by the Angostura dam," exactly what Saavedra and his ilk were trying to avoid.[54] Based in part on what he had seen in Mexico, Sanjinés developed a Jeffersonian vision tailored to the Bolivian reality that he felt would work well in Cochabamba. Further elaborating on his 1932 program in 1945, Sanjinés foresaw a state-led agrarian reform that would strengthen the position of smallholding peasants by providing them with land and property titles to nurture their confidence and "amor por la tierra" as well as ample irrigation water so that they could produce multiple harvests a year. The smallholders would continue to have some large estates for neighbors, but only those whose owners were willing to make their land productive. In the Altiplano the state would convert indigenous communal holdings into large cooperatives partnered with the state in order to ensure that they "produce efficiently."[55] In short, Sanjinés believed that his efforts to bring the Mexican engineers to Cochabamba had helped lay the basis for a major overhaul of the land and water property regime. As time would tell, he was right.

Sanjinés and Saavedra's differing positions on land reform mirrored debates among the three most prominent antioligarchic parties in the 1940s. The most radical program was that of the Trotskyist Partido Obrero Revolucionario (POR), a party of revolutionary miners founded in exile in Argentina that called for a combined "bourgeois democratic" and "proletarian socialist" revolution led by workers and peasants to establish a proletarian government. This revolution would usher in democratic reforms, establish workers' control over mines, "liquidate large agricultural properties" (feudos), and recognize land takeovers by "Indian serfs" (el siervo indígena) who would "resolve the land problem, and with it the much-debated 'Indian problem.'"[56] The Bolivian Miners' Federation adopted the POR's "Tesis de Pulacayo" at its 1946 congress.[57] The Soviet-leaning Partido de la Izquierda Revolucionaria (PIR) also called for a worker- and peasant–led revolution to nationalize mines, "liquidate feudal latifundios," abolish Indian servitude, and redistribute land—a task that PIR leader Ricardo Anaya said had to be "the work of peasants themselves." The "Indian problem," Anaya wrote in 1945, "we have said a thousand times, is a land problem." The party advocated a sweeping land reform to make the countryside more productive that would entail a "vast irrigation and technification plan" to benefit "all of those who now possess land, large and small."[58]

The Movimiento Nacionalista Revolucionario (MNR) leadership shared the PIR's goal of increasing agricultural productivity but called for a cross-class national revolution of Bolivia's "incipient bourgeoisie," middle classes, workers, and Indians. Socialist revolution, they argued, was not possible in a semicolonial country like Bolivia that lacked a working class capable of leading a revolution and establishing its own rule. MNR leader Walter Guevara Arze argued that nationalism was "the logical conclusion from a socialist perspective" in Bolivia and the nation's "only immediate hope." While some MNR leaders like Guevara Arze, Victor Paz Estenssoro, and Hernán Siles individually called for redistribution of large unproductive estates to peasants and indigenous communities, the party's platform merely advocated "incorporating into national life the millions of peasants marginalized from it" and "a law that would regulate the peasantry's labor."[59] As literary critic Angel Rama has noted, in the 1930s "the frustration of their expectations" for modernization led "urban intellectuals, labor leaders, and political voices of the lower middle sectors to take up the grievances of the countryside... and unfurl the banner of agrarian reform to rally support that would help them address demands and grievances of their own."[60] This was certainly the case in Bolivia. But in the 1940s most MNR leaders hoped they could modernize the country and integrate Indian peasants without redistributing land.

The PIR held more radical programmatic positions on proletarian-peasant revolution and agrarian reform than the MNR and sharply critiqued the MNR for not having pursued land redistribution while co-governing with Villarroel. But the

PIR's participation in the reactionary and repressive *sexenio* governments (1946–1952) discredited the party even among its own membership, leading to its demise. As historian Cole Blasier has explained, "the rapid succession of presidents and cabinet ministers during the sexenio was a symptom of the weaknesses of the traditional parties, their growing lack of popular support in the cities... and growing discontent in the mines."[61] In the late 1940s, as peasants, indigenous communities, and miners were staging revolts and strikes across the Altiplano and valleys, the PIR argued that socialist revolution would be premature. The PIR helped repress mineworkers' strikes and MNR electoral campaigns, pushing the theoretically more moderate MNR in a revolutionary direction. By the time the PIR proposed an agrarian reform institute that would redistribute land and "control irrigation schedules" in 1949, the party had lost credibility among the increasingly militant peasant and working classes.[62]

It was the reform-oriented MNR, not the revolutionary POR or PIR, that led a broad social revolution in 1952 and oversaw far-reaching land and water reform in the years that followed. But first they had to confront Cochabamba's Federación Rural whose *hacendado* members based their defense of private property in part on their expertise. According to an FRC representative, whereas *campesinos* had "never been contributors to progress," *patrones* possessed the "initiative" necessary to construct dams, irrigation works, and roads, and to experiment with new methods, studies, and machinery.[63] Not surprisingly, the FRC leader's improvement discourse failed to acknowledge the role of state institutions, Mexican engineers, and *colono* and *piquero* farmers in designing and building irrigation dams and systems.

EXPROPRIATING THE CHAPISIRCA LAKES

The attempt to make water more accessible through state-led engineering extended to cities as well. The Chaco War as well as *minifundio* (the predominance of landholdings barely large enough for subsistence) and water scarcity in the countryside led large numbers of veterans and peasants to migrate to department capitals after the war. The city of Cochabamba, known for its agreeable climate and economic opportunities, was a popular destination.[64] As the city grew, the already overstretched urban water system failed to meet increasing demand or reach the periphery, leading to intense protest, especially during a drought in 1940. The military socialists took a dual approach to addressing scarcity and inequality, working to "rationalize" urban water use and engineering new water sources for the city. The prefecture's expropriation of privately owned mountain lake water to serve the city in 1940 exposed deep inequalities in the region's water tenure regime and offered both rural smallholders and urban water users an opportunity to make a dent in the water monopoly.

Disparities in urban water access intensified as the city grew after the war. The urban population almost quadrupled from 21,900 in 1900 to approximately 80,000 in 1950. At the same time, city limits expanded, especially to the north and south, with the help of an improved transportation system and the arrival of automobiles.[65] Rapid population growth produced a housing crisis that encouraged and was exacerbated by intense speculation in urban property and housing in the decade after the war's conclusion.[66] By 1945, just 76 percent of the city's residents lived in the now more densely populated city center (the "casco viejo"), compared with nearly all of the city's residents at the turn of the century.[67] The other quarter now lived in a series of small densely populated pockets outside the center surrounded by corn and vegetable fields with little-to-no access to city services.

Like in other Latin American cities at this time, basic urban citizenship rights like drinking water and sewerage services were not guaranteed. Residents either accessed water in their homes, at public spigots, or at informal and often contaminated sources. Neighborhoods that were longer established whiter, wealthier, and closer to the cordillera had the best water access. While in the northern section of the *casco viejo* more than 70 percent of homes enjoyed all three basic services (water, sewage, and electricity), in the poorer more indigenous southern section the figure only reached 50 percent (Map 6). In the newer peripheral neighborhoods coverage was minimal, but not all peripheral areas were equally neglected. Northern neighborhoods dotted with new chalets housing the city's rich and prestigious drew on mountainside springs or drilled artesian wells, while poorer more indigenous residents of western and especially southern neighborhoods further from water sources often had to drink contaminated irrigation water. One municipal functionary, protesting its lack of services, called the Zona Sud "the most wretched area of the city."[68]

Water scarcity and unequal access generated protest across the city in the late 1930s and early 1940s. Established neighborhoods complained of shortages and contamination, new peripheral neighborhoods petitioned for municipal water coverage and protested when spigots ran dry, and investors and developers complained of the failure of water and sewage service to keep up with urban growth.[69] Petitions for water connections poured into the water office from across the periphery, especially from the Zona Sud.[70] Frustrated residents also aired complaints about the housing crisis, environmental contamination, high infant mortality rates, poor sanitary conditions, and the dearth of public services in local newspapers. *El País* agitated for attention to the issue, criticizing northern residents' use of public water to irrigate private fields and gardens, while other areas of the city, especially the Zona Sud, experienced extreme shortages.[71] Many of these complaints likely came from illiterate noncitizens who employed the services of notaries, public scribes, and reporters to make their claims.[72] New middle-class professional organizations like the Cochabamba Engineers Association, the Civic Committee,

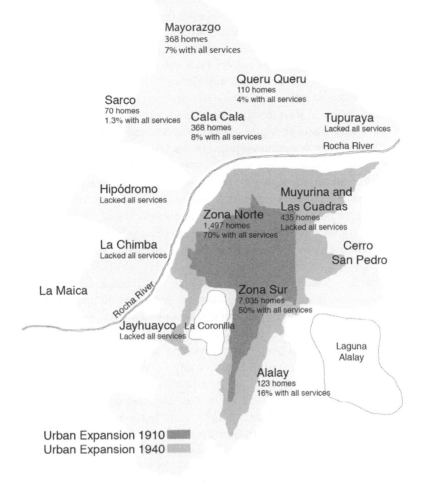

Mayorazgo
368 homes
7% with all services

Queru Queru
110 homes
4% with all services

Sarco
70 homes
1.3% with all services

Cala Cala
368 homes
8% with all services

Tupuraya
Lacked all services

Rocha River

Hipódromo
Lacked all services

Muyurina and
Las Cuadras
435 homes
Lacked all services

Zona Norte
1,497 homes
70% with all services

La Chimba
Lacked all services

Cerro
San Pedro

La Maica

Rocha River

Zona Sur
7,035 homes
50% with all services

Jayhuayco   La Coronilla
Lacked all services

Laguna
Alalay

Alalay
123 homes
16% with all services

Urban Expansion 1910
Urban Expansion 1940

MAP 6. Urban expansion and municipal water coverage, 1940. Map created by Jorge Camacho Saavedra.

and the Comité Pro-Cochabamba (CPC), cut their teeth petitioning the national government to oversee and provide loans for water projects.[73]

Military socialist officials blamed water scarcity on inappropriate and excessive use and attempted to restrict consumption. In part, this approach had a populist logic that faulted wealthy northern-area residents for using the public supply to water their fields, gardens, and orchards. On this basis, water service operators sanctioned Arocagua-area estate owners they accused of siphoning off the public water supply in 1938, forbidding them from carrying out any "type of water use in areas around the filtration gallery that supplies the Cochabamba population" and reaffirming the city's "right to use these waters." An Arocagua installations guard found guilty of secretly selling municipal water to landowners was punished far more harshly with three months of forced labor in the Chapare.[74]

These episodes suggest that prefecture authorities continued efforts begun in the 1920s to prioritize urban residents' water needs over the water property rights of large landowners, at least in some cases. Many rural estate owners were based in the city center where they also owned property and therefore stood to gain from urban water supply expansion projects. But this reasoning could also be used to blame and punish poor water users. National Public Works Department engineer Ricardo Urquidi, for example, attributed the city's predicament above all to the "classic carelessness of our people, who let water flow freely from faucets and domestic reserve tanks." Anticipating later arguments about the "tragedy of the commons," Urquidi argued that the only way to effectively limit water consumption was to impose water meters so that "no one [would] use more than they truly need."[75]

The prefecture prohibited water use for purposes other than human consumption and imposed fines for watering gardens and fields, nonpayment, leaving faucets running, leaky pipes, and other unauthorized uses, warning that "infractions would be rigorously fined."[76] Water service administrators introduced water metering to prevent people from "wasting" water on gardens—odd given officials' professed desire to create a "garden city"—and required customers to install meters at their own expense.[77] El País editors opposed meters, predicting that "terrifying de-hygenization" would result, but the water service won out.[78] One city-center resident was fined for selling water to her neighbor to make chicha, while another on the city's eastern limits was penalized for watering a vegetable garden.[79] While the water in question was metered and paid for, water administrators considered using the public supply to make chicha or water a garden—generally women's activities—theft. Never mind that chicha taxes paid for water infrastructure and expropriations of the urban water supply itself.[80] By imposing water meters and water use restrictions, municipal officials aimed not only to stretch existing supply but also to demarcate the modern sanitary city that drank water from the agricultural countryside that used water for irrigation and chicha production. Even if fines and threats had been effective, existing sources would not have met urban demand. Cochabambino engineers, civic organizations, and the press argued that "a radical and definitive solution" to the city's water crisis would require a large-scale project to "capture the immense water flows that collect in vain in the mountains."[81]

Despite their penchant for limiting consumption, military socialist officials knew Cochabamba required more water to clean city streets, water parks, fuel nascent industry, and supply its growing and politicized population.[82] In June 1936, President Toro assigned administration and execution of all public works projects in Cochabamba to the new national Public Works Department, as did his successor, President Busch.[83] In September 1939, prefect Julio Arauco Prado announced a new water-capture project that he promised would turn Cochabamba into "what it should be: the garden-city of Bolivia."[84] Rather than faulting water users, his approach blamed shortages on shoddy infrastructure and insufficient supply, opening up the possibility of negotiations and perhaps confrontations with *hacendado* and smallholder water owners.

In December 1939, Prefect Arauco Prado commissioned a group of Cochabambino engineers to study water sources in the Tunari Mountains. The commission was led by Vicente Sánchez de Lozada, an engineer who had worked on the Arocagua expansion project in the 1920s. Based on a survey of the region's lakes, rivers, and underground water sources, Sánchez de Lozada recommended improving water capture in Arocagua by tapping additional ravines in the short term while simultaneously initiating a major project in the Tunari Mountains. For Sánchez de Lozada, water scarcity was not a natural phenomenon but rather the result of an inability to make rational use of what were in reality abundant regional water sources.[85] In his view, nature was cooperative and had "resolved the problem in part" by "providing natural water deposits such as lakes, rivers, and underground sources." The engineer's job was to take advantage of the waterscape's natural rhythms to capture, transport, and distribute these sources efficiently, in Cochabamba's case capturing and storing rainwater in natural reservoirs during the rainy season to distribute during the rest of the year.[86] Promising a more ambitious project in the mountains later, the water service took up Sánchez de Lozada's proposal to squeeze still more water from Arocagua ravines as its first postwar water-capture project between 1936 and 1938.[87]

Like in the 1920s, the project required expropriating land and water sources from a group of Arocagua property owners. This time, however, Arocagua estate owners who fiercely opposed the sale were led by the renowned Cochabamba-born and Swiss-educated engineer Julio Knaudt. Like Ramón Rivero, the municipal engineer and Arocagua landowner discussed in chapter 1, Knaudt was an urban-based former municipal official and engineer. Knaudt had designed the rerouting of the Rocha River to prevent flooding as well as Oruro's municipal water system.[88] Prefect Coronel Méndez wrote Knaudt personally in July 1936 informing him that the city's drinking water scarcity crisis impelled the departmental public works committee to appropriate half of Knaudt's flow for the five remaining months of the year. Although the engineer did not initially respond publicly, due (he said) to his dual roles as a public engineer and an affected water-owner, he soon came out against the project. At first, Knaudt claimed to oppose the project on technical grounds, arguing that the water service would "not be able to capture even half of the water that flows beneath the ravine" such that it made little sense to "deprive" Arocagua property owners "of what legitimately and legally belongs to them." He later claimed, however, that he did not oppose the project itself but rather objected to seizure of water without due process. He and other water owners demanded that authorities recognize their water property rights, and Knaudt personally demanded compensation for damages, claiming that the diversion of waters "belonging to me" had left his property dry.[89]

Knaudt, who had spent his career working to improve the city's hydraulic environment, here took an individualist position, much as Rivero had in the 1920s. As they had then, municipal officials scorned Arocagua landowners like Knaudt who, "believing that they have rights to those waters," made capturing water there difficult.[90] The episode contributed to a growing sentiment among water users and local officials in Cochabamba that the rural water monopoly was illegitimate and untenable. Although the expansion project tripled flow to the city, authorities and other observers concluded that a large-scale project in the mountains was necessary to meet the city's demand.[91] The question was who would have to sacrifice water in the mountains, smallholders fortunate enough to have modest irrigation rights or *hacendados* with water to spare?

A drought in 1940 turned concern about water shortages into panic. *El País* announced that Cochabamba had become the most "forsaken place on earth," would soon "die of thirst," and was facing "every imaginable sickness and a miserable state of hygienic practices even worse than in the Congo or on the Maginot Line."[92] While such alarmist comparisons to the horrors of Belgian colonialism or Nazi-besieged France overstated the case, water scarcity hit hard in the city's new peripheral neighborhoods.[93] Residents complained to newspapers about parched conditions on the periphery and epidemics like typhoid that had been in decline were making alarming comebacks in migrant neighborhoods due to poor water and sewage services.[94] The drought and water shortages pushed officials to impose new restrictions, repair infrastructure, and make good on their promise to capture mountain lake water for the city.[95] As one editorial put it, "It is absurd that Cochabamba should suffer from water scarcity when there are great water flows in its surrounding mountains that could easily be tapped with a little money and effort."[96] A proposal to temporarily treat water from the contaminated Laguna Alalay and the Angostura reservoir to increase the drinking water supply met with such intense opposition from farmers, doctors, the press, and others that officials quickly scrapped it.[97] "Everyone," *El Imparcial* reported, "agrees that water from the mountains should be chosen."[98]

Like the Angostura project, the prefecture's plan to expropriate mountain water for the city was another attempt to increase water access without challenging existing water property relations. As they had in previous decades, state officials asked

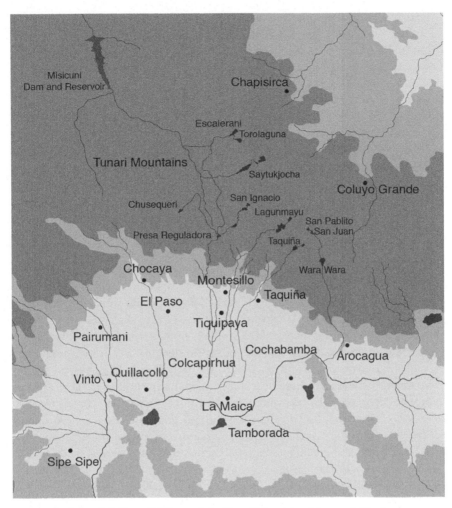

Misicuni
Dam and Reservoir

Chapisirca

Escalerani
Torolaguna

Tunari Mountains

Saytukjocha

Coluyo Grande

Chusequeri

San Ignacio
Lagunmayu

San Pablito
San Juan

Presa Reguladora
Taquiña

Chocaya
Montesillo
El Paso
Taquiña

Wara Wara

Tiquipaya

Pairumani

Cochabamba
Arocagua

Colcapirhua

Vinto   Quillacollo

La Maica

Tamborada

Sipe Sipe

MAP 7. Cochabamba's Central Valley and the Tunari Mountains. Map created by Jorge Camacho Saavedra.

rural water owners to sell their water sources to the water service. But this time they attempted to expropriate a large group of water owners that included both wealthy *hacendados* with water to spare and *piquero* smallholders who purchased water from their wealthy neighbors. The prefecture's first effort to acquire mountain water for the city began in July 1940 with the expropriation of the waters of the Chocaya, Montesillo, and Taquiña ravines (Map 7).[99] Located to the northwest of the city center and fed by various mountain lakes and natural springs, the ravines irrigated fields from Pairumani 20 kilometers to the city's northwest to Taquiña to its north.[100] The lakes Machu Mita, Lagunmayu, Capacachi, and Chapisirca flowed down the Montesillo ravine and irrigated farms in a vast area of Tiquipaya, while Lake Taquiña supplied the eponymous ravine that channeled its waters to the Taquiña hacienda, area *piqueros*, and the Taquiña beer factory. The expropriation requisitioned three-quarters of the ravines' flow, 150 liters per second, to meet the city's needs, leaving what remained for agriculture. Officials pledged that the project would allow the water service to provide each city resident with 120 liters of water per day, putting the city, in the prefect's words, "on par with London."[101]

While authorities promised that this was a short-term solution and that they would compensate water rights holders, both large and small landholders protested the prefecture's project. Large landholders in the Montesillo region, represented by Rafael Salamanca, son of the late president, claimed to speak on behalf of the eight hundred large and small landowners with rights to the water in question.[102] In a petition to the prefect, Salamanca and his fellow large landowners professed support for meeting the city's water needs but opposed this particular proposal as "ineffective" and "unjust" given that it would "devastate a vast and productive region."[103] Expressing fear that their properties would become "barren for lack of these waters," the petitioners accused the prefecture of "sacrificing the interests and lives of thousands of property holders and Indians [*propietarios e indígenas*]" who would have no choice but to flee this area whose production sustained the city and constituted a significant part of Cochabamba's wealth. They called on the prefect to find a solution that did not harm rural interests, suggesting expropriation of a nearby lake with only a handful of owners, or a ravine that was not used so extensively for irrigation, but without specifying any one in particular.

The case record also includes separate responses from individual landowning families of large and medium estates who called themselves water share owners. Encarnación Ahenke, for instance, referred to herself as the "property owner of mitas of the waters of Montesillo." Rafael Gumucio called himself "the owner of part of said waters that irrigate my properties." Policarpo Vargas testified that he and his wife Liboria "possess the water in question for a space of seven hours according to turns established according to customs."[104] Custom was widely cited in purchase-sale agreements to denote water rights tied to landed property.

Montesillo *piqueros* submitted a collective response that also opposed the expropriation, but with a different rationale and a sharper critique. They emphasized the extremely unequal distribution of water rights between the region's large landowners and *piqueros*, explaining that Montesillo water "was unequally distributed" such that "some of us have so little that it is not even enough to irrigate our small plots while others have such an abundance that...after irrigating their lands they have a surplus to sell—the infamous 'waters for sale' ['*aguas de venta*']." Unequal water tenure was "so extreme," they reported, "that we ourselves are often the buyers."[105] Use of the term "infamous" suggests broad *piquero* discontent with unequal water distribution and the rates they had to pay to "rent" water from *hacendados*. While Rafael Salamanca, whose family had water to spare, was perhaps angling for an expropriation his family could profit from, smallholders' opposition to expropriation owed to their desire to hold on to their hard-won and minimal rights.

Like Salamanca, the *piqueros* suggested expropriating lakes owned by a small group of owners. But they specifically recommended the Salamanca family's Chapisirca Lakes, which they said had "such an immense flow and are of such high quality" that they could both supply the city and irrigate their owners' properties. The piqueros thus proposed that the city buy the Salamancas' surplus water instead of carrying out a broad expropriation that failed to take into account cultivators' unequal water holdings. For the *piqueros*, expropriation of their already inadequate mitas would mean sure ruin.[106] Whereas the state had purchased *hacendados'* water in the past, this was the first time that officials had expropriated smallholders with water access issues of their own.[107]

Just as the case exposed lines of tension within the countryside and between the countryside and the city, it also exhibited the growth of a new class of urban professionals and statesmen without ties to the landed aristocracy willing to challenge the rural water monopoly. This group included municipal officials, engineers, and contractors like Antonio Zimmerman and the proprietors of Mavrich & Company, who submitted bids to carry out the project to the prefecture. Zimmerman warned that water scarcity would soon make life impossible for city residents and occasion disease if supply of "this principal element of life" did not increase quickly, emphasizing his own patriotism and commitment to the people of Cochabamba and challenging the "selfishness" of property owners who opposed the project.[108] Mavrich proclaimed that the water-starved city "could only be supplied by close mountain waters" and that the Montesillo ravine was most suitable.[109]

Prefect Julio Arauco Prado rejected Zimmerman and Mavrich's proposals and in fact scraped the Chocaya-Montesillo-Taquiña proposal altogether, likely due to the hostility of Montesillo and Taquiña *piqueros*.[110] Arauco Prado had offered them water from the nearly complete Angostura reservoir to replace their expropriated sources, but the promise of valley waters, considered less pure and valuable than their own, failed to entice them. Not only did the *piqueros* halt the expropriation, they also convinced the prefect to expropriate the Salamancas' Chapisirca Lakes instead. To explain his decision, Arauco Prado echoed the Montesillo smallholders' arguments—that the owners rented rather than used the Chapisirca Lakes' waters, that their expropriation would cause less damage to regional agriculture than expropriating the others, that their quantity was comparable to the lakes that fed the Chocaya, Montesillo, and Taquiña ravines, and that work could begin more quickly since there were fewer owners to expropriate.[111] Perhaps in an effort to preempt potential opposition from the Salamancas, the prefecture declared that "an entire city that would be affected and a population's right to drinking water supply is always superior to any other claim."[112]

The Chapisirca Lakes are located in high reaches of the Cordillera Tunari north of the Central Valley, more than 1,000 meters above the city of Cochabamba and 40 kilometers from the city center. Escalerani, the largest of the group, had been dammed before the Chaco War while the other two to its north, Toro-laguna and an unnamed third, remained "natural." At the time of the expropriation in 1941, the lakes were owned by the heirs of deceased and discredited former president Daniel Salamanca (1931–1934), who was widely blamed for leading the country into the Chaco War. Salamanca had inherited the lakes along with the Montesillo hacienda and the adjoining Chapisirca ranch from his father Jorge in 1904 as well as thirty-nine shares in the Colón beer factory, a quarter of the rights to the Marquina Lakes, and various other properties from his mother, Manuela, in 1928.[113] Thanks to the 1906 water law, Salamanca inherited water sources as accessories to his landed property. His mother's will specified that each property came with "all of the rights, improvements, fences, buildings, water sources, shares, rights of way, and additions made by past owners."[114] Salamanca's five children—Laura, Raquel, Leonor, Hernán, and Rafael—inherited his land and water sources upon his death in 1935. Rights to the Chapisirca Lakes were divided evenly among them.[115]

The Salamancas had negotiated over the lakes' waters before. In 1939, Raquel Salamanca attempted to stop Antonio Zimmerman from fishing them. Zimmerman conceded that the lakes were the Salamanca siblings' property but claimed that their father had granted him permission to utilize the waters before his death and argued that a 1936 Supreme Court decree conceded him the water. Raquel Salamanca made a strong defense of water as private property, arguing that the national state did not have the authority to grant a concession of privately owned water and that the 1936 decree was therefore illegal. She cited the 1906 water law that she claimed "consecrates my property rights," quoting Article 168 that stated, "Fishing in streams, ponds, lakes, and pools is not permitted without the permission of the owner."[116] Both prefect Julio Arauco Prado and national authorities in Sucre ruled in favor of Zimmerman and against the Salamancas, an indication that the tide was beginning to turn against *hacendados* like the Salamancas in the military socialist period. The decision made a small but concrete advance against the doctrine of water as private property, confirming the state's right to make water concessions. At the same time, all parties agreed that the water in question belonged to the Salamancas and that their permission was required for its use.

The Salamanca siblings were amenable to selling the lakes to the city, a less cumbersome and more profitable business than annual water sales to their none-too-grateful *piquero* neighbors, but they negotiated forcefully to win a high price. The siblings professed their desire to "assist in the use of the Chapisirca Lakes for the residents of the city" and agreement that "the vital necessity of providing our city with enough water" outweighed any damage to their own interests that the expropriation might incur. But their lawyer also emphasized "the enormous importance that the Chapisirca waters" had for their properties and "the harm that denying them use of this water would cause" not only them "but also the agricultural interests of the department." In the Salamancas and prefecture negotiators' sparring over how to appraise the lakes, one debate was whether the Salamancas should be compensated solely for the value of the lakes or for the damage that their loss would cause to their agricultural properties as well. Although the expropriation decree stated that they did not utilize the lakes, the Salamancas claimed that they used a significant portion of their water to irritate their own properties and thus argued that they should be compensated for both the lakes' "intrinsic value and the damage that their irrigated properties would suffer." The state appraiser, Wilfredo Milner, retorted that the Salamancas would still have water from other sources and that therefore they should be compensated for the value of the lakes' water alone. Another question was whether the Salamancas should be compensated for infrastructural improvements like Lake Escalerani's dam.[117]

The most heated debate was over the price of water itself. While Milner used Laguna Alalay's rental rate, the Salamancas countered that they should be compensated for their "clear and potable" water at a rate that was almost twice that of the low-lying "muddy, salty, and stagnant waters of Alalay." As they fired back sardonically, "It is odd that the state assessor did not fix the value of Chapisirca water in relation to the waters of Colomi, Ayopaya, or the Chapare," sites far away from Cochabamba's Central Valley. Milner disagreed, and reported that he had "reliable information that the amount actually collected by the owners is less than the official rate."[118]

Luis Quiroga, the head of the national hydraulic service who served as the arbitrator, arrived at an intermediate solution. He mostly sided with the Salamancas but with important exceptions. He took into account infrastructure and depreciation and used the rental rate the Salamancas charged to their neighbors. But he distinguished between the water they rented and the water they used themselves, affording them the higher price only for the waters they sold. But the nature of water and the water market made it difficult to determine how much the Salamancas should be compensated. As Quiroga pointed out, sale prices fluctuated, the proportion the Salamancas used versus what they sold varied from year to year, and irrigation water's value depended on what was being grown among other factors. Despite his professed reluctance to do so, however, Quiroga took pains to calculate the value of the lakes' waters. Milner had appraised the waters at Bs. 1.5 million, the Salamancas' assessor at Bs. 5.5 million. Quiroga's assessment, just under Bs. 2.9 million, met the Salamancas halfway.[119] The siblings accepted the revised offer.

The failed expropriation of Chocaya, Montesillo, and Taquiña and the successful Chapisirca expropriation demonstrate both the advances and the limits of water reform in late 1930s and early 1940s. The national, prefecture, and municipal governments were united in their willingness to more aggressively confront powerful rural water monopolists and sympathetic to the interests of *piquero* water owners. Under pressure from *piqueros*, officials avoided expropriating *piquero* water rights holders whom the Angostura project was meant to help. But authorities still needed to negotiate with *hacendados* who continued to own the region's most important water sources to gain new water sources for the city. While the Chapisirca expropriation obtained the most significant sources from rural water owners thus far, the Salamancas capitalized on the city's water crisis to sell their surplus water at a high price. The sale occurred just before the arrival of irrigation water from the newly finished Angostura reservoir that would likely have depreciated the market value of the water, they sold to their water-poor *piquero* neighbors. The continued power of rural water monopolists like the Salamancas showed that a more radical challenge would be required to make hacienda water available to rural smallholders and residents of the growing city.

THE STAKES OF MUNICIPALIZATION

Despite the Chapisirca expropriation, the department capital continued to face water supply problems. In the face of continued shortages, a rift developed between an older generation of civil engineers employed by the prefecture's water service and a younger group of Cochabambino architect-planners hired by the municipal government to develop an urban master plan. The conflict culminated in a battle over whether to "municipalize" the city's water service by transferring it from the prefecture to the municipality.

The growth of industry, commerce, and banking after the Chaco War generated a more powerful and city-oriented commercial and industrial elite and an expanded professional middle class with growing numbers of engineers, architects, and builders.[120] While less tied to haciendas for their livelihoods, many still had family and property ties to estates. Both prefecture engineers and municipal architect-planners were part of this urban middle class. Their quarrel owed to diverging visions for how to modernize the city and the region. While the prefecture engineers sought practical immediate solutions to regional issues, the municipal architect-planners sought to completely remake the city and the region.

Prefecture officials adopted two approaches to increase water supply to the city after the Chapisirca expropriation. One was to incorporate new neighborhoods into the municipal network in exchange for the neighborhoods' water rights and infrastructure. As the city grew into the foothills of the Tunari Mountains, urban developers and groups of residents purchased land from *hacendados* along with the parcels' water rights. In Tirani, for example, tin mining tycoon Simón Patiño owned several haciendas along with the San Juan and San Pablito Lakes in the mountains above. While waiting for Chapisirca conduct infrastructure to be installed, the prefecture traded Chapisirca Lake water for San Juan and San Pablito Lake water, which was channeled to Arocagua for the city's use.[121] The Patiño family then sold a hacienda and half of the San Juan Lakes to the military housing development Haras Nacional and three other haciendas and the other half of the lakes to Eduardo and Encarnación Plaza.[122] The sale included all "uses [usos], customs [costumbres], improvements [mejoras], and easements [servidumbres]."[123]

When the prefecture returned the San Juan Lakes to their owners, officials reserved the right to acquire Haras Nacional's half of the lakes for the city's water service once the area fully urbanized.[124] Through these kinds of arrangements, neighborhoods traded their water sources for incorporation into the municipal water service. Peripheral neighborhoods without their own water sources lacked this opportunity. Developers took advantage of the water service's willingness to incorporate new neighborhoods with water sources to neglect their contractual commitments to their clients to install distribution infrastructure.[125] Public water service also benefited land developers, who were often former hacendados, by increasing the market value of their land.[126]

The second approach was to engineer the newly acquired Chapisirca Lakes to increase their capacity and supply and to renovate and expand conduct and distribution infrastructure. The water service contracted prominent Cochabambino engineers Carlos Saavedra, the national irrigation service engineer who had worked on the Angostura project, and Alfredo Marrón to design improved water collection and transport infrastructure in Chapisirca. They proposed the construction of canals to capture and channel rainwater runoff to the lakes during the rainy season and a higher dam on Lake Escalerani to collect additional flows from smaller neighboring lakes. The engineers estimated that the project would allow the water service to provide 200 liters per resident until 1980, when the city would have around 140,000 residents.[127] Water service administrators were pleased with the study but did not implement it due to insufficient funding and the conflict under way over municipalization. As of late 1949, the Chapisirca project was incomplete, frustrating Cochabambinos waiting for improved water service.[128]

In the mid-1940s older civil engineers like Saavedra and Marrón faced off with a group of young Cochabambino architects trained in modernist urban and regional planning at the University of Chile in the 1930s. The group of architects was led by Franklin Anaya and Jorge Urquidi and included Gustavo Knaudt, Daniel Bustos, and Hugo Ferrufino, among others. While the engineers advocated practical technical solutions to planning challenges like public works projects, the architects argued for developing a theoretical vision and an urban plan from which practical action would flow. The architects accused the engineers of being uninterested in resolving urban problems and having no background in urbanism. If modernist urban planner Le Corbusier was famous for declaring that "the design of cities was too important to be left to the citizens," the Cochabambino architects were convinced that the design of cities was too important to be entrusted to engineers.[129] The bitter fight divided the Consejo de Urbanismo, forcing it to close in 1946.

The mayor's office hired the young architects to head new municipal offices of architecture, urbanism, and public works. Under the leadership of Jorge Urquidi, head of the new Municipal Architecture Department, and Franklin Anaya, director of the Municipal Office of Public Works, the modernist planner-architects vigorously attacked the existing city—its narrow streets, poor hygiene, adobe buildings, and faulty public services—and developed an ambitious urban master plan.[130] While professed modernists, the planner-architects drew on various planning frameworks to model a hybrid modernist-regionalist-garden city. From Ebenezer Howard and other garden city adherents, they borrowed and reshaped the ideas of satellite cities and harmony and close proximity between labor and work, proposing satellite cities in Quillacollo, Valle Hermoso, Sacaba, and Cliza and collective farms and ranches in rural centers. Following Patrick Geddes's regionalist survey methodology, they strove to harmonize the city's relationship with the larger region. As Urquidi later reflected, we tried to "determine the maximum potential of the whole region, including the city of Cochabamba and the surrounding valleys, without provoking a socio-economic or ecological disequilibrium."[131] But Urquidi and his collaborators subordinated these characteristics to a modernist logic of rationality, efficiency, and antidemocratic expert-led urban planning, leaving the radical social visions of the other frameworks behind. As was often the case with the Garden City movement elsewhere, the Cochabambino planners combined idealism with a top-down approach.[132]

Drawing on Le Corbusier's ideas, the planners tried to integrate industry, agriculture, and the population's needs (especially housing) in the region through the organization of space. In the countryside they wanted to revolutionize agriculture by replacing haciendas with productive and efficient capitalist farms. To prevent excessive rural-to-urban migration and distribute the population between the city and the countryside, they proposed distributing the population among "population nuclei" and establishing different zones for agriculture, industry, forests, residences, tourism, and vacation areas. To remake the city center, following Le Corbusier, they planned to demolish the old center's buildings, widen streets, and establish a network of major roadways to circumvent and penetrate the city. In true Corbusian fashion, they proposed three concentric urban rings: the inner ring for commerce and transport terminals, a second ring for neighborhood units, and a third that would limit the expansion of the city. Each ring would contain markets, universities, parks, forests, semirural and rural areas, and high-, middle-, and low-income housing. This plan would foster the growth of light industry and provide for the needs of factory owners, and workers would live separately but in harmony. Urquidi and his colleagues estimated that the project would take anywhere between six and twenty-two years—time they did not realize they lacked.

The architect-planners completed their master plan in late 1949 and a municipal order approved it in February 1950. But its most important aspects—the roadway system, the hierarchy of streets in the *casco viejo*, the neighborhood units— never left the drawing board.[133] And despite the planners' focus on limiting the city's population and territorial growth, the city's numbers and reach continued to grow. Cochabambino architect and historian Humberto Solares has argued that the Urquidi generation mechanically transplanted foreign ideas "to a social milieu completely distinct from industrial capitalist societies."[134] But the problem was not that planners mechanically transplanted outside ideas. The architect-planners reworked, adapted, and combined them according what they considered to be the Cochabamba region's needs and best path for its modernization. Rather, the planners' grave error was their belief that the plan would make reality—that a small group of enlightened architect-planners could remake urban society without a mass movement behind or alongside them. They adopted the garden city model's physical forms but ignored the social processes at the heart of Howard's model: community building, local management and self-government, freedom and cooperation, entrepreneurship, and the "social city." They likewise ignored Geddes's goals of completely remaking social and political life on the basis of cooperation among free individuals, creating an actively experienced environment, and promoting production for producers themselves.[135]

It was naïve at best to think that the city's popular classes could be planned into their place and that Cochabamba society could operate in differential harmony in the face of stark inequalities. The planners ignored the land market, the chicha market, the popular market, the artisan economy, and urban and rural plebians themselves because they considered them antimodern. In fact, they sought to build their modern city on the backs of people they considered backward. As Solares has written, these were the "modernist fantasies of an oligarchic society that on the surface appeared innovative but that at its heart did not renounce its colonial privileges."[136]

The architect-planners' vision was a revolution on paper. A social revolution on the ground would soon come that would leave the planners behind. Their shortcoming was not that they were not too idealistic. It was that they were too removed from the forces that could make the kinds of changes they sought—and that their ideals were elitist. Even Le Corbusier had reminded his followers that the plan was "only one of the elements of this whole that constitutes the region."[137] The failure of their plans to make reality meant that Cochabamba's *cuidad jardín* came to signify a city with gardens and parks, a promise fulfilled only in better-off northern neighborhoods.[138]

The only aspect of their plan that was implemented was municipalization of urban water, sewage, and paving services. The Urquidi team emphasized from the beginning that a major consequence of population growth in Cochabamba was "lack of water and sewerage." They noted that building had been more intense in the northern zone due to its greater water resources and promoted the municipalization of urban water, sewage, and paving services, until then run by the prefecture. Not only did they consider municipal services to be naturally the responsibility of the municipality, they wanted these services to be treated jointly and in concert within a broader plan rather than individually.[139]

In arguing for transfer of the water service to municipal control, municipal officials and a number of vocal critics charged the prefecture with mismanagement. Officials from seemingly every municipal office, from the director of public works to the city's lawyer to its treasurer, wrote long reports supporting municipalization. They charged that the prefecture had failed to keep up with urban growth, that its water and sewerage services were failing, and that municipal services were naturally the domain of the municipal government. Urquidi charged that the prefecture carried out "mere decorative projects" to create "illusions of urban progress" while "practically abandoning basic services such as water and sewage" that "are invisible because they are underground." He proposed acquiring Corani Lake, located 60 kilometers northeast of the city center where the eastern end of the Tunari Mountains divides the Cochabamba Valley from the lush tropical Chapare region to the city's north.[140] This was likely the first proposal for the Corani project that took on new life in the 1970s and 1990s. Of all these public figures, Urquidi came the closest to critiquing unequal access within the city. "The people are dying of thirst and relieve themselves anywhere they can," he wrote. "The popular classes endure all of the anguish of such primitive living conditions."[141] Jesus Aguayo, an engineer who had worked on the Chapisirca project, alleged that Escalerani was nothing more than a "miserable puddle" and called for purchasing another lake.[142]

Prefecture authorities struggling to hold onto the city's water service defended their record, charging that the municipal government lacked expertise and claiming it would pay inflated salaries but get nothing done.[143] Water service manager Eduardo Prudencio sustained that the water office had never failed to provide the city with sufficient water and that existing sources would be sufficient if residents used them responsibly, especially after Saavedra and Marrón's improvements were complete, and proposed additional water meters to enforce responsible use.[144] Shortages, he argued, owed to "excessive use" of the public supply to "water large gardens," wasteful household practices like "leaving faucets open for no reason," and abuses by businesses like a noodle factory accused of using the public water supply to make adobe bricks to construct its buildings.[145] Comité Pro-Cochabamba leaders concurred with Prudencio that many residents wasted water and proposed a fine whose proceeds would be divided between the municipality and whistleblowers "so that all Cochabamba residents would become jealous guardians of the public good." But the CPC could not overlook the fact that many residents left taps open because they only received water between 2:00 and 3:00 in the morning, often with such force that it blew faucets apart and flooded homes.[146]

Municipal officials won the fight. While other Latin American countries like Mexico and Argentina centralized water and sewerage services in the early to mid-twentieth century, in Bolivia municipalities gained control of what had been prefecture-controlled city water utilities at midcentury. Congress passed a law in December 1948 municipalizing Cochabamba's public services, including drinking water, sanitation, and paving. Santa Cruz followed suit in 1951.[147] In January 1950, Cochabamba's water service along with chicha tax proceeds and its other funding sources passed to the municipality.[148] As if to signal the prefecture's defeat, in 1949 a landslide destroyed Chapisirca water mains and heavy rains damaged infrastructure in both Chapisirca and Arocagua.[149] Meanwhile water scarcity remained a daily reality. El País reported in mid-1949 that "the city's residents are frankly bewildered by the scarcity of drinking water in spite of the fact that water service should have notably improved given that water now comes from both Arocagua and Chapisirca."[150]

Why, after a decade of large-scale hydraulic engineering, did the city still lack sufficient water? The Cochabambinos who endured and attempted to remedy urban water shortages tacked back and forth between blaming residents for irresponsible use and blaming authorities for insufficient hydraulic infrastructure. Although there was truth in both explanations, neither acknowledged that dramatically unequal water access in the city and the countryside owed to the nature of the regional water tenure regime. Poor neighborhoods lacked water not because residents were using the public water supply to produce chicha, make adobe bricks, or even water orchards. Rather, ongoing urban water shortages were the result of the unwillingness of state officials, military socialist and conservative alike, to mount a full-fledged challenge to rural water owners.

A 1936 El País editorial points to the promise and the limits of water reform in this period. In this optimistic moment of military socialist reform, the editors claimed that mountain water sources were plentiful enough to supply every home with enough water to drink and water a small garden so that "Cochabamba could truly become a garden city" instead of a "barren orchard." The editors called for redistributing water according to need—what they called a "socialist" approach.[151] With the Angostura irrigation project and Chapisirca Lakes expropriation, prefecture officials reorganized the water tenure regime and with the latter project redirected some hoarded water sources to the city. But officials stopped short of redistributing water according to water users' needs, instead hoping that engineering a new water source would be sufficient to increase agricultural production and that purchasing another one for the city would meet urban needs.

Whether municipalization would help democratize water tenure or governance remained to be seen. In the 1920s municipal officials had proven more willing to challenge the rural water monopoly to expand urban supply than prefecture officials. But in the late 1930s and early 1940s, prefecture officials hired by military socialist administrations had led water reform efforts in the countryside and the city. They responded to pressure from city residents to expand supply rather than merely limit consumption and to *piqueros'* proposal to expropriate the Salamanca family's Chapisirca Lakes. Modernist municipal planners also aimed to expand supply. But Urquidi's proposal to purchase an additional lake like Corani was no different from the prefecture's approach except that conveying water from far-off Corani would have been far more difficult than expanding Escalerani's supply as Saavedra and Marrón had proposed. Municipal officials seemed less rather than more likely to carry out projects to expand water access.

Neither prefecture nor municipal officials appeared willing to carry out non-consensual let alone uncompensated seizures of hacienda water sources. Prefecture engineers and urban officials' ties to the hacienda water monopoly were weaker than before the Chaco War but by no means severed. In contrast, hacienda *colonos*, a group none of these projects considered, were loyal to their water monopolist *patrones* only out of fear. Once that fear began to dissipate after the 1952 revolution, *colonos* seized hacienda land and water sources for themselves.

CONCLUSION

The period between the end of the Chaco War in 1935 and the 1952 Bolivian revolution was a pivotal moment for water tenure reform. Hydraulic engineering offered the reformist state a way to build its presence in Bolivia's cities and countryside, increase agricultural production, and improve life in the country's growing cities and impoverished countryside. Urban protest against scarcity pressured authorities to expand supply rather than solely restrict use, which pushed them to negotiate with and sometimes confront rural water monopolists and the entrenched system of private water tenure in the countryside. Rather than victimize rural smallholders and environments, growing national, prefectural, and municipal state power to expropriate hoarded regional water sources respected smallholders' growing power.

While officials aimed to avoid clashes with large landowners, water reform challenged the inviolability of private property. The Angostura and Chapisirca projects established that the state could expropriate land for irrigation and urban water supply projects, expropriate privately owned water sources for the country's growing cities, and generally reorganize the waterscape and water tenure in the public interest—all significant shifts from pro-*hacendado* policies of the past. Although property owners were compensated and promised water from Angostura, these cases established that the state had the right and indeed the responsibility to allocate water according to human need and national economic priorities. State authorities, urban planners, and hydraulic engineers tentatively applied a use-value approach that favored urban consumers and *piquero* smallholders over *hacendados* with private water property rights. In contrast to landed property, private water property was no longer sacred.

State officials used technology to both address and avoid dealing with inequality in water access in other arid and semiarid agricultural areas in the twentieth century.[152] James Ferguson and Tania Murray Li's research on technocratic approaches to development in Lesotho and Indonesia, respectively, found that development agents successfully depoliticized inequality and increased bureaucratic state power by rendering issues like employment, wages, housing, land, and water technical concerns rather than political questions of the distribution of wealth and resources.[153] Yet in her study of the Brazilian *sertão*, Eve Buckley found that technocratic drought alleviation efforts did not increase state power but rather shored up regional landlords' power.[154] What makes the history of state-led development in Cochabamba distinct is that humble water users, both in the city and countryside, began to win power over water and water policy. No one group—the state, regional elites, or rural and urban popular classes—won out in this period. The state's power as well as its *responsibility* to the rural and popular classes grew, and smallholders gained increased power to make demands and proposals of their own. Unlike in the Brazilian *sertão*, in Cochabamba there was somewhat of a reckoning with unequal water ownership. Reformist and conservative military governments attempted a technical fix of the kind that Buckley has written about, but it was more radical because it involved expropriating large water owners, in Chapisirca at the behest of smallholders.

Nevertheless, the rural water monopoly mostly endured. Technocratic water reform promised that water for all was possible without challenging private property too much. State-builders and engineers were confident that with technology and expertise they could harness nature to meet the nation's economic and social needs. Nature would provide abundant water sources under the guidance of state institutions. While they found the water monopoly inconvenient, officials worked within that reality, chipping away at rather than tackling unequal ownership of water sources or unequal distribution of water in the city head on. Expropriations for the Angostura and Chapisirca projects affected just a handful of water and landowners, most of whom were willing to be expropriated, and *hacendados* retained ownership of most of the region's water sources.

This latest effort to smooth over the contradiction between the private water monopoly and human need for water in the city and countryside could not resolve Cochabamba's water crisis. Even after these projects were complete, access to irrigation water and drinking water remained unequal and insufficient. Winning water for all, from the city center to its peripheries to *piqueros* and *colonos'* fields, would require redistributing existing privately owned water sources and thus confronting their *hacendado* owners. This blow to Cochabamba's *hacendados* came in the following decades of revolutionary upheaval. Whether accomplished through illegal land invasions or by more orderly but no less dramatic agrarian reform, hacienda owners lost land and with it control over water sources. It is to this story that we now turn.

3

Water for Those Who Use It

Agrarian Reform and Hydraulic Revolution

On August 2, 1953, seventeen months after the Movimiento Nacionalista Revolucionario (MNR) Party seized power, President Victor Paz Estenssoro signed agrarian reform, one of the centerpieces of the MNR's project, into law. He did not take this dramatic action in the capital La Paz, but instead traveled to the small agricultural village of Ucureña in Cochabamba's Valle Alto for the ceremony. Just after the president's land reform proclamation, the foreign relations minister, Walter Guevara Arze, took the stage and declared in Quechua: "The waters that before were rented or sold for agricultural production are now free and all have a right to them."[1] A native Cochabambino and cofounder of the MNR, Guevara understood that peasants' needs and demands included both land and water, and that hacienda owners dominated water resources even more than land in Cochabamba's valleys. Guevara's words articulated the MNR's promise that through agrarian reform the government would make water available to all.

The 1952 Bolivian revolution resulted in a substantial redistribution of wealth from landed elites, mine owners, and urban landlords to the Bolivian state and popular classes. In the late 1940s and early 1950s the MNR had adeptly drawn urban middle classes, factory workers, tin miners, and peasants into a broad coalition. When the army prevented the MNR from assuming the presidency after the party won national elections in 1951, party leaders organized an armed civilian popular uprising to take power by force. On 9 April 1952 party militants, urban factory workers, and members of the military police (*carabineros*) rose up against the military government. The next day, armed tin miners arrived in La Paz to support the insurrection. Soldiers joined the miners on the streets. In three days the rebels overthrew the government and installed exiled MNR leader Victor Paz

Estenssoro as president.[2] Power changes in Bolivia had occurred time and again through armed "revolutions" by opposition political parties.[3] What made the 1952 Bolivian revolution different was massive mobilization from below before, during, and after the April 1952 insurrection. Hacienda *colonos*, indigenous communities, tin miners, and urban workers drove the revolutionary process forward and shaped its course.

The MNR was led by a cadre of creole and mestizo middle-class men who wanted to modernize Bolivia along capitalist lines. How this would happen, however, was up for debate. *Colonos*, independent peasants, poor city dwellers, urban workers, miners, and others skillfully inserted themselves into these debates through mine and hacienda occupations, protests, petitions, union organizing, party politics, militia activity, campaigns, and other novel strategies. The interplay of MNR leaders' desire to modernize the economy, their need to rely on popular support to maintain power, and the revolutionary activity of popular groups led to the revolution's reforms. These reforms included the extension of citizenship rights to all Bolivians (including women and the illiterate), mine nationalization, agrarian reform, and urban reform (redistribution of housing).[4]

Scholars have long debated whether Latin America's major twentieth-century revolutions in Mexico, Bolivia, and Cuba were great triumphs or terrible betrayals. We should discard this dichotomy and rather view revolutions as processes that yield something between panacea and disaster.[5] The Bolivian revolution was neither. It delivered decently compensated but perilous jobs in the nationalized mines, significant but still limited and differentiated citizenship rights, acknowledgment and some redress of centuries of indigenous oppression along with new forms of subordination, substantial but insufficient agricultural land and credit, and water access to many but not to all.[6] The Bolivian revolution was revolutionary, not because the MNR was particularly radical in its original aims, but because peasants, indigenous communities, miners, and urban residents pushed the MNR project to its most radical conclusions and beyond.[7] The resulting reforms made significant improvements in people's lives, while old forms of exclusion persisted and new forms of marginalization emerged.[8]

Hydraulic justice was a major demand of the populace and a serious commitment of the revolutionary government with decisive consequences that have been overlooked ever since. Water reform in the years before the revolution committed the state to an active role in water provision and raised expectations that the revolutionary state should and would provide water for all. After the MNR came to power, *colonos*, *piqueros*, indigenous communities, and city dwellers demanded greater water access, pushing state officials to take more decisive action than in the past. Efforts to expand water access in the 1940s had increased supply by engineering new water sources and reorganizing water distribution but had mostly shied away from challenging the regional water monopoly and the sanctity of private water property rights. After the 1952 insurrection, in contrast, the MNR oversaw a sweeping agrarian reform that not only redistributed land but also transformed the water tenure regime by granting water sources to former estate workers, breaking rural landlords' control of important regional water sources, making major strides toward democratization of the region's water tenure regime, and creating new possibilities for urban access to these sources. Yet water reform favored some groups over others. As Cochabambinos struggled to improve their access to water in the revolutionary period, they based very different and often starkly opposed proposals for hydraulic development on the revolutionary promise of water for all, one of the revolution's most important and before now little-appreciated legacies.

MNR POLITICS AND POLICY IN THE COUNTRYSIDE

Although MNR leaders had been divided on the question of agrarian reform in the prerevolutionary period, indigenous communities and hacienda *colonos'* militant demands and actions after the insurrection forced their hand. By the early 1950s intellectuals and politicians had adopted an expanded cultural definition of *indio* synonymous with *campesino*. Yet, as historian Erwin Grieshaber has explained, there were two types of Indians: "one who still belonged to a solid communal tradition" and another "that dressed and spoke Indian but that observed western cultural norms."[9] While this dichotomy is perhaps too starkly posed, it usefully points to a divergence between Altiplano indigenous communities that had successfully resisted closure in the late nineteenth century and independent *piquero* smallholders and hacienda *colonos* in the valleys who had developed a mestizo identity starting in the colonial period.

At first, the MNR's approach evinced a conservative brand of *indigenismo* that sought to uplift peasants while keeping them in their (rural and unequal) place. A year after taking power, for instance, the MNR publication *Gaceta Campesina* avowed that "the child from the countryside should be educated like a child from the countryside, to live in the countryside and feel happy with life there."[10] As historian Ben Nobbs-Thiessen has written, "celebrating *the Indian* did not alter the degree to which the MNR imagined indigenous Bolivians as deficient rural subjects in need of transformation."[11] While the MNR's left wing, represented by the regime's "worker-ministers" Juan Lechín, minister of mines, and Ñuflo Chávez, minister of peasant affairs, called for "agrarian revolution," the MNR right opposed expropriation of hacienda lands beyond *colono* purchases of usufruct plots.[12] The party's most influential leaders—Victor Paz Estenssoro, Hernán Siles, and Walter Guevara Arze—were pragmatic centrists most concerned with jumpstarting economic growth by making agriculture more productive.[13]

Bolivia had one of Latin America's most unequal land tenure systems.[14] *Colonos* and indigenous communities' demands for hacienda redistribution and their unauthorized occupations, especially in Cochabamba, La Paz, and Oruro, forced the MNR to go beyond cultural approaches to embrace land redistribution as a means to both increase agricultural production and improve peasants' lives. As historian James Dunkerley has recounted, rural laborers, often in large numbers, attacked hacienda buildings around Lake Titikaka and in the Cochabamba Valley every week.[15] The battle for democracy within the party played out in particularly heated and dramatic ways in debates over whether and how to carry out land reform in Cochabamba.[16]

The MNR's agrarian reform program aimed to both placate indigenous and *colono* demands and strengthen the Bolivian economy, a project that party leaders, like their military socialist predecessors, saw as predicated on intensified agricultural production.[17] MNR leaders aimed to modernize agriculture and diversify the economy through peaceful, state-led reform. The party's development goals were similar to the Bohan Report's recommendations: diversification of the economy and improvement of infrastructure, especially roads, water, schools, and electricity.[18] Walter Guevara later commented that the party's aim was to achieve the results of the 1910 Mexican revolution "without ten years of Pancho Villa," failing to acknowledge that armed revolutionaries led by Zapata won agrarian reform during the Mexican revolution.[19]

Cochabamba's valleys were the among the most militant areas of peasant mobilization. Valle Alto *colonos* organized the country's first peasant union in 1936, carried out strikes and petitioned the national government for labor and property rights in the late 1930s and the 1940s, and invaded haciendas after the 1952 insurrection.[20] After attending the one-year agrarian reform anniversary celebration there in August 1954, anthropologist Ricard Patch wrote that "the redistribution of land in the Cochabamba Valleys was accomplished by the Indian people." It was them, not "a body of men in La Paz," who "had taken the houses, . . . the vehicles, [and] the seeds, and . . . divided everything up among themselves." It was not until 1954 or 1955, he reported, "that representatives of the Agrarian Reform Council [arrived] to try to put into some sort of order that which had already taken place."[21] Party officials censured unauthorized land occupations and promised that the state would soon lead an orderly and legal agrarian reform. At the "Semana de la Siembra" in early 1953, for example, peasant affairs minister Ñuflo Chávez urged "*orden en el agro*" (his emphasis) and instructed the peasantry of its patriotic obligation to produce food for urban workers and advance the revolution.[22] But it was *disorder* that pushed the MNR to carry out a more orderly agrarian reform.

Water was key to increasing agricultural production and improving life in the countryside. Peasants and indigenous communities knew this and so did MNR leaders. Peasants' most important claim was land, but along with land, whether explicitly or implicitly, *colonos*, smallholders, and indigenous communities demanded irrigation water to make effective use of their land. Rural land claims sometimes included explicit discussion of water, as in indigenous petitions preparing for the August 1952 Indigenous Congress just a few months after the insurrection. Comunarios from the Cantón Caiza in Potosí's Linares Province, for example, wrote the president asking for "special authorization to use plots with and without irrigation water that were not owned by anyone, given that some comunarios lacked land to work and provide for their families." Demonstrating agile ability to wield nationalist discourse for their own ends, *comunarios* couched the petition in the language of national revolution, ending with the declarations, "Viva Bolivia, Viva el M.N.R., Viva el Doctor Victor Paz Estenssoro, Viva el campesino."[23]

Many such petitions from the early months after the insurrection are now housed in the national archive's presidential files, including a Tarija peasant delegation's request that the government carry out a study of the Zola River's potential to irrigate the Guerrahuaico and Tolomosa Cantons and a letter from the Sindicato Agropecuario de Sora representing the ex-comunidad de Sora in Oruro's Dalence Province asking the president for "a water pump for irrigation of the property... in order to have a larger area to plant."[24] The evolution of the MNR's water policy flowed from attention to such demands as well as officials' recognition of the importance of water access to increasing agricultural production and fostering urban and industrial development.

In the months after the insurrection, MNR leaders developed a utilitarian conservationism that accommodated land and water redistribution in the service of efficient agricultural and industrial production.[25] Like in postrevolutionary Mexico, revolutionary leaders concluded that a utilitarian conservationist approach dedicated to efficiently using natural resources like land and water was required to develop the economy.[26] The MNR's approach emerged from fierce debates among Bolivian reformers and revolutionaries starting in the 1920s about how to marshal the country's oil, minerals, and land to fight economic underdevelopment and build a productive modern capitalist economy. As historian Kevin Young has argued, resource nationalism, which "prioritized protection of Bolivian resources" and vaguely implied equitable distribution, was a central component of revolutionary nationalism. In early decrees, laws, and publications, MNR policy makers advocated conserving water resources in order to foment agricultural production. Even before the first postinsurrection wave of peasant hacienda invasions in late 1952, Ñuflo Chávez declared on the 1952 Day of the Indian that all Bolivians have the right to "benefit from its riches" and envisioned an agrarian reform that would mechanize agriculture to increase efficiency and production.[27] As historian Ben Nobbs-Thiessen has written, MNR officials "envisioned a revolution in nature as a fundamental aspect of their political revolution."[28] This vision became more concrete as land invasions pressed Paz Estenssoro to create a commission to design an agrarian reform program.

MNR officials were willing to grant peasants land and water in exchange for peasants becoming productive contributors to the national economy. The decree establishing the Agrarian Reform Commission expressed the MNR's goals for countryside well. It tasked the body with planning for "a suitable distribution of land to elevate the peasantry's standard of living, intensify agricultural production, and develop the national economy" that would make "good use of and conserve natural resources."[29] The Agrarian Reform Commission included Partido de la Izqiuerda Revolucionaria (PIR) and Partido Obrero Revolucionario (POR) leaders, including *pirista* Arturo Urquidi, an agronomist and dean of Cochabamba's Universidad Mayor de San Simón who took a leading role in drafting the decree. The final document, in historian James Dunkerley's words, "bore the stamp of the PIR's objective of developing capitalism in Bolivia on the basis of medium-sized owner-worked or cooperative holdings."[30] For these Bolivian officials, rationalizing agricultural production through land and water redistribution would enable peasants to contribute to the nation's economy.[31]

The president thus tasked both the Peasant Affairs Ministry and the Agrarian Reform Commission with promoting a "sanitary-hygienic regime" with enough clean drinking water to create healthy peasant producers.[32] But more and more, the party had to tackle questions of wealth and property—land and water holdings—and their redistribution. While broadening access to some agricultural inputs necessary for the "mechanization and technification" of agriculture like seeds and tractors were questions of funds, access to water and land were matters of property.[33] More than in the pre-revolutionary reform period, pressure from below forced reformist officials, this time MNR leaders, to move beyond a technocratic approach to water reform to embrace a redistributionist one.

The MNR's strategy for increasing water access combined large-scale hydraulic infrastructure development with hacienda water redistribution. Like their military socialist predecessors, the MNR engineered new water sources by building dams across the country. The MNR inaugurated the inherited Angostura dam, which it named the Presa México, in April 1952, just days after seizing power, and completed Angostura's canal system in 1955.[34] But the party also committed itself to redistributing existing water sources and infrastructure, especially in the agricultural heartland of Cochabamba. Party leaders recognized that the agrarian reform project's success depended on its fate in Cochabamba and that success there would require democratizing irrigation water access. As *mnrista* Felix Eguino Zaballa wrote in the *Gaceta Campesina* in August 1952, "In certain valleys like the Cochabamba Valley, *minifundio* [extreme subdivision of agricultural properties] has become a major problem, especially when coupled with lack of water." Agrarian reform had to involve, he argued, "rational water distribution."[35] To this end, the president tasked the Agrarian Reform Commission with studying and reforming the country's "water tenure regime" ("régimen de aguas").

As the Agrarian Reform Commission's mandate makes clear, MNR leaders explicitly set out to reform and "rationalize" the country's water tenure regime by making water distribution more equitable and just. A subcommittee studied every aspect of the water regime, including property and use rights, actual use, dams, hydroelectric power, geography, and even the history of water use since the Incas. Its central task was to inventory and categorize the nation's water sources according to who owned them (the national state, municipalities, or private parties) and whether they could be appropriated ("afectarse") for irrigation, animal husbandry, forestry, industrial activity, or other purposes "essential to the wellbeing of the nation." Privately owned water sources already serving a "necessary purpose in service of the collectivity or nation" such as sources supplying reservoirs, hydro-electricity production for industry, or universities were to be excluded from expropriation so long as the user, whether a business, mining operation, railroad company, or other entity, respected laws to purify and recycle the water they used. But if a producing entity owned more water than it needed, the commission's directive indicated that the state could redirect the surplus for the greater good. Especially significant for the fate of Cochabamba's water monopoly, the plan cited the 1938 Constitution to deem water sources "found in the mountains and currently in the private domain" to be state waters subject to expropriation for irrigation service.[36] On the basis of these instructions, the commission produced an agrarian reform code that dramatically transformed Bolivia's water tenure regime.

Paz Estenssoro and Guevara Arze announced agrarian reform in Ucureña on 2 August 1953 in front of one hundred thousand potential beneficiaries from all over the nation.[37] The Agrarian Reform Decree Law set out a revolutionary water policy: nationalization of the country's water sources, abolition of the rural water market, equal rights to the flow necessary for all livestock raisers and agricultural producers, and the entire population's right to use drinking water sources.[38] The law's first article declared that "the soil, subsoil, and waters of the territory of the Republic belong by original right to the Bolivian nation." Its third article stated that the country's lakes and rivers, even if they had been opened by private parties, as well as "all forces that can be used for economic improvement, belong to the public domain."[39] On this basis the law abolished the rural water market, prohibiting "the sale or commercialization of water" and mandating that the surplus "in one area or property pass freely to benefit areas or properties that, lacking their own water sources, find themselves able to take advantage of this surplus."[40]

Even more radical was the law's promise that agrarian reform would redistribute water for irrigation, animal husbandry, and consumption. In the law's words, "agricultural and animal-raising properties shall use the *necessary flow* with *equal right* for production, irrigation, or watering holes," "populations have the right to use drinking water sources for domestic purposes," and "legally recognized towns have the right to request that the department capital's municipality specify how to access drinking water sources."[41] These provisions echoed the 1917 Mexican

FIGURE 5. Peasants and President Victor Paz Estenssoro celebrate Paz's signing of the Agrarian Reform Decree Law in Ucureña, 2 August 1953. Photo by Ramón Cordero. Colección "Cordero." Courtesy of the Museo de la Revolución Nacional, La Paz, Bolivia.

Constitution's Article 27 and postrevolutionary Mexican water policy discussed in chapter 2. These terms, especially guarantees of "equal rights" to "necessary flows," upended the private water property regime established by the 1879 water code that was elevated to law in 1906, promising water for those who need it alongside "land for those who work it." As geographer Karl Zimmerer has written, "The [agrarian] reform's slogan, 'The Land Belongs to the One Who Works It,' belied the widespread reliance of Bolivian agriculture on irrigation."[42] Indeed, agrarian reform provided for the redistribution of both land and water. The agrarian reform law made water for all the law of the land.

Shortly after introducing the agrarian reform law, the MNR launched a striking ideological attack on water owners. *El Pueblo*, the MNR-affiliated Cochabamba daily, ran an extensive editorial assailing "owners of drinking and irrigation water," calling them "dried-up," "soulless," and "merciless water pushers" and "bandits" who took advantage of the desperation of their neighbors to sell them water at the highest possible price. Comparing water sales to dispossession of peasant land at the end of the previous century, the article charged that "in Cochabamba, certain individuals perpetuate water banditry even to this day, harming not only their neighbors but the entire citizenry. Simply because a water source happens to pass through their property, they claim the right to deprive the city of water, and to exploit landowners who lack irrigation sources."[43]

The paper called water owners associations (juntas de propietarias de agua) that hacendados had formed to improve and manage shared water sources "entities created in oligarchic times for the defense of the interests of bossism [gamonalismo]."[44] It credited the agrarian reform law with "affirming, this time definitively and without equivocation, the principle of universal ownership of this elusive element."[45] After centuries of water dispossession and decades of the riparian system established by the 1879 water regulation and the 1906 water law, these attacks on private water owners and ownership were extraordinary. As with agriculture more broadly, the law outlined a central role for the state in allocating, conserving, and directing water use.

The MNR's utilitarian conservationism melded indigenismo with a redistributionist agrarian policy, holding that with land, irrigation water, and state direction, peasant and indigenous farmer communities could become productive contributors to the national economy. A series of articles in the issue of Gaceta Campesina released the same month as the law illustrated this coalescing perspective. The issue featured a six-page tribute to ancient Aymara hydraulic engineers who "planned and constructed magnificent irrigation works to channel water across great distances" and Tiwanaku's urban hydraulic engineers, "the most expert in the world for their time," who built "perfectly distributed covered underground aqueducts and canals to conduct drinking water to their sacred city." But the author deemed ancient Aymara knowledge long dead and held out little hope for its recuperation, despite contending that "Indians are hydraulic engineers by nature, or by instinct."[46]

Another article in the issue recognized colonos' hydraulic labor, listing "irrigation canal construction and repair" among their unpaid tasks but overlooked their design work. But other articles indicated that in the modern world, professionally trained state engineers built water works. Rational use of the nation's water sources required that agrarian courts re-allocate now nationally owned water sources to all farmers, but also that state-appointed (creole and mestizo) experts, not descendants of ancient Aymara (not to mention Quechua) engineers or colono builders, direct hydraulic development.[47] The agrarian reform law mandated continued use of "the system of irrigation mitas or turns" but tasked the state with ensuring water conservation.[48]

Despite the radical new law, agrarian reform cases sometimes took a decade or more to wind their way through the courts. Conflicts in these cases over land were also conflicts over water. Because hacienda land usually possessed an area's best irrigation water sources, winning a case meant securing both land and corresponding irrigation rights. To keep their land, estate owners had to prove that they had made productive use of it. Unproductive properties, or *latifundios*, were subject to redistribution. Agrarian cases first went before a local agrarian judge who ruled on how to characterize and allocate a property. The judge based this decision on information collected by rural inspectors regarding a property's size, water sources, irrigation systems, machinery, tools, fertilizers, and seed quality. The National Agrarian Reform Council (Consejo Nacional de Reforma Agraria, CNRA) then reviewed each case and made its own determination before sending it to the president.[49] The president usually signed any agrarian reform case that crossed his desk, leaving the real decisions to negotiations between landowners and peasant unions in local agrarian courts.[50] When these bodies decided to redistribute hacienda land, they also reassigned hacienda water sources.

Both *hacendados* and *colonos* were cognizant of the legal terms of water ownership and redistribution and seized on them to wage battles over hacienda property. The law instructed agrarian courts to base their decisions on whether hacienda owners had made productive use of their land and thus stipulated that the greater the availability of irrigation water, the more productive a property should be in order for its owners to keep some or all of their land. In valley areas like Cochabamba, properties with irrigation sources were expected to be even more productive and therefore had stricter limits on maximum holdings.[51] These criteria had important implications for *hacendados* in Cochabamba's Valle Bajo, Central Valley, and Sacaba Valley who owned large mountain lake reservoirs.

Colonos demanding redistribution often contended that an owner had not done enough to use or expand the property's irrigation water access. Landowners, in contrast, routinely argued that they lacked enough irrigation water to make their land more productive, used what irrigation rights they had, or purchased additional sources. Agrarian judges based their decisions in part on who they determined was correct about water use, frequently pointing to a property's water sources as evidence that it should have been more productive than it was. In the case of the hacienda Chullpas Quinto Suyo in Cochabamba's Valle Alto, for example, the estate owner testified that much of his land consisted of "dry parcels" that could not be cultivated and that he had purchased irrigation turns both for his own land and *colonos'* usufruct plots. Yet estate workers testified that the owner rarely purchased irrigation water and the court-appointed surveyor found that the property was, in his words, "surrounded by irrigation canals with abundant water in addition to the Huayculí River" and therefore should be considered "first quality." One *colono* testified that he and his fellow workers had to fetch water from the nearby town to deliver to the hacienda at 4:00 in the morning, a common complaint in Cochabamba agrarian reform cases. The agrarian courts ruled in favor of the *colonos*, concluding that the estate owner had failed to sufficiently invest in irrigation infrastructure and other improvements.[52]

The outcomes of agrarian reform cases transformed the water tenure regime by granting water sources to former estate workers and other beneficiaries. Water redistribution was a massive achievement, the most important step yet in democratizing water access and property. Through agrarian reform, former hacienda *colonos* and others won significant hacienda land and water sources away from their former overlords who had built their properties by usurping the land, water, labor, and hydraulic expertise of indigenous communities, smallholders, and *colonos* over centuries. As one former *colono* explained, "Before the customs were different than now: [we] did not have water to irrigate [our] farms, . . . the *patrón* sold water in turns, by the hour. Ever since the agrarian reform water is free and for all. . . . The agrarian reform law provided that and much more."[53]

But agrarian reform also reinscribed inequalities between estate owners and former workers, as was the case elsewhere in Latin America.[54] *Colonos* who won ownership of their usufruct plots won irrigation rights connected to them, but the courts often allowed landowners to keep the best hacienda land and with it the best irrigation rights. For instance, while Chullpas Quinto Suyo *colonos* won their case, the courts awarded sixteen hectares of land to the estate's owners and just one hectare to each *colono* worker—and the ex-*colonos* had to share the estate's water sources with the estate owner who had denied that these sources existed. The revolution's water reform also excluded other groups fighting to expand their water rights, especially *piqueros, arrimantes* (landless peasant laborers who worked for *colonos*), and city dwellers.[55] Land and water reform nevertheless revolutionized the lives of former *colonos*. Many *hacendados* allowed to hold on to some land and water sold their properties or fled, never to return.

EXPROPRIATING MOUNTAIN LAKES FOR THE CITY

At first the revolution made little impact on the city of Cochabamba's access to rural water sources. Despite significant water projects in the 1940s, the city's water supply remained insufficient to satisfy ever-growing demand, water quality was poor, and the distribution network was crumbling and limited in reach.[56] During the first postinsurrection dry season, municipal officials had to rely on the benevolence of water monopolists to supply the city when Chapisirca's Escalerani Lake ran dry in December 1952. City officials asked for assistance from the Rivero family, the owners of the Pacata Alta hacienda with rights to Lake Wara Wara discussed in chapter 1. While the Riveros offered the city temporary use of their lake's water free of charge, perhaps fearing expropriation, the deal was reminiscent of pre-revolutionary strategies of purchasing water from hacienda owners to expand urban supply.[57]

After the agrarian reform was announced in August 1953, MNR municipal officials seized on the law's promise of water for all to attempt to direct hacienda water sources to the city. In September 1953, Cochabamba's *mnrista* mayor Armando Montenegro expropriated the lakes San Juan, San Pablito, Saytukocha, San Ignacio, Lagunmayu, and Wara Wara and the ravines of Tiquipaya to serve the city (see Map 7). He attributed water scarcity to a consistent failure to take urgent action in the past, basing his decision on the agrarian reform law and citing its clause that "all of the ponds, lakes, rivers and all forces that can be used for economic improvement, even if they had been opened by private parties, are part of the public domain." Echoing the language of the law itself, he declared the municipality responsible for "providing an adequate solution to the city's emergency water shortage crisis" and "using the flows necessary to this end."[58] Montenegro's expropriation of mountainside lakes and rivers for the city was a far more significant attack on Cochabamba's water monopoly than previous expropriations and aimed to fulfill the agrarian reform's promise to redistribute hacienda water to both rural smallholders and urban residents.[59] The question was whether his declaration would translate into actual seizure of these sources for the city, and more generally who would gain access to hacienda sources and whether they would be sufficient to satisfy the demands of all of the region's water users.

Montenegro became mayor a year after the insurrection at a time of intense popular mobilization in the city. Migrants from the countryside were demanding housing, tenant union members were occupying privately owned rental properties, and residents across the city were protesting water scarcity, rationing, and limited service.[60] In response to these protests, the MNR introduced urban reform to distribute housing to thousands of families. The first decree in September 1953 expropriated agricultural land in the city's outskirts for workers demanding plots, especially teachers and miners. When renters demanded redistribution of what they called "hoarded housing" within the city, a second, August 1954 decree mandated expropriations inside city limits to "liberate" thousands, including teachers, veterans, and retired miners, from renting.[61] Yet urban reform exacerbated residential segregation by removing poor tenants from the city center where commercial rents were quickly surpassing residential rents, settling them in "villas" or "barrios marginales" on the urban periphery, especially in the Zona Sud. And the promise of housing in the city attracted migrants to Cochabamba, propelling an explosion of settlement on the city's periphery that exacerbated the urban water crisis.[62] The municipality incorporated new neighborhoods into city limits but mostly proved unable to enforce regulations requiring developers to provide basic services—or to provide those services itself.[63]

While water shortages had long been a major source of discontent among the city's popular classes, after the revolution residents mobilized more forcefully to demand action. As in the post-Chaco period, the geography of urban settlement

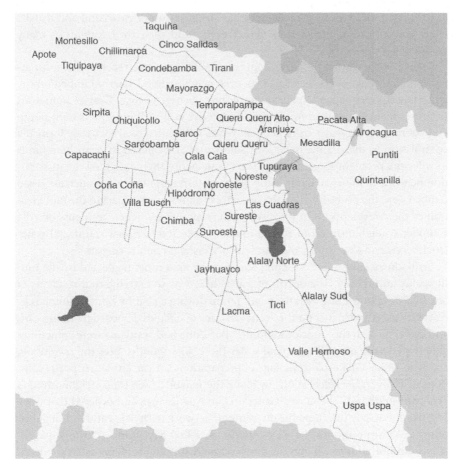

MAP 8. City of Cochabamba neighborhoods and zones. Map created by Jorge Camacho Saavedra.

shaped experiences of water scarcity and the nature of popular protest. In the center where network connections already existed, residents appealed for extended hours, improved quality, and increased pressure to bring water to upper floors.[64] In peripheral areas residents implored officials to extend the network, install public spigots, or at least provide municipal water truck service. In water-rich northern peripheral areas like Mayorazgo, Tupuraya, and Queru Queru, residents could often draw on natural springs or dig shallow artesian wells (Map 8). Petitions from these areas were common, usually requesting the installation of a public pump, but not nearly as desperate as those from drier areas to the east, west, and especially south.[65] In the early years after the revolution, neighborhoods were just beginning to organize to demand urban services like drinking water provision and usually tried to secure municipal service rather than build their own systems as many would in later decades.

Neighborhoods that protested aggressively seem to have received the most attention. Residents of the Las Cuadras–area neighborhood Barrio Gráfico on the eastern periphery began to petition for water coverage in 1952. Despite numerous promises from the mayor, in 1958 residents were still walking to a distant pump and petitioning for water truck service. When help failed to arrive, they formed a commission to discuss the issue with authorities and offered to contribute funds to solve the problem more quickly. The municipality then extended the distribution network to the area. By the early 1960s eastern neighborhoods such as Barrio Gráfico were the best served on the periphery thanks in large part to the mobilization of their residents.[66] On the city's western periphery, when residents of Villa Galindo, a neighborhood of retired miners, protested irregular municipal water truck service and rationing, the municipality installed public spigots.[67]

Arid, dusty, and poor, the Zona Sud was the area most neglected by the municipality and nature. The dearth of water there was so extreme that residents of one boarding house stormed the water pump during a visit by renters' union representatives. A journalist on the scene described "delighted" boarders filling cans and canteens with the "precious liquid."[68] But Zona Sud residents were sometimes able to persuade officials to extend water there. Just months after the revolution, residents of La Villa took advantage of preparations for the city's first postrevolutionary anniversary celebrations to invite the mayor to see their neighborhood's problems firsthand. The mayor visited in late August 1952 and ordered that work begin immediately to extend the distribution network to the area and install public pumps. Within a month the water service installed five pumps.[69] Municipal officials did not address all appeals, however, and supply problems often hindered their attempts to extend water service to the periphery.

Much like their predecessors, *mnrista* municipal authorities attempted to stretch limited water sources by restricting consumption. A month after the insurrection the mayor's office announced stricter rationing, organized a "permanent control and vigilance patrol" to enforce restrictions on water use in private fields and gardens, and installed a "libro de denuncias"—a complaint book—in its office where residents could inform on their neighbors and earn rewards from fine revenues.[70] Soon washing vehicles and washing floors were added to the list of prohibited water-using activities. During a drought in 1956, residents were required to repair their water fixtures or face fines.[71] The mayor and the press mercilessly attacked residents for wasting drinking water, accusing them of leaving water running in public taps and "using it to water gardens and fields rather than letting it attend to the needs of their neighbors who have to suffer from these abuses."[72] When crisis hit again in late 1958, the mayor "discovered" that residents were using municipal water to grow potatoes, corn, and other vegetables and called the cul-prits "selfish individuals" who had "forgotten that all of our children have the right to equitably consume water."[73]

Renewed efforts in these years to impose water meters reiterated this logic. In 1959 the municipality began to crack down on chalet owners in the Zona Norte who used municipal water rather than their own wells to fill their swimming pools. Municipal officials blamed water users' wasteful practices as much as drought, limited supply, and deteriorated transport and distribution infrastructure for the ongoing water crisis, making little effort to distinguish between the waste of those with enough water to fill swimming pools and those merely watering kitchen gar-dens.[74] But even as they blamed water users for shortages and tried to restrict con-sumption, officials worked to expand the city's water supply. Popular protest in the city and the opportunities presented by agrarian reform encouraged municipal officials to go after hacienda water sources to increase the city's supply, once again leading them into negotiations and confrontations with rural water owners, this time in radically different circumstances.

When Mayor Montenegro announced the expropriation of mountain lakes to serve the city, he assured their users that the waters being expropriated did not include "the normal irrigation turns" that would be "respected according to condi-tions established by custom."[75] Montenegro's pledge seems to indicate that he did not understand how water rights worked. In the case of the San Juan Lakes, for example, the owners of the Tirani hacienda, the Plaza family, had rights to half of the lakes' waters while Barrio Militar, a neighborhood to the south, had rights to the other half. The Plazas' sale of half their land to Barrio Militar included half of the hacienda's rights to the lakes San Juan and San Pablito. Their remaining rights were distributed among Plazas' own fields and colonos' plots.[76] How Montenegro thought the expropriation could avoid affecting irrigation rights is unclear, nor do available records reveal how the Plazas or other lake owners reacted to Montene-gro's announcement. What is clear, however, is that hacendado lake owners were soon up against far more formidable foes than the mayor—their colono workers. As Jose Gordillo has written, "The urban politicians took a long time to realize that the political center of gravity had moved from the cities to the countryside, and MNR militants mistakenly tried to continue directing the revolution from their desks."[77]

Colonos filed agrarian reform cases against the hacendado owners of all the lakes that Montenegro expropriated. The agrarian reform cases dealing with these lakes—San Juan, San Pablito, Wara Wara, Lagunmayu, and Saytukocha—have much to tell us about the role of water in agrarian reform litigation and about how agrarian reform transformed Cochabamba's water tenure regime and with it the nature of negotiations between the city and the countryside over water. These cases determined the fate of the most important irrigation water sources in the Valle Bajo, Central Valley, and Sacaba Valley. Despite Montenegro's bold pronouncement, the highly contested agrarian reform process, not the *mnrista* mayor, determined the fate of these lakes.

HYDRAULIC REVOLUTION

Although the Cochabamba countryside was quiet during the April 1952 insurrection, *colonos* and *piqueros* across the region mobilized by the thousands in the months after to demand land and water redistribution. Armed peasants invaded haciendas, sacked manor houses, blocked roads and railroads, and at one point "equipped with cudgels, axes, staves, and some rifles," entered the city center to demand release of arrested union leaders.[78] As agrarian activist Julio Butrón Mendoza has recounted, many *colono* unions invaded hacienda land to increase the size of their plots and thereby "establish precedents that would serve them" in the agrarian process.[79] Others waited for the MNR state to fulfill its promise to redistribute land and water.

Colono unions marched into cities and towns to press their demands. Butrón describes "thousands of campesinos from every province and rural corner of the country" marching on cities, "sometimes with the music of *zampoñas* [pan flutes]…, shooting off guns…, concentrating in the plazas, streets, and sports fields." In Cochabamba, he writes, "we entered the city the number of times that we believed necessary, showing off our numbers and our arms in their avenues and their busiest streets, firing our weapons into the sky." They occupied the stadium, Laguna Cuellar, Caracota's market, Plaza San Antonio, and all of the roads leading out of the city. "We crossed the city from one side to the other," he reports, "showing our human strength and determination to defend our rights against all those who opposed the resurgence of the *indio*." According to Butrón, no one in the cities joined them. Instead, many insulted their dress and purported smell and called them racist and derogatory names, including "*los mexicanos*." He recalls that "they thought about us even in their dreams and nightmares and did not forget about us for a single instant, whether kindly or not. Better if it was out of fear of our numbers, demands, and actions." He adds, "We saw that we could easily blockade the cities, and thereby cut off their supplies of food, drinking water, electricity, and other services."[80] This fascinating account hints at the way *campesinos* mobilized ethnicity and used their opponents' racism to their advantage to instill fear and gain respect.

The social geography of land and water tenure relations helped shape the political allegiances of *colonos* and *piqueros* in Cochabamba. In the Valle Alto large haciendas dominated more than in the region's other valleys, though many haciendas had subdivided in preceding decades.[81] Hacienda *colonos* there aligned themselves with the left wing of the MNR that favored land redistribution and called for agrarian *revolution*, where *colonos* unions would oversee the distribution of all hacienda land to their members. In the Valle Bajo, Central Valley, and Sacaba Valley, in contrast, smallholdings dominated but owners of large and medium estates nonetheless controlled most irrigation water sources, as discussed in previous chapters. According to Jose Gordillo, Catholic agrarian unions organized Valle Bajo *piqueros* to "break the monopoly of irrigation water held by *hacendados*."[82] Colonos in these valleys generally allied with the MNR's right wing, which had grudgingly accepted state-led land redistribution, and supported state-led land *reform*.[83]

In April 1954 provincial agrarian judges and rural councils were sworn in and, in June, began to hear cases. By this time, there were approximately thirty-five hundred agrarian unions in Cochabamba organized into forty *subcentrales* and fourteen *centrales*.[84] While *colonos* celebrated, urban elites, rural landowners, and local MNR leaders were less sanguine. The Comité Pro-Cochabamba called the agrarian reform "a monstrous attack on the right to property" and the prominent daily newspaper *Los Tiempos*, owned by active members of Cochabamba's Federación Rural, an association of large landowners, came out against land reform.[85] Peasants alleged that the MNR's Comando Departamental was attempting to sow divisions between the countryside and the city by spreading rumors that "the peasants are going to attack the city, . . . capture the CDM [Comando Departmental del MNR], [and] release the water from the [Angostura] dam to flood the city" before they "enter to sack it."[86] When local MNR leaders and the Federación Rural realized they could not prevent land reform, they tried to slow it down, arguing that preliminary studies and peasant education were necessary. In a similar vein, the minister of public works argued that the agrarian reform should "be carried out scientifically" in order "to create greater productivity."[87] A call for a "scientific" approach was often code for slow or little-to-no redistribution at all.

Tin miners from the Altiplano helped *colonos* bring agrarian reform cases forward in the Central Valley and Valle Bajo and often won land themselves. The Ministry of Peasant Affairs, the Central Obrera Boliviana (COB), and the miners' union (FSTMB), with the reluctant support of Cochabamba's peasant federation (Federación Sindical de Trabajadores Campesinos de Cochabamba, FSTCC), organized miners to work with *colonos* to present agrarian reform cases in hope of establishing peasant-miner cooperatives on expropriated haciendas. The new state mining company COMIBOL, eager to reduce its purportedly costly workforce, offered severance packages to miners willing to join the effort.[88] Gordillo has found that in the Valle Bajo "nearly half of land distribution beneficiaries were mineworkers from the nationalized Siglo XX, Catavi, and Colquiri mines."[89] He says *colonos* resented miners because the latter had no intention of farming but rather intended to exploit ex-*colonos* in the new cooperatives and later sell off land and water shares.[90] Miners' role in the agrarian cases discussed below, however, suggests that they may have been useful intermediaries in *colonos'* agrarian re-form petitions. FSTCC leaders also played a role in negotiating claims. As union leader Sinforoso Rivas Antezana has written, "When the presidents of the *juntas rurales* were named, the unions in various haciendas already had their paperwork prepared." Rivas's role was to get the union lawyer to approve the petition before submitting the file to the agrarian judge.[91] While national policy debates and local power dynamics shaped the agrarian reform process, savvy maneuvering on the ground was crucial to win land and water.

The San Juan Lakes

In June 1954, a few months after Montenegro announced the expropriations of the San Juan Lakes and several others, Tirani's fifty-eight *colono* workers filed an agrarian reform case claiming rights to their plots and the hacienda's water sources, San Juan and San Pablito (see Map 7). The San Juan Lakes had been used to irrigate local haciendas since at least 1880, when a group of *hacendados* formed the San Juan Lakes Water Users Society (Sociedad de Explotación de las Aguas de las Lagunas de San Juan), as discussed in chapter 1. Their heirs sold their shares and rights (*acciones y derechos*) to the Bolivian tin mining magnate Simón Patiño in 1934, when he purchased several area haciendas including Tirani. Patiño trans-ferred ownership to his children in 1941, but sibling infighting led to the lakes' auc-tion in 1945. Eduardo Plaza, the only bidder, bought the lakes, in addition to Tirani and two other Patiño properties, for a mere Bs. 1.2 million, a price so low that one observer remarked that it was as if Plaza had won the lottery.[92]

Tirani *colonos* had built the lakes' dams to increase their capacity and canals to control their flow in the 1920s and 1930s under the direction of *hacendados* and with the assistance of Catholic priests. As one resident recalled in a 2011 interview, "The first dams were constructed by our ancestors, our grandfathers in the time of *pongueaje* [indentured servitude] with the *patrones*."[93] From the 1920s to this day, Tirani *colonos* and their descendants have traveled up to the lakes annually to maintain and improve irrigation infrastructure. Before the revolution, entire families often made the 28-kilometer round-trip journey, traveling on foot and carrying food, chicha, coca, and other provisions on their backs. When they were lucky, horses, donkeys, or mules carried loads of tools and construction materials.

In April 1952 many Tirani *colonos* joined the revolution. "Someone would come in a yellow car and fire three shots. It was the way [the *colonos*] were summoned," recalled Josué Arias, who was ten years old at the time.[94] Organizers "would take them to different union subcentral offices, in Trojes or Quillacollo, where they would keep watch."[95] While at first the *colonos* kept working for the Plazas, after two years, Arias told me, the *colonos* "stopped going and the community rebelled."[96] When agrarian reform seemed imminent, descendants report that Tirani *colonos* bought their plots from the Plazas out of fear that the reform would fail to materialize or would later be reversed.[97] After it was announced, however, Tirani *colonos* immediately filed a case against the Plazas.

Tirani *colonos* alleged that the Plazas had treated them violently and had failed to take sufficient advantage of the estate's land and water resources. In their testimony *colonos* reported that they were often made to sleep outside, that Eduardo's bad-tempered wife Encarnación beat them, and that Eduardo had exiled *colono* union leaders to the Chapare, reduced plot sizes, taken several *colonos* to the police on false charges in order to dispossess them, and could always be found slinging a pistol.[98] Sixty years after the revolution one community elder recalled that "the *patrón* would come to supervise the irrigation turn on horseback, and he had a whip to punish anyone who stole his water."[99] *Colonos* still tell their children about this abuse. Josué Arias recounted to his son Joaquín that before the revolution the *colonos* were angry but submissive because the *patrones* had spies among them and could take away everything the colonos had.[100]

The local agrarian judge agreed with the *colonos* that the Plazas had abandoned large areas of the hacienda's productive land and an agrarian service agronomist's inspection confirmed that they used irrigation water poorly. Nevertheless, the final decision in November 1957 allowed the Plazas to retain 164 hectares and their chalet. The hacienda's fifty-eight *colonos* were granted their plots totaling approximately 70 hectares, additional land in the property's steep mountainside heights, and common use of the remaining cultivable and grazing land along with 2 hectares for a school and a recreation area. The courts ordered the owners and ex-*colonos* to share the property's water sources and maintain the mita turn system and instructed all of them to "contribute to the conservation, improvement, and maintenance of water infrastructure."[101] It is hard to imagine Eduardo or Encarnación climbing steep mountainside switchbacks to rebuild dams and canals, but they did not plan to. The Plazas had sold much of their land and half of the San Juan Lakes to Barrio Militar before the revolution and the municipality had then gained rights to Barrio Militar's half of the lakes through a 1951 agreement with the neighborhood. The final agrarian reform decision effectively legalized these transactions, splitting the hacienda's land between the ex-*colonos* and Barrio Militar, and the San Juan Lakes between the former tenants and the city.

In the years following the Tirani case's resolution, the ex-*colonos*' union and the municipality shared San Juan and San Pablito, with each considered owner of half the lakes' water.[102] The municipality captured water from the lakes over the course of forty days in the dry season when Escalerani, the city's principal water source, began to run dry and built a filtration gallery in Tirani to capture water descending from San Juan and San Pablito that was then diverted to the Cala Cala treatment plant.[103] This was the first instance of a water-sharing agreement between an ex-*colono* community and the city, but problems soon arose. Water service administrators complained in the early 1960s that water was not reaching the supply system because "peasants of the region divert water for their own use."[104] The relationship between Tirani and the city remained conflictive in the years and decades that followed, especially as water service officials vied to gain a greater share of the lakes' waters. The agrarian reform did allow the city to gain access to the San Juan Lakes, but not in the way that Mayor Montenegro had intended.

Lake Wara Wara

On September 27, 1954, Erasmo Pozo, general secretary of the Pacata Peasant Union, filed a case on behalf of fifteen *colonos* against the hacienda Pacata Alta's owner, Ricardo Rivero Torres, heir of Ramón Rivero who had sold water to the prefecture's urban water service in the 1920s. Like Tirani, Pacata Alta possessed abundant water sources, including Lake Wara Wara and the rivers and springs it fed, as well as irrigation infrastructure built by hacienda *colonos* earlier in the century.[105] And as in Tirani, Pacata Alta's water resources and irrigation infrastructure were key to classifying the land and determining the property's fate. In his decision nearly eight years after the case was filed, the local agrarian judge came down hard on the Rivero Torres family, finding that they had submitted their *colono* workers to "a regime of feudal exploitation" and failed to "enlist technical or mechanical assistance beyond rudimentary methods such as the Egyptian plow drawn by human blood" or to industrialize production despite favorable conditions. While most of the property was uncultivable land on the steep mountainside, the property's high mountain reaches were the site of Lake Wara Wara, in the judge's words, "one of the most important irrigation sources of Sacaba," and the hacienda was situated, as he pointed out, "along the banks of the Rocha River" near the Arocagua Springs that supplied the city.[106]

The presence of such a wealth of water sources strengthened the *colonos'* case that the owners had failed to capitalize on the area's geographic advantages to increase productivity. The judge also found that Ricardo's widow, Graciela Torrico, had violated the agrarian reform law by trying to sell off the property for urban plots before the case had concluded. The judge thus declared the property a *latifundio* and divided cultivable land among the *colonos*, other peasants, and a group of teachers. He assigned the remaining land—approximately 432 hectares "of grazing land, rivers, ravines, and roads, and the use of the waters of Lake Wara Wara"—to all of the beneficiaries for their collective use, especially for agriculture. Were this decision to stand, rights to Lake Wara Wara would belong exclusively to *colono*, peasant, and teacher beneficiaries and the ex-*hacendados* would be left without a single hectare or irrigation turn. Even the hacienda chalet was to become a social center.[107]

The National Agrarian Reform Council reversed the lower court's ruling. While the local judge had found the Riveros guilty of running a feudal labor system, the council found that "the relationship between the *patrón* and the peasants has al-

FIGURE 6. Lake Wara Wara in the 1920s. The people figured are likely hacienda *colonos* on an annual trip to maintain the lake's dam and irrigation canals. Photo by Rodolfo Torrico Zamudio. Courtesy of the Fundación Cultural Torrico Zumudio.

ways been based on cordiality, understanding, mutual cooperation, and uplifting the peasants' children." According to the council, Ricardo Rivero, an agronomist, had been a social reformer, an agrarian reform proponent, and had followed the law. The ex-*colonos* worked under a *colonato* system only until this labor system was abolished in the mid-1940s and ever since had been working "for salaries with the direct oversight and participation of the owners." Again, water was key to the decision. Incredibly, given the wealth of water sources it possessed, the CNRA concluded that some of the hacienda's productive land was not well cultivated because the property lacked adequate irrigation resources. The CNRA thus restored the hacienda's chalet, all of its arable land except for the *colonos*' plots, and 500 hectares of noncultivable land to the Riveros. The "true ex-*colonos*" became owners of their usufruct plots and the rest of the noncultivable land (368 hectares), and the rural teachers kept their 12 hectares while the landless peasant petitioners were excluded. The council assigned the property's water sources, including rivers, riverbeds, streams, and Lake Wara Wara, "for common use" of all parties, again prioritizing agricultural use. The president's final decision, handed down in May 1966, upheld the council's decision, ignoring Mayor Montenegro's expropriation and the city's needs completely.[108] It was not until the 1990s that the municipal water company (refounded as SEMAPA in the late 1960s) gained partial rights to Wara Wara by rebuilding its collapsed dam and by incorporating neighborhoods that had purchased land and water rights from ex-*hacendados* and ex-*colonos* in the decades following the agrarian reform case's resolution.

In both Tirani and Pacata Alta the agrarian reform's redistribution of hacienda water sources trumped Mayor Montenegro's 1953 expropriation of the haciendas' lakes. While the agrarian reform law mandated reallocation of hacienda water to both peasant producers and urban residents, in practice agrarian reform cases mostly divided hacienda water between estate owners and their former workers, excluding *piqueros*, landless peasants, and city dwellers. As migrants and groups of workers purchased hacienda and ex-hacienda land from ex-*hacendados* and ex-*colonos* to build urban neighborhoods in successive decades, however, they also purchased water rights, gradually urbanizing rights to San Juan, San Pablito, and Wara Wara.

Lagunmayu and Saytukocha

Unlike San Juan and Wara Wara, the lakes Lagunmayu and Saytukocha had long been co-owned at the time of Montenegro's expropriation (Map 9). Lagunmayu, situated in the mountains above Tiquipaya, is one of the region's oldest and most important irrigation water sources. The lake irrigates the northern, central, and southeastern areas of Tiquipaya and Coña Coña. Saytukocha, a lake with three times the capacity of Escalerani in the 1950s, was dammed in the late nineteenth century by *colono* workers of four *hacendados* from the southern section of Tiquipaya (Sirpita and Capacachi) with less favorable water access than their northern neighbors. The lake's waters irrigate the fields of these southern areas alone. Thus, while *hacendados* and *piqueros* shared rights to Lagunmayu, Saytukocha belonged exclusively to hacienda owners. Lagunmayu and Saytukocha's waters were therefore critical irrigation sources for several large estates, many smaller haciendas, and more than ten thousand *piquero* families when Montenegro expropriated them.[109] Efforts to expropriate these waters for the city had met with fierce resistance from both *hacendados* and *piquero* smallholders in the early 1940s, as discussed in chapter 2.

Through agrarian reform, hacienda *colonos* won rights to Lagunmayu and Saytukocha away from hacienda owners. In three of the four large Tiquipaya haciendas whose lands and waters were redistributed—Montesillo, Chilimarca, and Linde—hacienda *colonos* gained all of the properties' land and water rights. In Montesillo and Chilimarca former miners who had settled in the area led *colono* unions and brought agrarian reform cases forward on their behalf. Montesillo's

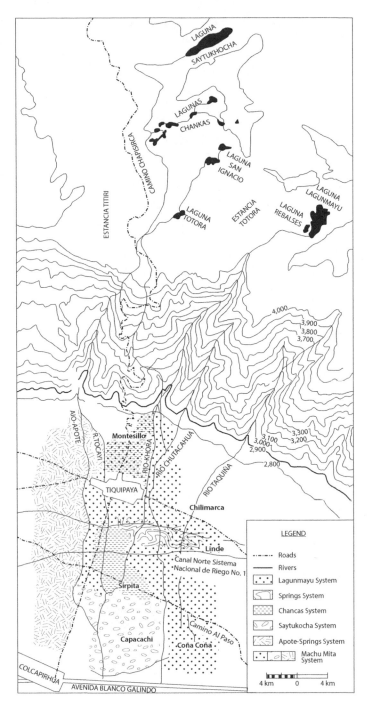

MAP 9.
Tiquipaya
haciendas
and irrigation
systems. Map
created by Fredy
Omar Fernandez
Quiroga. Zone
names added by
the author.

approximately fifty *colonos*, thirty *arrimantes*, and fifteen ex-miners paid owner Rafael Salamanca Bs. 65 million for all of the property's land and water rights. Agrarian reform institutions mediated thirty-four *colonos* and seventeen miners' purchase of the entire Chilimarca hacienda from the Guzmán family for the same price.[110] The Linde agrarian reform case ruling distributed land and water rights to a select group of the hacienda's workers (fourteen of thirty) who were considered land poor.[111] In all three former haciendas, ex-*colono* peasant unions took over administration of the haciendas' portion of the lakes' waters, which were mandated by the agrarian reform courts to be administered "according to existing customs and traditions."[112] In Coña Coña, the other large hacienda with rights to these lakes, *colonos* did not form a union and allowed owner Rafael Gumucio, who they considered to be a "good *patrón*," to keep all of his property other than their plots and to continue overseeing irrigation turn distribution. *Colono* union leaders testified that Gumucio ran a modern productive operation and treated his workers well.[113] In the face of Montesillo and Chilimarca's miner-led *colono* unions that had threatened to cut off water to lower-lying areas like Coña Coña, *colonos* seem to have deferred to their *patrón* to defend them.

Anthropologist Mareike Winchell has found that redistributive aid was a "source of virtue and authority" for *hacendados*, suggesting that a "good *patrón*" like Gumucio kept land, water, and authority over water distribution by fulfilling this expectation.[114] Irrigator union leader and historian Omar Fernández, in contrast, believes *colonos* in Coña Coña deferred to Gumucio because, unlike *hacendados* and miners, they did not yet have the ability to advocate for themselves ("el don de la palabra").[115] This does not explain why other *colonos* acted very differently, however. *Colonos*' differing approaches in the cases analyzed here suggest that they consciously employed different strategies and allies depending in part on their estate's proximity to water sources.

In all of these cases, *colonos* successfully used agrarian reform to win water rights from *hacendados*.[116] And, as in the cases dealing with San Juan and Wara Wara, none of the rulings acknowledged or allowed for Montenegro's expropriation of these lakes for the city. But the agrarian reform process reinscribed existing inequalities and erected new ones among Lagunmayu and Saytukocha rights holders. Hacienda owners who kept land and ex-*colonos* who had been hacienda administrators retained more land and water rights than most ex-*colonos* and agrarian reform excluded *piqueros*, leaving them with the same less-favorable water rights they had purchased from indigenous communities and haciendas in the late nineteenth century. Ironically, those who had escaped *colono* status decades earlier found themselves worse-off than those whom the agrarian reform had only recently freed from hacienda service. As a result, conflicts arose between *piquero* smallholders and ex-*colono* peasant communities over irrigation water. After agrarian reform ex-*colonos* enjoyed the more favorable irrigation rights that had belonged to estate owners. At times, they may have tried to appropriate *pique-ros'* water shares for themselves.[117] Tiquipaya *piqueros* accused ex-*colono* peasant union leaders of distributing water to their friends or the highest bidder and ex-*colono* water owners of hoarding water and "irrigating unnecessarily." As a result, they charged, "hundreds of *piqueros* are unable to plant given that they have no assurance whatsoever that there will be irrigation water available; those who sow anyway suffer considerable losses."[118] The agrarian's reform failed to acknowledge let alone remedy inequalities between *hacendados'* and *piqueros'* water rights, al-lowing *colonos* to inherit more favorable rights than piqueros and thus contribut-ing to a rivalry that continues to this day.[119]

City officials exploited and exacerbated the growing rift between now water-rich ex-*colono* communities and water-poor *piqueros* to gain access to Lagunmayu and Saytukocha by dealing with ex-*colonos* who led the lakes users' associations rather than their *piquero* rivals. When drought hit in late 1956, the mayor called on ex-*colono* peasant unions "that control the use of the waters of the mountains" to collaborate. Saytukocha and Lagunmayu's users' associations obliged, prompt-ing the mayor to praise them for their "selflessness" and collaborative spirit. But *piquero* members resented the city's use of Lagunmayu.[120] In 1958 *piquero* lake users formed the Comité de Agricultores Progresistas "in the spirit of the August second decree."[121] The committee vowed to "correct" irrigation water distribution and attacked the Comité Pro-Cochabamba (CPC), an elite urban civic organiza-tion, for its hypocrisy. While the CPC "oligarchs" had opposed the agrarian reform for violating private property rights, they were now committing the same offense by usurping Lagunmayu water from its "legitimate owners." As the Progressive Cultivators Committee put it, "To deny us use of our waters that we legitimately own will mean the death of the region. We have reviewed the contents of the agrarian reform law and we have not found any indication that the water meant to foment agriculture should be diverted to the city." The cultivators committee argued that the solution was not to supply the city by depriving the countryside but to expand the Chapisirca system, purchased for the city in 1941, by adding new lakes with enough water to supply the city's gardens and parks.[122] Criticizing the user association's sitting directorate for its inability to defend Lagunmayu against urban encroachment, the group put up its own slate and won control of the board in 1959.[123]

The episode is striking for several reasons. First, it reveals continued inequali-ties of water access and power among smallholders after the revolution, even within an association of lake-users. Second, it shows us that, like *colonos*, *hacenda-dos*, and Mayor Montenegro, *piqueros* too were reading and interpreting the 1953 agrarian reform law, which was indeed ambiguous on the question of urban water access, though not as vague as *piqueros* claimed. Finally, the affair is an early ex-ample of smallholders opposing urban encroachment on their water sources while also making informed urban hydraulic development proposals of their own that acknowledged the city's need for increased water supply. The new directorate led by the Progressive Cultivators Committee promised to balance agricultural and urban needs, but rather than cut the city off, both Lagunmayu and Saytukocha users continued to aid the city in times of crisis.

When the Chapisirca dam collapsed in March 1959, causing shortages in the department capital, Lagunmayu and Saytukocha's associations increased supply to the city. Later that year Lagunmayu users requested state funds to build Lagunmayu's dam higher and add water from neighboring lakes so it could provide water for urban and agricultural needs.[124] The additional lakes were also privately owned, so Lagunmayu users asked the state to expropriate them "for the benefit of Lagunmayu," an odd proposal in light of Lagunmayu users' argument that their lake was inalienable private property. As if conscious of the contradiction, they added that the expropriation would be made "with the express declaration to conserve its status as common private property [*propiedad común privada*]".[125] Indeed, this is what Lagunmayu and Saytukocha had long been—the "common private property" of a shifting array of groups, in the pre-revolutionary period of *hacendados* and *piquero* smallholders, after the revolution and water reform of ex-hacendados, *piqueros*, and ex-*colonos*. While the agrarian reform cases that redistributed Lagunmayu and Saytukocha ignored Montenegro's expropriation, Lagunmayu and Saytukocha's *piquero*, ex-*colono*, and ex-*hacendado* users consistently agreed to cede water to the city in exchange for water from La Angostura (and likely cash payments as well) throughout the revolutionary period and beyond.[126] Smallholders often made astute recommendations for ways to increase the city's water supply without infringing on their own.

Aftermath

The fate of these five lakes shows the powerful role of *colonos* in shaping the revolutionary process and democratizing the water tenure regime. The agrarian cases associated with these bodies of water overshadowed Cochabamba's *mnrista* Mayor Montenegro's expropriation to the point that it was never mentioned in case records or elsewhere again (as far as my research found), underscoring the importance of the highly contentious agrarian reform process in transforming Cochabamba's water tenure regime. *Colonos*, one of the region's most marginalized groups before the revolution, successfully claimed water sources and systems that they and their forebearers had built and maintained for several generations. At the same time, democratization was partial. Despite Guevara's Arze's pledge that agrarian reform would provide water to all, in the countryside *hacendados* kept disproportionate shares of their estates and water sources, water redistribution excluded independent peasants like the Montesillo *piqueros* discussed in chapter 2 who had stopped the state's expropriation of some of these same water sources in the early 1940s, and water reform mostly left out rural producers like *arrimantes* who lacked land and water altogether.

It was difficult for *colonos* who won land without irrigation rights to take advantage of newly won landholdings without state assistance to build irrigation infrastructure. In a 1997 interview, former *colono* and Valle Alto peasant leader Miguel Veizaga Guevara recounted that, after they received land, his community's goal "was to organize ourselves to least drill wells or build something like the Angostura dam. It was going to be something for our children." But Veizaga went on to explain that the government did not build irrigation works for them and that peasants were often unwilling or unable to invest requisite labor and funds.[127] Meanwhile, peasant unions were more concerned with defending land than with building hydraulic infrastructure.[128]

Despite the unevenness of agrarian reform's benefits, *piqueros* and ex-*colonos* built peasant unions together and developed a common *campesino* identity in the process of claiming and defending land and water after the revolution. As historian Christopher Boyer wrote in his study of postrevolutionary Michoacán, Mexico, rather than "a preconstituted fact," we should study "campesino identity as a product of historical processes."[129] Mestizo identity in Cochabamba had developed over several centuries as Spanish and creole landowners dispossessed indigenous communities' land and water holdings, community members left communities for haciendas and towns, and smallholders gained significant control over land and markets, as discussed in chapter 1. As Jose Gordillo's study of revolutionary-era Cochabamba peasant unions shows, *mestizaje* was a long-term subaltern process of resistance to colonial exploitation that took on new life after the revolution when Cochabambino rural toilers themselves embraced a mestizo *campesino* identity to claim equality and a degree of political autonomy. After the 1952 revolution, he writes, "these atomized valley peasants—who historically found in mestizaje...an escape route from elite and state pressures—experimented for the first time with...a collective identity as campesinos."[130] While *piqueros* and *colonos* remained conscious of their differing histories and water rights, they joined the same peasant unions. Organizing along class lines as *campesinos* allowed *piquero* and ex-*colono* smallholders to negotiate with revolutionary state officials in terms that officials understood.

In the Altiplano, indigenous communities had more successfully resisted community closure in the late nineteenth century and demands for community land restitution remained strong in the 1950s. Historian Carmen Soliz has shown that rather than victims of revolutionary reforms, as some scholars have portrayed them, altiplano indigenous communities won land restitution through agrarian reform.[131] In Cochabamba indigenous communities no longer existed. *Colono* and *piqueros'* demands there, as this chapter has shown, were aimed at gaining or increasing their land and water access. It made little sense in the 1950s for Cochabamba's *piqueros* and ex-*colonos* to embrace an indigenous identity that elites had used to malign them. Embracing *campesino* identity gave them claims to revolutionary citizenship and the right to political participation that it bestowed. It also offered an opportunity to reject the racism of those who disparaged them as "indios" by separating *indio* status from *campesino* identity once again. But identifying as mestizo *campesinos* did not require disavowing indigenous ancestry or culture. Cochabambino *campesinos* continued to speak Quechua, *campesina* women continued wear traditional clothing and hair styles inherited from colonial times, and *campesinos* continued to practice a syncretic Catholicism infused with indigenous beliefs. Mestizo identity also connected *campesinos* to urban and periurban workers, artisans, and market vendors. Cochabamba's urban and rural popular classes deemphasized ethnic identification after the revolution but did not reject it altogether.

Despite Montenegro's attempt to make good on Guevara Arze's promise, water redistribution mostly ignored residents of the growing city. While at times new urban workers' neighborhoods like Pacata Alta won land and water sources, water redistribution favored cultivators over other beneficiaries. The city's existing sources—the Arocagua Springs, the Chapisirca Lakes, half of the San Juan Lakes, and temporary use of flows from Lagunmayu and Saytukocha—were not enough to satisfy residents' growing demands. Now that hacienda sources had a new constellation of owners, it seemed that the municipal water service would have to look elsewhere to address city residents' appeals for greater water supply. Agrarian reform had redistributed hoarded water sources, but not to all.

BRIGADE TO CHAPISIRCA

Continued water shortages fueled renewed popular protest and new forms of popular action in the late 1950s and early 1960s. In the 1950s the municipal water service added 350–400 new connections to the distribution system each year without significantly increasing water sources. As a result, residents received poor quality water in scarce quantity from a deteriorated distribution network.[132] In 1960 the water network served less than a quarter of the city's territory and around half its population of 106,000.[133] After it became clear that neither Montenegro's expropriation nor agrarian reform would deliver hacienda lake water to the city, neighborhood groups, unionized workers, and the press mounted a campaign for increasing water supply and foreign funding for hydraulic development.

At first, neighborhood committees petitioned the municipality to extend and improve water access, especially on the periphery. By the early 1960s, however, neighborhood groups and unionized workers also began to take different kinds of direct action to access water, sometimes building their own supply and distribution systems and in one dramatic instance taking over a major hydraulic engineering project in the Tunari Mountains for several days in 1962. Urban neighborhood organizations and labor unions, much more than traditional and conservative civic organizations like the Pro-Cochabamba Committee or the Cochabamba Engineers Association, were the main protagonists in pressuring officials to secure more water and funding for hydraulic infrastructure in the late 1950s and early 1960s.

Neighborhood committees organized across the city to protest water scarcity and work to improve access in these years.[134] At first, they protested ongoing scarcity and called for municipal action. In the Zona Sud, the site of greatest protest over water scarcity, neighborhood associations objected to service cuts, complained when municipal wells ran dry, and organized protests when municipal water trucks increased rates in those areas lucky enough to have some form of municipal water service. In 1961, for example, a Zona Sud neighborhood committee representative reported that, after two weeks without water, housewives were wandering the streets searching for water. The representative criticized the municipality for wasting resources on festivals and receptions while "forgetting to provide the population with this important service."[135]

The municipality's inability to resolve water shortages prompted neighborhood residents to take direct action to access water. At times, residents volunteered their labor on municipal projects in exchange for water access and in other cases began to construct their own systems. The northern 14 de Septiembre neighborhood, for example, funded their water system with a loan from a local credit union, but nevertheless called the water crisis there "a problem that cannot be considered in isolation" that city leaders should address.[136] In such water-rich northern neighborhoods, neighborhood organizations were often able to purchase or simply take over water sources. The Tupuraya neighborhood committee, for instance, organized a team of one hundred men to direct excess water they claimed was spilling out of a nearby irrigation spring's eroded canals to the neighborhood's two thousand families who contributed to project costs and paid for connections. The neighborhood then traded its water and infrastructure for admission to the municipal water service.[137] This dynamic of leveraging local water sources and neighborhood-constructed systems to gain entrance into the municipal water system that had begun in the 1940s intensified as the city expanded further into outlying areas in the 1960s and subsequent decades. These strategies were in their infancy in this period, but the process of demanding water from the municipal government impelled residents to organize locally and solidify identities as neighborhoods, building on the experience of settling peripheral areas and foreshadowing autonomous organizing strategies they would use in the future when the municipal water service failed to incorporate them.

Ongoing water scarcity fueled increased discontent with the city's *mnrista* officials, even and perhaps especially among active MNR party members. MNR cells played an important role in organizing neighborhood committees and protesting water scarcity, especially in the Zona Sud where in one instance residents protested municipal authorities' "indifference" and reminded the mayor that Zona Sud residents paid property taxes and so deserved public services. In 1959 the head of the Zona Sud MNR cell and neighborhood mayor (*alcalde de barrio*) Raul Zalles asked Cochabamba's MNR newspaper *El Pueblo* to visit the neighborhood to witness its plight. After seeing that sewage filled the "black snake," as the Rocha River was called, and that residents lacked drinking water and electricity, the reporter concluded that "these simple and humble people do not have sufficient sway to achieve what others can obtain in a flash with a simple phone call."[138] A year later, after help failed to arrive, Zalles demanded the mayor visit the neighborhood and connect households to the network. How the municipality responded is unclear, but Zalles reported that despite shortages, inequalities, and the high cost of a direct connection, residents in his neighborhood with water access shared water with neighbors who lacked it.[139]

Despite the fact that *El Pueblo* was the MNR's official newspaper in Cochabamba, its editors and reporters were increasingly critical of municipal officials' approach to water scarcity.[140] While in the mid-1950s, the paper blamed consumers for wasting water, in the late 1950s and early 1960s it published resident complaints about unequal access like Zalles's and called on officials to extend service to the whole population.[141] Zalles's account of water sharing suggests that although uneven access to water across the city fomented competition and exploitation within neighborhoods, collective action and water-sharing practices flourished. Residents of the city's driest and poorest areas were most likely to form neighborhood organizations to combat water scarcity and therefore have the longest and strongest traditions of neighborhood organization in the city. Such neighborhood-level activity laid the basis for the seemingly spontaneous 1962 citywide take-over of the Chapisirca project.

In the face of *piquero* and ex-*colono* opposition to appropriation of their lakes, intense urban protest, population growth, and ongoing shortages, local and national MNR leaders and municipal water officials retooled their strategy for increasing urban water supply. After agrarian reform redistributed hacienda lakes to *colonos*, they shifted focus away from former hacienda sources toward large-scale hydraulic engineering projects. Much like the military socialists in the late 1930s, they attempted to apply a technical fix to the limits of water redistribution but had difficulty securing funding.

In the late 1950s municipal water service engineer Favio Cornejo revived Carlos Saavedra and Alfredo Marrón's 1949 Chapisirca expansion project.[142] Cornejo, educated in Argentina and Chile, took charge of the water service after its municipalization in 1950 when he was just thirty years old.[143] Cornejo proposed damming Lake Huara Huara and channeling its water to the Chapisirca system but lacked necessary funds. When the Corporación Boliviana de Fomento (Bolivian Development Corporation, CBF) ignored his request for assistance, Cornejo attempted to meter water use and increase rates to raise funds as his predecessor Eduardo Prudencio had done. But public outcry, concerns about the impacts on public health, and especially the objections of the Central Obrera Departamental (COD) that meters would increase costs for already impoverished residents defeated the scheme. Other funding proposals involved raising chicha taxes, asking for voluntary contributions, and forming an "investors' group" with individual, institutional, and municipal members. Cornejo even suggested surcharging movie tickets. The amount of money required, however, was far beyond the means of moviegoers, local investors, or even the national government. Although the water service started the project in 1959 with its own resources, it halted the project with less than half of the canal complete when it ran out of funds. Cochabamba mayor Héctor Cossio Salinas solicited financing from several Eastern European governments but aid ultimately came from the West.[144]

In the early 1960s the MNR deployed offers of assistance from the communist bloc to broker continued US aid.[145] These efforts took advantage of US fears that the 1959 Cuban revolution would inspire anti-US economic nationalism across the region. The centerpiece of US efforts to curb Cuban influence and stave off Cuban-style revolution in Latin America was the Alliance for Progress, established by US president John F. Kennedy in 1961. The program offered loans, direct aid, and technical support for infrastructure projects and social programs meant to improve quality of life and thereby dissuade beneficiary populations from supporting economic nationalism or socialist revolution. The program's slogan was "techo, trabajo y tierra, salud y escuela" ("housing, work and land, healthcare and schools"). At the same time, the US government funded counterinsurgency efforts to quash guerrilla movements and trained Latin American military personnel at the Latin American Training Center-Ground Division, established in the Panama Canal Zone in 1946 and renamed the School of the Americas in 1963.[146] Under pressure from several Latin American governments, the United States helped found the Inter-American Development Bank (IDB) in 1959, which provided loans for infrastructure projects as well.[147]

Bolivia had been a test case for US policy in Latin America for two decades.[148] The United States began providing aid in 1942 and increased it after the 1952 revolution in exchange for subservience to US dictates. As historian James Siekmeier has written, "Paz Estenssoro was the type of noncommunist, democratic, nationalist, pro-U.S. leader that the United States wanted to see throughout the Third World."[149] From 1952 to 1964, Bolivia received more US aid per capita than any other Latin American country and possibly more per capita assistance than any other country in the world besides Israel.[150] The MNR's pragmatic centrist wing, led by Victor Paz Estenssoro, accepted US aid for development projects that leaders hoped would eventually make future development assistance unnecessary and used US support to compete with the party's labor-left. Nevertheless, the relationship was, in Kenneth Lehman's words, "an unequal partnership." Whereas the US-sponsored coup that ousted progressive Guatemalan president Jacobo Arbenz in 1954 was a display of what could happen to Latin American nations that defied US mandates, Bolivia became a showcase for the largesse on offer for nations that acquiesced.

During Victor Paz's final term, the MNR negotiated an IDB loan to fund major urban drinking water expansion projects in La Paz, Oruro, and Cochabamba.[151] In October 1960 the public works minister wrote Cochabamba Mayor Cossio that the IDB loan would fund a "definitive solution" to Cochabamba's drinking water problem.[152] While loan and project negotiations between the government and the IDB were under way, Cochabamba residents staged the period's most dramatic collective action to confront water scarcity. To protest project delays, a two-hundred-worker "brigade" climbed the mountainside to take over work on the overdue Chapisirca project in December 1962. The day before their departure, the COD announced that the workers would build canals to channel additional water to the Chapisirca Lakes from its neighbors before returning to protest water and power shortages and support a teachers' strike on the city's streets the following week. Mayor Ramiro Villarroel Claure and water service manager Favio Cornejo tried to dissuade them, arguing that the real problem was lack of funds and that trained workers were already on the job, but the brigadiers remained undeterred.

On December 1 construction workers, transport operators, teachers, and municipal employees set off in ten trucks carrying tools and provisions donated by the Cooperativa de Empleados Públicos, ready to direct new water sources to the city. Among their ranks were blacksmiths, mining technicians, health officers, topographers, soil experts, a sixty-year-old worker, and a thirteen-year-old boy. Upon their return, brigadiers charged that officials' predictions "had been contradicted by reality" and that authorities were lying to the population about progress on the project. While municipal officials had warned that the volunteers would disorganize and confuse a fully equipped team of sixty municipal workers, the brigadiers found only six workers without tools on duty. COD general secretary Oscar Sanjinés reported that eighty-five volunteers worked tirelessly for twelve hours a day for two days, dynamiting open canals to connect two additional lakes to the Chapisirca system.[153] He also claimed that on their descent from Lagunmayu, workers had seen Tiquipaya residents and agriculturalists diverting water for their own use and that the municipality had canceled plans for drilling a battery of new wells.[154] The mayor countered that the workers would have been helpless without municipal employees' direction, city-owned equipment, and municipal engineers' plans; that many municipal workers were absent that day to celebrate Tiquipaya's anniversary; that Tiquipaya peasants were not redirecting Lagunmayu's water away from the city but rather had willingly ceded it to "cooperate in supplying water to the city"; and that the CBF was about to begin drilling wells. Water scarcity, the mayor assured *Prensa Libre* readers, was municipal officials' "constant concern."[155]

This remarkable event exhibits the intensity of late revolutionary-era urban ferment and mobilization around water access and hydraulic development. The renegade expedition of workers to the mountains shows how active the city's population was, how broader mobilization in the revolutionary period fed and was fed by demands for water, and how hard it was for the MNR to control grassroots formations in the late revolutionary period or to meet their demands. Seemingly in response to this forceful action, President Victor Paz Estenssoro announced to the people of Cochabamba, via a letter in *Prensa Libre*, that he had signed a loan agreement with the IDB and West Germany to fund a drinking water supply expansion project. The "definitive solution" to Cochabamba's drinking water problem, he assured Cochabambinos, was on the horizon.[156] Once again, the initiative for hydraulic development came from below.

While the IDB indicated that the loan would pay for the Chapisirca project, loan terms gave Bank officials rather than Bolivian authorities the power to choose new water sources.[157] The German firm Global Engineering, contracted by the IDB, determined that Chapisirca expansion could not meet future demand and proposed drilling deep wells in agricultural communities west of the city instead. The German engineers concluded that valley aquifers held "substantial volumes" of water and identified Vinto, a sparsely populated agricultural area 20 kilometers west of the city, as the most productive potential site. [158] On the surface Global Engineering's reasoning seemed to be about cost-benefit ratios, timing, capital outlay, location, and quality control. Wells in Vinto would provide more water than expanding Chapisirca, could be completed and paid for in stages as the population and demand grew, would be located west of the city where the population was growing fastest, and would provide water that was cleaner and easier to control than mountain sources. Mountain water was located in remote lake reservoirs, open canals exposed water to contamination and were difficult to maintain compared with the closed pipes that would drive aquifer water to the city, and turbulent mountain water required "complete treatment" in contrast to well water that only had to be chlorinated.

But engineers also chose wells as a technical solution to social contest over water. As Global Engineering's William Pauly wrote, "While in the mountains there is the possibility that cultivators will illegally divert water from the canals for irrigation, steel pipes from deep wells to the city present greater security against such illegal actions, as they will be laid underground and operated under pressure."[159] Indeed, well water would be safely out of peasants' reach, protected against their "illegal actions" by solid rock in 200-meter-deep aquifers before being pumped out of the ground and securely whisked away from the fields of Vinto and Quillacollo in closed underground pipes. For these engineers surface water sources lent themselves to theft while deep aquifer water could more easily become the exclusive domain of the city.

Wells were not the only possibility, however. Luis Calvo Soux, an engineer from Sucre who had adopted Cochabamba as his home, developed a proposal to dam the Misicuni River and direct its water from the Tunari Mountains to Cochabamba's valleys. He first came up with the idea in the 1940s while working for the water service and conducted a provisional study with funding from the engineering firm that he managed in the late 1950s. He envisioned three dams that would direct the waters of the Misicuni, Viscachas, and Putucuni Rivers to a 500-square-kilometer reservoir in the Misicuni Valley, 1,600 meters above the city. From there, a flow of 6,000 liters per second would pass through a 12-kilometer tunnel bored through the mountains to the edge of the Central Valley and fall 900 meters to produce hydroelectricity on its way to the valley's fields and treatment plants.[160] The available funds only allowed Calvo Soux to conduct what he called "barely a preliminary study," however, which the MNR government apparently ignored during an economic crisis when US advisers were pressuring the government to curb spending.[161] Despite these disappointments, support for the project grew in subsequent decades.

While some observers raised doubts about the wells project—that they would not produce enough water, that they might cost more than bringing water from the mountains, and that aquifers could dry up—and a few backed the Misicuni dam project as an alternative—most MNR officials and local engineers supported the Germans' Vinto wells proposal.[162] When he announced the study's recommendations in July 1964, Cochabamba mayor Eduardo Soriano Badani proclaimed that Global Engineering would solve Cochabamba's water problem within six months.[163]

The same month, fifty-two residents of the Villa Busch neighborhood west of the city, including a representative of the MNR armed cell René Barrientos Ortuño, submitted a petition requesting the mayor restore water truck service and drill a well there.[164] The petition is telling. It indicates that in mid-1964 water scarcity continued to plague urban residents and that they expected the municipality to extend water service to underserved areas. It also suggests that residents now saw the municipality as more likely to drill a neighborhood well or include them in a water truck route than to complete a large-scale dam project in the mountains, although desire for such a project was growing. The cell that made the request was named for General René Barrientos Ortuño, who had just been elected vice president in the 1964 elections that awarded Victor Paz Estenssoro a third term. Paz made Barrientos his running mate at the last minute in an effort to enlist military support for Paz's increasingly unpopular government.

THE FALL OF THE MNR

The MNR fell due to an inability to resolve contending visions within the revolutionary coalition in the face of economic crisis caused by the falling global prices of tin, Bolivia's main export. During the presidency of Hernán Siles Zuazo (1956–1960), the Bolivian government adopted the 1956–1957 Economic Stabilization Plan developed by US adviser George Jackson Eder, a deputy counsel at the International Telephone and Telegraph Company who had worked for a firm subsidiary in Argentina.[165] The plan prioritized balancing the national budget, resuming payments on foreign debt, and compensating former mine owners by cutting public spending, which were also goals of MNR moderates and the party's right wing. The results were disastrous: land redistribution slowed, financing infrastructure projects became more difficult, and the economy contracted. Austerity and repression of strikes against wage cuts and layoffs led many leftist leaders and militant miners to leave the party. As Eder himself admitted, the plan meant "the repudiation, at least tacitly, of virtually everything that the Revolutionary Government had done over the previous four years."[166] Assistance meant to facilitate economic independence and strengthen the party's center-right led the MNR government to rely on US economic aid and the military, further alienating party leaders from their base in a vicious circle of retrenchment and isolation.[167]

The MNR's willingness to use repression allowed Bolivia to become a posterchild for the US Alliance for Progress and win US development aid in the early 1960s. During his second term (1960–1964), Victor Paz Estenssoro and the United States teamed up to battle the Bolivian left, especially miners, students, and teachers. Paz deployed the military, secret police, and peasant and worker militias against miners who opposed harsh labor reforms required by the Triangular Plan's mine rehabilitation program.[168] He also deployed state security forces against university faculty and students, teachers, Communist Party members, and other leftists. As historian Thomas Field has written, the Alliance for Progress in Bolivia was "an aggressive modernization project implemented through armed force."[169]

The MNR's urban chauvinism and efforts to centralize control of peasants and their unions eroded support for the party in the Cochabamba countryside. Urban elites at times attempted to sow fear of the rural masses in the city by depicting depraved peasants ready to unleash floods on the city or cut off its water supply. Both rumors and actual peasant occupations produced what Jose Gordillo has called "collective hysteria" in cities and towns, setting the urban poor against the peasantry. In a 1993 interview an urban resident claimed that after the revolution peas-

ants came from "as far as Angostura to tear down the dam to flood the city of Cochabamba.... They wanted to do away with the whole world. It was too much!"[170]
At the same time, President Paz's dismissive treatment of Barrientos encouraged
the Cochabamba peasantry and military regiments to rally behind the general.[171]

Meanwhile, the military had been courting the peasantry. The MNR leadership
itself restored the power and credibility that the military had lost in the Chaco
War and the 1952 revolution by rebuilding the armed forces and employing them
to carry out nonmartial labor. In 1953 defense minister Luis Arteaga declared that
the armed forces' most important role was to "fight the war against misery and
the hunger of the people."[172] President Siles deployed the military to pacify the
Valle Alto during the 1959–1960 Ch'ampa Guerra, a conflict between rival peasant
unions.[173] Barrientos, a charismatic Cochabambino and native Quechua speaker,
personally directed the military's pacification campaign as well as the new US-
funded civic action program. Soldiers built schools, health posts, irrigation works,
and drinking water systems across the countryside.[174] Barrientos's brand of populist authoritarianism was built in part through infrastructure. As historian Molly
Geidel has written, "By involving the military, the U.S.-backed MNR government
blurred the line between military and civic life, militarizing development work
while softening the image of the re-empowered military."[175]

Military developmentalism helped lay the basis for the 1964 coup and the
Military-Peasant Pact (Pacto Militar Campesino, PMC), an agreement signed
in Ucureña on the anniversary of the 9 April revolution just before Paz Estenssoro's reelection in May 1964. In the pact, as historian Elizabeth Shesko has explained, "Barrientos, representing the military, and forty-eight peasant organizations pledged to work together to support Barrientos's candidacy for the vice
presidency, guarantee social peace, combat extreme doctrines, ensure economic
diversification, and defend the social, political, and economic interests of the
signees."[176] By the time Paz Estenssoro won a third term, the MNR was a mere shell
of the revolutionary coalition the party had once led. In James Dunkerley's words,
the 1964 elections united the right and left against the "ramshackle remnants of
a party that no longer possessed any popularity beyond that generated through
state patronage."[177] In fact, it was the military that most often delivered desired
improvement projects. Sergio Almaraz Paz, an MNR supporter-turned-critic, put
it well, "The revolution did not crumble from a single blow, it fell bit by bit, piece
by piece." The coup was "a shot fired into a corpse."[178]

In November 1964, Barrientos launched a military coup from Cochabamba that
overthrew the MNR and inaugurated nearly two decades of military dictatorship
in Bolivia. Yet historians are increasingly recognizing that the 1964 coup was less
of a rupture than scholars previously thought. The MNR government had become
quite repressive, the Military-Peasant Pact was signed, and violent US-backed
counterinsurgency efforts were under way in the mines before the coup. Unlike

the regimes that came to power in coups in Guatemala or Chile in 1954 and 1973 respectively, Barrientos's "Restorative Revolution" did not reverse the revolution's signature reforms. Much to Washington's relief, Barrientos became a faithful—and repressive—cold warrior. But the mines remained nationalized, universal citizenship rights endured, unresolved agrarian reform cases continued to make their way through the courts, and agrarian reform beneficiaries held on to their land and water holdings. In the years and decades that followed, a majority of Cochabambinos became convinced that a major dam project in the mountains would be the best way to fulfill the revolutionary promise of water for all.

MEMORIES AND LEGACIES OF THE REVOLUTION

In the early 1960s, MNR state agencies published evaluations of revolutionary reforms ten years on, celebrating their achievements. In the 1963 government publication *Diez años de reforma agraria en Bolivia, 1953–1963*, National Agrarian Reform Council president Raul Alfonso García ended with the following, worth quoting at length:

> With agrarian reform, not only have the productive forces been liberated, but also the powerful spiritual forces that are and will be the incentive for the growth of the nation. Proof of this is the extraordinary and widespread construction of schools,... roads, dams, and irrigation systems. All of these great endeavors were undertaken spontaneously by peasants themselves. The success of the agrarian reform owes to this patriotic attitude and conduct. The peasant of today possesses extreme energy to better himself and to be useful to his social community. His faith and trust are crucial for a better future. Through agrarian reform, the indigenous Bolivian has become dignified, achieved the quality of a human being, and reintegrated into the nation. "*El pongo con taquia*" [a peon rented out by his master as a laborer and supplier of dung] is no more than a grim memory.[179]

The paternalism and racism of this passage is astonishing if not surprising. But it is also striking that García credited peasants' own initiative, labor, and newfound access to land and irrigation water for the so-called entrance of the Indian into the ranks of the country's citizenry and the human race. He reminded readers that the agrarian reform's goals were not limited to land redistribution and increased agricultural production but also included "conservation of the country's natural resources"—namely its soil, subsoil, and water resources, through "adoption of indispensable scientific and technical methods."[180] This seemingly discordant combination of paternalism and redistributionism can only be explained by the revolutionary self-activity of Bolivian *colonos*, indigenous communities, and city dwellers. Demands for land and water along with the party's desperation to jumpstart the economy through increased agricultural production produced an ethos of state-guided redistribution, use, and conservation of land, soil, and water.

Agrarian reform revolutionized the nation's water tenure regime, dispossessing *hacendados* of water sources they had until then legally owned and delivering them to former estate tenants. By 1967, 7.2 percent of Bolivian land had been redistributed, the most extensive land reform in South America by that time.[181] As peasants and indigenous communities pushed the party to redistribute land to those who worked it and to its original owners, they also obliged the MNR to redistribute water. The text of the agrarian reform law promised to redirect hacienda water sources to all water users. All those contending for hacienda water sources in Cochabamba, including *colonos*, *hacendados*, *piqueros*, and the mayor, seized on the law to press their claims. But despite the law's expressed commitment to water for all, *colonos* won a greater portion of hacienda water sources than any other group in the revolutionary period. Their success owed to their power—their unions and leaders were experienced, well organized, militant, and willing to both take direct action and slog through years of litigation to win their land and water claims. *Colonos'* achievement was also a result of their ability to convince MNR officials that former tenants needed land and irrigation water to make themselves into the efficient and prosperous producers that the success of the MNR project depended on.

It is odd, then, that celebratory MNR publications neglected to mention water redistribution. Early 1960s state publications highlighted dam projects but failed to mention reallocation of hacienda water sources. In the beautifully designed and illustrated *Bolivia: 10 años de revolución*, published in 1962, an agrarian reform chapter section titled "Nueva Política de Aguas: Represas y Pozos" detailed progress on a series of irrigation dams, wells, and canals across the country, including Cochabamba's Angostura irrigation system.[182] While we can only guess at their reasoning, and it is possible they were unaware of this achievement, perhaps officials feared that drawing attention to hacienda water redistribution risked exposing failure to redistribute those sources to those like *piqueros*, *arrimantes*, and city dwellers still suffering from shortages.

The agrarian reform law promised to allocate requisitioned water sources to city residents as well, but this proved difficult to accomplish. MNR officials thus commissioned new proposals to respond to urban demands that accommodated the reality that ex-*colonos* had won control over these sources. At the same time, ordinary water users began to develop regional hydraulic development proposals to address continued shortages and disparities. Cochabambinos across the valley became convinced that there was plenty of water available if the national state could find the will to secure international funding and expertise to direct those sources to the valley. While *piqueros*, *colonos*, and city residents often sparred over existing sources, a growing cross-sector coalition began to demand large-scale infrastructure projects to provide more water to all groups. Rather than scarcity, they envisioned sharing a wealth of water resources.

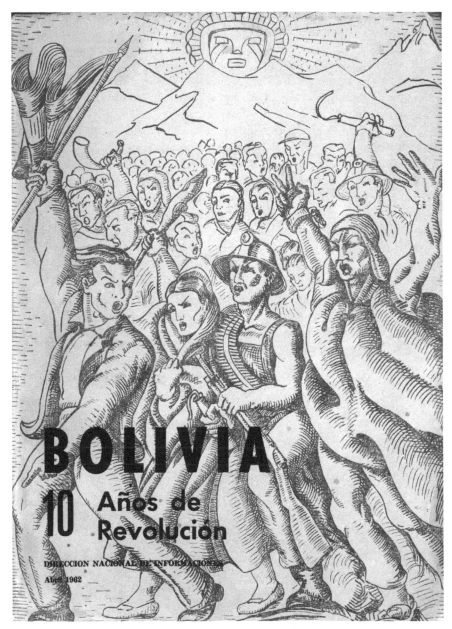

FIGURE 7. Cover of *Bolivia: 10 años de revolución (1952–1962)*, by Bolivia, Dirección Nacional de Información. Illustration by Fausto Aoiz (La Paz: Empresa Industrial Gráfica E. Burillo, 1962).

In the decades since agrarian reform, ex-*colono* communities have defended their hard-won gains. After winning land and water, ex-*colono* communities organized themselves into agricultural workers' unions along the territorial lines of former haciendas. Foreign, national, and local authorities' frequent efforts to tap ex-*colonos*' water sources for the city have met with militant resistance, a product of the confidence and power ex-*colono* communities gained through their revolutionary-era fights for land and water.

Peasants' power—both their ability to mobilize and their physical control of surface water sources—gained during the revolution has made state officials and foreign lenders and engineers wary of seeking surface water ever since. At the end of the revolutionary period and during the dictatorships of the 1960s and 1970s, international bankers and contractors and national and local authorities preferred to seek water in aquifers they believed could be more easily controlled and safeguarded from combative peasant cultivators. *Colonos, piqueros,* and urban dwellers, in contrast, argued for a dam project in the mountains that would increase water supply for both the city and countryside. After the radical promises of the early MNR gave way to pragmatism and then dictatorship, it became clear that agrarian reform would not distribute hacienda water sources widely. But Cochabambinos refused to give up on Guevara Arze's promise of water for all. Instead, they demanded even more ambitious regional hydraulic development to fulfill that revolutionary promise.

4
___

Popular Engineering

Hydraulic Governance and Expertise under Dictatorship

In September 1975, city water users organized a caravan to the Misicuni River in the mountains above Cochabamba to pressure national authorities to execute the ambitious Misicuni dam project. More than one thousand Cochabambinos made the journey. Two years later, peasant cultivators in the Valle Bajo community Vinto protested a plan to drill deep wells for the city that threatened their water sources. Not only were both actions effective, they occurred during the most repressive years of the Banzer dictatorship. Government troops had recently massacred upwards of two hundred peasant protestors in Cochabamba, suspended political parties, and put all labor, professional, business, and student associations under government control.[1] Bolivia's dictatorial regimes became increasingly more repressive from 1964 to 1982. But despite the risks, miners, students, peasants, urban water users, and many others pressured and confronted state institutions and forces throughout this period.

The 1964 coup ushered in nearly two decades of military rule with just brief moments of relief. Like in many other Latin American countries in the 1960s, Bolivia's dictatorships violently repressed labor, cracked down on students and leftists, and tried to control peasant organizations. And like their counterparts, René Barrientos (1964–1969) and especially Hugo Banzer (1971–1978) were, in historian Ben Nobbs-Thiessen's words, "enthralled by grandiose development initiatives, especially when they turned attention away from human rights abuses."[2] But unlike in other countries that experienced counterrevolutionary coups in this period, most notably Guatemala (1954) and Chile (1973), Bolivia's military regimes sustained revolutionary-era reforms. The dictatorships continued land and water redistribution, upheld state ownership of mines, and fortified a developmentalist state committed to urban and rural infrastructural development.

Bolivia's military regimes did not pretend to include workers or the left in their coalitions and meted out brutal repression. But they were more subject to popular pressure than is usually acknowledged. Scholars writing in the 1970 and 1980s blamed the betrayals of "reluctant" middle-class MNR revolutionaries for enabling the rise of dictatorship. But while they saw the 1964 coup as a decisive end to "the revolutionary phase of the National Revolution" and the beginning of a "long Thermidorian reaction," they nevertheless identified continuities: acceptance of "the National Revolution" and "fundamentalist nationalism," "firm commitment to Agrarian Reform and mobilization of the peasantry," and a close relationship with the United States.[3] New scholarship affirms significant continuity between the periods of MNR rule and dictatorship, emphasizing MNR repression in the early 1960s, and is beginning to reveal the ways popular groups pressured and constrained the military regimes.[4] The groups and actors contending for power after 1964 were engaged in fierce contests not only over what the revolution's legacy would be but also to some degree over what its *direction* would be, for dictators, peasants, workers, and leftists alike claimed that their regimes, unions, pacts, and activity were legitimate continuations or "restorations" of the 1952 revolution.

The history of water reform and hydraulic development in these years shows that rather than choosing between capitulation and repression, organized groups like peasant unions and neighborhood committees negotiated with the state under dictatorship, steering state action as much as they were able to meet their needs. While the dictatorships were less accountable to popular sectors than the MNR had been in the early revolutionary years, both city dwellers and peasants had room to maneuver, even after Banzer's 1974 "self-coup" (*auto-golpe*) and embrace of a more repressive model of rule.[5] Barrientos and later Banzer were receptive to pressure from mobilized water users to expand water access and democratize water governance. Rather than scuttle the Inter-American Development Bank (IDB) loan for urban water supply expansion in La Paz, Santa Cruz, and Cochabamba negotiated by the MNR, the Barrientos administration and the German contractor Global Engineering submitted the loan proposal in May 1965.

The IDB's arrival in Cochabamba in the 1960s marked a turning point. Before then, local groups and institutions had mostly engineered and managed water systems on their own, with the exceptions of occasional assistance from the national government starting in the 1890s and Mexican cooperation on the Angostura project in the early 1940s. Starting in the mid-1960s, international development banks and engineering firms began to finance and engineer hydraulic development and water provision in Cochabamba and other Bolivian cities. In the 1960s the World Bank focused on large public infrastructure projects like hydroelectric

dams and railways aimed at boosting economic growth in countries seeking development while the IDB funded urban and rural development projects like water,
sanitation, housing, and education aimed at improving everyday life.[6] In the 1970s
the World Bank under Robert McNamara followed the IDB's into social development as international lending in Latin America exploded.[7]

The IDB loan for urban water supply and distribution expansion in Cochabamba promised to end water scarcity and water segregation in the city. But loan
terms that expected water users to take on much of the financial responsibility
for improvements provoked controversy, prompting new rounds of mobilization
over water access and governance. As historian Amy Offner has argued, economic
practices usually associated with the 1980s-era Washington Consensus such as
privatization and self-help have an earlier history.[8]

The unfulfilled revolutionary-era promise of water for all fueled intense popular protest under dictatorship. Cochabambino water users were willing to take on
some responsibility for expanding water access, but they mobilized against policies that thrust that too much of the cost onto their shoulders. And now that the
limits of revolutionary water redistribution were clear, they embraced dam-build-
ing as a solution to water scarcity even as environmental movements elsewhere in
the world fiercely opposed them.[9] In their fights with the national government and
the IDB under dictatorship, Cochabambinos increased their control over regional
water sources, systems, and engineering and developed a sense of ownership over
the region's waterscape that, as much as they tried, dictators and the IDB were
mostly unable to restrain.

WATER FOR THE GROWING CITY

In the 1960s and 1970s, Latin America was one of the most urbanized regions
in the world.[10] Urban birth rates rose, death rates declined, and rural migrants
streamed into the region's cities. Midcentury modernization theory optimistically
saw urbanization as path to economic growth. When this growth failed to happen,
dependency theorists blamed the region's subordinated position in the international economy, others blamed the perverse contradictions of capitalist development and internal factors, while most lamented and feared the arrival of the rural
masses to the region's cities.[11] In the third quarter of the century, Cochabamba's
department capital grew rapidly from just over eighty thousand to more than two
hundred thousand.[12] Migrants escaping inadequate land, water, and credit access
in Cochabamba's agricultural provinces settled in areas that had been reserved for
green spaces or agriculture along the "axis of urbanization" from Quillacollo to Sacaba," often purchasing lots from developers (*loteadores*) who built neighborhoods
without basic services.[13] While city planners attempted to halt unplanned growth,
the urban land market was, in Cochabambino architect Humberto Solares's words,

the city's "great planner."[14] The result was creeping, low-density urban settlement and increasingly deficient and unequal provision of basic services.

While higher income earners enjoyed more consistent service, residents across the city faced insecure water access, the population's foremost grievance. Elites craved water for industrial expansion and the 48 percent of residents within the municipal distribution network complained of frequent rationing and service cuts.[15] Just a third of municipal customers had a direct connection inside their home; the rest accessed water at a connection in their building or at an outdoor tap.[16] During droughts, especially frequent in these years, these residents had to wait in long lines to receive municipal water rations. Outside the network some areas had public pumps that often served more than a hundred families each. In one Zona Sud neighborhood residents reported that they had to stand in pump lines with "cans, pots, and barrels" starting before dawn. As one resident commented, "the spectacle . . . is sad and unbelievable in a place said to be civilized."[17]

Since the municipality only operated six water trucks, most residents of periphery neighborhoods without pumps bought water from private water vendors called *aguateros*. While *aguateros* were supposed to keep rates low in exchange for access to municipal wells, protests against astronomical rates and municipal ineptitude often flared among their customers on the city's edges.[18] Underserved residents on the margins at times consumed water from crude wells, irrigation canals, and even pools of standing water, which at times caused conflicts with ex-*colono* communities.[19] Cochabamba suffered from especially poor access to drinking water supply compared with other Bolivian cities and urban areas in neighboring countries, which contributed to making it the city with the highest infant mortality rate in Bolivia.[20]

Water access disparities disproportionately affected poor women charged with childrearing and domestic responsibilities. It overwhelmingly fell on them to line up to pump water at 4:00 or 5:00 in the morning or to stay close to home to flag down the municipal water truck or an *aguatero*. As a result, women sometimes petitioned the mayor and water service administrators to witness and respond to their plight.[21] In 1968 women in the northern El Temporal neighborhood seized on a mayoral visit to demand water access. As the mayor's caravan descended a hilly street, women residents cried, "We want water!" and forced him to stop to hear their complaints. They told the mayor that on a typical morning three hundred people lined up along a nearby irrigation canal to collect water, which, they explained, "descends in weekly turns and is the only water source we have." The mayor explained that the area was outside city limits but promised to install a spigot. Unimpressed, the women responded, "What will we do with a spigot? We are more than 150 families of at least six people each."[22]

In the mid-1960s, as city residents protested water shortages, they also expanded water infrastructure neighborhood by neighborhood. New neighborhood associations insisted that the municipality regulate *aguateros* and expand municipal water truck service and called for extending the municipal distribution network. At the same time, they engineered projects of their own. With their own funds, materials, and labor, neighborhood residents expanded, repaired, and improved municipal service. When the municipality renovated the water distribution system in the Las Cuadras neighborhood in 1968, for example, residents there paid half the cost. The mayor's office held the deal up as a model for other neighborhoods, promising to "continue with these public works so long as residents assist and contribute as Calle Sucre residents have."[23]

Other new neighborhoods outside the city center's municipal network built independent water systems. In the teachers' neighborhood Barrio del Magisterio and the miners' neighborhood Juan XXIII west of the city, for instance, residents formed cooperatives that drilled wells and laid distribution infrastructure.[24] In Juan XXIII, founded by mine company workers from Northern Potosí's Siglo XX-Catavi mining center, residents at first collected water from a neighboring hacienda's artesian well in lard cans since, in one resident's words, "there were no buckets or anything else in those days." In 1968 neighborhood residents pooled their resources to drill a well and build a tank and then added wells, tanks, and connections as the neighborhood grew.[25] The neighborhood continues to operate this system independently to this day. Contributions by neighborhood residents to expanding urban water provision produced a sense of ownership over the city's water sources and infrastructure, especially in neighborhoods with independent systems like Juan XXIII.

At the same time that individual neighborhoods addressed water shortages on their own, civic organizations, a new neighborhood federation, and labor unions began to tackle this issue on a citywide basis in the late 1960s. Cochabamba's civic movement, dormant during the revolutionary period, revived after the 1964 coup. While some have attributed its resurgence to new opportunities for elites and the middle class under dictatorship, the civic movement included a strong popular component, as broad-based mobilization around water access attests.[26] In the late 1960s and the 1970s the Comité Pro-Cochabamba (CPC), the Junta de la Comunidad (JUNCO), the Federación de Juntas Vecinales (FEJUVE), the Central Obrera Departamental (COD), and the factory workers' union (the *fabriles*) combined forces to demand state action to improve water access and took action themselves.[27] In the process of organizing for water access, these civic, neighborhood, and labor organizations began to claim a right not only to receive water but also to participate in solving the city's water problems.

Starting in the mid-1960s, the FEJUVE claimed the right to represent residents in their water access complaints. When municipal authorities appointed "neighborhood mayors" (*alcaldes de barrio*) to address residents' complaints about service deficiencies, the FEJUVE declared that "the only legitimate neighborhood mayors are the presidents of neighborhood committees associated with the FE-JUVE, as they are elected by popular vote unlike neighborhood mayors who are appointed according to favoritism and political connections and have left us with bitter experiences." In addition to demanding extension of the municipal distribution network, FEJUVE leaders also helped residents expand water supply and distribution, in one instance helping drill wells in Zona Norte neighborhoods.[28]

While waiting for negotiations with the Inter-American Development Bank to conclude and funds to be disbursed, municipal authorities rationed water, restricted its use, and pursued small-scale supply projects. Like their predecessors, officials often blamed shortages on residents' "irrational" practices, especially during droughts. During the 1969 dry season, for instance, the new public water company SEMAPA announced strict controls to guarantee "rational" water consumption: inspectors visited homes to prevent "excess use" and fined and severed connections of those they found violating the rules. During drought years in the 1970s officials strictly enforced the ban on irrigating with municipal water, and city police monitored domestic water use.[29] Such controls were part of an ongoing effort that began in the 1940s to instill an ethic of responsible and moral water consumption practices and to thereby link citizenship to accountable water use. Officials held that "the average person does not voluntarily restrict his water use to allow sufficient water to flow to the humblest homes" and therefore sought to "instill in each citizen his responsibility" to restrict use of water "that is so lacking in various areas."[30]

While building a sense of solidarity among water users could have been productive, this rhetoric conveniently absolved state institutions of responsibility for ongoing water shortages, blaming municipal customers instead. In its final years of operation in the mid-1960s the municipal water service resumed work on the Chusequeri project, first proposed by Carlos Saavedra and Alfredo Marrón in the late 1940s, and took modest steps to extend the distribution network, but lacked the funds necessary to complete these projects.[31] As water shortages and public outcry intensified and loan negotiations with the IDB stalled, the municipality put dealing with water shortages on hold.[32]

President Barrientos and IDB representatives finally signed an $11 million loan agreement with the IDB in January 1968, prompting Cochabamba mayor Francisco Baldi to declare 1968 the "year of drinking water."[33] Upon signing the agreement for the long-awaited loan, Barrientos awarded IDB president Felipe Herrera, the Chilean economist who served as the Bank's first president, a Bolivian passport and pronounced him a Bolivian.[34] But Cochabamba's portion of the loan would not be disbursed for several years until the city met a number of conditions geared at ensuring repayment. The agreement required that the municipality found a new autonomous water company to administer Cochabamba's water and sewage services, that the new company raise rates, and that additional supply for the city come from new deep wells outside the city. These terms aimed to strengthen state control over water sources and management and to mold urban water users into passive paying customers.

The municipality met the first condition by founding the Servicio Municipal de Agua Potable y Alcantarillado (Municipal Water and Sanitation Service, SEMAPA) in 1967 before the loan agreement was signed. The other two conditions, however, met with intense opposition. In the late 1960s and the 1970s urban residents consistently fought rate increases and vied to control the new water company and determine the direction of hydraulic development. Most residents strongly opposed well drilling and argued for a major dam project in the mountains to increase supply instead. *Campesinos* joined them in opposition to deep wells, especially when their own irrigation wells were threatened, and also favored a dam project.

WATER RATES AND THE POPULAR ECONOMY

SEMAPA's founding in 1967 marked the beginning of more than three decades of struggle between Cochabambinos and water service officials over water rates, loan repayment, water service governance, and hydraulic development. The IDB pushed Cochabamba and other cities to found autonomous water companies so that water services would be free to raise rates and to more effectively collect payment. In these years the international aid community began to promote "self-help" approaches in development projects where beneficiaries contributed labor and materials.[35] In keeping with this emphasis, the IDB argued, despite long-standing practice, that SEMAPA customers rather than the national or local government should pay for all water service–related costs, including operations, loan repayment and interest, and local contributions to project costs. City residents strongly opposed rate increases in defense of what they called "the popular economy" and as part a larger fight for social control over SEMAPA and regional hydraulic development.

The fight over water rates that began in the late 1960s was at its root a debate about the nature of social citizenship: whether urban water users would become customers and "investors" who paid for service, repair, improvements, and loan obligations but were otherwise passive recipients of water service, or whether they would directly participate in water company management and hydraulic development and collectively own and manage independent and municipal water sources and systems.[36] In the 1960s and early 1970s the post–World War II developmental-state model, where governments oversaw the economy and social welfare, remained hegemonic. But as historian Amy Offner has shown, midcentury capitalist economies mixed elements of the free market and state planning. Like the self-help housing schemes in Colombia that Offner studies, rate hikes and the contribution of labor and funds by residents to the public water service in Cochabamba epitomized what Offner calls "the essential hybridity of the developmental state."[37] Devolution of responsibility from the state to "local" actors can take different forms. At times such measures allow the state to offload responsibility to localities, at others they respond to demands for local control of resources.

In Cochabamba, self-help in the water sector was not only introduced from above or outside but was negotiated between neighborhoods and SEMAPA. Building neighborhood water systems was a strategy of expanding the municipal network in some cases and managing water autonomously in those neighborhoods that remained independent. The water service responded to water user demands by coordinating some neighborhoods' work building water infrastructure. But it also offloaded significant responsibility onto them by drawing on their labor, funds, and water sources to expand supply and distribution. Indeed, self-help strategies in Cochabamba were forms of vernacular engineering where peripheral residents built neighborhood water systems themselves.

To meet IDB requirements, SEMAPA's architects reimagined water users as customers and investors, thereby shifting financial responsibility away from the state and financiers onto the population. Customers had representation on the company's board: three customer delegates, one from the Industrial and Commercial Chambers of Commerce, another from the FEJUVE, and a third directly elected by customers, joined three municipal board members (including the mayor as president). But this arrangement was likely meant to tame popular mobilization around water access. SEMAPA emphasized customers' financial responsibility for company operations and loan repayment over their participation. The bylaws transformed municipal water users into "investors" who could gain service and become "co-owners" by buying a connection—equated with a share in the company—and paying for service.[38] As Mayor Baldi put it at the loan signing ceremony, water charges would allow "the people themselves to pay back the investment."[39]

Water service fees had until then been very low and often went unpaid without sanction. Charges were just US$1.25 per connection per year, paid together with annual property taxes and split among as many as ten families who might share a connection.[40] As part of its feasibility study, Boyle conducted a survey to "investigate the potential for the people who will benefit from planned improvements to the drinking water system to cover the cost of these improvements and maintaining them." Boyle's guide was World Bank sanitation engineer Harold Shipman who, in a 1963 water and sewage symposium in Medellín, argued that water and sewage companies should charge twice their operation costs to cover loan and interest payments and produce enough of a surplus for system improvements.[41] Based on Boyle's findings, the Bank recommended a new *monthly* rate of US$1.50, more than 3 percent of an average family's $46 monthly income. While Bank representatives concluded that the proposed rates "reflect[ed] users' capacity to pay," they foresaw opposition. Anticipating that a "direct jump" would be "too much to be accepted without conflict by the population," the IDB recommended a gradual

FIGURE 8. Cochabamba mayor Francisco Baldi inspecting a water
project, 1967. *Los Tiempos*, 26 October 1967, 5.

increase over four years and the scaling of rates according to families' resources.[42]
The municipality announced in April 1967 that it would begin to charge a monthly
fee for each of the city's twelve thousand domestic connections to prove to the IDB
that Cochabamba would be able to repay the loan still escaping its grasp.[43]

Urban residents vehemently opposed water rate increases out of a strong conviction that the state should provide low-cost water service to all urban residents
and began to advocate a participatory model of urban water governance through
their efforts to hold the state to that obligation. City water users wanted the loan
but did not accept its terms. Given the failure of the loan to materialize or service
to improve, residents were loath to accept rate hikes. A 1966 census found that
60 percent of urban residents were willing to accept a water meter if service was
constant and pressure was high, while 11 percent said they "were not willing to
pay even a cent for drinking water."[44] Water users criticized the mayor for keeping them in the dark about loan terms, when it would be disbursed, and what
"its impact on the household economy" would be, "given that what is at stake is

the de-municipalization of the water service, which means that water will not be free."[45] Residents voiced concern that the new company would have the power to "establish and charge rates for service provision...without limit" and eliminate "free consumption that many areas of the city have become accustomed to."[46] As a *Prensa Libre* editorial warned, "To hand [the water service] over to an...entity that can impose rates above the people's means has grave risks for the future."[47] Fights over rate hikes intensified under Hugo Banzer's dictatorship in the 1970s.

In 1969, President René Barrientos died in a mysterious helicopter crash on his way to a peasant rally in Cochabamba. General Alfredo Ovando Candia, the air force commander who had been Barrientos's co-conspirator in the 1964 coup, seized power. Divisions in the military quickly forced the vacillating and autocratic Ovando to yield to the reform-minded general Juan José Torres in October 1970. Torres established closer relations with the socialist bloc, rescinded U.S. Steel's contract to operate the Matilde Mine, ejected US labor organizations and the US Peace Corps, and convened the July 1971 Popular Assembly—a body elected by workers and popular groups—to replace the legislature. The assembly responded to and inspired demands for the restoration of a revolutionary agenda. These moves led the United States to suspend aid and heightened divisions within the military, leading general Hugo Banzer Suárez to launch a coup with US support in August 1971.[48]

Upon taking power, Banzer banned the COB, the FSTMB, and all parties to the left of the MNR.[49] He then introduced an investment law in September 1971 that, as historian James Dunkerley has explained, "freed capital movement to enable substantial repatriation of profits, removed tariffs not only on capital goods... but also on primary materials, abolished taxes on production and manufactured exports, and laid down exceptionally generous terms for the assessment of capital depreciation."[50] The United States rewarded Banzer's government by quickly restoring and increasing economic and military aid. According to historian Kenneth Lehman, "U.S. aid jumped 600 percent during Banzer's first year in power and Bolivia received more military assistance than any other country in Latin America."[51] Nevertheless, the IDB continued to drag its feet on its loan disbursement to SEMAPA.

The IDB's paralysis even as SEMAPA raised rates angered civic, labor, and neighborhood organizations, who began to vie for control over SEMAPA. In the early 1970s, when IDB officials blamed SEMAPA's lack of legal autonomy for failure to disburse the loan, JUNCO president José de la Reza declared that JUNCO had "the support of all of the people's organizations of Cochabamba" to take over the effort to establish SEMAPA's independence and secure the IDB loan.[52] They demanded access to SEMAPA files to determine why the company had been unable to solve the drinking water problem and why the IDB had not disbursed the loan. When they discovered that SEMAPA still lacked legal status, JUNCO leaders demanded state officials take immediate action to meet IDB conditions and threatened to "mobilize the affected population" if they failed to do so.[53] In response, the mayor and SEMAPA's general manager met regularly with leaders of JUNCO, the Comité Pro-Cochabamba, the Comité Pro-Cochabamba Feminino (Women's Pro-Cochabamba Committee), and the FEJUVE to explain their efforts to address water scarcity, set priorities, and coordinate plans to improve water provision.

Once SEMAPA secured legal status, JUNCO and FEJUVE leaders leveraged the company's autonomy to protest national government intervention into its affairs. When the Urbanism and Housing Ministry appointed SEMAPA's new manager and reorganized the company in 1973, JUNCO, the Industrial and Commercial Chambers of Commerce, and the local press protested that SEMAPA's autonomy meant that Cochabambinos, not the central government, should oversee the company. A *Prensa Libre* editorial criticized the decision's "centralism," adding, "let's not talk about autonomy if there are going to be these kinds of abuses." JUNCO leaders condemned the national government's "obnoxious abuse of power," asked the government to consult the community on such matters in the future, and wrote a long letter to President Banzer on the subject.[54] Remarkably, the central government ceded to the demand for local control, suspending the appointment.[55]

With the 15 January 1974 deadline for using the loan money approaching, just $1 million of the promised $3.8 million disbursed, little progress on loan-funded projects, and even the IDB concluding that water service and waterborne disease were worse than before the loan agreement had been signed, civic leaders, SEMAPA's general manager, and the Banzer administration worked to renegotiate the IDB loan.[56] According to JUNCO leaders, in the five years since the agreement was signed, the real value of the $5.5 million loan (including the local contribution) had depreciated by $1.5 million. If its term was not extended, Cochabamba risked losing 60 percent of the loan. SEMAPA's dynamic new general manager, Severo Vega, applied for a new $7 million loan in March 1974 to replace the expired one but knew that if customers did not start paying their bills, the Bank would not grant the loan, or even if it did, would not disburse it.[57] The IDB gave Vega just fifteen days to implement a new rate structure.[58] The health of the Bolivian economy and Banzer's assurances that the national government would fund the local contribution convinced the Bank to grant the loan.[59]

Banzer oversaw an economic boom based on increased world oil and tin prices as well as Bolivia's first significant natural gas and agricultural exports. Growth between 1973 and 1975 averaged 6.8 percent, tin and oil export earnings increased, and exports diversified to include lowland agribusiness products like cotton and sugar. But these gains for some entailed costs for others. International Monetary Fund (IMF) devaluation requirements increased the cost of living by 39 percent without corresponding wage increases. Removals and reductions of state subsidies on goods and services hurt broad swaths of the population, occasioning protests from workers and peasants.[60]

Although historian Herbert Klein has noted that the Banzer regime "granted more land and benefited more peasant families than any previous regime, military or civilian," Banzer rejected peasant demands for credit, price supports, and other government assistance and imposed price caps on produce.[61] When twenty thousand peasants gathered in the Valle Alto village of Tolata in protest, Banzer ordered in troops who killed or "disappeared" upwards of two hundred peasants.[62] The January 1974 "Massacre of the Valley," as it became known, marked the end of the Military-Peasant Pact, the military's alliance with the country's peasant unions that commenced in 1964, pushing peasants into opposition to Banzer's government. The strength of the economy, impatience with popular pressure, and the emergence of dictatorships in neighboring countries prompted Banzer's November 1974 self-coup. He closed the legislature, imposed direct government control on labor organizations, and adopted a more violent approach in the mold of other new Southern Cone dictatorships.

Within days the IDB agreed to grant a $10 million loan on better terms than the earlier loan on the strict condition that SEMAPA establish and implement a new water rate structure.[63] Whereas the 1967 project overview had addressed the question in just a few paragraphs, the new 1974 project description devoted multiple pages to the issue. The loan contract, signed in March 1975, stipulated that SEMAPA had six months to "put into place a tariff regime acceptable to the Bank," nine months to show that it had "organized effective billing mechanisms," two years to "present a plan for promotion and education about the project among the beneficiary population," and three years to begin to "collect at least 80 percent of its bills" annually.[64] SEMAPA officials dutifully established a new rate structure that significantly raised costs to water users, making them responsible for paying all of the costs associated with the provision and improvement of service, including operation and maintenance, loan payments and interest, and water system improvement and expansion. If all went according to plan, by 1980 residents would be paying nearly 8 percent of their monthly income in water charges.[65]

The question was how to get the population to pay. The Pan American Health Organization (PAHO) determined that the population was unwilling to pay increased rates because SEMAPA had not "educated" them or "convinced them to collaborate." The organization recommended a "face-to-face" campaign to win the population over to rates increases.[66] To this end, the new IDB loan earmarked funds for an educational campaign to facilitate acceptance of rate increases.[67] It was up to Vega to make this happen. To convince customers to pay, he stressed that the new rate structure was based on a scientific study and established by supreme decree, arguing that taxes would never be enough to sustain SEMAPA. He warned that failure to pay would put the IDB loan at risk. These technocratic, economistic, and legalistic arguments were meant to establish not only the legitimacy of the new rates but also that there was no alternative.[68]

Vega drew on a liberal model of citizenship in which the citizen contributes to and participates in public life through regular payment for public services such as water. Like Mayor Baldi a few years earlier, Vega emphasized that paying service fees gave the population an opportunity to "support a complete drinking water solution" and claimed that payment from those with service would allow SEMAPA to extend the distribution network to the poorest areas of the city lacking service and exploited by aguateros. As Vega put it, "with the satisfactory service that SEMAPA will gradually provide," residents of the Zona Sud "will spend less and will have more and better-quality water that does not spread infectious diseases."[69] Paying higher rates would enlist SEMAPA customers in service of the collective good. Yet there was a clear tension between establishing personal responsibility on the one hand and a sense of collective interest on the other.[70] Vega's liberal model of citizenship had a redistributionist twist but asked consumers to replace the state as the company's "investors."

The population did not take well to the new rates. Neither the municipality nor the prefecture before it had succeeded in charging in any meaningful way for water. Now that the new IDB-sponsored water company seemed serious about making customers pay, they rebelled. Residents were incensed that SEMAPA and the IDB expected them to pay for water projects that the Bank had committed to funding, and to make payments on a loan that had not even been disbursed. In 1975 a reporter called the water company "the entity most resisted by public opinion."[71] A citizenship model that prescribed monthly cash payment for water service was foreign to Cochabamba. The population could accept charges for services like electricity and road paving, if begrudgingly, as it considered them modern luxuries. Water, however, as was repeated again and again, was a basic necessity vital for life. While Vega contended that paying higher rates was the only way to break a vicious cycle in which the company was unable to provide service due to lack of funds and residents were unwilling to pay because they did not receive sufficient water, residents argued that they should not be required to pay until service improved.

Residents suspected that SEMAPA and the IDB wanted them to pay charges beyond the cost of service and loan payments. The Comité Pro-Cochabamba calculated that the new rates would generate proceeds that far exceeded obligations to the IDB, leading some to accuse SEMAPA of adopting a "profit-seeking approach" ("espiritu commercial"). As a *Prensa Libre* editorial sarcastically remarked, SEMAPA "is now a respectable bureaucratic institution of more than a hundred employees whose most important role is not supply and service improvement but perfection of coercive methods to impose rates."[72] While the international financial and aid apparatus promoted "self-help" in this period of professed state-led development and international aid, Cochabambinos believed that the state and international lenders should fund service improvements, not the cash- and water-starved population.[73]

Civic and neighborhood organizations argued that once SEMAPA improved service, it should charge customers according to their ability to pay. JUNCO's sixty member organizations declared that they would only pay if "rates were minimal" and once "supply reached all areas, not only those with expensive homes with pools and plumbing, but also areas discriminated against where humble residents barely have one or two faucets." They demanded a sliding rate scale, emphasizing that the "popular economy" was already stressed.[74] Labor unions protested that meager incomes left families without enough food, especially since they already paid other utility bills. FEJUVE leaders agreed, sustaining that "due to current wage and salary freezes, the salaried sector, which makes up the majority of property owners, cannot pay the new higher rates." Letters to the editor from residents across the city testified to their inability and unwillingness to pay for water service renovation. As one letter put it, "without jobs that generate even minimal incomes...Cochabamba cannot support the new burden of sustaining a service that until now has not received a single dollar of foreign investment." Authorities, residents charged, had no right to ask the people to pay for water given their failure to create jobs, not to mention their dealings with "mercantilist" institutions like the IDB.[75] Residents also opposed basing rates on home values that did not correspond to residents' means or consumption. In spite of its earlier opposition, the FEJUVE called for installing water meters, indirectly rejecting Vega's call for more privileged hydraulic citizens to fund the work necessary to extend coverage.[76] Given their experience and knowledge of water politics in the city, SEMAPA customers had no reason to believe that their payments would be used to extend distribution to all.

SEMAPA customers' opposition to rate increases also owed to authorities' failure to consult them. When the mayor and SEMAPA officials invited the public to a meeting about the reasons for raising rates, the Pro-Cochabamba Committee responded that the population should have been consulted before new rates were imposed, not once people were already paying them due to fear of losing service. Adding insult to injury, the two hundred people who showed up for the gathering were made to wait an hour before being directed to a new location where the meeting had already concluded. Outraged, residents charged officials with the deliberate "humiliation of the people," reiterating that peripheral neighborhoods were not opposed to charges but to the "elevated sums being charged." JUNCO leaders called on SEMAPA's general manager to negotiate with them over the rate structure and vowed that their members would not pay their bills until an agreement was reached. Indeed, according its own reports, SEMAPA was unable to persuade more than 40 percent of the population to pay the new charges. Usually no more than 30 percent of customers were paying their bills at one time.[77] By 1975 the IDB had not disbursed any of funds pledged in January 1968, even as Bank officials were overseeing hydraulic development and the loan was allegedly accruing interest.

Residents often made decisions not to pay collectively. The neighborhood committee of Avenida Simon López, for instance, wrote to *Prensa Libre* calling SEMAPA's charges "totally unacceptable" given that they had been established "without consultation." After doing their own calculations of workers' salaries, taxes, and other service payments, the residents decided not to pay their water bills, which they called "an attack against the popular economy." They protested that "heads of household who were mostly white- and blue-collar workers could barely pay for the day's meal, let alone other impositions," and announced that they would call on civic organizations to "come out in defense of the people's economy."[78] Rather than accept officials' admonition that the way to participate was to pay, in this remarkable collective payment strike, municipal customers pressured authorities by refusing to pay instead.

Residents of neighborhoods that had built their own systems considered the new tariff structure to be outright theft. Neighborhood committee representatives of Barrio Petrolero in the Zona Sud, for instance, complained that SEMAPA had not helped "in the slightest" with the installation of their neighborhood's distribution network. Residents had purchased 5,000 meters of pipes, enlisted Yacimientos Petrolíferos Fiscales Bolivianos (YPFB) workers to lay them, and even so paid SEMAPA Bs. 300 per home for connection rights. Nevertheless, the neighborhood seldom received water. As the neighborhood association's president explained, "Despite SEMAPA's promises to provide drinking water ... the few times that water has flowed here have been true miracles." The committee's president pronounced SEMAPA's charges illegal, a sentiment shared by residents of new neighborhoods across the periphery. As a *Prensa Libre* editorial put it, "Extensive areas of new neighborhoods where residents organized cooperatives to provide water service are experiencing yet another injustice in being charged a duty on their own systems that they installed themselves."[79]

The FEJUVE, whose members included homeowners on the city's periphery "who had been obliged to install public services at their own cost," warned that "this economic sacrifice better be compensated by way of a significant rate reduction." FEJUVE leaders called for the installation of water meters and in the meantime a fixed rate for "homeowners on the margins who had installed water service with their own resources."[80] Installation of water meters thus became a popular demand from the city's periphery aimed at addressing unequal water access and SEMAPA's failure to keep its promise to provide service in exchange for incorporation of independent neighborhood water sources and distribution systems.

As the clamor got louder, SEMAPA tried to get tough. The water company made threats to cut service; issued deadlines for payment, regularizing connections, and signing contracts; and declared that water payments should be made to SEMAPA (rather than to the municipality as before). But since the company lacked the technical capacity to shut off water to individual homes, not to mention abolish independent water systems, there were no real consequences to nonpayment. The only credible threat SEMAPA could make was that families who did not pay their bills would not be connected to the promised future distribution network until they paid. Lacking means to cut off rate dodgers, SEMAPA and municipal authorities pleaded with residents to pay their bills and petitioned the Bank for more time. Officials promised residents that once the new network was complete, they would install water meters, take income into account in determining rates, and consider the proposal to charge the periphery less, but to little avail. By early 1976, SEMAPA was collecting only 33 percent of what the IDB wanted residents to pay, putting the loan in jeopardy. Officials especially condemned residents of the Zona Norte for their unwillingness to pay despite enjoying the best water access in the city and denounced popular groups like factory workers for nonpayment as well. Even the urbanization and housing minister scolded Cochabamba's citizenry for shirking its responsibility. The message was clear—the way to participate was to pay.[81]

SEMAPA failed to convince most residents to pay their bills. In late 1976, JUNCO and the CPC reiterated instructions to their members not to pay.[82] By May 1977 only 30 percent of SEMAPA customers were paying.[83] Out of desperation, SEMAPA asked the mayor's office to charge water debtors when they paid their property taxes. The mayor agreed, in effect reverting to the old payment system, but this was hardly a solution.[84] The only option left to SEMAPA was to attempt a technical fix by installing a new distribution network that would give them the power to cut off service and undercut the main excuse for nonpayment: deficient service. Well drilling was set to begin with IDB funds in August 1977, but a series of obstacles arose.[85] By demanding the right for their representatives to participate in determining rate structures and other water management issues and by refusing to pay their bills, Cochabambinos won a stalemate on rates increases and a seat at the table when major decisions about water management were made.

CARAVAN TO MISICUNI

Cochabambinos inserted themselves into debates about hydraulic development through intense protest and mobilization around where to obtain new water sources for the city in these years, strongly opposing the IDB's requirement that new water sources come from valley aquifers and promoting a dam project in the mountains instead. The 1968 loan agreement required that funds be used to drill new deep wells in the Cochabamba Valley and explicitly rejected proposals to draw on mountain water. Bank officials reasoned that aquifer water was purer than surface water and so did not require treatment. They also figured that wells would be cheaper and therefore facilitate a more modest loan more likely to be repaid.[86] Although it was true that cordillera projects would have required higher initial investment than wells that could be dug on an as-needed basis, and that well water required less intensive treatment, the Bank further concluded against all evidence that Cochabamba's "surface water sources [had] been developed to their maximum capacity." Documents that were confidential at the time reveal that, in addition to cost and quality concerns, Bank officials also backed deep wells as a way to "protect" water from "theft" by peasant cultivators and avoid negotiations with peasants who held rights to mountain lakes.[87]

Cochabamba's civic, neighborhood, and labor organizations strongly opposed well drilling and demanded that the IDB fund dam projects in the mountains instead. Private well owners, among the city's wealthiest residents, feared that deep wells would interfere with their own by lowering the water table.[88] They argued that they had "consolidated preferential use rights" to underground water sources that "no one should interfere with or diminish."[89] Comité Pro-Cochabamba president René Cuadros supported well owners, sustaining that "the fear is just; the wells could dry up...hurting their owners' and the collective interest." So did Antonio Valdivieso, owner of the valley's oldest well-drilling company.[90] Wells opponents argued that wells would deplete valley aquifers, employ foreign technology and personnel, and generate profits abroad. Mountain lakes and rivers, in contrast, enjoyed "permanent" flows thanks to seasonal rains, and damming them would utilize and benefit Bolivia's own experts and laborers.[91] As one editorial put it, "the benefits of surface water from the mountains are undeniable; it is there to be seen and available to whoever wants to bring it."[92] Urban well owners' claims to prior use rights of underground water sources and concerns about SEMAPA tapping them echoed in the countryside, where small-scale farmers in the western reaches of the valley would clash with SEMAPA over underground water sources a decade later.

Starting in the late 1960s, proponents of sourcing mountain water united behind the Proyecto Múltiple Misicuni as a democratic alternative to the IDB-Banzer plan to drill deep wells for the city's exclusive use. When Luis Calvo Soux first began to promote the project in the late 1950s, urban reformers and peasants were still confident that distribution of hoarded hacienda water sources would resolve water scarcity and inequality. While the MNR had shelved the project, the essential features of the project that Calvo Soux had proposed—the rivers in question, the Misicuni valley reservoir, the tunnel through the mountains, and the multiuse dimension—endured (Map 10). Large numbers of Cochabambinos began to take an interest in the project after the MNR fell and it became clear that agrarian reform would not redistribute hacienda water sources to all.

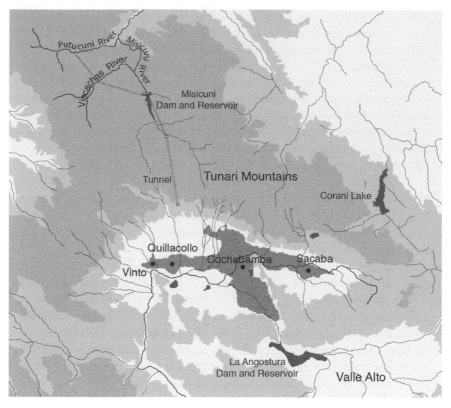

MAP 10. The Misicuni project. Map created by Jorge Camacho Saavedra.

From the late 1960s to the mid-1970s the coalition demanding realization of the Misicuni project grew from a nucleus of urban engineers and civic leaders into a broad cross-class alliance of city elites and professionals, urban popular groups, and rural smallholders. Among these supporters was the Comité Pro-Cochabamba, whose leadership was anxious to avoid conflict with Lagunmayu and Saytukocha rights holders protesting the city's use of their water and to develop a source exclusively for the city's use. In 1967, CPC leaders called for new studies and asked Luis Calvo Soux to help them look into the project themselves.[93] The newspaper *Los Tiempos*, owned by the wealthy landowning Canelas family, described Misicuni's waters as some of the purest and most abundant in the world and held the project up as "the hope of Cochabamba."[94] Peasant unions first endorsed the Misicuni project in the early 1960s, when one leader praised the Misicuni River as a "flow of great magnitude, fed by immense tributaries."[95] From the late 1960s on, Central Valley peasant unions forcefully opposed plans to drill deep wells for the city and demanded engineering studies of the Misicuni project, offering to contribute funds and labor.[96]

In 1973 peasant union leaders visited Misicuni and expressed "alarm" at the "hurdles" that authorities put in the project's way.[97] The project was appealing to smallholders because it promised to provide irrigation water for eleven thousand peasant households and drinking water to the city without threatening their existing water sources.[98] By the early 1970s several local mayors and state governors had inspected the project site and asked for national government support. Left-leaning military president Juan José Torres (1970–1971) responded favorably by appointing Calvo Soux to head the Cochabamba's new regional development corporation CORDECO, founded in 1970. Calvo Soux declared Misicuni his top priority, commissioned a preliminary study, and contracted the French firm Sté Fréjusienne d'Électricité (SOFRELEC) to carry out prefeasibility studies. He had little time to maneuver, however, before losing his position following Hugo Banzer's August 1971 coup.[99]

Banzer's support for the Misicuni project and Cochabamba's development more generally was tepid. The economic boom allowed his government to invest in large-scale national infrastructural development, from rural electrification to urban water and sanitation. Cochabamba's development ranked low among his priorities, however. His administration's "1971–1991 National Development Strategy" cast La Paz as the country's "dominant pole," Santa Cruz and Oruro as "poles of development," Chuquisaca and Tarija as "agro-industrial poles," and Cochabamba as the "pole of services." Cochabamba was situated between two more economically dynamic regions: the mining regions in La Paz, Oruro, and Potosí to the west and the petroleum, natural gas, and agro-export–producing departments of Santa Cruz and Tarija to the east. Banzer resolved that Cochabamba should link these two regions, serve as a way station between them, and service them by providing cheap labor, hydroelectricity, and foodstuffs, and by refining petroleum.[100]

This might mean that Banzer would support the Misicuni project, but there was no guarantee. At first, the Banzer administration seemed committed to the Misicuni project. When SOFRELEC completed its prefeasibility study in 1975, Banzer emphasized the project's potential to stimulate agricultural and industrial production, in line with his economic goals. Nevertheless, the Banzer administration ultimately prioritized export-oriented agriculture in the eastern lowlands over development in Cochabamba, ignoring water shortages and postponing the Misicuni project in favor of the Rositas hydroelectric project in Santa Cruz instead.[101]

With the national government once again sidelining their region, urban elites and popular groups rallied behind the Misicuni project with greater intensity and in the process built a broad new civic movement. CORDECO's new general manager and JUNCO leaders argued that the Misicuni project would increase agricultural production and industrial activity while defusing social tension in the countryside. The factory workers' union called Misicuni the "starting point for Cochabamba's development," and both JUNCO and the Cochabamba Women's Union sent representatives to La Paz to lobby the president.[102] JUNCO's Misicuni campaign culminated in a massive open assembly where member organizations demanded that the government immediately commence feasibility studies and allow JUNCO to execute the project alongside CORDECO.[103] For these Cocha- bambinos the Misicuni project offered an opportunity to improve their livelihoods on their own terms. While Banzer promised to review the prefeasibility studies, commit some funds to the project, and seek additional funds for a feasibility study from the Andean Development Corporation, local groups doubted the seriousness of his commitment, especially since his national development plan for 1976–1980 excluded the project.[104]

In a dramatic show of force, the city's now broad and democratic civic move- ment organized a caravan to Misicuni in September 1975 to promote "awareness of the Misicuni project's importance."[105] Local authorities joined in: Cochabamba mayor Humberto Coronel Rivas announced plans to visit Misicuni "to promote the interests of Cochabambinos to national authorities," SEMAPA officials pledged to lead a tour of the "hydraulic possibilities of the Misicuni watershed" once the caravan arrived at the site, and other state agencies, civic groups and clubs, and the chambers of commerce sent representatives.[106] Caravan organizers expected only one hundred participants, but at dawn on the departure date more than one thousand men, women, and children converged on Cochabamba's central plaza. Caravanners wound their way up a steep mountainside road and on to Misi- cuni, where they listened to a priest perform mass and to local authorities make speeches. JUNCO's president was pleased with the "massive turnout" that he said demonstrated "the people's consciousness of the Misicuni project's potential to achieve their long-desired development."[107] For this coalition, development meant not only fomenting agricultural and industrial production but also meeting basic human needs.

President Banzer did not attend, but within a month his government secured a $2 million loan for feasibility studies from the Andean Development Corporation. *Los Tiempos* reported that the loan was a direct result of the JUNCO-organized caravan, which the newspaper called "a resounding success due to the 'multitu- dinous' participation of Cochabamba's people."[108] Euphoric, JUNCO's president declared that "all Cochabambinos should unite around this popular aspiration, supporting…this project that will free us from underdevelopment and neglect."[109] A year later, the national government founded the Asociación Misicuni (reorga- nized as the Empresa Misicuni in the 1990s) to oversee feasibility studies, which a Canadian firm conducted from 1977 to 1979.[110]

The 1975 caravan to Misicuni was one of the high points of popular mobilization around water access in this period. Like the 1962 worker brigade to Chapisirca, city residents took to the mountains to demand that the municipal water service and municipal and national governments increase water supply to the city, and to insist that increased supply come from mountain lakes whose water they considered to be more abundant, renewable, and reliable sources than aquifer water that the IDB insisted on. Just as important as the content of their proposal was the fact that they felt that they had the right to make it and were confident to pressure the Banzer government in this way. While it is unclear whether peasants were among the caravanners, they soon mounted intense opposition to drilling deep wells in their communities for exclusive urban use and championed the Misicuni project as an alternative in a 1977 conflict known as the region's first "guerra de los pozos."

THE 1977 "WAR OF THE WELLS"

Peasant opposition to deep-well drilling and commitment to the Misicuni project culminated in the 1977 "guerra de los pozos," the first of many conflicts between peasant unions and the national government, international development banks, and local and foreign contractors over plans to drill deep wells in peasant communities from the late 1970s through the early 2000s. Conflict arose in 1976 after President Banzer launched an emergency water project to supply the city of Cochabamba during a drought. The nationally appointed emergency committee studied a number of proposals to tap mountain sources, the Misicuni project among them, but ruled out water capture in the mountains for its high cost and lengthy construction period. Instead, the committee recommended drilling ten deep wells in Vinto, an agricultural community 20 kilometers west of the city center populated by peasants of *colono* and *piquero* parentage and migrants from other parts of the country. Although Banzer emphasized that this was only a partial solution not meant to replace the Misicuni project, Vinto peasants saw the deep wells as a threat to their own groundwater sources and to the Misicuni project.[111]

The agrarian reform's redistribution of hacienda water sources to former estate workers had left the city in a difficult position. Now rather than purchasing water from wealthy landowners with water sources to spare, the city had to contend with peasants who owned lakes and springs that once belonged to *hacendados*. When it became clear that existing sources would not be enough to supply the city during the 1977 drought, the city bought more water from the owners of Lagunmayu and Saytukocha and struck a deal with the owners of Lake Wara Wara, whose dam had collapsed a few years earlier, to build them a new dam in exchange for a portion of their water.[112] But conflicts with peasants over these sources continued and their depleted reserves were insufficient to meet demand.[113] By drilling deep wells into aquifers whose water they assumed was state property, the national government and SEMAPA, like the IDB a decade earlier, hoped to circumvent peasant water owners. But Vinto peasants considered these aquifer sources to be theirs and mobilized in unprecedented ways to keep control over them. While both rural and urban popular groups were calling for the Misicuni project, an indication of the potential to overcome divisions, the decision by authorities to pursue deep wells in Vinto deepened the urban-rural rift.

Banzer's decision to provide emergency aid to the city responded to pressure from city residents. At the drought's onset, Cochabamba newspapers published alarming accounts of residents' plight. *Prensa Libre* reported San Miguel neighborhood residents' accounts of drinking contaminated water from Laguna Alalay, "filtering it through handkerchiefs," since private water truck operators preferred to sell their limited supply in larger quantities. The article relayed the account of a woman who approached an *aguatero* with a bucket only to be told, "There is no water; we only bring it for the *chicherías* because we have a contract with them." Others claimed that *aguateros* told them, "Go ahead and die. It's not our fault."[114] The Comité Pro-Cochabamba censured SEMAPA for its "indifference and its complete lack of human sensibility in the face of Cochabamba's grave drinking water scarcity problem," calling its authorities "incapable and incompetent."[115]

Even the mayor called for reorganization of SEMAPA's technical staff. As it turned out, SEMAPA only employed a few specialized engineers and did not count a single planner or economist among its staff. When SEMAPA personnel protested that "their work [was] not recognized by the people and their sacrifice [was] misunderstood," *Prensa Libre* rejoined, "All of the citizenry asks itself, *what* completed tasks and *what* sacrifice? The ineptitude of these functionaries is quite clear as the problem has existed for fifty years without a solution of any kind while we wait for divine intervention to allow us to use water accumulating in the cordillera." The CPC accused SEMAPA officials of lying about the seriousness of scarcity and JUNCO demanded "a thoughtfully considered and researched emergency plan with national government assistance." CPC leaders called on the prefect to convoke the emergency committee that Banzer had by then appointed and to declare the Cochabamba Valley an "emergency zone" until a solution to the drought was found.[116] In response, the mayor prohibited water truck sales to *chicherías* and car washes and ordered *aguateros*, whose supply came from municipal wells, to distribute water to all areas of the city, placing police officers in water trucks to enforce the new regulations. Banzer responded to pressure as well.[117] After founding the emergency committee in January 1977, the president pledged Bs. 12 million to fund an emergency plan and promised to personally supervise its execution.[118]

The emergency committee rejected all proposals to use mountain sources, ostensibly due to concerns about high costs, unpredictable water supply, and lengthy projected completion times. Composed of representatives from the mayor's office, the prefecture, SEMAPA, CORDECO, the national electricity company ENDE, the state oil company YPFB, and the Bolivian Geological Service (Servicio Geológico de Bolivia, GEOBOL)—all run by military officers—the committee instead recommended drilling a battery of ten wells in Vinto, the same project that had been rejected in favor of drilling wells in the city a decade earlier.[119] Banzer accepted their recommendation and charged YPFB with well drilling and aqueduct construction, GEOBOL with carrying out geological studies and drilling additional wells in El Paso, and the Seventh Army Division with assisting them.[120] The Seventh Army Division's Barrientos Regiment immediately went to work on the Chusequeri project, digging through 1,500 meters of hard rock in just twelve days to complete a canal. YPFB's general manager Delfín Pozo promised to finish the Vinto project by October, and SEMAPA's general manager Edgar Claure Paz announced that the population would have enough water for at least the next year.[121] The contrast with the IDB loan procurement process, not to mention the Misicuni project, could not have been starker. The government's "extensive considerations" of the Vinto project had taken less than a month.

While political and technical conditions may have been favorable, social conditions were more challenging. The emergency committee's report had warned that the new deep wells for the city could interfere with existing shallow irrigation wells used by area peasants and provoke their opposition and recommended compensating them with new wells. The engineers made clear that "the visible disadvantage of this project [was] that it could affect the production of some of the region's [existing] wells" and that "necessary measures need[ed] to be taken to address this delicate issue." Explaining the aquifer's structure, the report described its "thick sedimentary strata" as "permeable...layers covered by fine sediment."[122] The report's authors took for granted that the aquifer's layers were interconnected and therefore considered it very likely that the new deep wells would lower the water table, leaving existing shallow irrigation wells dry. Yet when rumors began to spread in Vinto that the new deep wells would interfere with old community wells, these same state engineers assured peasants there that new wells would tap deep layers of the aquifer that were sealed off from the upper layers that fed existing irrigation wells. And it seems that they kept secret the location of the drilling sites to defuse protest.[123]

Despite these assurances, by August Vinto peasants reported that their wells' production had decreased by 75 percent.[124] When SEMAPA, YPFB, and Seventh Division authorities ignored their complaints, Vinto residents formed the Pro-Vinto Committee and attempted to stop the project.[125] In open mass meetings and petitions, Vinto peasants called on state authorities to guarantee consistent water supply, drill additional wells for community use, connect them to the new water main, and immediately begin work on the Misicuni project.[126] While agrarian reform had granted some hacienda land to former tin miners who sometimes developed land and sold water, most of those protesting SEMAPA's wells proposal seem to have been ex-*colono* and *piquero* smallholders.

Faced with the threat of the project's paralysis, local authorities attempted to pit urban residents against the mobilized Vinto peasants and leveraged their own status and expertise to try to discredit and demobilize the peasantry. SEMAPA's Claure warned that halting the project would cause "serious harm" to the city's 250,000 residents and asked the national government to "adopt *medidas de caso*"—a euphemism for violent repression—as did Cochabamba mayor Humberto Coronel Rivas, who urged the national government to intervene to "save the people of Cochabamba."[127] Indeed, urban and rural water users were at odds on this question.[128] Banzer's favor of the city over the countryside in this instance was further evidence of the Military-Peasant Pact's demise.

In their dealings with Vinteños, state engineers represented themselves as experts and therefore the only legitimate bearers of correct technical information. Peasants were, at best, receivers of information provided to them by engineers and, at worst, ignorant and incapable of understanding the nature of the aquifer. When peasants initially complained to the Seventh Division's commander, he told them that their position lacked a "solid basis" and scolded them not to "emit opinions without understanding the causes [of the problem]."[129] In Claure's effort to convince national authorities to intervene, he reported that he had "technically explained and demonstrated to Vinto's inhabitants that drilling a battery of wells will not diminish their sources' flow," claiming that their wells were less productive due to the drought.[130] Given that the emergency committee, which included four YPFB engineers, had predicted that the new wells would very likely interfere with existing ones, it is doubtful that SEMAPA and YPFB engineers believed their own claims that the new wells' use of the aquifer's deeper layers would leave irrigation wells' sources untouched.

Vinteños had moral and technical arguments of their own. They took issue with the assumption that the city's water needs were more important than theirs, asserting "the fundamental rights of any people and pueblo to preserve life, health, and security" and declaring that "water is the property of the community" ("el agua es patrimonio del lugar").[131] On the primary technical question, they maintained that the aquifer's layers were interconnected so that pumping water from deeper layers would deplete upper layers' water as well. Their conclusions drew on long-term experience as well as recent observations. In a letter to SEMAPA, the Pro-Vinto Committee reported that "after the [new] wells were drilled, it became clear that there is filtration and communication among the layers, such that the population's wells are completely dry." Committee representatives pointed out that state authorities, despite their supposedly technical arguments, had not conducted a single technical study of groundwater resources.[132] The allegedly unsophisticated peasants came to the same conclusions as the emergency committee's engineers and every other study of the Central Valley's underground water resources before and since.[133]

The 1977 Vinto wells conflict recast the relationship between SEMAPA and the Valle Bajo peasantry. Vinto peasants did not stop the drilling, but they won significant concessions from the state. In a still binding agreement, SEMAPA officials agreed to guarantee "the normal and complete supply of drinking water to the population of Vinto" through a water main connection and to resolve any "inconvenience or difficulty" that the new wells might occasion.[134] Through this conflict, peasants strengthened their unions, their rights to underground water sources, and their resolve to confront SEMAPA's efforts to appropriate these sources. They also made clear their unequivocal support for the Misicuni project. Vinteños' success in pressuring SEMAPA helped consolidate a more powerful sense of ownership over wells and underground water sources that fortified peasant claims to water ownership across the region. This "wells for wells" accord became a model for future negotiations over well drilling in agricultural communities west of the city (see chapter 5). This move bolstered the demands of the Confederación Sindical Única de Trabajadores Campesinos de Bolivia (CSUTCB) that state institutions provide services, including water access and management, in rural areas across the country.[135]

By November 1977, as promised, the emergency plan projects were complete. In less than a year, national government institutions, primarily YPFB and the army, drilled wells in Vinto, El Paso, and Coña Coña, dug an aqueduct to connect the wells to the city, built a new water storage tank, and completed the Chusequeri project that had been under way but incomplete for decades, more than doubling the city's water flow from 350 liters per second to 810 liters per second.[136] Incredibly, the military government succeeded in doing more in one year than SEMAPA and the IDB had been able to accomplish in more than a decade. The project's inauguration was timed to coincide with a popular rally in support of Banzer's reelection, but a month later four women and fourteen children from the Siglo XX-Catavi mining center initiated a hunger strike that along with pressure from peasant groups led to Banzer's resignation.[137]

FROM DICTATORSHIP TO DEMOCRACY

The hunger strike set off a series of events that forced Banzer from power in July 1978, making his regime the first to fall in this era of Southern Cone dictatorships. By then, the gap between rich and poor had widened, oil exports and growth levels had fallen, and cotton and sugar exports had declined.[138] Opening the economy did not attract the level of foreign direct investment Banzer had hoped for, forcing his government to finance growth through foreign loans. Debt increased from $781 million in 1971 to an incredible $3.1 billion by the end of 1978, a scale, as James Dunkerley has noted, "appreciable even by the unenviable standards of the region."[139] Unrest among students, miners, and peasants was met with increasingly severe repression.[140] While protests had pushed Banzer to call elections, a new military junta took charge instead. A series of military and civilian governments held power between 1978 and 1980 before a coup by army general Luis García Meza Tejada. García Meza's short-lived "government of national reconstruction" from July 1980 to August 1981 was in reality a regime of state (military and paramilitary) terror linked to cocaine trafficking, making it the most brutal of Bolivia's military regimes in this era.

Bolivia's political crisis stemmed from and exacerbated its economic crisis. In the 1970s debtor countries faced rising interest rates, loan recalls, and commercial banks unwilling to extend new credit. By the early 1980s many Latin American countries could not repay their loans and found little sympathy in Washington, DC, in London, or on Wall Street. The IMF managed the debt crisis by offering new loans in exchange for financial restructuring. IMF requirements that debtor countries privatize state industries and decrease government spending by laying off public workers and cutting public sector wages made debtor countries responsible for solving the debt crisis without assistance from lenders. They were only able to repay existing loans with interest by taking on new ones, such that total debt mounted. As international relations scholar Ngaire Woods has written, "the result was good for the banks but disastrous for the debtors."[141]

Bolivia's reliance on export earnings and foreign loans made its economy vulnerable to global recession and debt crisis. As the global economy went into recession, legal export earnings declined sharply.[142] The García Meza regime's preparations for negotiations with the IMF included a January 1981 economic package that froze wages and cut price subsidies and public spending. These measures unleashed protests that the regime brutally repressed, including through torture and murder of activist leaders.[143] After García Meza ceded power to yet another junta in July 1981, the IMF granted Bolivia a $220 million loan.[144] In a demonstration organized by the COB in La Paz in October 1982, one hundred thousand protestors demanded a return to civilian rule. Congress installed Hernán Siles Zuazo and Jaime Paz Zamora, who had been elected on the ticket of a left electoral coalition called the Unidad Democrática y Popular (UDP) ticket in 1980, as president and vice president. This ended nearly two decades of military rule and made Bolivia one of the first Latin American countries to reestablish democracy.[145] Siles issued six separate economic packages in an effort to address the debt crisis, spiraling inflation, and economic collapse.[146]

In the chaotic years between the fall of the Banzer dictatorship in 1978 and reestablishment of stable democratic governance in 1985, Cochabambino water users built on earlier mobilization to strengthen their control over hydraulic engineering and governance. Urban civic organizations mobilized once the 1978 emergency projects were complete to pressure SEMAPA to use the IDB loan to improve the distribution system and extend it to new neighborhoods on the periphery.

But SEMAPA officials opted to pump the new wells' water to the city's already well-watered north instead of heeding Zona Sud leaders' calls to pump it directly to their neighborhoods. In response, the FEJUVE passed a resolution demanding SEMAPA immediately extend the distribution network to the Zona Sud and fine private water truck operators who failed to meet their obligations, declaring a "state of emergency in neighborhood committee ranks until their demands were met."[147] SEMAPA officials bowed to these demands, crediting the "intense pressure from neighborhood committees of areas without drinking water service" for their decision to sign an agreement to work in the city's "least-technically-advisable area."[148]

Rather than do the work itself, however, SEMAPA contracted the Chilean construction firm Hartley and Co. for city-center distribution network renovation and the Ecuadoran firm Monolítica to build the network out to the periphery. While Monolítica's work mostly proceeded smoothly, Hartley personnel arrived without adequate equipment or personnel, tore up streets across the city rather than proceed zone-by-zone as civic organizations had requested, laid faulty imported pipes, failed to pay subcontractors who soon halted work, and finally abandoned the project and fled the country.[149] JUNCO, the FEJUVE, and Cochabamba's engineers and architects' associations called for legal action against those responsible and demanded SEMAPA's restructuring, threatening to blockade the city "to demand a solution to the serious drinking water problem Cochabamba's population was suffering."[150] In response, the minister of urbanism removed SEMAPA's general manager, agreed to "completely restructure" SEMAPA, established a special commission to oversee SEMAPA's daily operations, promised to personally inspect SEMAPA projects regularly, and brought charges against former SEMAPA general manager Edgar Claure Paz and former mayor Humberto Coronel Rivas, among others.[151] SEMAPA customers also protested new rate increases in these years, calling hikes of up to 500 percent criminal and immoral, especially given residents' contributions to the extension of the distribution network.[152]

SEMAPA finished the abandoned city-center project itself in 1981, which raises the question of why it had contracted foreign firms to start with. Despite the Hartley scandal, between 1978 and 1983 the city's water distribution network grew from 75,000 meters of pipeline serving 96,000 residents to a 320,000-meter-network serving 217,000 residents, including around 100,000 previously excluded periphery residents.[153] In SEMAPA's final report to the IDB, officials concluded that the Bolivian companies "worked more efficiently and more responsibly than the foreign ones" whose personnel had shown "complete ignorance of the Bolivian context."[154] Already in the early 1980s, many Cochabambinos, including SEMAPA officials, wondered whether working with international loans and contractors did more harm than good.

Despite the emergency projects and distribution network overhaul, the water crisis deepened in the early 1980s. By 1980 SEMAPA's cordillera reservoirs were empty and in 1982–1983 an El Niño–triggered drought, more severe than any since the great drought of 1877–1879, led SEMAPA to ration water.[155] Fewer than half of Muyurina and Vinto's wells were operating by 1983 due to high metallic content and disrepair. They were, after all, emergency measures never meant to definitively solve Cochabamba's water supply problem. The distribution system still covered only 60 percent of municipal territory and 70 percent of the municipality's population even before the 1982–1983 drought depleted supply and fueled exodus from the Bolivian countryside to cities. Residents of many neighborhoods on the outskirts of the city of Cochabamba pooled their resources or sought outside assistance to build independent systems as SEMAPA struggled to supply existing customers. SEMAPA purchased additional water from Lagunmayu and Saytukocha owners in exchange for more water from La Angostura and infrastructure improvement projects and brokered deals with owners of other lakes, but conflict with lake owners resumed.[156] In 1985, for instance, Cochabamba's peasant union federation threatened to close valves and destroy pipes and canals to cut off water from Lake Escalerani to the city.[157] All agreed that Cochabamba's ongoing water crisis demanded a far more ambitious solution than had been executed previously. Now more than ever, the popular hope remained Misicuni.

CONCLUSION

Cochabamba's civil society mobilized more actively around water access in this period than ever before, demonstrating the power of disruption to win their demands. Although the dictatorships controlled local institutions and imposed wells, intense civic mobilization and criticism in the press suggests that there were spaces for popular agitation and dissent. The Banzer government's willingness to fund and organize water provision improvements indicates that his regime was more vulnerable to popular demands coming from the city and even from the countryside after the 1974 rupture of the Military-Peasant Pact than often assumed. Banzer's regime proved more capable of providing funds and solutions than previous governments, due in part to the export boom and international credit flows. As historian Kenneth Lehman has written, "labor, peasants, and the political parties were never fully silenced or made impotent by Banzer, and they waited impatiently in the wings to reassert their demands."[158] Indeed, Cochabambino water users asserted demands and made major gains in broadening vernacular hydraulic governance during Banzer's dictatorship.

The fight for local democratic control of SEMAPA and economic practices usually associated with the 1980s and 1990s date back to the company's founding and early years of operation. Already in the late 1960s and the 1970s, the IDB and SEMAPA tried to shift economic and moral responsibility for water provision onto water users who they attempted to reconstitute as customers and "investors." But water users treated questions of water sources, rates, meters, distribution, and loan terms as social and political questions, however much authorities, engineers, and lenders tried to bill them as technical matters. They expected state and international investors, not customers, to fund operational costs, make loan and interest payments, and improve and extend service. Through creative forms of protest and direct action, the region's water users inserted themselves into debates about urban water development and won a seat at the table where water service decisions were made—from Cochabamba to La Paz to Washington. While popular groups did not win all of their specific demands, they slowed efforts to impose rate hikes and obliged the IDB, SEMAPA, and the state to compensate peasants for well-drilling, to seek water in the Tunari Mountains, to move forward with the Misicuni project, and to extend distribution. In the process they gained greater control over water sources and systems and developed a participatory model of urban governance rooted in a collective and redistributive idea of social citizenship at odds with the embryonic neoliberal model advanced by the Banzer government and the IDB.[159]

The Misicuni project's advance through feasibility studies was a key legacy of broad mobilization around water access in the 1970s. What was at stake in these debates was not only the Misicuni project itself, but also the larger question of what development would mean and who would set priorities. Smallholders and city residents, drawing on their own knowledge, saw Misicuni as a techno-fix to their water problems that would confer the benefits of modernity just as much of the developed world turned away from dams. They argued that it should not be judged strictly by economic criteria but rather by what one official called its "social profitability"—namely its potential to improve people's lives.[160] National authorities and IDB officials, and later World Bank representatives, in contrast, insisted on economic profitability.[161] By the end of the 1970s a broad cross-class regional movement had consolidated behind the project as a democratic alternative to deep-well drilling that would provide water to all instead of only to those with power and resources to drill the deepest wells. Urban and rural mobilization was decisive in persuading the national government to commission the 1975 prefeasibility study, the 1979 feasibility study, and the 1987 final design study, all against the initial wishes of the IDB.[162] Already by the 1970s one could say, as geographers Nina Laurie and Simon Marvin would write in the late 1990s, that "Misicuni had become emblematic of the region's identity and hopes for the future."[163] The campaign for the Misicuni project was an effort to gain popular control over regional water governance and to fulfill the revolution's promise of water for all.

Urban and rural populations' experiences working and wrestling with SEMAPA, the Inter-American Development Bank, and foreign contractors were still fresh as the country entered a period of political and economic "stabilization" after Victor Paz Estenssoro was reelected to the presidency in 1985. Rather than revive a state-led development model, Paz Estenssoro began to dismantle the social welfare state, wreaking havoc on many Bolivians' livelihoods. In Cochabamba water users had experience fighting efforts to shift responsibility for public services onto their shoulders. Cochabambinos had built a popular hydraulic society across the valley well before the battles over water appropriation and privatization in the neoliberal period.

5

The Water Is Ours

Water Privatization and War in Neoliberal Bolivia

Bolivia reestablished democratic rule in the 1980s, but the political parties that ruled the country from 1985 to the early 2000s mostly represented the nation's elites. In 1997, after he won a plurality of votes in the presidential elections, Congress chose former dictator Hugo Banzer as president. All of the country's establishment parties were committed to privatizing state-owned enterprises and public services. But while Banzer's predecessors sold off state resources with little resistance, Banzer's attempt to privatize water in Cochabamba occasioned a war.

Bolivia's return to democracy between 1982 and 1985 occurred, perhaps not coincidentally, during trying economic times. Like other Latin American countries, Bolivia's exports slumped while foreign debt ballooned. By 1983 debt service required an outlay equivalent to more than a third of total exports while inflation skyrocketed.[1] Inability to deal with economic crisis made South American dictators like Bolivia's Luis García Meza more vulnerable to growing pro-democracy movements demanding their ouster. But despite a democratic mandate, President Hernán Siles Zuazo (1982–1985) was unable to stabilize the economy either, leading him to hold early elections in July 1985 that brought the MNR's Victor Paz Estenssoro back to the presidency. Rather than return to state-led economic development of the kind his first administration implemented after the 1952 revolution, however, Paz Estenssoro introduced neoliberal economic reforms. Convinced by neoliberal economic theory's contention that state retreat from the economy would help Bolivia's to stabilize and grow, Paz Estenssoro and international financial organizations dismantled the remnants of Bolivia's social welfare state and restructured the Bolivian economy along strict neoliberal lines, making Bolivia the first Latin American country to pursue neoliberal reform under democracy.[2]

Bolivia's New Economic Policy (NEP) successfully reigned in inflation and reduced the deficit but threw the economy into recession, leaving Bolivia's workers
and poor to bear the colossal burden of these policies. Tens of thousands of public
sector jobs with decent salaries and good benefits disappeared, incomes plum-
meted, and purchasing power declined. The growing informal and coca-cocaine
sectors absorbed some of those thrown out of work but not all.[3] Bolivia's leading
center, left, and right parties nevertheless pursued neoliberal economic restructuring while in power during this period of "pacted democracy" in which the dominant parties ruled in coalition with each other.[4] The centrist MNR's Paz Estenssoro (1985–1989) hired US economist Jeffrey Sachs to help devise the NEP, which
slashed state spending in part by closing state-owned mines and firing twenty
thousand state-employed miners. Despite protests, Paz Estenssoro's nephew, Jaime
Paz Zamora (1989–1993) of the ostensibly leftist Movimiento de la Izquierda Revolucionaria (MIR) party upheld his uncle's approach. The MNR's Gonzalo Sánchez
de Lozada (1993–1997), who had implemented the NEP as Paz Estenssoro's planning minister, oversaw sales of the state oil and gas company (YPFB), national
electric company (ENDE), communications company (ENTEL), and national airline (LAB) through "capitalization" schemes where the government retained 50
percent ownership. Then in 1997, when Banzer returned to power as the candidate
of the rightist Acción Democrática Nacionalista (ADN) party, he privatized water.

The architects of neoliberal water policy in Bolivia aimed to privatize municipal
water utilities, as is well-known. But this was just one component of a broader effort to dispossess the population of water sources and systems as well as the social
right to steer water management and hydraulic engineering. The campaign to "rationalize" the national water sector was most aggressive in Cochabamba for it was
there that water access was most contentious and water users were most powerful.
National and local officials ordered extensive hydraulic studies, new rate increases,
new deep wells, and selective incorporation of peripheral neighborhoods in an
attempt to bring water governance under state and lending-institution control.
Bolivian authorities and international actors, aware of past conflicts over rate hikes
and well-drilling, adopted new strategies to deal with so-called barriers to rationalization, using environmental crises to justify intensified international intervention, unpopular policies, and ultimately privatization. As scholars have noted, implementing decentralization often entailed aggressive government intervention.[5]

Efforts to restructure the water sector ignited new rounds of popular organization and protest in Cochabamba in the 1990s. SEMAPA customers challenged new
rate hikes, peripheral neighborhoods protested exclusion from SEMAPA service
and constructed independent water systems, and smallholders resisted new well-
drilling plans. Although urban, peripheral, and rural popular groups had largely
waged their fights over water access separately in previous decades, in the 1990s
the question of whether to compete or unite over water access was posed more

sharply. Peasants and city residents directly confronted each other in this decade's "well wars" but also united when privatization threatened water users' control of sources and systems in the city, periphery, and countryside. In these fights with international lenders, the national government, SEMAPA, and each other, Cochabamba water users defended their ownership of water sources and systems and their right to participate in service management and hydraulic engineering. These conflicts built on past experiences and fueled the Water War in 1999–2000.

WATER SECTOR RATIONALIZATION IN THE CITY

Two intense droughts in 1982–1983 and 1987–1992 and the closure of state mines produced an exodus from the countryside and highlands to the cities and tropics in the 1980s and 1990s. Many migrants settled on the outskirts of Cochabamba's capital, where the population doubled from 1976 to 1992 and continued to grow rapidly thereafter.[6] With drought depleting the city's reserves, SEMAPA was unprepared to meet the needs of its existing customers, 55 percent of the city's population, let alone expand the network to the 30 percent who relied on shallow wells, natural springs, or private water vendors. A full 15 percent of the city's water users belonged to independent systems.[7] Water utilities in La Paz, Oruro, and Santa Cruz, in contrast, covered more than 72 percent of residents in their municipalities.[8] Scholars have shown that government subsidies for water and sanitation services disproportionally benefit wealthier residents of Latin American cities, a phenomenon geographers Simon Marvin and Nina Laurie have called "negative redistribution."[9] Cochabamba exhibits this tendency to an extreme (Map 11).

Renewed urban water scarcity crises led the national government to make new international partnerships to fund, design, and carry out multimillion-dollar-emergency projects that brought an influx of foreign bankers, engineers, and capital to Cochabamba's water sector. Through these emergency projects, officials aimed to provide greater water to the population and to acquire information necessary to exert greater control over sources and users. The Inter-American Development Bank remained a key player in Cochabamba's urban drinking water sector in the 1990s, and the government found a number of new partners for water sector assistance, including the Japanese International Cooperation Agency (JICA) and the governments of Argentina, France, and the French city of Nantes.[10] But the World Bank became the most important international financial institution (IFI) in Bolivia's water sector in these years. The Paz Zamora administration took out a $35 million World Bank loan in 1990 for urban drinking water system improvement in La Paz, Santa Cruz, and Cochabamba; $20 million was designated for new deep wells, renovations, and network expansion in Cochabamba.[11] The World Bank's recommended program for water sector "rationalization" had three components: decentralizing governance, increasing knowledge, and tightening control.[12]

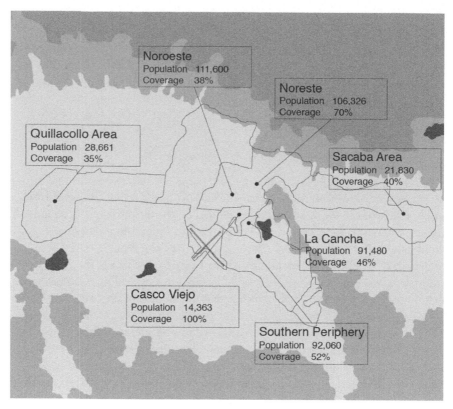

Noroeste
Population 111,600
Coverage   38%

Noreste
Population 106,326
Coverage   70%

Quillacollo Area
Population 28,661
Coverage   35%

Sacaba Area
Population 21,830
Coverage   40%

La Cancha
Population 91,480
Coverage   46%

Casco Viejo
Population 14,363
Coverage   100%

Southern Periphery
Population 92,060
Coverage   52%

MAP 11. Cochabamba metropolitan area water coverage, 1994. Map created by Jorge Camacho Saavedra.

In Bolivia neoliberal reforms promised to democratize governance by devolving authority to municipalities and an expanded citizenry. The 1994 Ley de Participación Popular (LPP) and the 1995 Ley de Decentralización expanded the number of municipalities in Bolivia from a few dozen to more than three hundred, allocated them one-fifth of state revenues, opened up hundreds of new elected positions, and recognized more than thirteen thousand Organizaciones Territoriales de Base (OTBs) to oversee local government.[13] These reforms, along with election rather than appointment of mayors starting in 1985, led existing political parties to pay attention to local demands and led to the rise of new popular and indigenous political parties. These included media personality Carlos Palenque's Consciousness of the Fatherland (CONDEPA), beer industrialist Max Fernández's Unidad Cívica Solidaridad (UCS), Felipe Quispe's Movimiento Indígena Pachakuti (MIP), and the Asamblea por la Soberanía de los Pueblos (ASP) that became the Movimiento al Socialismo (MAS) led by coca union leader Evo Morales.[14]

The Sánchez de Lozada administration also oversaw constitutional reforms that recognized Bolivia as multiethnic and pluricultural, a new agrarian reform law ("Ley INRA") (1996) that provided for collective titling of indigenous territories, and the Ley de Reform Educativa (1994) that promoted teaching indigenous languages and culture in schools. Peasants and indigenous people took advantage of these opportunities to run for office and occupy new patronage jobs as municipal politics took on a new vibrancy in the 1990s.[15] But while multicultural and decentralizing reforms responded to demands from regions, peasants, and indigenous groups, "neoliberal multiculturalism" was double-edged. As anthropologist Nancy Postero has written, the government "intended the reforms as a palliative for the larger structural adjustments it imposed."[16] The reforms fit with the World Bank's neoliberal agenda that wove structural adjustment and social and environmental reform together, what sociologist Michael Goldman has called "green neoliberalism." In response to social movement critique of the human and environmental costs of large-scale development projects, the World Bank began to require social and environmental assessments of projects that often served as cover for approving projects that Bank and national officials deemed beneficial for the nation's economy.[17]

As it did elsewhere, the World Bank conditioned loans to Bolivia on water sector reforms that would enable the government and lenders to exert greater control over water sources, infrastructure, rates, and governance.[18] As discussed in chapter 4, water sector policies usually associated with neoliberalism like decentralization, self-help schemes, and full-cost pricing for water provision have a longer history. But earlier efforts in the water sector had been comparatively mild, and water users had opposed them with much success. In the 1990s the Bank moved away from funding large infrastructure projects, focusing instead on institutional restructuring to ensure efficiency and cost recovery to make water utilities attractive to investors.[19] In Bolivia negotiations with the World Bank led to the establishment of the new Superintendency of Basic Sanitation (Superintendencia de Sanitación Básica, SISAB) to regulate the water and sanitation sector and distribute concessions and licenses. These reforms aimed to facilitate privatization, private sector management of water provision, and commercialization, and treated water as a commodity with an economic value rather than as a social good or right.[20]

To prepare for loan-funded urban water projects in Cochabamba, state institutions and foreign engineering firms conducted numerous studies of aquifers west of the city center in these years. The large number of water-related studies that the Regional Development Corporation of Cochabamba (Corporación de Desarrollo de Cochabamba, CORDECO) carried out analyzing rainfall, watershed dynamics, and aquifer structures and counting and classifying wells speaks to the intensity of the state's drive to make the waterscape legible. In 1987, CORDECO created a Hydraulic Resources Division whose mission was to address "irrational use and management of superficial and underground water sources for domestic and industrial use" and to "generate, increase, and bring up to date basic hydro-meteorological, cartographic, and natural-resource-related information."[21] By 1988, CORDECO was planning or conducting ten hydraulic studies. The same year, the prefecture adopted a new regulation aimed at "imposing rational administration of available water and appropriate management of wastewater in defense of this resource and the environment."[22]

Eight different studies carried out by multiple institutions from 1988 to 1994 probed the size, quality, and behavior of the valley's aquifers on the one hand and the number, location, and ownership of the valley's wells on the other.[23] One of these was CORDECO's three-year effort to inventory the western valley's more than one thousand wells.[24] A 1994 study by the French engineering firm SEU-RECA aimed to identify aquifers that could "be used to quickly resolve the city's water supply problems" and make "efficient administration of these underground water resources" possible. It inventoried more than fifteen hundred wells and recommended drilling new deep wells in Vinto, Sipe Sipe, and El Paso to provide water to the city.[25] Armed with this information, SEMAPA once again embarked on a well-drilling mission. Like in 1977, SEMAPA and its partners decided to drill new deep wells in Valle Bajo agricultural communities to solve the city's water crisis. But this time SEMAPA, the national state, and IFIs were better prepared to strengthen state control over aquifers and contend with smallholders.

Like their IADB counterparts in the 1970s, World Bank officials held that improving water service required shifting the financial burden from the state to water utilities and their customers. The national government and the World Bank thus introduced a new water service regulatory framework requiring water utilities to improve cost recovery by automatically raising rates quarterly in line with inflation, promising that the poor would still be able to afford water. But Bank officials recognized SEMAPA would need to provide more water to its customers to justify rate increases and would therefore require new water sources. The Bank expected self-financed supply expansion, infrastructure renovations, and improved distribution to attract private investment. As an internal World Bank report put it, "adequacy of the infrastructure sector (water, sewage, power and transportation services) heavily influences the productive potential of private investment."[26] In other words, the Bank was asking SEMAPA customers to finance overhaul and expansion of water supply and provision in order to attract private investment. Why they would need private investment at that point was unclear.

Water scarcity and rationing, new rate hikes, and continued delays on the Misicuni project prompted renewed and more militant protests in the city in the 1990s. Like in the 1970s, debates over water rates revolved around the question of what should come first, improved service or increased rate charges. SEMAPA was under greater pressure from international lenders to increase rates, but residents still refused to pay their bills given shortages and inequitable distribution of water. They rallied repeatedly against rationing and rate hikes and in favor of the Misicuni project in these years, demanding that the national government and international lenders, fund the project and other improvements. While requisite studies had been carried out in the 1970s, the Misicuni project had yet to break ground.

The first citywide protest over water scarcity and the Misicuni project in this period was the December 1992 Marcha por el Agua y la Vida. Fearing that authorities had lied about the Misicuni project's progress "as part of an electoral strategy to win votes in the upcoming general elections" and that funding shortages had halted the Misicuni project, the FEJUVE, the Central Obrera Departamental (COD), and the Civic Committee declared that they would not allow Paz Zamora's government "to play around with the interests and hopes of the people" and threatened to call a general strike if the government did not immediately explain itself.[27] When it became clear that the project lacked funding, the Civic Committee threatened roadblocks and a general strike if the government did not quickly secure funding.[28] When the national planning minister announced Italian government financing, a national meeting of regional neighborhood federations demanded authorities begin work on the Misicuni project immediately and threatened to call a state of emergency if they refused.[29]

Another conflict over water rates ensued in 1993 when SEMAPA officials announced a 30 percent rate hike. Officials claimed the increase was necessary to raise the $100 million local contribution for the Misicuni project, fund emergency wells in El Paso, and avoid bankruptcy and closure. SEMAPA's general manager Roberto Prada explained that the Misicuni project's "feasibility depends on the value of water," by which he meant that its profitability depended on raising the price of water.[30] The Municipal Council, civic organizations, and the press called these claims "absurd," in the words of a Los Tiempos editorial penned by its owner Carlos Canelas. They lambasted officials for failing to consider the economic situation of a population already dealing with "incredible and unacceptable rationing…in the city with the highest inflation rate in the country," as Canelas put it.[31] The Municipal Council at first refused to ratify the rate increase but agreed to an initial round of price increases on the condition that proceeds be used to fund the El Paso wells project. But when council members learned that the World Bank was requiring that SEMAPA's rates be indexed to the dollar, they refused to approve further increases, denouncing the company's effort to "lay the burden of its poor management on the backs of the people."[32] The FEJUVE and unions said they would accept rate increases only once the company resolved water scarcity. This pressure forced SEMAPA to back down.[33]

The company increased rates again the following year after the 1994 Capitalization Law established that national regulatory bodies, not municipalities or utility companies, would set rates for public services, despite the government's theoretical support for decentralization.[34] As Nancy Postero has written, "although neoliberalism's advocates often argue that the main goal of neoliberalism is to pare down the state, the Bolivian version has always been tied to an ambitious state-building project."[35] In response, the COD protested, the FEJUVE instructed affiliates not to pay their bills, and the Municipal Council's Oscar Terceros criticized the hike as the work of "pressures put on SEMAPA by the government and foreign financial institutions."[36] While SEMAPA justified the increase as necessary to extend service to the periphery, FEJUVE representatives countered that poor peripheral residents would be the hardest hit. As the FEJUVE's Eloy Luján put it, these kinds of measures "will further impoverish residents already on the brink of misery."[37] SEMAPA seems to have maintained the increase, but the company did not attempt another, despite pressure from the World Bank, for another two years.

In early 1996, SEMAPA officials succumbed to Bank pressure to raise rates, sparking a new conflict. SEMAPA's new general manager Gustavo Mendez defended the rate increases as necessary to demonstrate the company's ability to raise its $15 million local contribution and avoid losing $44 million in international loans (including $10 million from the World Bank, $6 million from the French government, and $20 million from the IDB) for projects already under way, including extension of the network to the Zona Sud.[38] Cochabamba mayor Manfred Reyes Villa, president of SEMAPA's board, defended the increase as necessary to strengthen SEMAPA financially to avoid capitalization. Now that the World Bank had put SEMAPA "between a rock and a hard place" ("entre la cruz y la espada"), Reyes Villa reasoned, SEMAPA had to raise rates to avoid a capitalized SEMAPA "aimed at turning profits rather than providing a public service."[39]

But this appeal to antiprivatization sentiment failed to convince most SEMAPA customers. Some residents reported that SEMAPA had raised its rates as much as 600 percent and that when they could not pay in time the company imposed multiple fines. As one resident complained, "We do not receive water but the bill for service arrives right on time and if payment is late by even a day or two fines are applied immediately." FEJUVE representatives called the hike a "tremendously abusive attack on the lean economy of the population," called water a "vital element for life," and announced a state of emergency.[40] Luján indicated that neighborhood committees were prepared to block city streets and avenues and wage a massive hunger strike "capable of reversing this injustice committed against the poorest sectors of Cochabamba."[41] In the face of these threats, SEMAPA again backed down.

Successful resistance to water rate hikes frustrated authorities from Cochabamba to Washington, DC. These new rounds in a long-standing conflict over water rates exposed the contradiction between the rhetoric of decentralization and the reality of (attempted) state control. As Michael Goldman has written about this period, "the Bank's interventions [were] not only expanding the role of the state, but [were] helping to produce a different type of state altogether."[42] Cochabamba's urban residents saw their contributions of funds, labor, infrastructure, and water sources as more than sufficient to justify their expectations for decent service and system expansion. These contributions had allowed the SEMAPA supply and distribution system to function and grow. While officials claimed that rate hikes were necessary to secure loans to expand service, even with these loans SEMAPA consistently failed to extend service to the city's outer areas, particularly to the Zona Sud, where residents faced drought, water scarcity, and rate hike fights of their own.

VERNACULAR ENGINEERING ON THE PERIPHERY

While SEMAPA officials promised to use loans to extend service to the city's expanding periphery, in practice they adopted a more discriminating approach, working to incorporate neighborhoods with their own water sources and infrastructure into the SEMAPA system while continuing to exclude neighborhoods that lacked them. Adding insult to injury, the municipality watered gardens and parks in the city center and wealthy northern neighborhoods under the slogan "Cochabamba ciudad jardín" as the periphery grew.[43] As in earlier decades, municipal officials were unable control new settlement. Drought and mine closures led Quechua speakers from Cochabamba's provinces and mineworkers and Aymara-speaking peasants from the Altiplano to settle illicitly on the city's outskirts. In 1993 the municipal government considered 80 percent of periphery neighborhoods where 40 percent of the city's residents lived illegal "red zones." As a result, these neighborhoods largely governed themselves, in part by building independent water systems.[44]

Migrants who settled on the city's water-rich northern edges purchased land from former hacienda owners or agrarian reform beneficiaries that frequently included water rights. Through such purchases and agreements with ex-*colono* and ex-*hacendado* water rights' holders, water cooperatives inherited water rights redistributed through agrarian reform in the 1950s and 1960s. Some of these neighborhoods secured funding from USAID and technical assistance from SEMAPA to build water systems. Others relied entirely on their own funds, labor, and expertise to build drinking water systems complete with wells, tanks, and home connections. Many of these neighborhoods turned their systems over to SEMAPA in exchange for inclusion in its network. SEMAPA gained important water rights and indirectly benefited from the agrarian reform through these agreements, acquiring water rights by making deals with neighborhoods that had purchased them from ex-*hacendados* and agrarian reform beneficiaries. In SEMAPA's agreement with the drinking water committee of the Puntiti neighborhood northeast of the city, for instance, residents ceded their rights to a portion of Lake Wara Wara's water to the company in exchange for a new drinking water system for the neighborhood.[45]

Neighborhoods without water sources could participate in SEMAPA's "self-help program" by contributing 50 to 80 percent of the cost of extending the network into their area. These scenarios were generally limited to the city's northern edges in the Tunari foothills where water sources were close and abundant. In these ways SEMAPA extended coverage and increased its supply on the city's northern edges with little financial outlay, and residents there became SEMAPA customers by contributing funds, materials, labor, and neighborhood-owned water sources and infrastructure.[46] It is no wonder then that residents of these neighborhoods consider these pockets of SEMAPA's network to be their own.[47]

Other water cooperatives with water sources chose to remain independent to maintain more secure access than they thought SEMAPA would provide. In the 1990s neighborhoods northeast of the city founded new water cooperatives, often with the assistance of neighborhood Catholic parishes. Residents of the Quintanilla neighborhood a few kilometers northeast of the city center, for instance, formed the Cooperativa de Agua Potable y Alcantarillado "Quintanilla Ltda." with encouragement and assistance from their neighborhood's parish priest. The cooperative gained rights to mountainside springs and mountain lakes through agreements with ex-*colono* agrarian reform beneficiaries and through an arrangement with the daughter of the Arocagua hacienda's former owners. According to the cooperative's president, Jesús Salazár, these agreements and cooperative members' seasonal labor to maintain dams, canals, and other installations make them co-owners of these mountain water lakes and springs. As Salazár put it in a 2011 interview, "We became owners [of our water sources] through uses and customs and the maintenance work that we carry out every year. The work is wonderful, truly historic work."[48]

Accessing water on the further reaches of the northern periphery, outside SEMAPA's designated coverage area, was more challenging. In Chilimarca, northeast of the city center in the Tiquipaya municipality, altiplano tin miners bought lots sight-unseen from developers only to arrive and find that neither the municipal government nor the smallholders who lived there recognized their property rights. Migrants recall that while the MNR supported smallholders' claims to disputed land, Banzer's ADN, Municipal Council president Gonzalo "Chaly" Terceros of the center-right Nueva Fuerza Republicana (NFR) party, and Max Fernández's UCS supported the migrants' ultimately successful efforts to legalize their land claims.[49] These sponsors helped bring electricity and transportation to the neighborhood, but not water. Guadalupe Yacupaico, who migrated with her husband from the Colquri mine in La Paz, recalls that settlers collected water that smelled like dirt from irrigation canals. As she explained, "since Chilimarca was farmland and there was no one living around the canals, we just took the water."

She remembers carrying rocks and cement to Chutakjawa, a mountainside spring, to line canals to channel water to their settlement. "The work in Chutakjawa was terrible," she said. "The community of miners carried cement to the mountain on their backs" and "pregnant women miscarried because they helped. Thanks to this labor we have water."[50]

Memories of employing community resources to build neighborhood water systems run strong among older residents. But Santiago Torrez, Chilimarca's young water system administrator who moved there from a Cochabamba province as a child, explained in a 2007 interview that the nongovernmental organization MAP International and the Bolivian government's Fondo Nacional de Inversión Social helped fund water projects. Because smallholders had rights to Chutakjawa, migrants made an agreement with the Taquiña beer factory to use water from the Taquiña River instead. Together, company and neighborhood representatives designed a tunnel to bring water from the river to the new settlements, but residents did the work. While older residents emphasize smallholders' hostility, Torrez told me that some smallholders allowed the newcomers to use their water and "even fought with their fellow comunarios" over the issue. As smallholders sold land to newcomers, Torrez explained, the number of small farmers and the amount of farmland deminished. "Sometimes they have nothing to irrigate and water flows in the streets," he said. Migrants and smallholders who wanted to help them argued that the ancestral principle of reciprocity should guide them. Torrez saw the divide between *comunarios* and migrants fade as they became friends and intermixed in various ways. A *comunario*'s child might live in one of the new neighborhoods, Torrez said, so denying a neighbor water "would mean denying it to one's own people."[51]

Drought and mine closures also led to informal settlements in the arid Zona Sud where accessing water was much more difficult. In the 1980s and 1990s new groups of migrants "invaded" agricultural land where they formed neighborhoods that fended for themselves as they worked to gain municipal recognition. Zona Sud residents organized neighborhood committees to petition the municipality for roads, transportation, schools, and water. Success often owed to residents' offers to "cooperate" with the municipality by supplying materials and labor. Cochabamba's municipal government established satellite offices in Zona Sud neighborhoods in the 1990s to rationalize governance and land tenure. As anthropologist Daniel Goldstein has written, "In an apparent contradiction, by decentralizing state authority the Bolivian government seems to have created a more effective system for extending state control."[52] But while the municipality legalized property claims, extended roads, and built schools, SEMAPA only incorporated a small section of the vast Southern Zone. Despite housing around a third of the population (113,000 people), the four Zona Sud districts received only 0.66 percent of municipal investment in 1999.[53] In the face of municipal neglect, many neighborhoods pursued a dual strategy of pressuring SEMAPA to extend service while forming independent water committees to secure water in the meantime. There were 120 water committees there by the early 2000s, though not all were active.[54]

One of the most successful Zona Sud water committees was organized by residents of the neighborhood Villa Sebastián Pagador, located in Valle Hermoso, 5 kilometers south of the city center. Before the 1952 Bolivian revolution, all of Valle Hermoso was owned by the Tardío family. After the revolution former hacienda *colonos* who won land parcels through agrarian reform sold them to a cooperative that in turn sold the land to speculators who then sold lots to Aymara settlers from Oruro who began to arrive in the 1960s. The municipal government considered all of these sales illegal.[55] Like in Chilimarca, residents used their own funds and labor to build water systems and solicited assistance from outside entities. At first, as neighborhood leader Hipólito Condori recounted in a 2007 interview, "we used to go to the city to buy water, or had it given to us there." Marches and blockades won them paved streets, streetlights, and electricity, but their protests did not yield water.

When I spoke with him in 2007, Esteban Yanez, a water committee leader, explained that "since [authorities] did not want to hear about the water problem, the idea of having our own water and water committees was born."[56] The Villa Pagador water committee, formed in 1990, drilled a well. They found water, but "it was salty and smelled horrible," Condori recalled. The difficulties led neighborhood leaders to seek outside resources. The World Bank chose Villa Pagador for a pilot project, funding studies that determined that the neighborhood's groundwater was unsuitable. The Bank therefore funded the drilling of wells on the other side of the San Pedro hills in Quintanilla instead.[57] But the project only benefited more established residents who blocked a plan to install public spigots that would have made water available to others, thereby exacerbating divisions in the community.[58]

Zona Sud neighborhoods further from the city center like Primero de Mayo, a 13-kilometer trip from the city center, did not expect SEMAPA's network to reach them. When the first migrant families arrived there in 1985, they brought water on foot from a hillside spring a kilometer away. But tapping this source provoked conflict with neighboring farmers who used it for agriculture and raising livestock. Primero de Mayo resident Isadora Alemán told me that their new neighbors treated migrants like her poorly at first. "They looked at us like we were from another world because they were *cochalos* [Cochabambinos] and they called us campesinos." She recalled the "cochalos" grabbing migrants, insulting the food they ate, and prohibiting them from using the spring, saying "it's ours." The migrants' solution was to improve water capture at the spring so they could claim the additional water. According to Alemán, "husbands and wives worked together, even at night, to build the tank" so that water "would not be wasted." Although she says that they always invited the "cochalos" to help them, they always declined. Her husband, Antonio Heredia, president of the neighborhood organization when we spoke, told me that whereas the "originarios" (roughly "original inhabitants") carried water by donkey, the migrants drilled a well, built a tank, laid pipes, and installed home connections and water meters with help from the Swedish government. The "originarios were surprised that we were able to do all of that and little by little they built the same kinds of systems."[59] Here, the "cochalo" "originarios," a term that usually refers to indigenous people, cast migrants as more indigenous than themselves.

Abraham Grandydier, whose family arrived with the first group of migrants when he was young, told a different story that emphasizes cooperation among the different groups that converged in and around Primero de Mayo. Grandydier became a neighborhood leader in the late 1990s and organizer of the Zona Sud water committee network ASICA-Sur (Asociación de Sistemas Comunitarios de Agua del Sur) in the early 2000s. In his view Primero de Mayo's water committee was successful because it brought together miners and peasants who shared "a concept of solidarity" and fused syndical and communitarian traditions as they constructed communal water systems. Grandydier recounted that miners and peasants built "communitarian drinking water systems that were administered collectively and communally" on the basis of the belief that "water belongs to all." Miners brought knowledge about how to transport water from far sources, and peasants knew how to administer it collectively. He attributes these improvement projects not to conflict with the spring's owners, but rather to migrants' desire to "pipe water to our houses just like we had in the mines." Water sources, he told me, were "places of brotherhood, recognition, and friendship because older people, children, young people, men, and women all went there ... to meet each other, get to know one another, and play." But Grandydier worries that individualist practices like building tanks and laying pipes to "protect" water sources have eroded communitarianism.[60]

Many peripheral neighborhoods have projected a collective indigenous identity in bids to gain external financial and technical assistance for water projects. But residents' experiences in these three areas highlight their complex relationships to indigeneity, place, and each other. As anthropologist Robert Albro has written, many Bolivians and especially Cochabambinos recognize and express pride in their indigenous heritage "while not being fully defined by it."[61] A story told to me by Miguel Palma Chambi, a former tin miner and union leader who migrated from the Huanuni mine to Chilimarca where he became a neighborhood leader, bears this out. At a funeral in Huanuni, Palma's father arrived wearing *abarcas* (sandals made from leather and tire treads) and a *q'epi* (a satchel made of woven cloth), items worn by indigenous peasants. He embraced his father and introduced him to his co-workers, who also embraced him and congratulated him for educating his son, now their leader. Palma concluded, "I am proud to identify myself [with my father]. I come out of that....I have no reason to disavow my father."[62] The story illustrates both Pavia's pride in his indigenous heritage as well as the distance he feels he has traveled from those roots.

Others, including many Aymara-speaking residents of Villa Pagador, fervently identify as indigenous. One Villa Pagador resident told me that the Aymara culture that migrants brought to the neighborhood was "more advanced than the culture of the Quechuas" who were already there. Yet Villa Pagador's Aymara migrants were hardly a homogeneous group. Some hailed from the Oruro countryside, others from the department capital, and still others from the mines.[63] Many miners were born in the countryside and maintained ties or residences there even as they worked alongside Quechua-speaking miners from Cochabamba. When they arrived in Villa Pagador, the Orureños settled next to Quechua-speaking cochalos who had their own complex relationship with indigenous identity. As Albro writes, "In a cultural world complicated by intense mixtures and categorical intimacies and in a political environment of the ascendancy of indigenous identity, people continue to reimagine the right relation among parts."[64]

Many Zona Sud neighborhoods managed to build independent water distribution systems through a combination of residents' resources and external financial and technical assistance from Catholic parishes, the World Bank, foreign countries such as Italy, and NGOs like Fundación Pro Habitat.[65] The residents of Valle Hermoso, Villa San Andrés, Villa San Miguel, and Santa Vera Cruz, for example, made contributions and received assistance from the Santa Vera Cruz Catholic parish to drill wells in the 1990s. As Father Javier Velasco, a priest involved in this effort, recalled, "the residents rose to the challenge of not having water, contributed family resources, and against all technical and geological advice drilled a well until it hit water, which thank God was abundant."[66] But in this arid and polluted zone, far from the Tunari Mountains' lakes and springs, it was easier to build tanks and lay pipes than to find a secure water source. While neighborhoods like Villa Pagador and Primero de Mayo were able to tap a nearby spring or drill a well, groundwater contamination from agricultural and industrial activity forced many neighborhoods with storage and distribution infrastructure to purchase water "in bulk" from SEMAPA.[67]

Most Zona Sud neighborhoods lacked both sources and infrastructure and had no choice but to purchase water from private water vendors (aguateros). Of the roughly 30 percent of city residents that purchased their water from private vendors in the 1990s, the vast majority lived in the Zona Sud.[68] According to architect and water researcher Carmen Ledo, water trucks supplied 95 percent of residents in the Zona Sud's three most urbanized districts in these years.[69] Aguateros charged as much as 25 times what SEMAPA charged and their customers were at far greater risk for water-borne disease than those with SEMAPA connections.

Water vendors did not test or treat their product nor did municipal officials regulate this sector. To receive and store water, residents purchased large metal drums often previously used for industrial purposes that they placed outside, close to the road. In these dry and windy hillside neighborhoods, dirt and fecal materials quickly coated the surface of water that was simultaneously absorbing rusty metal and chemicals from the barrel itself. These conditions, the direct result of exclusion from municipal water service, produced infant mortality rates far higher than in the rest of the city.[70] The FEJUVE repeatedly protested "extortion" by "wicked sellers" whose untreated water and astronomical prices "threatened public health and the family economy," at times instructing members with SEMAPA service not to pay their bills to pressure the company to extend service to the periphery.[71] Authorities usually ignored such complaints.[72]

At first, residents of Zona Sud gained water access through vernacular engineering out of necessity rather than desire. While more fortunate neighborhoods close to the city center with water sources of their own chose whether to join SEMAPA or not, Zona Sud water committees discussed here had no choice but to self-govern. If SEMAPA service had been available, they would no doubt have used it. As Goldstein clarifies, Zona Sud residents were "struggling not to 'resist' state authority but in protest against a perceived failure of the state; what they desire is not autonomy but greater inclusion...to gain the very practical benefits that membership in the modern city and nation is said to entail."[73] Yet exclusion has generated vernacular water governance in the Zona Sud as well as ambivalence about whether to turn autonomous systems over to SEMAPA should that opportunity arise.

THE ECOLOGY OF WELLS

SEMAPA's well-drilling program provoked numerous conflicts in the late 1980s and the 1990s. In the 1977 Vinto wells conflict, debate had revolved around the aquifer's structure, peasant organizations and state institutions clashed, and threats of violence were minimal. In the late 1980s and the 1990s, conflicts over wells intensified. Both peasants and state officials deployed increasingly sophisticated legal, technical, ecological, and moral arguments, urban popular groups got involved, and all sides threatened to use force. As urban-rural conflicts over water intensified, the state's uneasy relationship with rural water rights holders became increasing fraught. In its effort to "rationalize" water tenure, the state attempted to become the primary regulator and owner of water sources and systems at the very moment that indigenous and peasant communities were demanding recognition of territorial rights locally, nationally, and internationally. Valley peasants relied on water to produce corn, wheat, and alfalfa as well as newer products like fruit, milk, poultry, and flowers.[74] They mobilized forcefully against SEMAPA well projects in these years, winning significant concessions from the company and frustrating SEMAPA, national, and World Bank officials' efforts to dispossess them of water rights.

SEMAPA's first emergency project was a new well field in El Paso, a rural community in the Quillacollo municipality (see Map 7). Officials predicted that the wells would provide an additional 140 liters per second to the city by the end of 1987. El Paso peasant opposition, however, delayed the project and sparked a new debate over well drilling. Like in 1977, SEMAPA and CORDECO officials argued that the new wells would not affect existing irrigation wells and tried to discredit the "oversensitive" peasants' "erroneous and unfounded" claims by appealing to "scientific-technical" studies.[75] But officials' campaign to gain control over aquifer water was now far more aggressive. Appealing to the hydrological studies by prestigious institutions discussed above, officials argued that the water SEMAPA would pump was minimal compared to the area's extensive reserves and contended in moral terms that the needs of four hundred thousand city residents trumped those of "a few people" obstructing the general good.[76] SEMAPA general manager Roberto Prada billed the project as the only way to overcome the deficit quickly and affordably and warned that its failure would cause serious water supply problems across the city.[77] Prada reminded El Paso peasants that water legally belonged to the Bolivian state such that "no one could claim private water ownership" and on this basis reasoned that the state should "regulate the use of this resource for the general good."[78] The undersecretary of urbanism summed up the state's position succinctly: "Only through rational exploitation of hydraulic resources will a solution that harms no one be achieved."[79]

SEMAPA's legal, technical, and moral arguments held little sway in the countryside but resonated deeply in the city. Water scarcity during the drought in the late 1980s and early 1990s led Cochabamba's Municipal Council and urban popular groups to vocally back well-drilling in the provinces. The Municipal Council president called the El Paso peasants' attitude "dictatorial and criminal" and the situation an example of "the negative aspects of the democratic system in which [one group's] authoritarianism could put the survival of an entire population at risk."[80] As the conflict wore on, the COD and the *fabriles* formed a commission to dialogue with El Paso peasants to try to convince them to agree to the wells.[81] Both the peasants and the state threatened force as the conflict escalated. In October 1988 peasants stormed the municipal building where negotiations were taking place between provincial and SEMAPA officials, allegedly cursing and trying to attack Prada and others.[82] Later they prevented SEMAPA officials and workers from entering the well site to begin work, leading to the project's temporary suspension and a new study of the area's water resources.[83]

When peasants rejected the accord brokered between municipal and SEMAPA officials, the prefect threatened to "apply the force of the law" and warned that if they did not sign the agreement, he would send the police to oversee the project's execution since "no one could claim ownership of surface or underground water sources that have no owner other than the state." He further warned that if the peasants physically impeded the project, they would have no one to blame but themselves for the presumably bloody consequences.[84] As state institutions had predicted, the study concluded that the local population "wasted" underground water sources while the new well field would help to establish better, more rational use. Not only would the project "not affect aquifers," its authors claimed, it would "prevent water table losses" produced by "irrational exploitation of underground flows" and even "facilitate the necessary replenishment of all aquifers in the area."[85] In other words, replacing shallow wells for local use with deep wells for the city would somehow make more water available for all.

SEMAPA and El Paso leaders signed an agreement in May 1989 that permitted SEMAPA to drill three new wells for urban supply in exchange for two additional wells and technical assistance for the community.[86] The wells were complete by June and providing 100 liters per second to SEMAPA customers by October. The prefect thanked the El Paso community for their support in "alleviating the anguish of many families who lack sufficient water."[87] But, at the wells' inauguration, Prada reminded attendees that the project had only been possible after "overcoming problems created by peasant opposition."[88] A few months later, peasants took over pumping stations and cut off flow to the city, complaining that the new wells had reduced and muddied their own well water. After the conflict was resolved, the police took charge of the wells to prevent further "sabotage."[89]

Both proponents and opponents of wells made ecological arguments as social movements, the United Nations, NGOs, international financial institutions, and neoliberal governments were taking up environmental questions worldwide. The United Nations Conference on the Environment and Development held in Rio de Janeiro in 1992 both responded to and influenced developments already under way in Latin American countries like Bolivia. Like the UN, the World Bank, and other Latin American governments, the Bolivian government adopted ecological discourses and reforms in response to social movement pressure, fashioning what Michael Goldman has called an "environmental state."[90] In 1990 lowland indigenous groups organized the March for Territory and Dignity from the lowlands to the national capital demanding autonomous control of their territories and resources.[91] A year later, the Paz Zamora administration created the Secretariat of the Environment.[92] In 1993 the Sánchez de Lozada administration established the Ministry of Sustainable Development and the Environment and tasked it with fostering "harmonious development of the country" by "taking care of the environment, maintaining and recuperating renewable natural resources, and promoting rational economic use." Protecting air, land, and water sources, officials reasoned, would require "applying economic incentives." Like midcentury statutes discussed in earlier chapters, the law creating this ministry asserted national state ownership of water sources, designating them "patrimony of the state."[93]

This context shaped a conflict over SEMAPA's efforts to drill new wells in the Vinto–Sipe Sipe area in 1994. This time technical arguments turned ecological, urban popular groups got involved more directly, disputes over state versus community water ownership intensified, and threats of violence and confrontation increased. SEMAPA now claimed that existing irrigation wells hurt the environment. SEMAPA general manager Gustavo Mendez alleged that the valley's five thousand "clandestine" shallow wells overexploited shallow aquifers, "putting the area at risk for sinking and even seismic activity." He singled out the valley's three thousand to four thousand shallow irrigation wells as the cause of its "ruin." Mendez promised to line the first 400 meters of SEMAPA's 600-meter-deep well with cement so as not to draw on shallow layers of the aquifer and thereby protect existing wells and springs according to "principles of sustainable development."[94]

Provincial and peasant organizations opposed to SEMAPA's plans also employed ecological arguments, drawing on nearly two decades of experience with SEMAPA's deep wells. The Association of Irrigation Systems of Tiquipaya-Colcapirhua, founded in 1992, and new antiwells committees argued that it was SEMAPA's overexploitation of local aquifers that was irrational, not proliferation of shallow irrigation wells. One resident reported that whereas before well-drilling, Vinto had been a "vergel"—a lush, fertile place—"there is now no guarantee that planting will yield a crop."[95] Another charged that since Vinto had become "a simple supplier of water for the city," its aquifers had emptied, its springs had disappeared, and once abundant vegetation and agricultural production had diminished.[96] They also claimed, in the words of a Comité de Defensa Ambiental representative, that the wells had caused "fractures in the land, a clear symptom of soil erosion," and cited independent geological studies predicting that "drilling wells 100, 200, 600 meters deep or more could provoke seismic movements like the Sipe Sipe earthquake of 1909."[97]

Omar Fernández, president of the Association of Irrigation Systems of Tiquipaya-Colcapirhua and a member of the Comité de Defensa de los Recursos Hídricos, argued that SEMAPA's deep wells were contributing to desertification and environmental deterioration. SEMAPA's "irrational exploitation of these hydraulic resources," he said, had "robbed the soil and dried up springs and underground flows." Fernández cited "serious studies, conducted free of economic and political interests," which demonstrated that the "famous French experts" hired by SEMAPA had "lied in their studies, exaggerating the supposed potential of aquifer resources in the Central and Lower Valleys."[98] Both SEMAPA officials and antiwells activists agreed that some wells were harmful; the question was whose.

Opponents of SEMAPA's well-drilling plan—who included peasant unions, irrigators, ranchers, chicken famers, neighborhood and civic committees, teachers, and bus drivers from Sipe Sipe, Vinto, El Paso, and Quillacollo—invited a group of professionals to form a technical advisory council to study the potential impacts of the plan. The council included several engineers, an educational psychologist, and Marcelo Delgadillo, an architect from Vinto who comes from a family of small farmers and helped found the Comité de Defensa Ambiental de Cochabamba in 1992. According to Delgadillo, well opposition group leaders obtained the French study and others carried out by GEOBOL, the German Development Agency (GTZ), the Servicio Geológico Minero (SERGEOMIN), the Universidad Mayor de San Simón (UMSS), and the Empresa Misicuni. After analyzing the studies, Delgadillo recounts, the Technical Advisory Council concluded that SEMAPA's deep wells would likely "dry up existing wells that supplied agriculture, cattle, poultry, and other farming," reduce evaporation, and exacerbate the drought the area was already experiencing.[99]

The conflict culminated in the decade's second March for Water and Life. Early on the morning of 7 October 1994, more than three thousand peasants from one hundred communities in the Valle Bajo departed from Vinto, chanting against well drilling. Banners expressed opposition to wells and demanded execution of the Misicuni project as an alternative that would satisfy both urban and rural water needs. Community organization members from Sipe Sipe, Vinto, Quillacollo, Colcapirhua, and Tiquipaya called on authorities to execute the Misicuni project and pledged $50 and a week of labor each toward its realization.[100] Fernández alleged that since the 1970s, "well-drilling policy [had] aimed to postpone the Misicuni project."[101] The antiwells movement's ecological arguments were on full display during the march. A representative of the Comité de Defensa Ambiental de Vinto y Sipe Sipe declared that two hundred communities opposed well drilling in "defense of endangered natural resources." Another organizer told a reporter that "by rejecting more drilling we are defending the agricultural production, ecology, and environment of these areas that are the envy of the region for their high productivity and idyllic landscapes that could be harmed by drilling." Protestors threatened to block interdepartmental highways and cut off water to the city if authorities failed to respond.[102]

Supporters of the deep wells project, including local, national, and World Bank authorities as well as urban civic and neighborhood groups, were determined to overcome peasant opposition. In anticipation of the march, the FEJUVE had called on city residents "to remain united and strong against the opposition of the Vinteños" and pledged to use "medidas de hecho," a euphemism for force, if necessary. FEJUVE president Eloy Luján announced that the new deep wells were "essential to alleviating the thirst of the city" and that FEJUVE members would not allow for "interference" with them. He called for dialogue and compromise, offering to "explain" to the marchers that "studies affirmed that sedimentation and ancient rock made the layers up to 400 meters deep impermeable," technical ar-

FIGURE 9. March from Vinto and Sipe Sipe to Cochabamba, October 1994. *Los Tiempos*, 8 October 1994.

guments that echoed state and foreign experts' positions. If they continued with their "mistaken critiques," however, Luján warned that FEJUVE members "would find themselves obliged to block marchers' access to the city, potentially provoking a confrontation."[103] SEMAPA general manager Gustavo Mendez accused the peasantry of blocking Cochabamba's modernization and progress, in effect calling them backward: "It is incomprehensible that in the twentieth century, the age of technology, space exploration, social modernization, application of scientific discoveries to improve the quality of human life and…the evolution of consciousness and intellect," that Cochabamba "should continue delaying this opportunity for change and progress due to the negative attitude of certain inhabitants toward regional plans and projects."[104]

The threatened confrontation never took place, but conflict intensified after the march. The Sánchez de Lozada administration declared a state of emergency and imprisoned several members of the Technical Advisory Council in the eastern Beni department where the Banzer regime had banished opponents in the 1970s.[105] Two weeks later, an unidentified gunman fired at an El Paso well, cutting off water to many city neighborhoods.[106] Vinto and Sipe Sipe community members threatened to march to the city again and block the highway between Cochabamba and Oruro. As Amador Olivera, a spokesperson for the Comité de Defensa Ambiental de Vinto y Sipe Sipe, told the press, "if the well-drilling effort continues, we will be obliged to resist with all means available to us, including mobilizations and blockades."[107] Soon thereafter, a meeting of Vinto and Sipe Sipe peasant union representatives, the Vinto Civic Committee, and the Comité de Defensa Ambiental de Vinto y Sipe Sipe declared their "right to use all means available to us" to oppose well drilling and that SEMAPA would bear "responsibility for the potentially fatal consequences."[108]

Amador Olivera avowed that although "we are conscious that we live in a civilized country, when dialogue fails there are other tools at our disposal."[109] When the mayor of Sipe Sipe signed an agreement with SEMAPA without consulting the community, a popular assembly called for his resignation, marched to his office, stoned the building, and demanded that he come out to explain himself. The mayor appeared on the balcony, where he ripped up a copy of the agreement and offered to resign.[110] When SEMAPA and CORDECO officials called in the military to oversee well drilling, peasants threatened to bar access to the well site and confront soldiers and police.[111] *Los Tiempos* reporters found hundreds of peasants blocking roads. A Comité de Defensa Ambiental leader told them that if authorities continued to try to drill a well in the area, the officials would "have to pass over our dead bodies" because the peasants were "defending life, their children's future, and departmental food security." Others said they would be happy to fill prisons to block drilling.[112] Widespread antiwells sentiment in the Valle Bajo pushed MIR and CONDEPA leaders to oppose SEMAPA wells in competing bids for municipal office there.[113]

After two weeks of peasant protest, the government lifted the state of emergency and released detainees. SEMAPA abandoned its plan to drill wells in Vinto and Sipe Sipe, drilling a well on military property with police protection in El Paso instead. While El Paso peasants also opposed SEMAPA's plans, they yielded to SEMAPA in exchange for a water system, one of many such exchanges made in this period.[114] The World Bank's report at the close of its $35 million, three-city drinking water project in 1998 deemed the Santa Cruz project a success, La Paz's a partial success, and Cochabamba's a failure. Only 77 percent of planned works were built in Cochabamba, and the water supply increase fell short of the Bank's goal. World Bank officials blamed the outcome on "physical opposition of farmers to the drilling of new wells [that] would deprive them of water for irrigation in favor of water supply to the urban sector," inadvertently admitting that the farmers' technical position was correct.[115]

While supporters of wells saw them as necessary to achieve the promises of modernity in the city, their opponents decried this exclusionary vision and threatened to act violently if a more inclusive plan such as the Misicuni project was not adopted. As Daniel Goldstein has written about attempted extrajudicial lynching in the Zona Sud, "the 'attempt' is to gain the attention of the authorities through the threat of violence more than it is the actual commission of the violent act itself."[116] Although wells opponents did use some physical force, *threat* of force was their main weapon. By threatening to sabotage wells and cut off water to the city, Valle Bajo peasants appropriated elite and urban views of their savagery for their own ends, simultaneously performing powerlessness and demonstrating power. This approach was reminiscent of Cochabamba peasant mobilizations during the 1952 revolution. Urban authorities and residents also threatened force, and state authorities used it, in the 1980s and 1990s with little reproach outside the Valle Bajo.

The question of who owned the water under El Paso, Vinto, and Sipe Sipe was at the heart of these conflicts. While state officials asserted the state's legal ownership of water sources, peasants claimed historical rights to the water sources known as "usos y costumbres." Interestingly, Valle Bajo peasant communities and former *hacendado* elites found common cause on this question. *Los Tiempos*, owned by the Canelas family that retained some of their expropriated haciendas' land and water sources, defended peasant claims to water ownership. "It is no wonder that Vinto and Sipe Sipe's representative organizations decided to defend their underground water resources," an editorial read. "Although according to the Constitution, the subsoil and all of its riches and usable resources belong to the state, it is no less certain that the inhabitants of the provinces like those of the capital city make up the state."[117] Peasants employed this "we too are the state" discourse to defend water rights (see chapter 6 for further discussion). Cochabamba's other major daily, *Opinión*, by contrast, fumed that "water sources, whether surface or subterranean, do not belong to individuals or to groups. They belong to the state, which has every right to use them however it sees fit to benefit communities."[118] To the chagrin of *Opinión*'s editors and SEMAPA authorities, the state once again had failed to establish itself as the rightful owner and manager of the Cochabamba Valley's underground water sources.

Well conflicts spurred the founding of the Cochabamba Irrigators' Federation (Federación Departamental Cochabambina de Organizaciones Regantes, FEDECOR) in 1997. These irrigators were smallholders, whether of *piquero* or ex-*colono* extraction, not already organized by the Federación Sindical Única de Trabajadores Campesinos de Cochabamba (FSUTCC), which FEDECOR leaders saw as controlled by dominant political parties. Until the 1990s irrigators had organized on the basis of a shared water source.[119] The first irrigators association, the Association of Irrigation Systems of Tiquipaya-Colcapirhua mentioned earlier in the chapter, formed in 1992 in response to decentralization reforms that gave municipalities authority over irrigation systems and concern that a new water law would further threaten peasants' water rights and open the door to privatization.[120] Others formed in the years after. FEDECOR brought these associations together into a departmental federation to defend irrigators' historical rights against well drilling and municipalization. As FEDECOR founder Omar Fernández explained, "we created our irrigation systems and water sources through our own efforts, and they resulted from an important historic struggle of our forefathers, so we could not so easily hand them over to the municipalities."[121] The Federación Única, as its name would suggest, was none too pleased with the emergence of this new organization.[122]

Irrigators appealed to the concept of *usos y costumbres* to vindicate historical rights to water sources not codified by law or in property titles. Based on interviews and workshops in the four valleys where they work, FEDECOR leaders Omar Fernández and Carmen Peredo have defined *usos y costumbres* as "the natural rights that God gave man. Water is the *Pachamama* [Mother Earth] and *Wirakhocha* [Creator God] that is neither person nor spirit but rather the land that gives us life and its blood that is the water that allows for human life." Invoking ancestral rights and referring to mid-twentieth-century agrarian reform that redistributed hacienda land and water, they describe *usos y costumbres* as the "rights of our forefathers, the original inhabitants [*originarios*] . . . inherited from our parents and grandparents who inherited them from the hacienda owners [*patrones*]."[123]

Fernández was born in Tiquipaya and married into an agricultural family in 1982. His wife Dora Pardo Fuentes's family owned agricultural land with water rights in the Montesillo area of Tiquipaya where Fernández and Pardo worked the land, fulfilled labor obligations necessary to maintain their irrigation rights, and became certified Montesillo irrigators. Fernández later earned a degree in economics at the Universidad Mayor de San Simón. His outstanding 1996 undergraduate thesis traced the history of Tiquipaya's water rights regime. He was thus well equipped to develop FEDECOR's position that historical labor confers water rights. Fernández served as president of Tiquipaya's Drinking Water Committee, treasury secretary for the Lagunmayu irrigation system, and president of the Tiquipaya-Colcapirhua Irrigators Association that he helped to found in 1992 before becoming FEDECOR's president upon its founding in 1997.[124]

While FEDECOR's *usos y costumbres* discourse sometimes portrays water rights as inviolable, *usos y costumbres* have changed over time, as Fernández and Peredo's reference to the region's vanquished hacienda owners suggests and Fernández's research shows. Irrigators have fought over water among themselves and, as geographer Thomas Perreault has argued, the concept of *usos y costumbres* masks and justifies inequalities among them.[125]

In stressing ancestral rights, irrigators often highlighted their indigenous heritage. While critics claim that irrigators only began to appeal to "Andean identity frames" in the 1990s, *usos y costumbres* and the Andean water ritual practices that they are rooted in have a longer history.[126] Fernández holds that the term itself had long been used Tiquipaya before the 1990s. As this book has shown, purchase-sale agreements, water owners' responses to attempted expropriations, and agrarian reform decisions used various combinations of the terms uses, customs, improvements, and easements from as early as the 1940s. This bears out irrigators' deeper claim that water rights have changed over time as the region's water users have negotiated water rights among themselves through social struggle, negotiation, and compromise. They have at times involved the state in their fights, most notably in revolutionary-era agrarian reform cases.

To this day, irrigator and peasant water-owning communities meet regularly to make decisions and perform collective labor. In Tiquipaya, annual assemblies, monthly meetings, irrigation system cleaning days, and yearly trips to mountain lakes and dams are set in the calendar "according to custom," says Fernández. Labor assignments correspond to a family's origins—whether it descends from *piqueros* or *colonos*, for instance—and "the work is a collective celebration [*una fiesta y un compartimiento comunitario*]." Fernández explains that when laborers ascend the mountainside to lakes and dams each year, "they perform a *k'oa* [a ritual offering to the Pachamama], converse with the water with great respect, and ask for and thank the water." He told me that the lake can get angry and punish or even eat the workers. Irrigators consider water "a living being that has a head, body, and tail" whose parts correspond to the source's main outlet, and upstream and downstream communities.[127]

In Vinto urban residents and smallholders also carry out collective labor to clean rivers, canals, and ditches, and to dig trenches and lay pipes in a system of mutual and obligatory community labor organized according to principles of reciprocity (*ayni*). Marcelo Delgadillo, a lifelong resident of Vinto, told me that work on water infrastructure often begins with a *challa*, an offering to the Pachamama to ask her blessing for the project. Laborers celebrate the workday's end with an *aptapi*, a shared meal where all contribute, a *k'oa*, and native dances (*danzas autóctonas*).[128] These ritual practices surrounding hydraulic labor did not begin in the 1990s but rather have their own deep history.[129] What changed in the 1990s was that ethnic identity became politicized and a tool to defend and claim territory, natural resources, and rights. This helps explain why Bolivia experienced, in anthropologist Carwil Bjork-James's words, a "revival of indigenous self-identification" in the 1990s.[130]

Cochabambino smallholders' defense of community water rights and management flowed from and contributed to new international and national laws recognizing indigenous and peasant communities' rights to use and control natural resources. The International Labor Organization (ILO)'s 1989 Convention 169, ratified in Bolivia in 1991, and Bolivia's 1994 Popular Participation Law gave legal status to indigenous and peasant communities and recognized their historical rights to manage their territories and natural resources.[131] The 1996 "Ley INRA" affirmed communities' rights to manage their natural resources according to traditional practices and recognized communities' right to participate in renewable use of natural resources in accordance with ILO Convention 169.[132] The new approach turned an existing gap between Bolivian law and practice into a contradiction within the law itself. While the new statutes recognized indigenous and peasant communities' management of "their" natural resources, the constitution held that natural resources such as water belonged to the national state, the 1999 Municipalities Law gave municipalities the right to manage rivers and springs, and the post–Water War 2000 Drinking Water and Sanitation Law established the state as the owner of all national hydraulic resources. Nevertheless, myriad water rights holders like irrigator cooperatives, peasant unions, ex-*hacendado* families, independent neighborhoods, and SEMAPA customers now had greater legal backing for their property rights claims.

In the 1950s the revolutionary coalition had supported state management of oil and mines, what historian Kevin Young has called "resource nationalism." Whether to support state management of water in the 1990s was a more complicated question. Even in the 1950s, peasants mostly demanded water redistribution, not state management. In the 1990s residents of excluded Zona Sud neighborhoods demanded SEMAPA service but expressed ambivalence about inclusion in a city that had historically erased, criminalized, and maligned them. Smallholders had even less reason to trust that state institutions would look out for their interests.

THE PATRIMONY OF COCHABAMBA

City center, peripheral, and rural water users' conflicts with SEMAPA from the 1970s through the 1990s ironically prepared the Cochabamba Valley's population to defend the company against privatization in the late 1990s. President Gonzalo Sánchez de Lozada's administration first announced its intention to turn SEMAPA over to a private company in July 1996, when the World Bank and the IDB demanded that SEMAPA privatize in order to keep its loans. The Capitalization Ministry announced that it would begin the bidding process immediately and passed a decree reorganizing SEMAPA's directorate, removing the mayor as board president and replacing him with a presidential appointee, and transforming SEMAPA into a "metropolitan" company that would service the broader region. Whether the result would be privatization, capitalization, or a concession was unclear.

These unilateral actions set off protests in Cochabamba and fierce debates about municipal autonomy and water property. At first, local protest was over the process of privatization rather than privatization itself. The mayor, Manfred Reyes Villa (1993–2000), and the Civic Committee agreed that private sector investment was necessary to improve water service and supported a concession arrangement in which a private company would rent SEMAPA for forty years. In exchange for making a profit, the company would invest a significant sum to improve and extend service. But on the operative questions—who the private company would rent SEMAPA from, how much it should be required to invest, how much it should be allowed to raise rates, where increased water sources should come from, and who should oversee the concession process—the national government and municipal officials parted ways. Popular groups, in contrast, were opposed to privatization altogether. A little-remembered yearlong antiprivatization struggle from 1996 to 1997 combined legal action with popular mobilization to fight Sánchez de Lozada, the World Bank, and the IDB's effort to privatize SEMAPA.

The main issue was who owned SEMAPA and its assets. While the Sánchez de Lozada administration considered water sources and even infrastructure to be national state property, the broad cross-class movement that arose throughout the valley to define the terms of and ultimately oppose privatization contended that the population owned water sources and systems. They appealed to the concept of "patrimony" that refers, as Robert Albro has explained, to "collective inheritance or property," including collective rights to natural resources like water. These claims drew on the 1985 Municipalities Law that defined municipal resources as patrimony and the 1994 Ley de Participación Popular that established the category of cultural patrimony.[133]

Reyes Villa, a member of Banzer's ADN party and rival of President Sánchez de Lozada, criticized the government for "seizing the proprietary rights of the population."[134] When the Cochabamba prefect, a presidential appointee, argued that national government contributions had been so great that SEMAPA was 85 percent national state property, Reyes Villa retorted that "it was absurd to talk about patrimony in percentages," adding that "SEMAPA was born and remains a municipal institution."[135] The Civic Committee rejected privatization without local consent, affirming that the company was a "product of Cochabambinos' sacrifices" meant to serve them alone, and that the committee would not let SEMAPA become "a company for profit."[136] The Cochabamba Engineers Association demanded local oversight over the privatization process, arguing that SEMAPA along with its infrastructure and water sources were the "patrimony of Cochabambinos" who alone should determine the company's future.[137] While these organizations opposed the government's undemocratic approach, they ultimately agreed that SEMAPA should be privatized.

Popular urban organizations opposed national control over privatization and were more skeptical than the mayor and civic committee elites about privatization itself. The FEJUVE and the SEMAPA workers union opposed privatization in any form. Privatization, they argued, would constitute theft of Cochabamba's patrimony—both SEMAPA and the local water supply—and make water unaffordable. SEMAPA workers also feared that they would lose their jobs. Charging the World Bank with "using the loan as blackmail for privatization" and claiming SEMAPA as the "patrimony of Cochabamba's people," the SEMAPA workers' union declared a state of emergency and permanent mobilization against privatization.[138] The union claimed that 70 percent of SEMAPA belonged to its customers because the company had been "consolidated on the basis of the self-help system." When the new board of directors arrived for their first meeting, SEMAPA workers blocked the entrance to the company compound with a tractor.[139] Residents of the El Temporal neighborhood, the site of SEMAPA's headquarters, declared their own state of emergency and called on the Civic Committee, the FEJUVE, and professional organizations to join them in "defense of Cochabamba's patrimony."[140] FEJUVE leaders agreed that privatization was theft of "Cochabamba's patrimony" and feared that only the wealthy would be able to afford water.[141] Criticizing the Civic Committee for what he called its passive attitude, FEJUVE leader Eloy Luján announced that the organization would "make its own decisions, convoking residents to take to the streets against privatization."[142] Yet the FEJUVE soon agreed to support a concession if the government met its demands and guaranteed local participation in the process.

Rural groups, including provincial officials and peasant organizations exhausted but emboldened from ongoing "well wars," strongly opposed the plan to turn SEMAPA into a metropolitan company. Provincial civic committees declared that the national state should "assume responsibility for improving the quality of life of the population" without "appropriating the modest patrimonies of municipalities that had managed to build decentralized water companies and drinking water cooperatives in the face of longstanding abandonment by the central government."[143] Like their neighbors in the capital, they feared theft of their water sources and systems and inflated prices for drinking and irrigation water, appealing to the principle of municipal autonomy enshrined in the 1985 Municipalities Law to make their case.

All of these groups united against privatization in the decade's third Marcha por el Agua y la Vida in March 1997. The marchers supported Reyes Villa's lawsuit against the federal government demanding the reversal of SEMAPA's reorganizing and the end of privatization negotiations without local participation. The march was organized by Cochabamba's new Departmental Water Commission that was comprised of representatives from the prefecture, the mayor's office, the Municipal Council, the Civic Committee, Empresa Misicuni, SEMAPA, the FEJUVE, and the Society of Engineers. The COD, the transport union, the SEMAPA union, the university student union, the small business owner's federation, the Federación de Gremialistas, and local congressional representatives also helped organize the march. The commission asked the government to postpone bidding until it dealt with local concerns, especially fear that local funds and foreign financing totaling $60 million would be handed over to the concessionary. The commission demanded that the concessionary be required to carry out the Misicuni project as the city's new water source instead of developing the Corani reservoir, which had been dammed in the 1960s in a World Bank–funded hydroelectric project.[144] While the governing MNR party of President Sánchez de Lozada supported the Corani project, which they argued could provide as much water as Misicuni at lower cost with less risk, opposition parties including Cochabamba mayor Manfred Reyes Villa's NFR backed Misicuni.[145]

Organizers and participants' statements, placards, and chants displayed their consciousness of Cochabambinos' long-standing contributions to expanding water access and their belief that the fruits of water users' labor belonged to them. The march flyer declared that "all of the patrimony accumulated by SEMAPA comes from contributions by the people, generated by ongoing rate increases and the original contribution by the municipality." The transport union, which provided free transportation to the march, declared, "we cannot allow our patrimony...to be handed over to foreigners who will subordinate us as they please."[146] Luján predicted that the march would be "multitudinaria" because "we Cochabambinos are tired of plans being carried out at our expense and efforts to take over our patrimony."[147] The mayor called on the population to mobilize against the "política entreguista" ("sell-out policies") of the Sánchez de Lozada government and its plans to "liquidate Misicuni."[148] Artisans, transport workers, students, housewives, retirees, teachers, workers, and local politicians brandished placards reading "SEMAPA no se vende, mueran los políticos capitalistas" and "El agua es vida, el MNR es muerte." They chanted in unison "Viva Cochabamba, SEMAPA, y Misicuni!" and "Corruptos, escuchen, SEMAPA no se vende."[149] These were the slogans of Cochabamba's popular hydraulic society.

As marchers flowed into the September 14th Plaza, the mayor proclaimed, "SEMAPA belongs to the Cochabambinos," and avowed that Cochabamba would not allow its water company to be "stolen" or the Misicuni project to be "buried."[150] A Transport Federation leader referred to the project as "life for Cochabambinos" and threatened a twenty-four-hour civic strike if the government did not answer the marchers' demands.[151] When the government failed to meet them, the strike went forward. A bustling assembly of teachers, factory workers, press union members, FEJUVE representatives, mayor's office functionaries, and Catholic priests organized a hunger strike to protest the government's intransigence.[152]

By June it was clear that the concession was in trouble. The Supreme Court stripped the government of its legal authority to oversee bidding on SEMAPA's concession during its deliberations. When it seemed that President Sánchez de Lozada planned to visit the city to sign contracts anyway, Reyes Villa barred the president and his entourage from using city streets that "belonged exclusively to the municipality."[153] Capitalization minister Alfonso Revollo, concerned that potential investors might be scared off by local opposition, wrote to the companies who had submitted proposals alerting them that bidding would be suspended until the Supreme Court emitted its decision.[154] World Bank representatives were also concerned. During a loan project supervision visit, Bank officials expressed doubt that the concession would be successful, now blaming the national government's unilateral approach and concurring with Cochabamba officials and protestors that "water and sewage services are municipal."[155] The World Bank resolved that it would cooperate in "strengthening" SEMAPA and other urban water services only once national and municipal officials coordinated with each other, as if the Bank had played no role in the national government's intrusive approach.[156] Meanwhile, a commission of Cochabamba municipal authorities and representatives was en route to Sucre to explain "the spirit of Cochabamba's demand" to Supreme Court justices.[157]

In June 1997 the Bolivian Supreme Court nullified the bidding process. In spite of ongoing conflict between the city and the countryside over water and between SEMAPA and its customers over rates, the population united against the threat to local autonomy, the "family economy," and the Misicuni project, forcing the national government to work with local authorities, promise affordable rates, and require the concessionary to carry out the Misicuni project. A month after the Supreme Court handed down its decision, Sánchez de Lozada issued a decree recognizing SEMAPA as a decentralized company belonging to the Cochabamba municipality, returning the SEMAPA Board of Directors chairmanship to the mayor, and establishing provincial representation on the directorate.[158] The decree represented a victory for Reyes Villa and for Cochabambinos who claimed that SEMAPA belonged to the municipality.

Incredibly, the World Bank concluded from this experience that it should condition future loans for water projects on private sector involvement in service management and delivery. The Bank's 1998 project completion report blamed the failure of privatization on "local political intervention" at odds with the best interests of the public, implying that Reyes Villa and the Civic Committee had opposed privatization and the Corani project out of self-interest.[159] Although this was undoubtedly true, it does not explain why the public rallied behind them. Bank officials concluded that improving service would require privatizing SEMAPA and tapping an affordable new water source like the Corani reservoir rather than carrying out the expensive Misicuni project. They worried that the protestors' victory in forcing the government to require the concessionary to carry out the Misicuni project had put the concession at risk because its high cost would deter companies from bidding. Despite the conditions imposed from Cochabamba, the national government remained committed to privatizing SEMAPA.

In the late 1980s and the 1990s, Cochabamba water users fought SEMAPA over rates, exclusion, and wells. State institutions and their international partners went to great lengths to exert authority over water sources, systems, and rates as part of a broader mission to "rationalize" the water sector. SEMAPA often acted as an arm of the state and an emissary of international financial organizations. But water users also defended SEMAPA against privatization. In these fights water users strengthened their organizations, formed new ones, and defended control over water sources, systems, and projects they considered their own. When a former dictator, banks that had been pushing deep wells and rate hikes, and a United States–based transnational tried to dispossess Cochabambinos of hard-won water sources and infrastructure, peasants, periphery residents, and SEMAPA customers were ready to confront them.

CONTRACTING AGUAS DEL TUNARI

By the time the government initiated a new bidding process in 1998, former dictator Hugo Banzer had retaken the presidency—this time legally. Congress chose Banzer as president after he won a plurality (22.3 percent of the vote) in the 1997 elections. In exchange, Banzer formed a mega-coalition government that included his ADN party along with the MIR, NFR, UCS, and CONDEPA—every significant party except the MNR. With Banzer's victory the winds shifted in favor of the Misicuni project. But, like his predecessor, Banzer was committed to water sector privatization. Banzer's ally Manfred Reyes Villa, who had won three consecutive mayoral elections in Cochabamba with more than 50 percent of the vote, and the NFR-led Cochabamba Civic Committee helped facilitate the government's contract with Aguas del Tunari. This coalition seemed to think that by advancing the Misicuni project, it could both score points against Sánchez de Lozada and the MNR and get Cochabamba's population on board with privatization. They were correct on the first point, sorely mistaken on the latter.

Tensions had continued to simmer after the 1997 victory for local autonomy. While the Civic Committee accepted the government's concession plan and urged the population to accept it in order to create an "atmosphere of international confidence," the FEJUVE demanded to know what privatization would mean for water rates.[160] In July 1998, as residents faced continued water rationing, the national government imposed a rate hike with the explicit aim of making SEMAPA "more attractive" to potential international investors. In response, the FEJUVE declared a state of emergency and the Civic Committee proclaimed that it would not accept a new increase until the Misicuni project was complete.[161] Cochabambinos objected when they learned that the concession authorized an additional 40 percent rate hike, 20 percent upon concession and an additional 20 percent upon completion of the Misicuni project's first phase.[162] In reply, national water superintendent Luis Uzín warned that if they wanted water, and especially if they wanted Misicuni, "Cochabambinos would have to make sacrifices."[163] National authorities had little room to maneuver as the World Bank had explicitly conditioned its loans on the prohibition of any state subsidies for water rates in Cochabamba.

While rate hikes and renewed plans for privatization were under way, Valle Bajo agricultural communities faced off with SEMAPA in a new conflict over wells in 1998. As they had previously, state officials and engineers presented themselves as experts, claiming that water table levels had reached an "equilibrium" and that additional deep wells were the only solution to water scarcity in the city. El Paso and Vinto farmers along with urban environmental activists countered that existing wells had already lowered the water table and damaged crops. A team of inspectors from the Valle Bajo found that new deep wells would "destroy homes" and cause "cracked soil, desertification, and homes to sink into the earth at any moment." A Valle Bajo Irrigators Association report concluded that while SEMAPA had invested $30 million in wells, none of the wells produced more than 50 liters per second.[164] SEMAPA officials answered that drilling was a "technical, scientific question" that should be addressed by engineers and blamed drought and cracked land on El Niño effects like erosion. When thousands of peasants blockaded Cochabamba's main highway waving the Bolivian flag and *wiphalas*—checked, multicolor flags representing native peoples of the Andes—they were met with rubber bullets and teargas.[165]

Although Cochabamba's Human Rights Assembly and the COB condemned police violence, FEJUVE representatives and some Zona Sud neighborhood leaders supported well drilling and demanded that authorities "punish instigators."[166] When SEMAPA moved to drill wells on military property in El Paso, peasant leaders threatened to remove drilling equipment from the site, cut off water to SEMAPA, and crucify themselves along Avenida Blanco Galindo. Thousands of peasants vowing to "defend our natural resources" used machinery, trucks, logs, and stones to block the roads leading out of Cochabamba.[167] Peasant unions expressed sympathy for the suffering of city residents but urged officials to pursue Misicuni instead. FEJUVE representatives nevertheless claimed that opposition to well-drilling was "political" and threatened to "confront groups in the Valle Bajo in order to obtain water for our children."[168] With President Banzer's support and under police protection, SEMAPA drilled several wells on military property in El Paso. Frustrated peasants vowed to petition the government for exclusive rights to surface and underground water on the basis of "ancestral uses and customs."[169]

Meanwhile, the Bolivian legislature was drafting a new water law that would define the terms of privatization. Aware that the law would likely affect irrigators' water rights, FEDECOR followed this process closely—and got involved. The federation held workshops on the proposed water law starting in 1998, inviting national authorities to explain the draft legislation and hear irrigators discuss "what *usos y costumbres* were for us." When irrigators learned that the proposed law did not protect *usos y costumbres*, FEDECOR formed a commission to draft its own law. FEDECOR's proposal rejected the commercialization of water, declared water a social right, demanded respect for *usos y costumbres* and community management, and called for government-issued water property titles definitively recognizing water property rights as well as the right to tap additional water sources as needed.[170] In August 1998 twenty thousand irrigators converged on Cochabamba's main plaza to deliver their proposal to the Cochabamba congressional brigade. They were joined by cocaleros and Evo Morales, then a congressman and head of the *cocaleros*' union federation, who marched from Cochabamba's tropical Chapare region to support the irrigators' proposal.[171] Over the next year FEDECOR continued to hold workshops in Cochabamba's four principal valleys, where federation leaders learned more about the region's systems of *usos y costumbres*. They recount that government officials also held workshops in these communities, not to consult irrigators and peasants but to promote the draft law even as irrigators were fighting SEMAPA over new deep wells.[172]

When the government opened bidding for the contract to administer water in Cochabamba, Civic Committee, FEJUVE, and other officials applauded. Civic Committee president Edgar Montaño declared bidding signaled "a future of hope" for Cochabamba. FEJUVE president Alfredo Gómez García avowed that the "historic decision" to initiate bidding "showed President Banzer's willingness to solve Cochabamba's water crisis structurally." Cochabamba "should be happy," he said, at this "new step toward realization of the Misicuni project" and "modernization" of SEMAPA that would together bring "abundant water." Even provincial civic committees were pleased, deeming bidding "a passport for promoting development and support of the whole department, due to the great benefits that the water, irrigation, and electricity will bring." Cochabamba congressman Oscar Torrico considered the decision an effort "to end a half century of betrayals, delays, and swindles" and "begin new phase of Cochabamba's development."[173]

Only one company submitted a bid, an international consortium registered in the Cayman Islands called Aguas del Tunari. The consortium was comprised of International Waters, a subsidiary of the construction firms Bechtel (US) and Edison (Italy) that held 55 percent of shares, the Spanish construction company Abengoa that held 25 percent, and four Bolivian contractors that held 5 percent each. Fearful that they would lose their only bidder, government representatives negotiated the terms of the contract directly with consortium executives, sweetening the deal's terms. The contract guaranteed the company a 15–17 percent return and gave the company exclusive rights to provide and charge for drinking water and sewerage services, set water rates, sell irrigation and bulk water, and use the region's water sources. The agreement also cut the Misicuni project down to what the Society of Engineers called a "bonsai" version. Lowering the required height of the dam from 120 meters to 90 meters meant postponing the project's irrigation component and reducing the amount of water and electricity it would provide.[174] In theory, the contract even prohibited rainwater collection, as immortalized in William Finnegan's *New Yorker* article "Leasing the Rain," one of the first reports on the Water War in the United States, and the Spanish film *También la lluvia* (*Even the Rain*).[175]

As the public learned about the contract's terms, water users began to organize. In July 1999 a group of Cochabamba professionals, environmentalists, and urban water committees formed the Committee for the Defense of Water and the Popular Economy (Comité de Defensa del Agua y la Economía Popular, CODAEP) in opposition to rate hikes and other terms. Members of the Cochabamba Society of Engineers played a leading role in CODAEP. Unlike in the past, the society now opposed SEMAPA's plans to drill additional deep wells due to their high cost, low productivity, and harmful effects.[176] FEDECOR followed contract negotiations closely and had been on alert about the implications of SEMAPA's privatization since its founding. The federation continued to hold workshops on the proposed water law and worked with CODAEP to warn the population about rate hikes as contract negotiations continued.

In September 1999 the Bolivian government signed the contract with Aguas del Tunari, awarding the consortium a forty-year concession for water provision in Cochabamba.[177] The following month, Congress passed Ley 2029 de Agua Potable y Alcantarillado Sanitario (not a general water law as planned) that gave the contract legal backing and a legal framework. The law established that "private entities could participate in water and sanitation service provision" and gave concessionaries exclusive rights to provide water in concession areas, thereby prohibiting the collection of water without permission from the newly established national water authority SISAB. It established that zones serving more than ten thousand inhabitants could be granted in concessions to private companies for forty years. Nonconcessionary zones with fewer than ten thousand users could apply for licenses valid for just five years. The law also gave concessionaries the right to use public goods "free of charge," including "soil, subsoil, air, roads, streets, plazas, and any others required to provide service."[178] Finally, it threatened not only service cuts but also legal sanction for failure to pay bills.[179] The law thus threatened expropriation of independent neighborhoods and irrigators' water sources and systems—and the interests of all of the groups that had been organizing around water in Cochabamba over previous decades who had often won their demands while organizing separately. Like hydraulic studies conducted in preparation for privatization, these provisions appealed to rationality and efficiency to justify privatization.[180] By November 1999, Aguas del Tunari had taken over SEMAPA's offices and operations.

As with other reforms, the reality of concentrating power in the hands of national regulators, a private transnational company, and IFIs like the World Bank contradicted the rhetoric and logic of decentralization. The new national regulation system, aimed at facilitating private sector involvement in the water sector, replaced mechanisms for consumer and municipal control over quality and rates. To justify giving concessionaries exclusive provision rights in concession areas, state authorities endorsed the idea of a "natural monopoly" in the water sector at odds with the capitalist principle of free-market competition.[181] They also argued that private sector involvement and national oversight was needed because municipalities had not provided good service. But private companies like Aguas del Tunari planned to improve service—and make a profit—by raising rates, something SEMAPA had tried and mostly failed to do for three decades.

Law 2029 and the contract with Aguas del Tunari alarmed Cochabamba's in-dependent water owners, including members of neighborhood water cooperatives and committees on the city's periphery and irrigators in the countryside. They feared Aguas del Tunari would charge them to use their own water sources and systems and that any alternative water provision system could be considered ille-gal.[182] When the contract was signed, FEDECOR leaders tried but failed to obtain a copy. "The only thing we knew was that they were giving all of SEMAPA's water to Aguas del Tunari," FEDECOR leader Omar Fernández later wrote.[183] Just after Law 2029 was passed, FEDECOR held one of its workshops on the water law. Once participants learned of the passage of Law 2029, they became "very angry" and the seminar "became an assembly."[184]

FEDECOR opposed the contract and the law for four reasons. First, irrigators objected to the separate and unequal systems of forty-year concessions for com-panies like Aguas del Tunari and five-year licenses for water rights holders like the irrigators and the fact that national authorities controlled concession grants and licensing. As Omar Fernández declared at the time, "We who are owners and have worked our wells, embankments, and lakes, are only going to be able to take out a license for five years." At the end of five years, "we could lose our property rights."[185] Second, they criticized authorities for failing to consult water users who would be affected by the new water regime. Third, they opposed paring down the Misicuni project. They worried that if Misicuni did eventually provide irrigation water, agro-industrialists would be able to pay steep prices but irrigators would not.[186] Fourth, they feared that allowing Aguas del Tunari to widen its conces-sion area to include Quillacollo and Sacaba without additional authorization, and granting the company the right to develop any additional water sources it deemed necessary to expand service, endangered water sources used by irrigators.[187] As Fernández warned at the time, "the contract opens the possibility that the conces-sionary could have free access to any water source...without taking into account its use by communities and peoples."[188]

On November 4, FEDECOR organized blockades across the region to broad-cast irrigators' concerns and measure their forces. Irrigators and neighborhood committees mobilized in large numbers in the Valle Bajo, the Central Valley, and Sacaba and in smaller but significant numbers in the Valle Alto, where irrigator unions had been less militant. In Vinto irrigators decided to overrule their leader-ship and continue their blockade after the planned twenty-four hours were up, demanding that national authorities come to negotiate with them directly. The na-tional water superintendent arrived and signed an accord agreeing to suspend well drilling and respect irrigators' water sources. But FEDECOR leaders soon learned that the accord could not trump Law 2029 or the contract. Meanwhile, police and soldiers forced irrigators to shut down their blockades. At this point, according to Fernández, the irrigators realized they needed allies to win changes to the contract and the law.[189] FEDECOR leaders reached out to urban organizations affected by rate hikes and threats to periurban water systems, including the COD, the *fabiles*, the teachers union, provincial civic committees, and CODAEP. On November 12 around twenty organizations from across the region formed the Coordinadora de Defensa del Agua y de la Vida (Coordinating Committee for the Defense of Water and Life). There were some conspicuous absences, however.

The Civic Committee, the FEJUVE, the transport union, and the FSUTCC at first backed Law 2029 and the contract. These organizations were all aligned with Manfred Reyes Villa and his NFR party and therefore with the national governing coalition that had negotiated the contract.[190] According to FEDECOR leaders, FEJUVE president José Orellana even accompanied Aguas de Tunari personnel to neighborhood meetings where they talked up the advantages of the contract.[191] Once rates shot up and protests began to mount, Mayor Reyes Villa broke with the governing coalition, claiming to have been "deceived."[192] The FEJUVE and the Civic Committee followed suit but called for renegotiation, not annulment of the contract. As one group of analysts explained, "the Civic Committee maintained its support for the concession process and for negotiating peacefully so that the water company would not abandon the city because the committee was convinced that this would be a great loss for the region.[193] As opposition to the contract and the law grew, the Civic Committee lost legitimacy due its support of the contract, its leaders' ties to the NFR, and its efforts to discredit the Coordinadora and position itself as the only legitimate body for the government to negotiate with.

Among the 2000 Water War's key participants were SEMAPA customers, members of water committees and cooperatives on the urban periphery, and irrigators, groups that had been divided on water issues in the past. When the Coordinadora called its first protest in December, Coordinadora spokesperson Oscar Olivera recalls that organizers assumed the turnout would be small given that, as he put it, "the interests of city dwellers and country dwellers had often been opposed" since "increased supply of city water came at the expense of water for the farmers." On the day of the protest, however, ten thousand peasants, provincial town residents, periphery dwellers, and SEMAPA customers filled the streets.[194] For the first time since the 1952 Bolivian revolution, urban and rural popular groups mobilized together around a common cause, this time to defend collective ownership of water sources and infrastructure.

COCHABAMBA'S 2000 WATER WAR

This account of the Water War starts in the countryside where organization against the new water regime began and then spirals inward to the Zona Sud, the northern periphery, and the city center to flesh out motivations on the ground across the region before chronicling the Water War and its outcome. Although different constituencies had differing histories and ways of accessing water depending in large part on where they lived, they all considered themselves owners of the region's water sources and infrastructure and opposed privatization on this basis.

Irrigators from the Valle Bajo and Central Valley were the first to mobilize against the water law and among the first to oppose the contract with Aguas del Tunari. Irrigator associations organize their members to collectively build, maintain, and manage water and require strict discipline to ensure that that every family participates in labor and management. As sociologist Lorgio Orellana Aillón has poignantly observed, "frequent meetings and assemblies dealing with irrigation issues and collective labor to dig and clean canals...help unify what the excessive division of land had succeeded in dividing."[195] FEDECOR leaders attribute these careful decisions about water in part to respect for Mother Earth. As FEDECOR leaders Fernández and Peredo have written, "We have to take care of water because the Pachamama could become angry."[196]

While some scholars consider such use of "Andean identity frames" and links to "the past and 'Andean heritage'" to be "strategic" or "imagined," this book has shown that irrigators' invocation of ancestral uses and customs references historical processes of rights allocation and property rights acquisition through inheritance, purchase, revolutionary-era redistribution, and labor.[197] Irrigators played a central role in the Water War due to their claims to water sources and systems that they built and managed and their experience defending water rights against earlier national government, SEMAPA, and IFI efforts to dispossess them.[198] Irrigators were not only experts in building and maintaining water systems, they also became authorities on water law. This experience proved crucial during the Water War when, as FEDECOR leaders later put it, they gave the broader population confidence "that the people too can make laws."[199]

Like irrigators, residents of provincial towns like Quillacollo, Vinto, and Sipe Sipe mobilized against Aguas de Tunari's takeover of wells that urban neighborhoods administered autonomously. Angelo Paredes and Rodrigo Cruz, leaders of the Quillacollo Federation of Retired Miners, recounted that the government and the company's argument that subsoil resources like aquifer water belonged to the state served as "legal camouflage" for their efforts to "confiscate wells that [irrigators] and neighborhoods administered in associations or small groups" and "charge us for water that we supplied to ourselves." In their view the wells were collective private property.[200]

Residents of Zona Sud neighborhoods with their own water sources and systems like Villa Pagador participated in the Water War en masse. As Villa Pagador resident and water committee representative Esteban Yanez explained, "When Aguas del Tunari arrived, they wanted to charge us to use our wells, so the Zona Sud got angry. In the countryside too they wanted to charge people to use water from mountain springs. They even wanted to charge for rainwater." He and others recalled that residents went to the city center every day to protest. "We were gassed, there were bullets, but we still went every day and finally everyone [in the neighborhood] began to understand and cooked for those protesting in the streets."[201] Primero de Mayo resident and leader Antonio Heredia attributed his neighborhood's mobilization to the fact that the contract made Aguas del Tunari "the owners of our water systems that they had not paid a single Boliviano for." Like Yanez, Heredia emphasized shared interests with irrigators. The Zona Sud and irrigators joined "the Water War because we opposed the company making itself the owner of our wells," he told me. "In this way we made history." Heredia attributed his neighborhood's involvement to "the revolutionary character" that miners "carry in our blood." In his view miners' experiences and culture made them natural leaders in the fight against water privatization. "We taught the people how to act according to solidarity, how to participate in assemblies," Heredia told me. "Every time there was a conflict, we always held a large assembly and oriented and informed the people. These practices came from the mines."[202] His wife Isadora Alemán recounted that twenty to thirty vans carrying Primero de Mayo men and women went to marches in the city center "anytime the loudspeaker convoked us."[203]

ASICA-Sur president and Primero de Mayo resident Abraham Grandydier agreed that miners played a crucial role but credits the Water War's victory to the fusion of and overlap between miners and peasants' experiences. For Grandydier, the way families took turns going to protests and operating barricades owed to Andean peasant traditions of community work (*minka*) and reciprocity (*ayni*) and collective organization flowed from miners and peasants' common syndical experience. Like FEDECOR leaders, Grandydier also referenced the place of water in Andean cosmovision. "In the Water War, there was this vision of the Pachamama, the Mother Earth, who calls to her children. In the Andean cosmovision, water is the sacred blood of the Pachamama, of the earth, which nourishes us and without which we cannot live."[204] It would be a mistake, as some researchers have done, to dismiss such framing as somehow false. In the years preceding and following the 2000 Water War, many Cochabambinos identified long-standing values and practices as part of a broader Andean indigenous cultural world, whether or not they had before. Those values took on new meaning in the context of the struggle over privatization.

Neighborhoods on the northern periphery also rose up against what they saw as dispossession. The ex-*colono* community Tirani, whose residents are members of the Cochabamba peasant federation, descended from the foothills into the valley much as they had in 1952 to join blockades in Cala Cala. Joaquín Arias, who was twenty-four years old at the time, recounted, "They told us they were going to give us new canals and improve infrastructure. But the problem was they were going to charge us for water."[205] In Chilimarca, Teodoro García Hinojosa explained that residents protested privatization because "water is a natural resource. The people asked, 'if God gives it to us how can they do this?' Water comes from a spring. They wanted to enclose it in a pipe and then sell it to us. So the people began to react and said we are not going to allow this."[206] Zenón Mercado attributed Chilimarca residents' opposition to their work building water systems. "Here we had worked for nine years trying to get official authorization" to use sources and canals "we had worked hard to excavate. We had paid all of the costs of cement, sand, and other materials and paid a quota of $95" to create the system.

According to Miguel Palma Chambi, when the Coordinadora called marches, "everyone [in Chilimarca] participated. Everyone went on foot to fight."[207] Guadalupe Yacupaico recounted, "We all took turns, especially the women, who suffered greatly. We even slept there" in the city center.[208] Residents of Nuestra Señora de Guadalupe, another neighborhood on the northern periphery, also saw privatization as theft of their property. There, resident Agustín Rojas explained, "We rose up against Aguas del Tunari because the concession gave them our water project. We who had invested our money and had worked personally had to give it to someone who had done nothing and who on top of that was going to charge us to use it! Aguas del Tunari did not have any capital other than that which we had given them."[209]

Cocaleros, organized in the Seis Federaciones del Trópico, and their leader Evo Morales supported the Coordinadora from the beginning of the conflict. As Marcela Olivera told me, "many cocaleros live on the periphery of the city" so their "communitarian water systems were affected as well."[210] Like opponents of water privatization, *cocaleros* in the Chapare were fighting for their livelihoods and against what they saw as plunder of their natural resources by the national government and powerful foreign interests. The Water War offered Evo Morales and his MAS party an opportunity to increase their visibility in the department capital and across the country. While Coordinadora spokespeople proudly denied having electoral ambitions, Evo Morales was a congressman working to build a national profile.

The foremost grievance of city-center residents with SEMAPA service was rate hikes. According to Bechtel, the poorest residents' rates only went up 10 percent, the highest increases of 106 percent were reserved for the heaviest water users, and extreme increases owed not to dramatic changes in water rates but rather to increased water use made possible by the increased supply Aguas del Tunari provided. The company justified what they claimed were modest rate increases as necessary to pay for the Misicuni dam, SEMAPA's debt, and a water treatment plant, among other contract requirements.[211] Protesting customers, however, reported rate increases of upwards of 200 percent across the board. [212]

As Juan Sánchez Ayala, a lawyer who participated in the Water War, explained, "The government sold water to transnational companies without consulting the people, a policy that benefited big companies at the expense of the people. Water bills that had been Bs. 20 or 30 previously suddenly charged Bs. 120 to Bs. 150 or Bs. 200."[213] Scholars Humberto Vargas and Tom Kruse have cited examples of families whose bills increased as much as 285 percent.[214] Furthermore, many neighborhoods with SEMAPA service had been incorporated into the municipal system in exchange for water sources and distribution systems that residents had purchased and constructed themselves.

While the FEJUVE leadership supported privatization and supported Civic Committee efforts to discredit the Coordinadora, a newly formed parallel federation called FEJUVE-Pueblo rallied 199 neighborhood committees in a December 13 march against rate increases and joined the Coordinadora. During the Water War, neighborhood residents erected barricades, took turns keeping watch and feeding blockaders, and participated in mass meetings, marches, and other actions.[215] SEMAPA customers were loath to accept national water superintendent Luis Uzín's argument that higher rates were necessary to fund expansion to the city's poorest areas.[216] After all, officials had made this argument for thirty years without having adequately expanded distribution—and obtaining foreign capital for supply and distribution expansion was the rationale for privatization.

The factory workers union was the only urban union to play a prominent role in the Coordinadora and the Water War.[217] Coordinadora representatives attribute the union's leadership role to the "open-door" policy it had developed to reach Cochabamba's large unorganized informal working class.[218] This work made the union visible to large sectors of the population and gave it, in *fabriles* leader Oscar Olivera's words, "credibility with the people." The *fabriles'* central role in coordinating the Water War flowed from factory workers' unique position at the intersection of the informal unorganized workforce and organized labor, and of the city and the countryside. While there were forty thousand to fifty thousand factory workers in Cochabamba, only around six thousand were unionized. Factories are located on the city's outskirts, so factory workers often live in rural communities where they own land and possess water rights as members of peasant unions or irrigators associations. As a result, there was a "natural alliance," in Olivera's words, between irrigators and factory workers. Workers not directly connected to the countryside, like Olivera himself, began to learn about irrigators' "collective property, their drinking water systems that they had created with so much effort." During the Water War, the *fabriles* organized protests in each factory and helped coordinate peasants, provincial town residents, peripheral neighborhoods, and city-center residents to take collective action.[219]

The Coordinadora met at the *fabriles'* office, conveniently located on the corner of the main September 14th Plaza where mass meetings and protests occurred and marches converged. Olivera recounted that "little by little, as the hosts, we began to direct the assemblies and to speak in the name of the Coordinadora." Coordinadora leaders called themselves "spokespeople" to stress their accountability to the masses. Olivera, who became the Coordinadora's most prominent spokesperson, emphasized "we are not leaders, we are spokespeople and a product of a social movement."[220]

Olivera was born in Oruro in 1955 and migrated to Cochabamba while he was still a child. He began working in factories at sixteen years old. In 1978 he started working at the Manaco shoe factory in Quillacollo, where he became involved in the union. While Olivera values the syndical experience he and the *fabriles* brought to the Coordinadora, he and other representatives worked to make the Coordinadora more responsive and accountable to its base and less hierarchical than many Bolivian unions. Sociologist Carlos Crespo has praised Coordinadora representatives for their "great capacity to listen," a quality he says "had been lost among political and union leaders."[221] Coordinadora activists opposed gaining legal status so that, in the words of one representative, if "the popular movement stopped supporting the Coordinadora at some point, it would no longer exist."[222]

Like FEDECOR and periurban water committee representatives, Coordinadora representatives connected the fight over water to a long history of indigenous rebellion against imperial dispossession. According to a Coordinadora statement, this history showed "that it was impossible to create an integrated society with a solid basis of cultural equality without recognition of indigenous nations' rights and demands to autonomous forms of government in their extensive territories."[223] The hundreds of thousands of Cochabambinos who participated in the Water War were a diverse group that included people who identified in ways not easily reducible in ethnic terms. Some considered themselves mestizos, perhaps with indigenous heritage. Others considered themselves Aymaras. Still others *campesinos* or *regantes* (irrigators). While most *campesinos* and *regantes* speak Quechua as their first language and many freely mix Spanish and Quechua in conversation and meetings, few would call themselves Quechuas. They usually identify instead as *campesinos* or *regantes* and rural and periurban women sometimes call themselves *cholas* or *cholitas*. Each of these terms carries class, spatial, and ethnocultural implications. As anthropologist Olivia Harris has written about Bolivian cultural identity generally, "everything is mixed but not everything is mestizo."[224]

The Coordinadora's references to indigenous struggles reflected the population's connections to indigenous heritage and culture and linked Cochabamba's fight for water to other Bolivian social movements. As Robert Albro has explained in his study of urban politics in Quillacollo, there is a "popular, working-class, urban indigenous" world in Cochabamba "not necessarily recognizable in territorial or even collective terms."[225] The Water War coincided with other protests across the country, including police and health workers' strikes and altiplano Aymara community mobilizations against the proposed water law and the Ley INRA.[226]

Coordinated collective action among these different groups and government intransience turned the conflict into a war between the national government and the region's water users. In the months that followed the first mass rally in December 1999, a series of open mass meetings (*cabildos*), citizen strikes, rallies, and marches demanded that the government terminate the contract with Aguas del Tunari, repeal Ley 2029, and force the company to reverse rate hikes. The first "battle" occurred in January 2000 when the Coordinadora called on residents to refuse to pay their hiked water bills and a *cabildo* of thousands of participants called an indefinite citizen strike and blockade that lasted four days. The Civic Committee called a parallel twenty-four-hour strike against rate hikes that merged with the blockade. The strikers gave the government three months to meet their demands. When the government refused and police met protestors with teargas, residents burned their water bills in the plaza.[227]

The second battle took place in February when the Coordinadora called a demonstration it called "the takeover of Cochabamba" ("la toma de Cochabamba"). While organizers assured authorities that they meant "takeover" symbolically and that the protest would be peaceful, the government deployed the military's Special Security Forces, known as the "dálmatas" ("dalmatians") for their black-and-white uniforms, from La Paz to police the city. The marches began at various points around the city. Valle Bajo and Central Valley residents congregated at the overpass west of the city, Zona Norte and northern periphery residents gathered in the Cala Cala neighborhood, Sud Zud residents met on the southern end of the city's large outdoor market, Valle Alto marchers converged just south of the city, and Sacaba Valley residents converged at the Muyurina Bridge.[228] Before the marchers had even set off, the *dálmatas* launched teargas and began clubbing protesters.

Meanwhile, in a blatant attempt to divide urban and rural protestors, a plane dropped fliers reading, "compañeros campesinos, the government recognizes that the water belongs to you. You are being deceived. Go back to you communities."[229] In the face of repression that recalled the days when Banzer ruled as a dictator, city residents spontaneously fed protestors, gave them vinegar to reduce the effects of teargas, and threw paper and cardboard from their windows for them to burn.[230] The government agreed to a temporary rate freeze but otherwise ignored protestors' demands. In March the Coordinadora organized a popular referendum on the contract, a new tactic within Bolivian social movements. At voting stations across the region, more than sixty thousand people voluntarily cast votes. The vast majority rejected the contract with Aguas del Tunari and the 1999 water law.[231]

The final showdown took place over eight days in April after the three-month deadline passed without any response from the government. On April 4 one hundred thousand Cochabambinos heeded the Coordinadora's call to the streets. They shut down the city and surrounding region and faced brutal repression from the military and police. Rather than deter them, many participants reported that repression inspired greater numbers of people to fight harder and united people

FIGURE 10. Crowd gathered in Cochabamba's 14 de Septiembre Plaza during the last battles of the Water War in April 2000. Photo by Tom Kruse.

from the wealthiest neighborhoods to the poorest corners of the periphery and countryside. Juan Sánchez Ayala recalled that "in every neighborhood, people came out with their banners" and residents distributed food, water, and vinegar. "It was all about solidarity," he said. "People didn't get tired. They marched for hours."[232] Concurrent actions took place in the Chapare, La Paz, El Alto, and the Altiplano.[233] After a week of marches, rallies, and *cabildos* to determine next steps, meetings with government officials facilitated by the Catholic Church, the occupation of the offices of Agua del Tunari and the Civic Committee, detention of Coordinadora representatives, and violent clashes with the military and police that left seventeen-year-old Victor Hugo Daza dead and more than one hundred people wounded, the government agreed to rescind the contract with Aguas de Tunari and modify Ley 2029 according to the Coordinadora's demands. Meanwhile, protestors tore down the Aguas del Tunari sign and replaced it with one that read "Aguas del Pueblo."[234]

Coordinadora strategy deftly combined direct action with a willingness to negotiate and compromise.[235] Its actions creatively combined classic forms of protest, including marches, strikes, and blockades, with new kinds of spectacular direct action like the symbolic takeover of the city, burning water bills, graffiti, and popular referendums.[236] *Cabildos* dated back to early nineteenth-century independence movements, but Water War *cabildos* were far larger and far more diverse than their late colonial predecessors. The more the government refused to meet the movement's demands, the more radical those demands became. The Coordinadora coordinated action among a multitude of water users who claimed collective ownership of the region's lakes, springs, wells, dams, canals, pipes, and tanks and had experience managing and defending them.

CONCLUSION

The victory of an antiprivatization movement in a relatively small city in South America's poorest country against the World Bank, the Inter-American Development Bank, a transnational consortium, and the Bolivian national government at first seems unlikely. But the history of social struggle over water in the Cochabamba Valley reveals the origin of this power. Unlike previous privatizations in Bolivia, water privatization in Cochabamba did not merely privatize a state-owned industry or public service. Ley 2029 and the contract with Aguas del Tunari expropriated resources owned and managed not only by the municipal water service SEMAPA but also by peasant communities, irrigators' unions, and urban neighborhoods and residents with long-standing claims to the water sources and systems being privatized. Neoliberalism found its weakest link in Cochabamba's water sector because it threatened collective ownership of the region's water sources and systems.

The Water War brought together groups with extensive experience engineering and managing water sources and systems and defending access to them. While they had vied over water access in the past, during the Water War peasants, irrigators, provincial and peripheral neighborhoods, and SEMAPA customers united to defend water systems they considered collective property. Their power rested on significant control over water sources, infrastructure, engineering, and governance established over decades of social struggle, organization, labor, and investment. The 2000 Water War was the culmination of a long history of social struggle over water. The movement's slogan "¡El agua es nuestra, carajo!" ("The water is ours, damn it!") embodies this history. Over the course of the twentieth century, popular groups in Cochabamba had built a popular hydraulic society in which rural, peripheral, and urban residents owned and managed water sources and systems and set the terms of hydraulic development. In the Water War they built on their experience and expertise. They organized not only to defend that popular hydraulic society but also to pursue an alternative vision of modernity with abundant water for all that would necessitate subsidized water for all of the region's water users, cost recovery be damned.[237]

By bridging their differences and forging solidarity over access to a scarce and vital resource, Cochabambinos opened up the possibility of establishing a more

FIGURE 11. Banner reading "¡El agua es nuestra, carajo!" ("The water is ours, damn it!") hangs from the balcony of the Central Obrera Departmental (COD) building in Cochabamba's 14 de Septiembre Plaza during the final mobilizations of the Water War, April 2000. Photo by Tom Kruse.

bottom-up, direct, and participatory democracy. Bolivia's "return to democracy" in 1982 was more an arrival at an impoverished form of democracy where elite political parties sacrificed the well-being of the majority on the altar of economic stability. Between 1985 and 2003 state violence during protests in Bolivia led to 280 deaths, 700 injuries, and more than 10,000 illegal detentions, leading some observers to call Bolivian democracy a "democradura," an elected government that ruled like a dictatorship.[238] In the 1990s and early 2000s Bolivian social movements deepened democracy, drawing on the experience of the 1952 revolution but also introducing new concerns and approaches. In the 1990s those fights were largely defensive struggles against a powerful array forces that included the national government, the United States, and international financial institutions. That changed in 2000.

During the Water War, Cochabambinos pried open political space on the streets and in the plazas, overcoming and perhaps healing divisions among residents of the city, periphery, and countryside. Yet the alliance among urban, periurban, provincial, and rural groups was precarious, based in part on shared interests but also on a common threat to collectively but nonetheless exclusively owned water sources and systems. The challenge would be to maintain an approach based on solidarity after defeating privatization.

After the War

Water and the Making of Plurinational Bolivia

Cochabamba's 2000 Water War was transformative locally, nationally, and internationally. In Cochabamba it created a model for bottom-up, participatory, and direct democracy in the water sector and politics more generally. In Bolivia the defeat of water privatization was the first reversal of a neoliberal privatization and a major victory for the country's "new social movements." It opened a five-year period of social movement mobilization that brought down two presidents, paving the way for the election of Evo Morales, the country's first indigenous president, in 2005. In the Andes, and Latin America more broadly, the Water War and Morales's rise to power were part of a new period of social upheaval and election of leftist "Pink Tide" governments. Around the world opponents of water privatization heralded the Water War as an example to emulate and an indication that the tide was turning against neoliberal globalization. Meanwhile, privatization proponents studied the conflict to rethink their approaches.

Defeating privatization was a major triumph for Cochabamba's popular hydraulic society. Cochabambinos restored control over water sources and systems to the municipal water company SEMAPA and myriad water cooperatives and committees across the valley. In these same years the Misicuni dam project broke ground after two decades of popular demands. These successes have not, however, secured water for all. The problems facing the valley before 2000 have endured. SEMAPA still only serves the wealthier half of the city, residents of the Zona Sud still pay astronomical rates to private water vendors, and water rights are still distributed unequally in the countryside. As Cochabambinos wrestled with these realities in the two decades after the Water War, a central question was who was best prepared to deal with these inequities: state institutions, independent associations of water users, or some combination?

In the years after the Water War and during Morales's presidency (2006–2019), Cochabamba water activists called for a constitutional assembly to refound Bolivia as a plurinational state. Having united and mobilized different groups across class, ethnic, and spatial lines, the Coordinadora offered a model for a grassroots representative body that could democratize access to the commons and public goods and establish just stewardship of natural resources. In his campaign Morales promised to convoke such an assembly and once he was president made good on that promise. The resulting 2009 constitution refounded the country as the Plurinational State of Bolivia in recognition of the nation's indigenous peoples. Rights enshrined in the new charter included autonomous control over territory and resources like water.

In the Morales years a tension at the heart of the Water War came to the fore: should the state take responsibility for social welfare, or should responsibilities like water provision devolve to civil society organizations such as neighborhood committees and irrigators associations? At issue was not only what entities were best prepared to provide and improve water service but also whether and to what extent state power and popular interests could converge. While in many ways the Morales government continued earlier efforts to consolidate state power over local resources like water sources and infrastructure, water users had more room to maneuver than in the past. Not only did popular mobilization frequently check state power; at times, the agenda of popular groups coincided with the agenda of the state, leading popular actors to align with the MAS-led government. This chapter discusses the aftermath and impact of the Water War locally, nationally, and globally and examines water politics during Morales's presidency.

REFOUNDING SEMAPA

The Water War produced immediate legislative results. On April 11, 2000, the Bolivian Congress passed a new Drinking Water and Sanitation Services Act that made thirty-six modifications to Ley 2029, the November 1999 law that set off the Water War. The new Ley 2066, drafted by a working group of legislators and Coordinadora leaders, promised universal access to efficient, reliable, high-quality, sustainable, and affordable drinking water and sanitation services provided to beneficiaries according to "socio-economic criteria and social equity."[1] The law importantly recognized that a diversity of organizations provided water and sanitation services. These providers, denominated in the law as Water and Sanitation Service Providers (Entidades Prestadoras de Servicios de Agua Potable y Alcantarillado Sanitario, EPSAs), include public municipal companies, private companies, cooperatives, civil associations, indigenous communities, peasant unions, and independent water committees and systems.[2] The law also recognized *usos y costumbres*, defined in its text as "social and community hydraulic resource use and management practices for providing drinking water and sanitation services based on socially agreed-upon natural authorities, procedures, and norms of originary and indigenous peoples, indigenous and peasant organizations, and peasant unions."[3] Ley 2066 thus offered the possibility of legal recognition of vernacular hydraulic governance according to historic uses and customs to Bolivia's more than five thousand independent water systems.[4] But there was a contradiction at the heart of this law with a long history that foreshadowed tensions to come.

While the law recognized historical claims to autonomous water management, independent water systems' ability to operate was subject to state approval. An EPSA had to first gain legal status and then apply to the Water and Sanitation Superintendency (SISAB), the new national regulatory agency, for a license or registry to continue using water and providing services.[5] And like all statutes dating back to the 1938 Constitution, the law declared water sources the original property of the state.[6] While the law implicitly recognized that usos y costumbres had historically determined how water rights were allocated, from then on national authorities planned to exercise oversight.

The 2004 Irrigation Law (Ley 2878), passed in response to FEDECOR's proposal, also embodied this contradiction. Under Ley 2878, irrigators' unions won legal recognition and protection for their historical and collective rights. But the law granted the national state unprecedented authority over irrigation water rights allocation without helping smallholders who did not have historic claims. The governing board of the new Servicio Nacional de Riego (SENARI) now had the power to recognize, grant, and revoke irrigation water use rights to "indigenous and originary peoples, indigenous and peasant communities, and peasant associations, organizations, and unions...according to their usos y costumbres."[7] Such intervention in rights allocation is fundamentally at odds with a key aspect of *usos y costumbres*: that water-using communities and entities determine allocation and settle disputes. Furthermore, formalizing rights freezes a hitherto historical process at a particular moment in time, codifying inequalities within and among water-using communities and thereby hollowing out the core of *usos y costumbres*—their flexibility according to changing agreements among users.[8]

Tensions were pronounced in Cochabamba's city center as water activists attempted to democratize SEMAPA. After Aguas del Tunari's departure, local officials, activists, and water users experimented with new governance arrangements in the water sector. Municipal officials along with Coordinadora leaders retook control of the company, establishing an interim board of directors including Coordinadora leaders that immediately reset water rates at pre-privatization levels. While municipal officials were content to regain control of the utility, Coordinadora leaders proposed creating a new "self-managed social company" owned by its users.[9] As they wrote at the time, "The Coordinadora's assembly affirms that collective wealth such as water should be... managed by those who use it."[10] They envisioned water users themselves, not Coordinadora leaders, managing the company.[11] As a Coordinadora statement avowed, "decision-making power... should reside in the organized structures of painstakingly built neighborhoods, water committees, and unions."[12] Coordinadora leaders thus proposed that a majority of SEMAPA's board be elected by the community and that drinking water committees be established in every neighborhood.

Although the governing structure of SEMAPA changed somewhat, reforms fell short of Coordinadora activists' vision. The effort to reconstitute SEMAPA as "social property" met with stiff resistance from municipal and SEMAPA officials who argued that trained experts were better prepared than the average citizen to manage water. One former SEMAPA general manager opposed participatory management because, in his words, "this country... has not yet reached [the] maturity of First World countries."[13] Water committees within the city center did not materialize and activists had to settle for three community-elected seats on a seven-member board.[14] Omar Fernández attributes the outcome to activists not having generated support for social control over SEMAPA "at the grassroots."[15] Indeed, by the time restructuring efforts occurred, the Coordinadora's power to mobilize water users had waned. In the first elections fewer than 4 percent of those eligible voted, and by 2010 the community seats were vacant.

Coordinadora activists and SEMAPA community representatives nevertheless worked diligently to build a more socially responsive municipal water company. Father Luis Sánchez Gómez, who represented Zona Sud residents on SEMAPA's board from 2002 to 2004, urged the board to clarify the relationship between SEMAPA and independent Zona Sud neighborhood water systems. He and others proposed establishing a comanagement arrangement in which SEMAPA "provides them with water and they distribute it throughout their neighborhoods using their own networks."[16] In late 2002, Cochabamba water activists held an International Seminar in Support of SEMAPA with representatives of organizations from Brazil, the United States, and Canada. Participants discussed rate structure reform, SEMAPA's relationship with independent systems, and how to increase supply and extend water and sewage networks, avoid dependence on foreign investors, protect ecosystems, and facilitate community involvement.[17]

Nevertheless, SEMAPA did not become a community-governed institution. Instead, it remained a bureaucratic, top-down, sometimes corrupt, and often inefficient public company dependent on international loans and private contractors. At the time of its reconstitution SEMAPA held $18 million in debt and lacked capital to fund service improvements and expansion.[18] Biannual public accountability meetings have been poorly publicized and poorly attended, decisions about the company's plans are made by managers and engineers, and the company has often failed to consult neighborhoods affected by its expansion projects.[19] One midlevel manager commented in 2011 that although things have improved, corruption and a culture of leaving projects unfinished persists. To purge these tendencies, he told me, "everyone would have to be fired, myself included." He added, "Everything should be technical, not political," meaning that service improvement rather than personal interests should guide SEMAPA's work.[20] Despite these difficulties, the company has attempted to address corruption and losses (around 50 percent of its supply is lost due to infrastructural deficiencies and illicit connections) and expand service. And Cochabamba water users have found other ways to make themselves heard, including on the international stage.

THE WATER WAR GOES GLOBAL

Cochabamba's dispute with Aguas del Tunari did not end with the contract's termination in April 2000. After attempts to reach an amicable agreement failed, Aguas del Tunari consortium members filed suit against Bolivia with the World Bank's International Center for Settlement of Investment Disputes (ICSID) in 2002 demanding $25 million in damages and another $25 million in lost profits. After the contract was canceled, Aguas del Tunari had transferred ownership of its assets from the Cayman Islands to the Netherlands with whom the Bolivia had signed the Netherlands-Bolivia Bilateral Trade Agreement (BIT) in 1992. Despite the Bolivian government's protest, the majority of the ICSID Tribunal voted to allow the claim to proceed under the terms of the BIT. Bolivia, the consortium, and the World Bank each chose one of the ICSID's three judges.[21]

For the first time in the ICSID's history, a third party petitioned for the right to intervene in the proceedings.[22] The petitioners included the Coordinadora and Oscar Olivera, the Cochabamba irrigators' union FEDECOR and Omar Fernández, a network of Zona Sud water committees called SEMAPA Sur and its founder Father Luis Sánchez, and the Dutch environmentalist group Friends of the Earth. The petitioners based their request on their "direct interest in the subject matter of this claim," the "lack of transparency that traditionally attends international arbitral processes," their "unique expertise and knowledge" related to the case, and widespread international support for their petition. The Coordinadora reasoned that the "tens of thousands of citizens of Cochabamba" it represented would have to pay severe rate increases and lose access to "affordable and equitable access to water" if the ICSID saddled SEMAPA with compensating the company.

FEDECOR argued that the livelihoods of its members, "thousands of small-scale producer families," would be threatened if a precedent was established "that rights to use and manage water could be undermined at any time by transnational corporations using secretive international processes." SEMAPA Sur contended that compensating Aguas del Tunari would destroy plans to extend SEMAPA coverage "in ways that complement, not threaten, local systems." The petitioners contended that the World Bank was not a neutral party given that the Bank had made privatization a condition for debt relief and water system expansion financing and that World Bank president James Wolfensohn had publicly supported rate increases during the conflict. Therefore the tribunal could not make an impartial decision without the petitioners' participation.[23] The popular groups that had won a place in water governance and defended autonomous control over water sources and systems in Cochabamba were now attempting to do the same on the world stage.

While the ICSID denied the request, activists forced Aguas del Tunari consortium members International Waters, Bechtel's water subsidiary, and Abengoa to drop their case through an international activist campaign. Coordinadora activists benefited from relationships with international solidarity activists, including Jim Shultz, head of the Cochabamba-based Democracy Center originally founded in Shultz's native San Francisco. The Democracy Center publicized the Water War through a newsletter, circulated over email via a dial-up Internet connection, and spearheaded a campaign to bombard Bechtel and Abengoa with emails demanding that they withdraw their case at the ICSID.[24] Oscar Olivera also built relationships with international activists on tours and at global conferences. He began his October and November 2000 tour of the United States and Canada in Washington, DC, where the Institute for Policy Studies awarded him the Letelier-Moffitt Prize. On a return trip in 2002, Olivera led a protest march to Bechtel's headquarters in San Francisco. Activists shut down Bechtel's headquarters in San Francisco on two occasions, both Bechtel and Abengoa received thousands of emails, and citizen groups from forty-three countries signed a petition demanding that the World Bank open the case to public participation.[25] Olivera also collaborated with US activist Tom Lewis to publish a book in 2004 that publicized the Water War in the United States.[26]

In December 2005, four years after filing suit, International Waters and Abengoa agreed to accept two Bolivianos (the equivalent of around $0.25) for their combined 80 percent share of the company's stock.[27] According to Bolivia's lead negotiator, Bechtel CEO Riley Bechtel decided that the "case wasn't worth the damage to the company's reputation."[28] A joint statement issued by the Bolivian government and Aguas del Tunari's international shareholders maintained that "the concession was terminated only because of the civil unrest and the state of emergency in Cochabamba and not because of any act done or not done by the international shareholders of Aguas del Tunari."[29] These positions inadvertently recognized the role of Cochabambino water users in expelling Aguas del Tunari and in preventing consortium members from winning compensation.

The Water War seems to have pushed the World Bank to rethink water privatization. A Bank report evaluating the failure of privatization in Cochabamba blamed "political interference" but acknowledged that farmers' opposition owed to fear that "new wells would jeopardize their irrigation water" and that municipal customers opposed higher tariffs in the context of rationing. The report concluded that "privatization is not a panacea," that a "pragmatic approach tailored to local circumstances should be adopted for effective institutional development," and that "private sector participation in the [water] sector must demonstrate tangible benefits."[30] A 2009 article coauthored by a World Bank analyst found that Latin American cities where water service had been privatized had no better service than those served by public utilities, even though privatized companies raised rates in order to eliminate subsidies and "earn a fair return on their capital."[31] And a 2017 World Bank–commissioned paper found that small user-operated systems and big public utilities complement each other in cities with water supply difficulties. Rather than recommend privatization, the report concluded that governments should oversee coordination efforts.[32]

Across the world, antiprivatization movements adopted the September 2000 "Cochabamba Declaration" as a rallying cry and hailed the Water War as proof that neoliberal policies could be defeated. The document proclaimed water sacred, a "fundamental human right," and a resource "best protected by local communities and citizens."[33] While some international activists focused more on the Water War's success in restoring public administration of urban drinking water service and others highlighted the successful defense of independent water systems, all agreed that the Water War was an important victory for community control over water against corporate profiteering.[34] As Indian activist Vandana Shiva wrote in her preface to Olivera's book ¡Cochabamba!, "Bolivia's Water War and water democracy is not just an inspiration for us all. It also provides political education for every community struggling to reclaim their commons and public spaces in this age of corporate globalization."[35] Activists and scholars have drawn on Cochabamba's experience to argue for reclaiming natural resources for human need rather than corporate profit.

For many Global Justice activists, the Water War offered a new model of fighting corporate globalization that involved organizing both unionized and informal workers in a "multitude form" around what Olivera called "basic conditions for life and social reproduction."[36] As weakened labor movements struggled to confront neoliberal assaults on unions, the number of unorganized informal workers in the Global South grew. At the same time that public services and natural resources were privatized, work-place resistance and economic demands seemed to become outmoded due to downsizing and outsourcing. In his 1999 book La mirada horizontal, Uruguayan journalist and political theorist Raúl Zibechi critiqued the twentieth-century left and labor movements as subservient to capital and the state and celebrated innovative forms of struggle emerging from new "democratic, horizontal, participatory, and autonomous grassroots organizations."[37] Bolivia's 2000–2005 uprisings, especially the Water War, seemed to bear out Zibechi's horizontalism thesis and helped him develop it further. In his 2010 book *Dispersing Power*, a study of community and revolution focused on El Alto, Zibechi argues that "community administration of water" in Cochabamba exemplifies "a society without a state" with "a multiplicity of indivisible communities."[38]

So too, the Coordinadora's role in the Water War bolstered social theorists Michael Hardt and Antonio Negri's theory of the multitude, which they defined as "an open and expansive network in which all differences can be expressed freely and equally" and "that provides the means of encounter so that we can work and live in common."[39] Although these thinkers concurred with sociologist John Holloway that social movements should "change the world without taking power," others like Argentine theorist Claudio Katz warned that "refusing to take over the state preserves the status quo and consolidates the impoverishment of the dispossessed."[40] Whether social movements should contend for state power and if so, how, became urgent questions in Bolivia in the early 2000s that generated debates and differences among Cochabamba water activists.

Soon after the Water War, Coordinadora activists called for a national constituent assembly to refound the nation in the interest of Bolivia's poor, working-class, and indigenous majority, echoing the demand of lowland indigenous organizations during national marches in the 1990s. Coordinadora activists first called for a constituent assembly in September 2000 at the moment when protesters in the Altiplano were demanding annulment of the Ley INRA and withdrawal of the water law then before Congress, *cocaleros* were protesting forced coca eradication in the Chapare, and teachers and students were demonstrating in El Alto and La Paz.[41] The goal of a constituent assembly was to scale up from the experience of the Water War to demand, in Oscar Olivera's words, "full social justice." This could only be achieved, Olivera argued, by "forging a new democracy" that is "neither delegated nor representative, but authentic, participatory, direct, and without intermediaries."[42] Cochabambinos' experiences managing water and defeating privatization produced a belief that ordinary people could create public institutions, laws, and a new constitution to create a more just and equal society. As Olivera wrote at the time, the "experience of managing public affairs in a specific area—the distribution of water"—is "rebuilding people's confidence in their ability to see to their own needs."[43] While they were not the first to make it, Coordinadora activists were well positioned to introduce the proposal for a constituent assembly to social movements around the country.

The Coordinadora gradually dissolved in the years after the Water War. Although member organizations continued to coordinate joint actions at times, they mostly returned to working independently. One possible explanation for the Coordinadora's short life is that it had successfully eliminated the common threat to collective water sources, systems, and governance that privatization had posed.[44] But it also owed to political differences among Coordinadora leaders over how to relate to Evo Morales's government. While some leaders distanced themselves from state-sponsored reform efforts, others participated in the new Water Ministry (which had been proposed by water activists), the Constituent Assembly, and the legislature.[45] The heir of the Coordinadora, an NGO called Fundación Abril, was founded in 2002 by Olivera with the winnings from his 2001 Goldman Environmental Prize. Fundación Abril is dedicated creating a society based on "the exercise of economic democracy" that "preserves and recuperates water as a common good."[46] Although Olivera and many other Cochabamba water activists maintained their independence from the Morales administration and the MAS party, others worked within the government to try to forge a new democracy.

FROM THE STREETS TO THE PALACIO QUEMADO

During the five years of social upheaval following the Water War, two lines of thinking on state power emerged within Bolivia's left and indigenous social movements. One set of activists, including many who participated in the Water War, was wary of electoral strategies. Another group, led by Morales, championed an electoral approach. Through strikes, roadblocks, rallies, and marches, from the Altiplano to the valleys to the lowlands, social movements built enough power to defeat the parties that had implemented neoliberal restructuring, first on the streets and then at the polls.

Morales's participation in the Water War helped him gain a national platform. As Cochabamba water activist Abraham Grandydier told me, "Before the Water War Evo Morales was isolated in the Chapare." Thanks to his participation in the Water War, people across the country began "to see him as a leader fighting on behalf of humble people."[47] After being expelled from Congress on charges that he was responsible for violent *cocalero* protests that led to the death of five soldiers, Morales ran for president in 2002, garnering an astonishing 21 percent of the vote, only 1.5 percentage points behind the winner, Gonzalo Sánchez de Lozada. Another indigenous candidate, Rafael Quispe, won 5 percent of the vote, meaning that for the first time most of the indigenous majority voted for indigenous candidates.[48] As a result, the number of indigenous legislators grew from 10 to 52 out of a total of 130.[49] Like Banzer in 1997, Sánchez de Lozada won the runoff in Congress and formed a weak governing coalition with other establishment parties committed to privatization.

At the turn of the twenty-first century, Bolivian social movements staged uprisings opposing privatization, foreign control over natural resources, and other policies that increased the cost of living. As scholar Benjamin Kohl has explained, "opposition groups were able to tie a common nationalist thread around what (to outsiders) often seemed disparate" issues, including coca eradication, gas nationalization, and water privatization.[50] These were all questions of control over natural resources. In 2002 *cocaleros* confronted state eradication efforts and violence, earning them sympathy and support across the country. In February 2003 a wide array of groups protested new taxes imposed by the Sánchez de Lozada administration in response to International Monetary Fund (IMF) pressure to reduce the national deficit. Military repression in what became known as the Tax Revolt left twenty-three people dead.[51] In October 2003 protests erupted against a government plan to allow a transnational consortium to export gas through Chile to Mexico and the United States.[52]

Mobilizations in El Alto, La Paz, altiplano communities, and other parts of the country were coordinated by the Coordinadora Nacional por la Defensa y Recuperación del Gas, a network that Oscar Olivera helped form in July 2003. Protesters called for nationalization of gas (the state oil and gas company YPFB had been privatized in 1996), refining it in Bolivia, using proceeds to improve living conditions, and refounding the country through a constituent assembly, a set of demands that became known as the October Agenda.[53] After state forces violently repressed protesters, killing seventy-three people and injuring hundreds more, Sánchez de Lozada fled Bolivia for the United States.[54] Vice president Carlos Mesa assumed the presidency, promising to reform the hydrocarbons industry, call a constituent assembly, and refrain from using force against demonstrators.[55]

Conflict over water privatization arose in La Paz and El Alto in these years as well. In 1997, at the behest of the World Bank, the Bolivian government had granted a thirty-year concession to administer the two cities' water service to an international consortium called Aguas del Illimani South America (AISA). The consortium's lead member was the French water company Suez, which held 55 percent of shares. IFIs considered the contract to be "pro-poor" because of its focus on expanding connections. Although the company did increase connections, it did so within the contracted service area where customers could afford to pay and excluded hard-to-reach areas of El Alto home to the metropolitan area's poorest residents. Even within the "served area," high connection costs left seventy thousand residents without service.[56] In total, around two hundred thousand *alteños* lacked connections.[57] While protests against Aguas del Illimani began soon after the concession was granted, in 2004 and 2005 El Alto's FEJUVE built on the momentum of the Gas War to organize large mobilizations demanding cancellation of the contract due to high rates, poor service, and exclusion.[58] Like in Cochabamba, El Alto water users rejected privatization in favor of local control over water provision.

Strikes, blockades, and a massive protest march in January 2005 pushed President Mesa to cancel the contract. He did so through legal channels to avoid liability, however, which meant paying the consortium indemnification. The Morales administration later agreed to pay investors $5.5 million in compensation and assume all of the company's debt.[59] After AISA's departure the Water Ministry heeded the proposal made by FEJUVE–El Alto to set up commissions including water activists and to reorganize the public water utility as a transparent and participatory "social water company."[60] The new company, EPSAS, was founded in 2007 with the mission to extend "water to all." A decade later, EPSAS had extended coverage, but not to all.[61] In addition to budget deficits and dependence on foreign loans, the company is up against drier dry seasons and wetter wet seasons as glaciers that supply the metropolitan area melt.[62]

Ultimately, Mesa's ability to smooth over the rift between economic and political elites and social movements failed. His administration organized a referendum in 2004 on hydrocarbon industry reform, but it circumvented the issue of nationalization, leading many activists including Oscar Olivera to nullify their ballots.[63] Moreover, the promised constituent assembly never materialized. In May 2005 renewed protests calling for oil and gas nationalization and a constituent assembly broke out, forcing Mesa to resign.[64] A series of caretaker presidents ruled the country until new elections were held in December.

In each moment of social mobilization, from the Coca War to the Tax War to the Gas War to El Alto's Water War, Coordinadora and FEDECOR activists helped coordinate resistance. Over these years social movements and organizations around Bolivia adopted Cochabamba water activists' proposal, first made by lowland indigenous groups, for a revolutionary constituent assembly to decolonize Bolivia and refound the nation on the basis of collective rights to wealth and resources.[65] In 2004 some of the most important organizations behind the 2000–2005 left-indigenous revolutionary cycle formed the Unity Pact (Pacto de Unidad) to push for a constituent assembly.[66] The Unity Pact called for drafting a new constitution that would "completely refound the Bolivian State" as "an inclusive and plurinational state that would allow for building a shared country."[67] Creating a new economic model and promoting collective ownership of natural resources like land and water were foremost among their goals. Activists called the transformative agenda social movements proposed and the means they used to implement it the "proceso de cambio" ("the process of change").

In the first decade of the new millennium, from Bolivia to India, water became a symbol of the struggle against international financial institutions and transnational corporations. This symbolism was perhaps most beautifully captured in the short animated movie *Abuela Grillo* (*Grandmother Cricket*), a 2009 Bolivian-Danish collaboration inspired by a myth of the Ayoreo people, who are indigenous to the Bolivian lowlands.[68] In the movie, protestors in La Paz defeat large-suited blockheads who have kidnapped Grandmother Cricket and stolen the rain that her songs bring. Other than the suits' grunts and the demonstrators' protests and cheers, the only sound is Bolivian singer Luzmila Carpio's voice singing a song in Quechua asking the "soft little rain" to never cease. Like news of the Bolivian water wars, the video circulated around the globe. Released the same year that Bolivia ratified a new constitution refounding the country as a plurinational state, the movie celebrated the victories against water privatization in Cochabamba and La Paz–El Alto and looked forward to a future where communities would control life-sustaining natural resources.

WATER GOVERNANCE IN PLURINATIONAL BOLIVIA

Evo Morales rode the tide of social upheaval to the presidency, promising to "rule by obeying" the organizations and communities that made his election possible. At his January 2006 inauguration in Tiwanaku, a pre-Columbian ceremonial center, Morales pledged to respect and restore indigenous and peasant communities' autonomous control over their territories and the natural resources within them. He vowed to restore state control over extractive industries and deliver public services like drinking water in order to provide for citizens' well-being. More generally, Morales and the MAS positioned themselves as the defenders of the Pachamama, Mother Earth, and proponents of the principle of *vivir bien* (living well in harmony with nature). While Morales's commitment to public water provision sounded like a fulfillment of social movement demands, state intervention in water management brought the contradiction between community autonomy and state authority to the fore during his presidency. As anthropologist Arturo Escobar wrote in 2009, a key question for MAS leaders was whether they could "maintain their redistributive and anti-neoliberal policies while opening up more decidedly to the autonomous views and demands of social movements."[69]

Morales fulfilled his commitment to convoke a constituent assembly soon after taking office. But while activists had proposed that the constituent assembly "be convoked by society itself" and that social movements, unions, neighborhood associations, and other civil society groups elect representatives, political parties dominated the assembly and Morales's MAS party accepted the demand of the traditional parties that key articles pass with a two-thirds' majority.[70] The Constituent Assembly took place in Sucre from August 2006 to December 2007 amid threats and racist verbal and physical attacks on indigenous participants.[71] Despite intimidation and limits on its participation, the Unity Pact made a proposal based on social movement organizations' demands. Although neither Cochabamba Coordinadora nor Fundación Abril representatives participated in the Constituent Assembly, FEDECOR leader Omar Fernández promoted water reform at the assembly through the National Association of Irrigators and Communitarian Drinking Water Systems (Asociación Nacional de Regantes y Sistemas Comunitarios de Agua Potable y Saneamiento, ANARESCAPYS) he helped found in 2004.[72]

The Unity Pact proposed that water be considered a social good and a human right and that it be administered by a combination of public, place-based, and indigenous and peasant community organizations. Its first constitutional proposal included articles prohibiting water concessions, privatization, and exportation.

Other terms required the state to consult with indigenous and peasant communities around water use and to guarantee sustainable water use and equitable distribution, "prioritizing women, the elderly, indigenous people, and the poor."[73] The 2007 "consensus version" afforded more power and responsibility to the state. But it still insisted that "water resources and watersheds within the territories of indigenous, originary, peasant, and Afro-descended nations and peoples be managed according to their own rules, procedures, practices, uses, and customs." It also stipulated that public drinking water utilities "incorporate participation, co-management, and social control of users according to their own norms and procedures."[74] There was thus a tension in Unity Pact proposals between calls for the state to take responsibility for water provision and place-based community management.

The resulting constitution, ratified in a January 2009 popular referendum, refounded the nation as the Plurinational State of Bolivia, recognizing the rights of Bolivia's indigenous peoples and nations. The preamble credits the 2000 and 2003 Water Wars with inspiring the creation of a new state based on "collective coexistence with access to water, work, education, health, and housing for all."[75] The new charter affirms that "all people have the right to water" and to "universal and equitable access to basic services," including drinking water provision, and that "access to water and sanitation is a human right." Water and sanitation services therefore can neither be offered in concession nor privatized but rather are subject to a system of licenses and registries according to law.[76]

Like the Unity Pact proposal, the constitution embodies friction between state authority and community control: the text declares that water sources fall under the "exclusive jurisdiction of the central state" *and* that "indigenous, originary, peasant autonomies have control over irrigation systems, hydraulic resources, and water sources within their jurisdictions." Declaring water "a fundamental right for life," the charter charges the national state with "promoting use and access to water on the basis of principles of solidarity, complementarity, reciprocity, equity, diversity, and sustainability"; prioritizing the use of "water for life"; guaranteeing "water access to all inhabitants" with social participation; and prioritizing "conservation, protection, preservation, restauration, sustainable use, and integrated management" of water resources. Although it requires the national state to "recognize, respect, and protect uses and customs of communities, their local authorities, and indigenous and peasant organizations over water rights, management, and sustainable administration," the power and responsibility to provide and oversee water access and management lies with the state.[77]

The perspectives of Cochabamba water activists on the Constituent Assembly and whether to participate in the Morales administration diverged. Omar Fernández actively participated in the assembly and credits activists for approval of articles guaranteeing universal and equitable access to water, prohibiting water privatization, and recognizing water as a fundamental right necessary for life.

These principles served as the basis for new water legislation, proposed in 2011 by Unity Pact organizations, which the Bolivian legislature has yet to pass as of this writing.[78] Fernández worked both at the grassroots through irrigators organizations to develop and promote the law, within the legislature as an elected senator (2006–2009) to pass it, and then as coordinator of the Kanata Metropolitan Region from 2014 to 2016 to "protect and recuperate aquifer recharge areas."[79] Olivera, in contrast, accused the "impostor" Morales government of "confiscating and undermining" the *proceso de cambio* by, among other things, drafting the Constituent Assembly law behind closed doors and allowing political parties to appoint *asambleístas* "a dedo" such that the "new constitution did not have effective participation of the people."[80]

The 2012 Law for the Rights of Mother Earth took the new constitution's mandates further, tasking the state with ensuring equitable distribution of natural resources in order to establish a just society. The text established that the state should "reduce differences in Bolivian people's access to land, water, forests, biodiversity, and other components of Mother Earth" and to guarantee the "right of water for life" to build "a just, equitable, and solidarity-based society without material, social, or spiritual poverty." The commitments to eliminate "concentrations of landed property in the hands of private property owners or businesses" and establish "equitable conditions of access to water for consumption, irrigation, and industrial use" reflected the ambition and optimism of the times.[81] With the 2009 Constitution and the 2012 Law of Mother Earth, water for all became the law of the land.[82] But the question of what bodies should oversee water provision remained contentious.

At the urging of the Morales administration and water activists, the United Nations General Assembly declared water access a human right in July 2010. After campaigning for adoption of a constitutional right to water in Bolivia, Bolivia's ambassador to the United Nations, Pablo Solón, pushed for the United Nations to adopt it as well.[83] The UN resolution recognized "the right to safe and clean drinking water and sanitation as a human right" and called on states and international organizations to finance efforts to "provide safe, clean, accessible, and affordable drinking water and sanitation for all."[84] At global water forums in Kyoto, Istanbul, and Mexico, Bolivian and international water activists had pressured the UN to declare water access a human right to give citizens a legal basis for demanding that states supply water and opposing initiatives like privatization that curtail water access. As anthropologist Andrea Ballestero has written, "activists and community organizations" that promote treating water as a human right are "arguing against its mercantilization." They insist "that the prices charged for water" should not "follow market rationalities, take advantage of people, [or] generate profits" and see recognition of the human right to water as synonymous with its recognition as a public good.[85]

Yet others worried that the right to water might prioritize human use over ecosystems, could conflict with existing water rights regimes, and would not necessarily prevent privatization. Indeed, at the Fourth World Water Forum in Mexico City in 2006 a group of private water companies declared their support for the right to water. Soon after, Nestlé's CEO disavowed his earlier opposition and began to call himself a devoted supporter of the human right to water. As a result, as Ballestero has noted, "the boundary between a human right and a commodity" became "blurrier than ever" and many water activists came to see "human rights as weak anticapitalist tools."[86] Critics also argue that rights-based approaches establish the state rather than communities as the rightful guardians of natural resources like water.[87]

The Morales administration's efforts to put the human right to water into practice in Bolivia involved both assistance to and interference with nonstate water operators. Upon taking office, Morales promised to invest $528 million in water and sanitation between 2006 and 2010 and his 2006–2010 National Development Plan promised to increase water access for consumption, irrigation, and production in a policy called "Agua para Todos."[88] The plan aimed to extend drinking water service to 1.9 million of the 2.3 million Bolivians lacking it and to provide water to small farmers without rights while respecting *usos y costumbres*. The "Mi Agua" program provided $300,000 to each municipality for improvement of community water systems. In 2019 the Ministry of the Environment and Water reported that since 2006, the government had invested $292 million in drinking water and sanitation projects and another $141 million in irrigation and hydraulic resources projects, increasing drinking water access from 71 percent to 86 percent (95 percent in urban areas, 67 percent in rural areas) of households and putting 258,145 hectares of land under irrigation, benefiting 234,708 families.[89] Those numbers did not reflect issues with quality and quantity or reports of poor project execution, however.[90] Furthermore, government projects at times threatened the historic rights of smallholders and periurban water cooperatives that Morales had vowed to protect. Provision of Mi Agua funds, for instance, was contingent on municipalization of community water systems.[91]

Some Cochabambino water activists and scholars opposed enshrining the human right to water in Bolivian law. They stressed that the right to water that they fought for in the Water War was not a state-granted right to become paying public water utility customers but rather the right to autonomously govern water sources and distribution systems, whether they be irrigation systems, neighborhood systems, or municipal systems. As Oscar Olivera wrote in 2011, "In 2000, the people did not fight for water to be recognized as a human right. This is a pretty term on paper and for the north, but it goes against the concept of water as the blood of the Mother Earth, that water is a living being and a generous gift from Mother Earth for all living beings, including the earth itself, mountains, plants, and animals."[92]

For Olivera and other like-minded water activists, water for all meant water for all living beings. In a 2012 interview, however, Olivera called the inclusion of the human right to water in the constitutions of countries like Bolivia, Ecuador, and Uruguay "an important step" that should spread to other countries.[93]

Regardless of their position on the question of the human right to water, most Cochabamba water activists opposed the way MAS-led state institutions used the human right to water as a pretext for interfering with community control over water. Cochabambino sociologist and water activist Carlos Crespo has argued that "the principle of a human right to water serves to legitimate, in a new context, the long history of the destruction of water commons by the Bolivian state."[94] While Omar Fernández and other FEDECOR leaders' water law proposal stated that water is a "fundamental right for life" and a human right, Fernández opposed government mandates that community water systems share water "with businesses and other entities" that did not "take into account the drinking water system's capacity, above all the quantity of the source." In taking this approach, he says, the state offloaded "its responsibility according to the constitution to provide water" onto community systems.[95]

Human rights discourse and practice in Latin America came out of the experience of dictatorship in the 1960s, 1970s, and 1980s that led activists to look for ways to defend citizens against state terror. Adopting a human-rights approach was controversial among Latin American activists who, as historian Patrick William Kelly has written, fell on a "sliding scale between outright rejection and forthright embrace." Although some worried that wealthy countries and elites would employ human rights as an "ideological weapon" to depoliticize state violence and "mut[e] concerns over economic injustice," others found in it a "versatile vocabulary" they could use to build national campaigns and transnational solidarity movements to combat state violence.[96] Human rights activists appealed to international law to push international governing bodies like the United Nations and the Organization of American States to intervene in national affairs to protect human rights. Since then, as historian Jessica Stites Mor has pointed out, indigenous scholars, feminists, and others have critiqued human rights frameworks as rooted in a "Western model of political and economic development... that values individualism over community."[97]

Bolivian water activists have made similar critiques, adding that human rights privilege states over communities and people over ecosystems and other living beings.[98] At times, like their predecessors, Bolivian water activists have used human rights language strategically to make their demands legible to Bolivian lawmakers, global justice activists, and international governing bodies despite their reservations about this approach. But Bolivian water activists have also drawn on other grammars of rights with deep roots in Bolivia, including historical use, property, and governance rights. Olivera's seemingly contradictory position recognizes that rights-based approaches can mean different things and are applied in diverse ways. The shift from proudly declaring the human right to water in the 2000 Cochabamba Declaration to criticizing it a decade later can be explained by international water companies' appropriation of this discourse and the Morales administration's use of this principle to justify state appropriation of collectively owned water sources and systems.[99]

The key question in the water sector during the Morales presidency, which these critiques signal, was how and whether it was possible to expand water access to all while respecting autonomous community-administered water systems and rights. The Morales administration responded to popular demands for better water access in ways that, if successful, would strengthen state institutions. Like the project of legal decolonization that anthropologist Mark Goodale has studied, Morales's water policy "sought to salvage the instrumentalities of state power."[100] While critics alleged that MAS-led state institutions used the right to water enshrined in the 2009 Bolivian Constitution as a pretext to interfere with and dispossess autonomous water systems, MAS officials argued that it was sometimes necessary to challenge existing systems of rights allocation in order to provide water to all. After his administration secured passage of the new constitution and defeated violent opponents like separatists in the eastern "media luna" departments in 2009, the Morales government began to turn away from its commitments to social movements and a politics of liberation to fashion a pragmatic neodevelopmentalist state instead.[101]

"WE TOO ARE THE STATE": WATER GOVERNANCE IN COCHABAMBA UNDER MORALES

The tension between state authority and community autonomy enshrined in the constitution and environmental legislation reflected and contributed to ongoing conflicts over water in Cochabamba. As MAS-led state institutions expanded the state's reach in the water sector, water committees, cooperatives, and rural communities pushed back. But not all conflicts were between public institutions and community-run systems. Some involved competition between public water utilities. Others pitted different groups of water users against each other. Four axes of conflict over water access in Cochabamba during the Morales presidency illuminate the complex social geography of water governance in these years.

One type of conflict was between municipal water companies and neighborhood water committees that lacked independent water sources. With Japanese funding, SEMAPA extended coverage to northeastern Zona Sud neighborhoods. President Morales inaugurated the project in 2011, closing the event by turning on a water spigot that had been installed on the stage and spraying audience members.[102] But most of the Zona Sud remained outside the network by the end of Morales's presidency. Some water committees there built water storage and distribution infrastructure and purchased water from SEMAPA or private water vendors to supply their autonomous systems. Zona Sud water committees in these areas clashed with SEMAPA managers over prices and exclusion. In a SEMAPA public accountability meeting in 2011, for instance, Zona Sud representatives disrupted the proceedings, charging that SEMAPA had not made any serious plans to extend service. One neighborhood representative exclaimed, "We can talk about [the city center] not having water in the future but in the southeastern zone we have never had sufficient basic services." When a SEMAPA official replied that Misicuni would solve Cochabamba's water problems, the Zona Sud contingent shouted, "When?" Around forty people walked out, vowing to return when the board was ready to seriously discuss expansion.[103]

The architects of the IDB-funded Metropolitan Master Plan indicated that Misicuni water would supply these systems, but questions remained as to whether SEMAPA or neighborhood water committees would manage them. SEMAPA officials charged that many of these systems were poorly constructed and expressed reluctance to incorporate them into SEMAPA's network.[104] Abraham Grandydier, president of the Zona Sud water committee network ASICA-Sur (renamed ASICASUDD-EPSAS in 2010), envisioned a "public-collective" comanagement model that would allow water committees to continue administering their own systems with water from Misicuni.[105] But during the Morales presidency, ASICASUDD lost significant international funding and began to rely on MAS-run state institutions, weakening network and member committee autonomy.[106]

A second set of disputes arose between municipal water companies and peri-urban neighborhood water cooperatives that possess their own water sources. In Sacaba, the municipality just east of Cochabamba, for instance, the MAS-run municipal government tried to seize the independent water sources and distribution systems of neighborhood water cooperatives in order to build a new municipal water company there called EMAPAS (Empresa Municipal de Agua Potable y Alcantarillado de Sacaba). Municipal water officials appealed to the human right to water to justify incorporating the cooperatives into the EMAPAS system, arguing that the cooperatives exclude those who cannot pay steep entry costs.[107] The Quintanilla, Arocagua, and Puntiti water cooperatives date to the early 1990s, when these neighborhoods built water distribution systems and made agreements with irrigators to gain water sources.[108] Cooperative members and irrigators, concerned that EMAPAS's municipalization plan threatened their water rights, organized a joint march against the plan in September 2011. One of the march's organizers, Sebastián Chambi, explained that irrigators and cooperative members had "done everything possible to ensure that they administer water themselves."[109]

Irrigators who won water through agrarian reform in Pacata Alta now share their historical rights not only with the Quintanilla, Arocagua, and Puntiti neighborhood water cooperatives but also with SEMAPA.[110] SEMAPA gained partial

FIGURE 12. March against the Sacaba water service's plan to "municipalize" neighborhood cooperatives and irrigators' water sources, Cochabamba, September 2011. Photo by author.

rights to Lake Wara Wara in exchange for rebuilding the lake's dam that collapsed in 1995. Irrigators have also negotiated with mountain communities where the lakes that irrigators use are located.[111] Before EMAPAS's bid for cooperatives' water sources and infrastructure, water-sharing agreements in this area were forged among mountain communities, valley cultivators, neighborhood residents, and SEMAPA representatives who all respected other groups' water rights claims, even when vying for a larger share.

FIGURE 13. Lake Wara Wara and its dam, May 2011. Photo by author.

A third series of quarrels were between SEMAPA, which serves the Cercado municipality, and other municipalities and rural communities where nearly all of SEMAPA's existing or desired water sources are located. SEMAPA shares rights to the lakes Wara Wara, San Juan, and San Pablito with ex-*colono* communities. While these water-sharing agreements worked fairly well, other relationships were more fraught. When SEMAPA attempted to expand the Wara Wara system to tap lakes higher in the cordillera, *comunarios* from Coluyo Grande, a community near these lakes, blocked them with support from the Sacaba municipality where the lakes are found. The SEMAPA representative in charge of these consultations recounted that the national Water Ministry required that the company negotiate with *comunarios* there who demanded schools, irrigation works, drinking water service, and cash payments in return for water access.[112] These negotiations failed. While SEMAPA's representative suspected that Sacaba made Coluyo Grande a better offer, a Sacaba water service official maintained that the community simply "preferred to give water to the Sacaba municipality that it belongs to."[113] To make matters even more complicated, SEMAPA is supposed to "return" sources like the portion of Lake Wara Wara that it uses to the municipalities they are located in once Misicuni water arrives.

Another site of SEMAPA-community confrontation was in Chapisirca, the site of the Escalerani Lakes where *comunarios* demanded compensation for animals

FIGURE 14. El Paso residents protest efforts by Cochabamba's
municipal water service SEMAPA and Quillacollo's municipal water
service EMAPAQ to take over wells drilled for El Paso in the 1990s, El
Paso, August 2011. Photo by author.

swept away in SEMAPA's canals, a new union building, and road improvements.
Comunarios cut off water to the city, or threatened to do so, multiple times in these
years and in 2010 captured SEMAPA general manager Julio Vargas and two other
officials to press their demands. Former SEMAPA engineer Armando Leygue
attributed the problem to Escalerani communities' marginalization. "SEMAPA
is the only institution that goes up there so it is the only one that they can ask

for what they need," he explained.[114] The abduction forced SEMAPA officials to agree to community demands, but officials said that the company did not have the means, equipment, or authority to pave roads or construct union buildings. Nevertheless, SEMAPA allocated funds to build infrastructure for the community for the first time the year after the incident and asked the national government to build a union hall.[115]

SEMAPA also faced opposition in El Paso where the company operates wells drilled in the 1970s, 1980s, and 1990s. Quillacollo's water company EMAPAQ demanded that SEMAPA turn the wells over for Quillacollo's use, while El Paso residents insisted that SEMAPA cede the wells to them in a three-way power struggle. While SEMAPA originally made agreements for well drilling directly with El Paso, the MAS-led Quillacollo municipality and water company began to claim jurisdiction over the area in the 2010s.[116] SEMAPA officials responded that losing the El Paso wells would imperil water access in the Zona Sud.[117] In August 2011, El Paso residents staged a civic strike in a bid to take over the wells. At a rally in El Paso's central plaza, speakers alternated between Quechua and Spanish, as is customary in the Cochabamba countryside. El Paso Comité de Vigilancia president Pasqual Mendoza declared, "We helped them in the Water War. Now it is our turn to recover our water." Another speaker proclaimed, "With the new constitution, the wells belong to us. We are the children of the forgotten ones." More ominously, he added, "The third water war will be in El Paso, *compañeros*."[118] Discussing the question of water ownership before the rally, Mendoza told me, "We are the legitimate owners of the water. We too are the state."[119] Peasants frequently asserted state status to claim ownership of water in these years.

Many SEMAPA officials saw the state as the rightful owner of the nation's water sources and expressed frustration with communities and municipalities that blocked the company's access to sources needed to improve and expand service. SEMAPA general manager Julio Vargas, referring to Coluyo Grande and El Paso residents, charged, "They don't understand that there are people in the Zona Sud who only get water once a week."[120] Referring to Sacaba, he added, "Up in the mountains, each municipality thinks it is the owner. But the municipality does not own subsoil resources."[121] An Empresa Misicuni engineer told me that these conflicts stemmed from the increased power that rural communities had under Morales's government. "This is good, but they have gotten more aggressive," he added.[122] Armando Leygue concurred: "Before the people from the countryside were truly marginalized and this was a terrible thing. Only people from the city had rights. The problem is that now they are being given rights at the expense of people from the city."[123] He contended that peasants and indigenous people were misinterpreting the constitution, taking it to mean that they owned water that in reality belonged to the state and everyone. They are "taking advantage of being peasants to force us to comply," he told me.[124] A SEMAPA lawyer maintained that the reason

FIGURE 15. Lake Wara Wara overlooking Cochabamba's Central
Valley, May 2011. Photo by author.

the state owns public goods like water "is obvious: the state needs to take charge
of administration to avoid chaos and conflicts." He lamented that, thanks to Morales's policies, "the population has begun to consider itself the owner of land and
all its accompanying resources."[125] These SEMAPA and Empresa Misicuni officials
saw themselves as the rightful managers of state-owned water sources and infrastructure with the expertise necessary to run and improve the region's systems.

Other SEMAPA officials voiced more nuanced positions that distinguished
between property and use rights and accepted community ownership. One

SEMAPA engineer, referring to Lake Wara Wara, expressed a novel view of *usos y costumbres* that included SEMAPA. "Everything has its owner, even the lake," he explained, "but *usos y costumbres* govern the property, too. So SEMAPA's use of the lakes is also protected by *usos y costumbres*."[126] A former SEMAPA general manager, referring to Arocagua irrigators, told me that "the users are the owners. SEMAPA just has rights to its water through an agreement with them."[127] A SEMAPA engineer who worked closely with the communities where SEMAPA sources are located and was captured along with Julio Vargas in Escalerani told me that the lakes San Juan and San Pablito belong to the Comunidad Tirani, not SEMAPA. He said that in Escalerani, "SEMAPA should pay the *comunarios*, build them infrastructure, and compensate them for water."[128] From this perspective, SEMAPA holds use rights to these water sources negotiated with the sources' owners—peasants and irrigators who won them in part through agrarian reform. It follows that, just as the state is the original owner of privately owned land, the state can cede water property rights to individuals, communities, neighborhoods, or public water companies, in effect allowing *usos y costumbres* to govern distribution. As Arocagua water manager Sebastián Chambi put it, "The constitution says very clearly that all natural resources belong to the state. *Usos y costumbres* belong to the people. We manage them in coordination with each other, without selfishness."[129]

Peasants' confidence to assert ownership over water sources in their jurisdictions grew during Morales's presidency, but their property claims were not new. Rural communities that won these sources through agrarian reform in the 1950s and 1960s have long claimed property rights. As Tirani union leader Javier Molina told me, "The right [to a water source] is given *cuando se ocupe*."[130] The Spanish verb *ocuparse* can mean "to take possession of," as in English, but it can also mean "to work on or take care of." For Cochabamba's rural water rights holders, both possession and generations of labor have cemented the community's water property rights.

Indeed, understanding *usos y costumbres* and water property claims requires a deep historical horizon. When communities in the foothills like Tirani claim water ownership on the basis of *usos y costumbres*, they are referring not to some abstract or timeless idea but rather to the labor that has gone into building and maintaining water infrastructure that created these sources over generations—and the social struggles that it took to win control over the products of this labor. Tirani *comunarios* with rights to San Juan and San Pablito and Arocagua irrigators with rights to Wara Wara won them through agrarian reform cases after the 1952 revolution that granted land and water ownership to estate workers. As former Tirani *juez de aguas* Benicio Portillo told me, "Just as the land returned to the *colonos*, the lakes with all of their *usos y costumbres* returned to the *colonos* as well."[131] Tirani community members consider themselves owners of these sources just as estate owners did before them. But unlike *hacendados*, ex-*colonos'* claims rest not only on property titles and riparian rights but also on labor.

Historical memory, passed down from the generation that experienced the revolution and agrarian reform, serves as the foundation of rights claims today. In interviews, elders who were in their early twenties in 1952 recounted annual trips to the lakes high in the mountains to repair dams and canals both before and after the revolution. As Fernanda Guzmán told me, "Nobody complained, but it was very hard work. Since the agrarian reform, water has been distributed just like land and we no longer work for the hacienda. The hacienda died."[132] Sergio Portillo succinctly expressed what many remembered: "The water was given to those who worked it, the comunarios."[133] Like this book's third chapter, these statements invite us to reframe the agrarian reform as granting not just land to those who work it but also water to those who use it.

Most Tirani *comunarios* do not identify as indigenous but nevertheless ground their claims to land and water in Andean heritage and practices of reciprocity and collective use, labor, and distribution embodied in *usos y costumbres* and rooted in pre-Columbian practices. One community leader born just before the revolution and agrarian reform in January 1952 recounted, "When I was little, we didn't have electricity or gas. We cooked with wood that we lit not with matches but with the spark of a rock, like the Incas. We are indigenous, descendants of the Incas." He emphasized that "the lakes belong to the community. The lakes were given to the union through agrarian reform."[134] Community members continue to carry out collective labor to maintain dams, canals, and other irrigation infrastructure. They perform *k'oas* and *ch'allas* asking permission from and thanking the Pachamama when they begin and finish a job. But, as Tirani's *juez de aguas* Cesar Suarez Velarde explained in an interview, participation in these ceremonies is optional given that many Tirani community members have become evangelical Christians.[135]

Once they became land and water owners in the 1950s with agrarian reform, Tirani *comunarios* reorganized irrigation turns and continued annual work trips to the lakes. Whereas before the reform the estate's fields received water every seven days and the *colonos'* every thirteen, afterward all plots began to receive water around every ten days.[136] Their descendants still manage water and maintain infrastructure in the same way. Tirani's irrigation turn schedule dates to this time. Families still send laborers on annual trips to repair dams and canals and pay monthly quotas for the system's upkeep. Failure to work or pay can mean losing water rights.[137] Community members reported in 2011 that another community had recently attempted to wrest the San Juan Lakes away from them but that they were able to resolve the conflict without confrontation. Ongoing labor and negotiations over water distribution make *usos y costumbres* a living and changing set of practices.

Piqueros' water rights also owe to a long history of collective use, labor, and organization. Like *colonos*, *piqueros* claim water rights on the basis of their historical labor damming lakes and building and maintaining irrigation works. But unlike *colonos*, some of their rights date back to the colonial era. According to Omar Fernández, "In users' association meetings to this day, they call names from the 1794 [water] distribution."[138] Revolutionary-era land and water reform mostly excluded *piqueros*, creating lasting inequalities, rivalries, and conflicts between *piqueros* and ex-*colonos*, as discussed in chapter 3. Fernández says that as a result *piqueros* often refuse to contribute an equal number of laborers to clean canals that they share with ex-*colono* communities.[139]

During the Morales presidency, smallholders began to identify with the state in a way they had not since the years following the 1952 Bolivian revolution. Asked about state ownership of water resources, Tirani union leader Dionisio Hurtado declared, "I believe that we are part of the state and so we are included in its owners."[140] Taquiña union leader Bonifacio Posada echoed this position. "The lake is within our territory, so we consider it to be ours," he told me. "When they say water is state property, we say we too are the state. I am a citizen of this state, so I too am the state."[141] In their discourse and interactions with MAS-led state institutions, Cochabamba water managers like Hurtado and Posada worked to reconcile not only the seeming contradiction between state water ownership and community management but more profoundly the tension between state governance and civil society autonomy, often finding common ground. But this "we too are the state" discourse goes beyond identification with a relatively friendly presidential administration. It also constitutes a claim to sovereignty. While scholars have studied indigenous assertions of statehood extensively, they have paid less attention to the ways that peasant communities have proclaimed state status.[142]

Finally, the tension between state responsibility for guaranteeing water access and community autonomy contributed to a fourth set of clashes between neighborhoods on the ever-expanding urban periphery and agricultural communities. Conflicts of this kind have exploded in Tiquipaya, a lush municipality set into the hillside northwest of the department capital where irrigation canals snake through fields and along city streets. Tiquipaya, once home to one of Cochabamba's five *pueblos reales de indios* until these communities were dismantled in the 1870s, became a patchwork of *piquero*, ex-*colono*, and ex-*hacendado* landholdings and irrigation systems after agrarian reform. In the 1980s and 1990s "relocated" miners who lost their jobs after state mine closures built ramshackle neighborhoods on former farm fields. In recent years, Tiquipaya has become a bedroom community for well-off professionals who work in the department capital and home to more humble migrants from other regions. As a result, Tiquipaya has gone from one of the valley's most important agricultural areas to one of its most urbanized.[143] The municipality failed to provide water service on its outskirts, leaving residents to fend for themselves.

As urban neighborhoods in Tiquipaya's water-rich foothills grew, conflicts arose between urban residents and peasant cultivators over water access. While the barrios alleged that peasants no longer needed as much water as they once did since so much agricultural land had urbanized, peasant unions argued that they needed more water than ever and that they were entitled to it due to their historical rights. One particularly intense conflict occurred in 2012 and 2013 over access to the Taquiña River. In 2012 the Ministry of the Environment and Water developed a project to direct river water to eleven neighborhoods called the Cinco Salidas Drinking Water System Improvement Plan. When the Taquiña peasant union with rights to the river protested, authorities responded that "el agua es de todos" ("the water belongs to everyone") and continued the project.[144]

The conflict turned violent in March 2013 when Taquiña peasants seized pipes that Cinco Salidas residents had installed to divert some of the river's flow away from peasants' fields toward their homes. In response, Cinco Salidas residents blocked roads, demanding the peasants return the pipes. A confrontation with rocks and dynamite ensued that left forty-five people injured. While Taquiña cultivators claimed historical rights to sources they said they needed to irrigate their fields and pointed out that the Taquiña beer company's use of the river had already reduced their flows, Cinco Salidas residents insisted they had a constitutional right to the river's water.[145] State authorities sided with neighborhood residents, contending, in the words of Cochabamba Gobernación lawyer Freddy San Milán, that "water is a natural resource that does not belong exclusively to anyone. It must benefit all."[146] The two sides reached an agreement, but the following year Cinco Salidas residents alleged that the Taquiña peasants' union was not fulfilling its obligations and that other neighborhoods had illegally drilled into Cinco Salidas pipes to connect to the system.[147] As these events reveal, the debate over the human right to water is not simply a state-community conflict. It also pits water rights holders against those lacking historical rights who have seized on the human right to water enshrined in the Bolivian Constitution and international law to demand water access—and to justify their efforts to capture water.

The Cinco Salidas dispute raises a difficult question: is it possible to respect historical rights based on collective labor while simultaneously responding to changing realities, needs, and demands? If so, how? The MAS government negotiated conflicts between historical claims and new ones by erecting new state institutions to oversee water distribution and mediate disputes that at times encroached on water users' historical rights and their power to make these agreements horizontally. Water cooperatives, peasant and irrigators unions, and water activist organizations like Fundación Abril demanded that water users be allowed to make these agreements directly, as they long had. But they have been less vocal about how to make water access correspond better to changing needs and realities. Categoric defense of the historical rights of those who have water access risks disregarding the needs of those who lack it in the present. As anthropologists Nicole Fabricant and Kathryn Hicks have written, water activists have had difficulty moving from resistance to privatization "to a truly democratic and participatory governance structure."[148] It also risks erasing the history of changes to water rights regimes won through social struggle, negotiation, and compromise.

The Misicuni dam project was supposed to be the answer to these problems. Like in the 1940s, engineering a new and abundant water source promised to assuage conflicts over existing ones. Promoters promised that it would improve water access for smallholders, periurban neighborhoods, and SEMAPA customers alike. After three decades of popular demands for the project, construction began in 1996 and concluded in 2017 under Morales.[149] The population collectively won realization of this project, but so far it has yet to benefit the valley's most needy water users. Delays, losses, and signs of corruption tainted the project in the public's eyes, infrastructure required to convey water to the region's neediest areas has yet to be built, it is still unclear how Misicuni water will be distributed, and it has yet to reach the Zona Sud or the countryside.[150] In his final campaign speech in Cochabamba before the 2019 presidential election, Morales pledged to further invest in Misicuni to increase water flow to the valley.[151] At this writing in late 2020 the promise of bending the Misicuni River's flow to the Cochabamba Valley to provide water to all remains unfulfilled.

On 10 November 2019, Evo Morales resigned as president of the Plurinational State of Bolivia after weeks of protests against alleged electoral fraud and clashes between his supporters and opponents on the streets. Two days before Morales's resignation, *comunarios* in the Tunari Mountains closed the valves of the Escalerani dam and peacefully occupied the Misicuni dam in defense of the president. The anti-Morales alliance Comunidad Ciudadana denounced the MAS-affiliated comunarios for their "cowardly" and "criminal attack against the Cochabamba population" that "violated human rights." Some urged authorities to militarize these areas to prevent actions that could cut off water to the valley.[152] In the days after Morales's resignation, Misicuni officials denied rumors that *comunarios* planned to flood the city but vowed to protect the dam. Meanwhile, soldiers surrounded SEMAPA's headquarters to prevent Morales supporters from attacking its offices to protest his ouster. Misicuni and SEMAPA officials negotiated with the *comunarios* and an agreement was soon reached.[153] This was just the latest instance of a long history of rural communities threatening to disrupt water flow to make political and economic demands. Like they had during the 1952 revolution, *campesinos* played on urban fear to bring attention to their communities' needs and views.

CONCLUSION

In the two decades after the Water War, Cochabambinos worked to democratize water governance and to make water access more equitable locally, nationally, and internationally. While they made some gains, inequities and deficiencies persist. The most significant structural inequality is that SEMAPA provides affordable water to the city's better-off neighborhoods while excluding most of the Zona Sud. Rates are low within the SEMAPA system due to decades of social organization and protest. As we have seen, many of the neighborhoods included in it originally traded infrastructure and supply for incorporation. Zona Sud neighborhoods lacking water sources to trade have not had the opportunity to make such exchanges.

While not on par with SEMAPA's exclusions or the broader failure of state institutions to prioritize hydraulic infrastructure projects, the disconnect between historical rights and current needs on the urban periphery and in rural areas also contributes to unequal water access. Cochabamba's periurban and rural water users have defended their water access against dispossession by powerful entities like SEMAPA, national state institutions, and global capital. But they have been less willing in recent years to give up water for their neighbors. This is understandable given that water users built and paid for these sources and systems and that they are one of the only tools that smallholders possess to pressure state authorities for development projects. Perhaps irrigators, peasants, and mountain communities would be more willing to cede water rights if state institutions treated them as water *property* rights and formally expropriated and compensated their owners accordingly. After all, many of them fought a revolution in 1952 to win them and war in 2000 to defend them. Legislative and institutional victories after the 2000 Water War have given water-using communities with their own sources and systems more protection and control, but sometimes at the expense of water users seeking access to those sources.

Cochabamba's 2000 Water War set off a wave of uprisings that led to Evo Morales's election. The MAS government transformed Bolivian politics by bringing indigenous people and women into positions of power, distributing oil and gas rents to broader sectors of the population, and restoring the state's commitment to providing for the basic needs of its citizens. Internationally, the Morales administration and Bolivian water activists supported other antiprivatization campaigns and efforts to expand water access. In Bolivia, in the name of the human right to water, MAS-led state institutions increased investment in the water sector and worked to make water more accessible in metropolitan areas like Cochabamba. But these efforts at times intruded on autonomous communitarian water systems and negotiation processes that Morales had vowed to protect. The conflicts over water access described in this chapter reveal the tension between state responsibility and community autonomy at the heart of the *proceso de cambio*. But they also gesture at something deeper.

The MAS's electoral path and Cochabamba water activists' grassroots approach reflected more than different strategies. They also revealed different visions for a more just and democratic society. The MAS under Morales adopted a developmentalist vision that depended on state direction, foreign capital investment, fossil fuel extraction, and commercial agriculture to broaden access to modernity's promises.[154] Many Cochabambino water activists, in contrast, envisioned a bottom-up democracy rooted in the self-activity and organization of the country's poor and working peoples. For them, refounding the country meant creating new constituent and legislative bodies elected from the grassroots and social control over natural resources like water.[155] While the Morales administration was intent on centralizing water provision under state direction, water activists worked to strengthen what Water War leader Oscar Olivera called the "social tapestry" of community and public water systems "built from below."[156] These were not binary positions, however, but rather two ends on a continuum within the *proceso de cambio* where many people fell in between. This explains why community water system members both defended their autonomy and demanded the state execute the Misicuni dam project.

The vision that won out nationally was Evo's. But his administration's hegemonic agenda was always aspirational, especially in the water sector. In practice, public and community water systems coexisted, and their managers clashed, negotiated, and collaborated. State efforts at times opened opportunities for peasants, irrigators, periurban residents, and SEMAPA customers to strengthen social control over water sources and systems. Water users who stood to lose water rights generally opposed state intervention, while those who lacked rights often welcomed it. Yet contending groups agreed that state involvement should occur on local water users' own terms, and that secure access to plentiful and clean water was necessary to survive and improve their lives. Together they contributed to broader demands for social and economic justice that dictators had repressed and neoliberal governments had whittled away. In so doing, they helped make Bolivian democracy more bottom-up and more just.

Conclusion

Water for All

By late 2020, four of the Tirani community elders I had spoken with in 2011 had passed away, and Justina, my Quechua translator and research assistant there, had moved to Brazil. But most of my informants remained and continued to defend community ownership of the San Juan Lakes, most recently in a conflict with another community whose members had allegedly ruptured the lakes' accumulation membranes. Meanwhile, after thirty years in community and public service, Omar Fernández was devoting himself to his fields, irrigating his fava bean, pea, green bean, and corn plants with water from the centuries-old Machu Mita and Lagunmayu irrigation systems and newer ones.[1]

This book has told the story of water dispossession and reconquest over 140 years, from 1877 to 2019. It began by examining how rural elites took advantage of drought, famine, indigenous community closure, and liberal state policies to construct a water monopoly in the late nineteenth century. It explored how coalitions of reformers and water users dismantled that monopoly in the years before and after the 1952 Bolivian revolution. The revolutionary-era promise of water for all and the limits of its realization gave rise to a diversity of experiments in popular water management that make Cochabamba and Bolivia unique. After the revolution, *piqueros*, ex-*colonos*, periurban neighborhood residents, and municipal customers worked to expand water access and influence planning, management, and, of course, billing. In the process they built a popular hydraulic society to defend the gains and deal with the limits of revolutionary water reform. As this history shows, water claims and uses are neither timeless nor are they new inventions. Rather, they have a deep and complex history rooted in community, labor, and social struggle.

The tensions between state institutions and water-user communities over management traced throughout this book exemplify a contradiction at the heart of twentieth- and twenty-first-century revolutionary projects: revolutionary leaders who profess commitments to community and worker autonomy and management of natural resources and industry but in practice take custodial, civilizing, and at times repressive approaches to their bases, particularly poor, working-class, and rural peoples. Initially, the main axis of conflict in Latin America's twentieth-century revolutions was between revolutionary coalitions and the oligarchies they displaced. Upon victory, however, conflicts within the leadership and between leaders and bases of revolutionary coalitions came to the fore. In Mexico revolutionary leaders entrusted stewardship of the environment and the economy to professional, state-employed foresters, agronomists, and engineers who restricted worker and rural communities' management of oil, land, forests, and water sources.[2] In postrevolutionary Cuba, Fidel Castro's government simultaneously pursued conservation and harnessed nature to develop the state-socialist economy. Like their Bolivian and Mexican counterparts, Cuban officials saw water conservation through dam and reservoir construction as central to combatting drought and increasing agricultural production.[3] In all three countries the revolutionary state strove to rationalize water management and distribution in the service of national economic development.

But revolutionary state water rationalization programs also aimed to foster social justice and opened up opportunities for water users to win greater access to water and control over its provision. Many rural toilers gained irrigated land for the first time through revolutionary-era agrarian reform, and city residents gained greater access to previously hoarded hacienda water sources. Nevertheless, water redistribution and dam projects extending water access in Mexico and Bolivia excluded large numbers of rural cultivators and city residents. While the Mexican and Cuban revolutions empowered the reconstituted state more than the revolutionary masses, in Bolivia peasants, miners, and urban workers who carried out the revolution won far greater power than their Mexican and Cuban counterparts. This was particularly the case in the water sector. The Bolivian state—under MNR, dictator, neoliberal, and MAS rule—has attempted to wrest that control away from water users ever since. In Cochabamba these efforts mostly failed as water users defended and expanded their power.

Revolutions are not events. They are processes contested and carried out by diverse groups who turn a moment of crisis into an opportunity to press long-standing demands and pursue visions of a more just future. Revolutionary leaders, despite their pronouncements and claims, do not own or control these developments. Nor have state institutions or formal experts dictated approaches to technical questions like hydraulic development and water provision, even in times of relative calm. In Bolivia, as early as the 1940s, peasants, estate workers, and city dwellers offered proposals of their own to expand and more equitably distribute water supply. Water users drew on revolutionary language and promises to demand that the state fulfill its promise and obligation to provide water for all *and* to defend and develop community sources, systems, and management.

This history suggests that the Bolivian state has not been weak in the water sector due to incompetence or lethargy. Nor have Bolivians rejected a relationship with state institutions.[4] Rather, ordinary water users have often dictated where, when, and how the state has intervened. For Bolivians, and especially for Cochabambinos, water is different than electricity, roads, transportation, and other services. It is not a luxury but rather a basic necessity for survival and a decent life that the state should either guarantee or allow communities to provide for themselves. State and international financial institutions have attempted to deliver that service by increasing state (and in the late 1990s private) control over water sources, infrastructure, planning, and provision and increasing rates according to a liberal model of citizenship. Water users, in contrast, have developed a collective model of social citizenship where they own, plan, build, and manage water sources and systems—and state involvement—themselves. To do so, they have drawn on ancestral customs and formulated new organizations and practices. But the popular hydraulic society that Cochabambinos built nevertheless remains unequal. Although Bolivians have won incredible power over water over the past century, it has not yielded ample water access for all.

To more equitably distribute water sources, water rights need to be flexible and continuously reallocated through democratic and inclusive processes. Some Cochabamba water activists have proposed creating a new body modeled on the Coordinadora de Defensa del Agua y de la Vida that emerged during the 2000 Water War with representatives of all water-using groups, institutions, and communities.[5] Such a body could work to respect community autonomy and historical rights while also taking a holistic valleywide approach that accounts for changing needs and realities. It could also decide what role the state plays in this process. What is needed is not only vernacular governance within particular systems but also democratic governance over water sources and equitable distribution across the region based on a radical politics of solidarity. In the absence of a new *coordinadora* and in the face of deep inequalities, however, it is no wonder that rural and periurban collectives guard their property and that rural communities threaten flow to the city to press their demands. As this book has shown, the "right to interrupt" is a form of participation and power that these communities have cultivated for decades.[6]

If there is one lesson that Bolivia's water history can offer, in Bolivia and beyond, it is that redistribution of wealth, resources, and decision-making power is required to guarantee water as well as employment, housing, transportation, education, electricity, sanitation, and basic safety and dignity to all. To echo the late

US historian Howard Zinn, transforming society depends less on who sits in the Palacio Quemado, as important as that is, and more on who is marching, blockading, and occupying—and on who plans, engineers, builds, repairs, accesses, and controls resources, infrastructure, and wealth.[7]

Cochabamba's popular hydraulic society, governed by water users themselves, will endure and evolve. Cochabambinos built it through revolution and in spite of dictators and guarded it against privatization and state intrusion. In the process Cochabambinos helped galvanize movements for social justice across Bolivia and around the world. The capacity of ordinary Bolivians to collectively manage common resources like water, organize to defend their interests and win their demands, and dictate to power will carry on. The challenge going forward will be to build on existing forms of vernacular governance and expertise to pursue a vision of equitable and plentiful water access for all.

Maximum Holdings under the 1953 Agrarian Reform Decree Law

Maximum Holdings for Small Properties

Altiplano Zone

Northern subzone alongside or with coverage from Lake Titikaka			10 hectares (ha.)
Central subzone with coverage from Lake Poopó			15 ha.
Southern subzone			35 ha.

	Irrigation	Dry	Wine-producing
Valley Zone			
Open valleys subzone	6 ha.	12 ha.	3 ha.
Closed valleys subzone	4 ha.	8 ha.	3 ha.
Municipal seats subzone	20 ha.		
Tropical Zone			
Yungas subzone			10 ha.
Santa Cruz subzone			50 ha.
Chaco subzone			80 ha.

Maximum Holdings for Medium Properties

Altiplano Zone

Northern subzone alongside Lake Titikaka	80 ha.
Northern subzone with coverage from Lake Titikaka	150 ha.
Central subzone with coverage from Lake Poopó	250 ha.
Southern subzone	350 ha.

	Irrigation	Dry	Wine-producing
Valley Zone			
Open valleys adjacent to the city of Cochabamba	50 ha.	100 ha.	24 ha.

(with coverage from the Angostura irrigation system and moist land in the Arani, Punata, Sacaba, and Caraza Valleys and the Jordán and Esteban Arze provinces)

	Irrigation	Dry	Wine-producing
Other open valleys	60 ha.	150 ha.	24 ha.

	In valley lands	On the mountainside	Hacienda total
Closed valleys	40 ha.	40 ha.	80 ha.
Valley municipal seats	200 ha.		
Tropical zone			
Yungas subzone	150 ha.		
Santa Cruz subzone	500 ha.		
Chaco subzone	600 ha.		
Agricultural tropical zone			
Beni, Pando, and Iturralde provinces of the La Paz department	500 ha.		

Maximum Holdings for Agricultural Enterprises

Zone with coverage from the lake	400 ha.
Andean, altiplano and puna	800 ha.
Open valleys not adjacent to the city of Cochabamba covered by the Angostura irrigation system	500 ha.
Closed valleys	80 ha.*
Tropical and subtropical zones in the east	2,000 ha.

* in cultivable land of the valley, in addition to 150 ha. on the mountainside

ABBREVIATIONS

ADN	Acción Democrática Nacionalista
AISA	Aguas del Illimani South America
ANARESCAPYS	Asociación Nacional de Regantes y Sistemas Comunitarios de Agua Potable y Saneamiento
ASICASUDD-EPSAS	Asociación de Sistemas Comunitarios de Agua del Sud, Departamental y Entidades Prestadoras de Serivico de Agua Potable y Alcantarillado Sanitario
ASICA-Sur	Asociación de Sistemas Comunitarios de Agua del Sur
ASP	Asamblea por la Soberanía de los Pueblos
BIT	Netherlands-Bolivia Bilateral Trade Agreement
CAF	Corporación Andina de Fomento
CBF	Corporación Boliviana de Fomento
CNI	Comisión Nacional de Irrigación (Mexico)
CNRA	Consejo Nacional de Reforma Agraria
COB	Central Obrera Boliviana
COD	Central Obrera Departamental (Cochabamba)
CODAEP	Comité de Defensa del Agua y la Economía Popular
COMIBOL	Corporación Minera de Bolivia
CONDEPA	Conciencia de Patria
CORDECO	Corporación de Desarrollo de Cochabamba
CORFADENA	Corporación de Desarrollo de las Fuerzas Armadas
CPC	Comité Pro-Cochabamba
CSUTCB	Confederación Sindical Única de Trabajadores Campesinos de Bolivia
EMAPAQ	Empresa Municipal de Agua Potable y Alcantarillado de Quillacollo
EMAPAS	Empresa Municipal de Agua Potable y Alcantarillado de Sacaba
ENDE	Empresa Nacional de Electricidad de Bolivia
ENTEL	Empresa Nacional de Telecomunicaciones
EPSA	Entidad Prestadora de Servicios de Agua Potable y Alcantarillado Sanitario

FEDECOR	Federación Departamental Cochabambina de Organizaciones Regantes
FEJUVE	Federación de Juntas Vecinales
FRC	Federación Rural de Cochabamba
FSTCC	Federación Sindical de Trabajadores Campesinos de Cochabamba
FSTMB	Federación Sindical de Trabajadores Mineros de Bolivia
FSUTCC	Federación Sindical Única de Trabajadores Campesinos de Cochabamba
GEOBOL	Servicio Geológico de Bolivia
GTZ	Gesellschaft für Technische Zusammenarbeit (German Technical Cooperation Agency)
ICSID	International Center for Settlement of Investment Disputes (World Bank)
IDB	Inter-American Development Bank
IFI	international financial institution
ILO	International Labour Organization
IMF	International Monetary Fund
INAVI	Instituto Nacional de Vivienda
INRA	Instituto Nacional de Reforma Agraria
JICA	Japanese International Cooperation Agency
JUNCO	Junta de la Comunidad
LAB	Lloyd Aéreo Boliviano
LPP	Ley de Participación Popular
MAS	Movimiento al Socialismo
MIP	Movimiento Indígena Pachakuti
MIR	Movimiento de la Izquierda Revolucionaria
MNR	Movimiento Nacionalista Revolucionario
NEP	New Economic Policy
NFR	Nueva Fuerza Republicana
OAS	Organization of American States
PAHO	Pan American Health Organization
PMC	Pacto Militar Campesino
SEMAPA	Servicio Municipal de Agua Potable y Alcantarillado (Cochabamba)
SENARI	Servicio Nacional de Riego
SERGEOMIN	Servicio Geológico y Minero
SISAB	Superintendencia de Sanitación Básica
SOE	state-owned enterprise
SOFRELEC	Sté Fréjusienne d'électricité (France)
UCS	Unidad Cívica Solidaridad
UDP	Unidad Democrática y Popular
UMSA	Universidad Mayor de San Andrés
UMSS	Universidad Mayor de San Simón
UNDP	United Nations Development Program
USAID	United States Agency for International Development
WHO	World Health Organization
YPFB	Yacimientos Petrolíferos Fiscales Bolivianos

NOTES

INTRODUCTION

1. Javier Molina, author interview, Tirani, 27 May 2011.

2. I use lowercase in "revolution" when discussing the 1952 Bolivian revolution to signal that I am not merely referring to the events of April 1952, the MNR's seizure of power, and the official reforms and MNR administrations from 1952 to 1964 but also to the more complex, bottom-up, and interactive processes in the halls of power and in fields, factories, and neighborhoods. Nor do I call it the Bolivian National Revolution (or the Bolivian national revolution). To use that title would echo the MNR's official propaganda and risk obscuring local and regional experiences.

3. Olivera and Lewis, ¡Cochabamba!, 34–44.

4. Barlow, Blue Covenant, 102–141.

5. Amann and Baer, "Neoliberalism and Its Consequences in Brazil."

6. Kohl and Farthing, Impasse in Bolivia, 109.

7. Webber, From Rebellion to Reform in Bolivia; Gutiérrez Aguilar, Rhythms of the Pachakuti.

8. Evo Morales Ayma, "Discurso Inaugural," 22 January 2006 (La Paz: Ministerio de Relaciones Exteriores y Cultos de Bolivia, 2006).

9. By "noninstitutionality," Gutiérrez means the body's unwillingness to become a legal entity subject to state regulation. Gutiérrez Aguilar, Rhythms of the Pachakuti, 17, 22–23.

10. Water War leader Oscar Olivera maintains in his account of the conflict that "the people look at water as something quite sacred." Olivera and Lewis, ¡Cochabamba!, 8.

11. Kohl and Farthing, Impasse in Bolivia, 149.

12. White, "Are You an Environmentalist?," 172.

13. Borsdorf and Stadel, The Andes, 11–12.

14. Borsdorf and Stadel, The Andes, 23, 61.

15. Borsdorf and Stadel, The Andes, 62.

16. Murra, *Formaciones económicas y políticas*, 59–116; Larson, *Cochabamba, 1550–1900*, 14–25.

17. Bray, "Water, Ritual, and Power in the Inca Empire."

18. Sherbondy, "Water Ideology in Inca Ethnogenesis," 57.

19. Murra, *Formaciones económicas y políticas*, 80–81.

20. Bray, "Water, Ritual, and Power in the Inca Empire," 167.

21. Bray, "Water, Ritual, and Power in the Inca Empire," 167, 187.

22. Sherbondy, "Water and Power in Inca Ethnogenesis," 72–73.

23. Nobbs-Thiessen, *Landscape of Migration*, 9–11.

24. Larson, *Cochabamba, 1550–1900*.

25. Bolivia is divided into nine departments.

26. The pools, ponds, and lakes that once formed in the valley's shallow depressions gave Cochabamba its name, derived from the Quechua *q'ocha pampa*, meaning "lake plateau" or the "valley of lakes." Navarro and Maldonado, *Geografía ecológica de Bolivia*.

27. Larson, *Cochabamba, 1550–1900*, 176; Jackson and Gordillo Claure, "Formación, crisis, y transformación," 727; Jackson, "Decline of the Hacienda," 262–263.

28. Viedma, *Descripción geográfica*.

29. Karl S. Zimmerer has found evidence that floodwater and canal irrigation in Cochabamba's Valle Alto "was in use at about AD 719 and that it functioned as early as 3,500 years before present (BP)." Zimmerer, "Origins of Andean Irrigation," 481–483.

30. Viedma as quoted in Larson, *Cochabamba, 1550–1900*, 289–290.

31. McDowell and Hess, "Accessing Adaptation," 346.

32. Averanga Mollinedo, *Aspectos generales de la población boliviana*, 58; CIA Factbook, www.cia.gov/library/publications/the-world-factbook/geos/print_bl.html, accessed 29 June 2020.

33. Pritchard, *Confluence*; Jørgensen, Jørgensen, and Pritchard, *New Natures*.

34. Marx and Engels, *German Ideology*, 47; Smith, *Uneven Development*, 32–35, 56; Foster, *Marx's Ecology*, 155–158, 165.

35. Boelens et al., "Hydrosocial Territories," 1–2.

36. Matthew Vitz employs an urban political ecology approach to similar questions in Mexico City. Vitz, *City on a Lake*, 8.

37. Mitchell, *Rule of Experts*, 19–53. See also Sutter, "Nature's Agents or Agents of Empire?"

38. Marx, *Eighteenth Brumaire of Louis Bonaparte*, 15. See also Fiege, *Irrigated Eden*; McCook, *States of Nature*; Mitchell, *Rule of Experts*; Pritchard, *Confluence*; Raffles, *In Amazonia*; Soluri, *Banana Cultures*; Wolfe, *Watering the Revolution*; Zhang, *The River, the Plain, and the State*.

39. Wittfogel, *Oriental Despotism*.

40. Worster, *Rivers of Empire*.

41. Worster, *Rivers of Empire*, 78–81.

42. Aboites Aguilar, *El agua de la nación*; Aboites Aguilar, *La decadencia del agua de la nación*; Fiege, *Irrigated Eden*; Lipsett-Rivera, *To Defend Our Water*; Mikhail, *Nature and Empire in Ottoman Egypt*; Mukerji, *Impossible Engineering*; Pisani, *Water and American Government*; Wolfe, *Watering the Revolution*.

43. Swyngedouw, *Social Power and the Urbanization of Water*; Anand, "Pressure."

44. Christina Jiménez's study of Morelia, Mexico, is an important exception. Jiménez, *Making an Urban Public*.

45. Gandy, *Concrete and Clay*; Gandy, *Fabric of Space*; Gandy, "Landscapes of Disaster"; Gandy, "Paris Sewers and the Rationalization of Urban Space"; Gandy, "Rethinking Urban Metabolism"; Kaika, *City of Flows*; Kaika and Swyngedouw, "Fetishizing the Modern City"; Loreto López, *Agua, poder urbano y metabolismo social*; Swyngedouw, *Social Power and the Urbanization of Water*.

46. Scott, *Seeing Like a State*, 5.

47. Scott, "High Modernist Social Engineering," 26–27, 33.

48. Gilbert, "Low Modernism and the Agrarian New Deal," 144.

49. Buckley, *Technocrats and the Politics of Drought*; Escobar, *Encountering Development*; Ferguson, *Anti-Politics Machine*; Li, *Will to Improve*.

50. Krupa and Nugent, *State Theory and Andean Politics*; Nugent, *Modernity at the Edge of Empire*.

51. Boelens, *Water, Power, and Identity*, 42; Boelens, Bustamante, and de Vos, "Legal Pluralism and the Politics of Inclusion"; Seemann, *Water Security, Justice and the Politics of Water Rights*, 27.

52. Here I build on Rudi Colloredo-Mansfeld's conception of "vernacular statecraft." Colloredo-Mansfeld, *Fighting Like a Community*, 6–7. The term "governance" captures the reality that both state and nonstate actors manage water systems. Horowitz and Watts, *Grassroots Environmental Governance*, 12.

53. Boelens, Perreault, and Vos, *Water Justice*, 3–4, emphasis in original.

54. Agrawal's exploration of what he calls "environmentality" also concerns the relationship between the state and local resource users but takes a more top-down approach. Agrawal, *Environmentality*.

55. Small-scale irrigation systems in Mexico that have maintained or gained some autonomy as the national government has centralized water governance exemplify this dynamic. Palerm Viqueira and Martínez Saldaña, *Antología sobre pequeño riego*.

56. Ostrom, *Governing the Commons*.

57. Holston, *Insurgent Citizenship*, 23. On water services, see Anand, *Hydraulic City*; Anand, "Pressure"; Anand, Gupta, and Appel, *Promise of Infrastructure*; Larkin, "Politics and Poetics of Infrastructure"; von Schnitzler, "Citizenship Prepaid"; von Schnitzler, *Democracy's Infrastructure*; von Schnitzler, "Traveling Technologies." On struggles of the urban poor for citizenship rights more generally, see Auyero and Swistun, *Flammable*; Fernandes, *Who Can Stop the Drums?*; Fischer, *Poverty of Rights*; Fischer, McCann, and Auyero, *Cities from Scratch*; Goldstein, *Owners of the Sidewalk*; Goldstein, *Spectacular City*; Murphy, *For a Proper Home*; Velasco, *Barrio Rising*.

58. I use the term "vernacular experts" rather than "citizen experts" to include those who do not possess full citizenship rights and to avoid confusion with efforts to facilitate public participation in scientific research such as those discussed in Buytaert et al., "Citizen Science in Hydrology and Water Resources."

59. Studies showing situated knowledge and practice to be the product of interactions between local community members and official authorities include Carey, *In the Shadow of Melting Glaciers*; González, *Zapotec Science*; Gross, "Between Party, People, and Profession"; Gross, *Farewell to the God of the Plague*; Mathews, *Instituting Nature*; Mukerji, *Im-*

possible Engineering; Pritchard, *Confluence*; Schmalzer, *Red Revolution, Green Revolution*; Scott, "Science for the West, Myth for the Rest?"; Simpson, de Loë, and Andrey, "Vernacular Knowledge and Water Management"; Soto Laveaga, *Jungle Laboratories*. On vernacular skill, knowledge, and technology, see also Carney, *Black Rice*; Eyferth, *Eating Rice from Bamboo Roots*; Mavhunga, *Transient Workspaces*; Orlove, Chiang, and Cane, "Forecasting Andean Rainfall"; Storey, *Guns, Race, and Power in Colonial South Africa*.

60. In adopting a broad definition of experts and expertise, this book joins a growing body of scholarship that takes a broad social approach to science and technology in Latin America. Chastain and Lorek, *Itineraries of Expertise*, 10. In addition to the *Itineraries of Expertise* collection and works cited above, see Barandiarán, *Science and Environment in Chile*; Hecht, *Entangled Geographies*; McCook, *States of Nature*; Medina, *Cybernetic Revolutionaries*; Medina, da Costa Marques, and Holmes, *Beyond Imported Magic*; Olsson, *Agrarian Crossings*; Schwartz, "Transforming the Tropics"; von Hardenberg et al., *Nature State*.

61. For an incisive critique of dichotomous views of "western" and "indigenous" science, see Agrawal, "Dismantling the Divide between Indigenous and Scientific Knowledge." On the origins of the "disregard for local knowledge," see Mehos and Moon, "Uses of Portability," 68. For contrasting views, see de la Cadena, *Earth Beings*; Escobar, *Territories of Difference*.

62. Appadurai, "Deep Democracy"; Grandin, *Last Colonial Massacre*, xv; Hines, "Power and Ethics of Vernacular Modernism."

63. Carse, *Beyond the Big Ditch*.

64. Carey, *In the Shadow of Melting Glaciers*; Gaonkar, "On Alternative Modernities"; Nugent, *Modernity at the Edge of Empire*; Wolfe, *Watering the Revolution*.

65. On alternative modernities, see Appadurai, *Modernity at Large*. For Bolivia, see Goodale, *Dilemmas of Modernity*.

66. Krupa and Nugent, *State Theory and Andean Politics*, 15; Tate, "The Aspirational State," 236.

67. Roseberry, "Hegemony and the Language of Contention," 360. See also Joseph and Nugent, "Popular Culture and State Formation in Revolutionary Mexico." I diverge from a strain of subaltern studies that considers subaltern practices to be autonomous from elite culture, and from a tendency among some Latin Americanist subaltern studies scholars to counterpose the state and the subaltern. For an example of a dualistic approach, see Rodríguez, "Reading Subalterns." For a sympathetic critique of Latin American subaltern studies, see Mallon, "Promise and Dilemma of Subaltern Studies." In the past few decades, historians have shown that Latin American subalterns have engaged state, market, nongovernmental, and other institutions to their own ends. Examples include Gould, *To Lead as Equals*; Larson, *Cochabamba, 1550–1900*; Mallon, *Defense of Community in Peru's Central Highlands*; Méndez, *Plebeian Republic*; Spaulding, *Huarochirí*.

68. Bjork-James, *Sovereign Street*, 214.

69. Li, *Will to Improve*.

70. On the relationship between academic production and political action in Bolivia, see Barragán, "Bridges and Chasms."

71. James, *Doña María's Story*, 242.

CHAPTER 1. WATER FOR THOSE WHO OWN IT

1. Rainfall in the agricultural year 1877–1878 was only 142.70 millimeters, concentrated in just twelve days, mostly at the beginning of the agricultural season. Average annual rainfall in Cochabamba since data collection began in 1942 has been 476.1 millimeters. "Lluvias," *El Heraldo*, 12 October 1877, 3; Henriques, "Análisis de los niveles de vida," 80.

2. By my calculations, based on information reported in Aceituno et al., "1877–1878 El Niño Episode," 404, and Pentimalli de Navarro and Rodríguez Ostria, "Las razones de la multitude," 19, at least 4,600 Cochabambinos died as a result of starvation and disease. Pentimalli de Navarro and Rodríguez Ostria report that 18,241 "indígenas" died and say that number does not account for those not buried in cemeteries. Pentimalli de Navarro and Rodríguez, "Las razones de la multitude," 17.

3. Davis, *Late Victorian Holocausts*, 7, 108–115; Aceituno et al., "1877–1878 El Niño Episode."

4. Davis, *Late Victorian Holocausts*, 11.

5. Sen, *Poverty and Famines*; Buckley, *Technocrats and the Politics of Drought*, 220.

6. Larson, *Cochabamba, 1550–1900*; Jackson, *Regional Markets and Agrarian Transformation*.

7. Rivera Cusicanqui, *Violencias (re)encubiertas en Bolivia*, 30.

8. Wachtel, "Mitimas of the Cochabamba Valley."

9. Zimmerer, "Rescaling Irrigation in Latin America."

10. Wachtel, "Mitimas of the Cochabamba Valley," 202.

11. Zimmerer, "Rescaling Irrigation in Latin America," 156; Larson, *Cochabamba, 1550–1900*, 291; Cochabamba Departamento de Cultura, *Repartimiento de tierras por el Inca Huayna Capac*, 10, 20–21.

12. Sherbondy, "Water and Power," 76.

13. Trawick, "Against the Privatization of Water," 982.

14. Rivera Cusicanqui, *Violencias (re)encubiertas en Bolivia*, 42.

15. Mumford, *Vertical Empire*, 113, 115; Larson, *Cochabamba, 1550–1900*, 147–148.

16. Jackson and Gordillo Claure, "Formación, crisis, y transformación," 734.

17. Jackson and Gordillo Claure, "Formación, crisis, y transformación," 734.

18. Larson, *Cochabamba, 1550–1900*, 157–161; Rodríguez Ostria, "Entre reformas y contrareformas," 287.

19. Larson, *Cochabamba, 1550–1900*, 88; Zimmer, "Rescaling Irrigation in Latin America," 164–167; Fernández Quiroga, "La relación tierra-agua," 20–21.

20. Jackson and Gordillo Claure, "Formación, crisis, y transformación," 759.

21. Spain and Consejo de Indias, *Recopilación de leyes*, 407.

22. Meyer, *Water in the Hispanic Southwest*, 120.

23. Platt, *Estado boliviano y ayllu andino*.

24. Larson, *Cochabamba, 1550–1900*, 145.

25. Zimmerer, "Rescaling Irrigation in Latin America," 165–166.

26. Jackson and Gordillo Claure, "Formación, crisis, y transformación," 731.

27. Larson, *Cochabamba, 1550–1900*, 137. In Bolivia (and colonial Upper Peru), *mestizaje* had more to do with economic, cultural, and geographical transitions than with racial "mix-

ture," though the latter has been important too. See Larson, *Cochabamba, 1550–1900*, 376; Thomson, "Was There Race in Colonial Latin America?"

28. Larson, *Cochabamba, 1550–1900*, 218–219; Jackson, *Regional Markets and Agrarian Transformation*, 17.

29. "Situación alarmante," *El Heraldo*, 8 February 1878, 1.

30. On similar dynamics in press coverage of climate disruptions in late nineteenth and early twentieth-century Mexico, see Wolfe, "Climate of Conflict."

31. Pentimalli de Navarro and Rodríguez Ostria, "Las razones de la multitud," 17.

32. Concejo Municipal de Cochabamba, "Memoria de 1878" (Cochabamba: Imprenta del Siglo), AHMC.

33. Querejazu Calvo, *Guano, salitre, sangre*, 255–258; Jackson, *Regional Markets and Agrarian Transformation*, 17–19.

34. Concejo Municipal, "Memoria de 1878"; Concejo Municipal de Cochabamba, "Memoria de 1879" (Cochabamba: Imprenta del Siglo), Biblioteca Arturo Costa de la Torre (BACT); "Miseria pública" and "Beneficencia," *El Heraldo*, 3 January 1879, 2.

35. On disease, racism, and hygiene in this period, see Zulawski, *Unequal Cures*, chapter 1.

36. "Plan de Subsistencias," *El Heraldo*, 22 April 1878, 1.

37. Consejo Municipal, "Memoria de 1878."

38. Pentimalli de Navarro and Rodríguez Ostria, "Las razones de la multitud," 19–20.

39. Pentimalli de Navarro and Rodríguez Ostria, "Las razones de la multitud," 20–22; Scott, *Moral Economy of the Peasant*.

40. Consejo Municipal, "Memoria de 1879."

41. Cushman, *Guano and the Opening of the Pacific World*, 73; Sater, *Andean Tragedy*, 2.

42. Sater, *Andean Tragedy*, 19.

43. Basadre, *Historia de la República del Perú*, vol. 8, 117.

44. Sater, *Andean Tragedy*, 1.

45. Klein, *Parties and Political Change in Bolivia*, 18–21; Klein, *Concise History of Bolivia*, 142–143; Langer, *Economic Change and Rural Resistance*, 36–51.

46. Klein, *Concise History of Bolivia*, 132–140.

47. Rodríguez Ostria, "Entre reformas y contrareformas," 307; Larson, *Trials of Nation Making*, 219; Government of Bolivia, "Disentailment and Its Discontents," in Thomson et al., *Bolivia Reader*, 184–185.

48. Two Lawyers from La Paz, "Transforming the Property Regime," in *Bolivia Reader*, ed. Thomson et al., 182.

49. Quoted in Francovich, *El pensamiento boliviano en el siglo XX*, 20.

50. Government of Bolivia, "'The Slow and Gradual Disappearance of the Indigenous Race,'" in *Bolivia Reader*, ed. Thomson et al., 251.

51. Gotkowitz, *Revolution for Our Rights*, 18; Larson, *Trials of Nation Making*, 218–229.

52. Gotkowitz, *Revolution for Our Rights*, 30.

53. Rivera Cusicanqui, *Oprimidos pero no vencidos*; Choque Canqui, *Sublevación y masacre de Jesús de Machaqa*; Mamani Condori, *Taraqu: 1866–1935*; Cárdenas, "La lucha de un pueblo"; Larson, *Trials of Nation Making*; Hylton, "Reverberations of Insurgency"; Ari Chachaki, *Earth Politics*.

54. Larson, *Cochabamba, 1550–1900*, 311. Rodríguez Ostria describes Cochabamba communities on the eve of the reform as "groups of dispersed islands protected under the fiscal category of indigenous community but in reality existing as a collection of small, clearly delimited peasant properties." On the eve of the reform, community landholdings in the Valle Bajo had already decreased by 36.4 percent from their creation by Toledo in 1573. Rodríguez Ostria, "Entre reformas y contrareformas," 288, 322.

55. Scholars have noted that the privatization process began in Cochabamba earlier than in the Altiplano, but most have not recognized the role of the drought in facilitating an earlier, more rapid, and less contentious disentailment there. See Gotkowitz, *Revolution for Our Rights*, 26.

56. Rodríguez Ostria, "Entre reformas y contrareformas," 320.

57. Larson, "Redeemed Indians, Barbarized Cholos"; Barragán, "Census and the Making of a Social 'Order,'" 113–114; Gordillo Claure, "Peasant Wars in Bolivia," 34.

58. Gotkowitz, *Revolution for Our Rights*; Hylton, "Reverberations of Insurgency"; Larson, *Cochabamba, 1550–1900*; Poole, *Vision, Race, and Modernity*; Stepan, *"Hour of Eugenics"*; Zulawski, *Unequal Cures*.

59. Harris, "Ethnic Identity and Market Relations," 361; Shesko, *Conscript Nation*, 32.

60. Barragán, "Census and the Making of a Social 'Order,'" 126, 129.

61. Bolivia, Decreto de 8 September 1879, Reglamento de aguas, Articles 41, 205, and 212, *Gaceta Oficial*.

62. Rodriguez Ostria, "Entre reformas y contrareformas," 316–317.

63. Gordillo Claure and Jackson, "Mestizaje y proceso de parcelización en la estructura agrarian de Cochabamba," 20.

64. Larson, *Cochabamba, 1550–1900*, 202–209; Jackson, *Regional Markets and Agrarian Transformation*, 75–77.

65. Jackson and Gordillo Claure, "Formación, crisis y transformación, 737.

66. Jackson, *Regional Markets and Agrarian Transformation*, 137–138. See also Gotkowitz, *Revolution for Our Rights*, 33.

67. According to Robert Jackson, whereas most elite families relied on hacienda income and were therefore vulnerable to fluctuations in agricultural prices, the Salamancas were among the few who invested in bank and mining stock and interest-bearing bonds. Jackson, "Decline of the Hacienda," 274.

68. Jackson, *Regional Markets and Agrarian Transformation*, 159–161.

69. "Juicio civil seguido por José Caraballo contra Francisco Guillen sobre entrega de aguas," 26 August 1878, Expedientes Republicanos Cochabamba, vol. 131, no. 7, fs. 676–723, AHMC.

70. "Títulos de las propiedades de Cala-Cala, Temporal, Tirani e Incahuacasca y las Lagunas de San Juan," AHDGC, Exp. Rep., 1946, vol. 344; "Testimonio de la escritura de venta judicial de los fundos del Temporal, Incahuarakaska, Tirani, así como de la mitad de las aguas de La Laguna San Juan," 24 December 1946, private files of a Tirani community member and descendent of Tirani colonos made available to the author in September 2011 (hereafter "Tirani Community Documents").

71. The name of the lake is also spelled "Lagun-mayu," "Lagun Mayu," "Lagunmayo,"

and so on. I use "Lagunmayu" consistently and have changed the spelling within quotations throughout.

72. Bustamante, "De las 'permanencias' y 'cambios,'" 16; Hendriks, "Negociación de intereses locales," 30; Maita Morales, "Estudio de las características de gestión," 60–61; Fredy Omar Fernández Quiroga, personal communication with author, October 2020.

73. Quiroga, "Una sentencia injusta."

74. Author interviews, Tirani, July and August 2011.

75. Raffles, *In Amazonia*, 34, 53–54, 61.

76. For a similar argument about Afro-Brazilian communities, see De la Torre, *People of the River*.

77. Lipsett-Rivera, *To Defend Our Water*, 8.

78. Bray, "Water, Ritual, and Power in the Inca Empire," 166.

79. Rama, *Lettered City*, 60.

80. Klein, *Parties and Political Change in Bolivia*, chapters 1–4, especially 59; Klein, *Concise History of Bolivia*, 144, 146, 153, 157; Larson, *Trials of Nation Making*, 203; Zulawski, *Unequal Cures*, 24.

81. On government public works proposals and projects, see Klein, *Parties and Political Change in Bolivia*, chapters 1–4.

82. Shesko, *Conscript Nation*, 23, 51, 3–56.

83. Goubert, *Conquest of Water*, 103. See also Melosi, *Sanitary City*, chapters 4–5; Melosi, *Precious Commodity*, chapter 2; Carse, *Beyond the Big Ditch*, 14.

84. Klein, *Parties and Political Change in Bolivia*, 8.

85. Gotkowitz, *Revolution for Our Rights*, 28.

86. Shesko, *Conscript Nation*, 23, 51–58.

87. Scholarship on popular uses of liberalism in the nineteenth-century Andes has shown that liberalism was not an exclusively elite project. Hylton, "Reverberations of Insurgency"; Larson, *Trials of Nation Making*; Mallon, *Defense of Community*; Méndez, *Plebeian Republic*. Christina Jiménez has extended this approach to cities. Jiménez, *Making an Urban Public*.

88. Rama, *Lettered City*.

89. "Sesión ordinaria de 7 noviembre 1930," *Gaceta Municipal*, AHMC; "Aguas Potables," *El Heraldo*, 10 May 1878, 1.

90. Concejo Departmental de Cochabamba, "Informe de 1876" (Cochabamba, Imprenta del Siglo), BACT; Concejo Departmental de Cochabamba, "Memoria de 1878" (Cochabamba: Imprenta del Siglo), BACT; "Sesión ordinaria de 9 abril 1891," *Gaceta Municipal*, AHMC; "Sesión ordinaria de 30 abril 1891," *Gaceta Municipal*, AHMC.

91. Concejo Municipal de Cochabamba, "Memoria de 1880" (Cochabamba: Imprenta del Siglo), BACT; Concejo Municipal de Cochabamba, "Memoria de 1881" (Cochabamba: Imprenta del Siglo), BACT; "Órden de 29 de diciembre de 1882," *Gaceta Oficial*; "Aguas de Arocagua," *El Comercio*, 28 November 1894, 3.

92. "Informe del Ingeniero Don Boloslao Mayerski," *Gaceta Municipal*, 19 March 1882, HUMSA.

93. Quotation from "El Concejo de Cochabamba a los Honorables Representantes del Departamento" (Cochabamba: Imprenta El Heraldo, September 1888), BACT. See also

"Provisión de Aguas Potables," *14 de Septiembre*, 6 May 1887, 2–3. For detailed coverage of these discussions, see Concejo Municipal and Ajuntamiento Departamental presidents' annual reports and *Gacetas Municipales*, 1882–1887, AHMC and BACT.

94. Bolivia, Resolución, 4 November 1891, *Gaceta Oficial*.

95. "Escritura de compra-venta de las aguas de Arocagua," 3 November 1891, published in "Aguas de Arocagua," *El Comercio*, 14 December 1894.

96. "Las fiestas de la inauguración," *El Heraldo*, 18 July 1896, 3. For detailed discussion of the project's progress, see daily press coverage in *El Heraldo* and *El Comercio* and *Gacetas Municipales*, 1893–1896, AHMC.

97. "Aguas de Arocagua: Expropiación of terrenos para cañería," AHDGC, Expedientes Republicanos (hereafter Exp. Rep.), 1895, vol. 84.

98. Solares Serrano, *La larga marcha de los cochabambinos*, 83–85.

99. Gotkowitz, *Revolution for Our Rights*; Hylton, Reverberations of Insurgency"; Kuenzli, *Acting Inca*; Rivera Cusicanqui, *Oprimidos pero no vencidos*.

100. Gotkowitz, *Revolution for Our Rights*, 37–43; Shesko, *Conscript Nation*, 25.

101. "Solicitud de Don Juan de la Cruz Torres sobre varios puntos referentes a la finca de Pacata," AHDGC, Exp. Rep., 1901, vol. 95; "Resolución de 20 julio 1910," *Digesto Municipal de Cochabamba 1900–1927*, AHMC.

102. "Sesión ordinaria de 27 junio 1898," *Gaceta Municipal*, AHMC; "Aguas potables," Resolución del Ministerio de Instrucción Pública y Fomento, Sucre, 23 August 1899.

103. "Aguas potables," Resolución del Ministerio de Fomento e Instrucción Pública, La Paz, 28 May 1902.

104. "Aguas potables de Cochabamba," Resolución del Ministerio de Instrucción Pública y Fomento, Sucre, 3 November 1897; "Aguas potables de Cochabamba," Resolución del Ministerio de Instrucción Pública y Fomento, Sucre, 13 July 1898.

105. Gandy, *Concrete and Clay*; Gandy, "Landscapes of Disaster"; Kaika, *City of Flows*; Melosi, *Sanitary City*; Swyngedouw, *Social Power and the Urbanization of Water*.

106. "Sesión extraordinaria de 18 enero 1901," *Gaceta Municipal*, AHMC; "Informe del Prefecto y Comandante General Zenón Cossío al señor Ministro de Gobierno y Justicia 1918–1919," HUMSA.

107. "Aguas de Arocagua: Ley de Reglamento del Servicio a Domicilio, 23 December 1913," AHDGC, Exp. Rep., 1926, vol. 170; "Aguas potables," Decreto Supremo, 17 February 1902; "Servicio de aguas," *El Comercial*, 12 April 1902, 3; "Sobre el servicio de aguas," *El Comercial*, 19 September 1902, 2; "Arrendamiento de aguas potables," *El Comercial*, 24 October 1902, 3.

108. "Agua potable: El origen de los pozos artesianos en el país," *Prensa Libre*, 31 July 1964, 3.

109. "Agua," *El Heraldo*, 10 November 1909, 3.

110. "Fuentes públicas" (editorial), *El Ferrocarril*, 21 August 1911, 2; "Fuentes públicas," *El Ferrocarril*, 19 December 1912, 3.

111. "Pelea por agua," *El Ferrocarril*, 8 November 1917, 3; "Aguas potables, al enemigo ni agua," *El Republicano*, 28 May 1920, 2.

112. Zenón Cossío, "Informe al Ministro de Gobierno y Fomento 1917–1918," HUMSA.

113. Bolivia "Aguas," Resolución Suprema, 24 March 1911, *Gaceta Oficial*.

114. Bolivia, "Aguas," Ley, 29 December 1912, *Gaceta Oficial*.

115. "Sesión ordinaria de 2 febrero 1913," *Gaceta Municipal*, AHMC; Natalio Arauco, "Discurso en la inauguración de las sesiones de 1916," *Gaceta Municipal*, AHMC.

116. "Sesión ordinaria de 23 agosto 1916," *Gaceta Municipal*, AHMC; *Memoria Municipal 1916* (Cochabamba: El Heraldo), AHMC.

117. "Pilas de San Antonio y San Sebastian," *El Heraldo*, 30 November 1897; "Fuente," *El Heraldo*, 13 August 1909, 3; "Otras fuentes," *El Ferrocarril*, 14 December 1910, 3; "Colaboración: El alcantarillado y el servicio de aguas," *El Heraldo*, 18 November 1920, 2, and 19 November 1920, 3.

118. Jiménez, *Making an Urban Public*, 86, 88–89.

119. Shesko, *Conscript Nation*, 56.

120. Klein, *Parties and Political Change in Bolivia*, 46.

121. Foss, "On Our Own Terms"; Giraudo and Martín-Sánchez, eds., *La ambivalente historia del indigenismo*; Gotkowitz, *Revolution for Our Rights*; Larson, *Trials of Nation Making*; Rosemblatt, *Science and Politics of Race*; "Rethinking Indigenismo on the American Continent."

122. Grieshaber, "Fluctuaciones en la definición del indio," 56.

123. Quoted in Thomson et al., *Bolivia Reader*, 248; Gotkowitz, *Revolution for Our Rights*, 58.

124. Choque Canqui, *Sublevación y masacre de Jesús de Machaqa*.

125. In 1921 his rivals, led by Daniel Salamanca, formed the Genuine Republican Party, splitting the young party in two. Klein, *Parties and Political Change in Bolivia*, 65–66.

126. Klein, *Concise History of Bolivia*, 163.

127. Klein, *Concise History of Bolivia*, 166.

128. "Aguas potables, al enemigo ni agua," *El Republicano*, 28 May 1920, 2.

129. "Por la salubridad pública," *El Republicano*, 12 February 1922, 5.

130. Ramón Rivero, "Informe de las labores del Concejo Municipal en 1918" (Cochabamba: El Mercurio), AHMC.

131. "Aguas de Arocagua," *El Republicano*, 2 August 1922, 2.

132. "Nomina de las concesiones de aguas de Arocagua," AHDGC, Exp. Rep., 1923, vol. 153; "Aguas de Arocagua," *El Heraldo*, 24 October 1922, 2.

133. "Aguas de Arocagua" (editorial), *El Heraldo*, 17 October 1922, 2.

134. "Nomina de las concesiones de aguas de Arocagua," AHDGC, Exp. Rep., 1923, vol. 153.

135. "Informe elevado por la Prefectura ante el Ministro de Fomento sobre las Aguas de Arocagua," *El Republicano*, 2 October 1922, 2–3.

136. "Una propuesta sui generis sobre aguas potables," *El Heraldo*, 8 September 1922, 3.

137. "La captación de aguas" (editorial), *El Heraldo*, 25 August 1924, 2.

138. "Los derechos del Estado sobre las vertientes de Arocagua" (editorial), *El Heraldo*, 27 August 1924, 2.

139. "Cochabamba y Arocagua" (editorial), *El Heraldo*, 6 February 1925, 2.

140. "Por los intereses de Cochabamba" (editorial), *El Heraldo*, 6 January 1925, 2.

141. "Expropiación de las Aguas Arocagua," AHDGC, Exp. Rep., 1924, vol. 157.

142. "Aguas potables" (editorial), *El Heraldo*, 26 April 1926, 2.

143. Other water expropriations for urban supply in the 1920s were far more amicable. These included the 1923 purchase of water from the fifteen owners of the La Isla property for the Recoleta neighborhood and the 1924 purchase of the Chorrillos Springs from Cleómedes Blanco for a standpipe in the Queru Queru plaza; another family there ceded their portion of Chorrillos water for free. "Ordenanza de 16 octubre 1923," *Originales del Digesto Municipal de Cochabamba 1900–1927*, AHMC; "Ordenanza municipal," *El Republicano*, 9 November 1923, 3; Luís Rodrígues G., *Memoria Municipal correspondiente a la gestión del año 1924* (Cochabamba: El Mercurio, 1925), AHMC; "Ordenanza de 19 noviembre 1924," *Originales del Digesto Municipal de Cochabamba 1900–1927*, AHMC.

144. Goubert, *Conquest of Water*, 200; Reisner, *Cadillac Desert*, 159.

145. Knudson, *Bolivia: Press and Revolution*, 74.

146. "Captación de aguas en Arocagua," *El Republicano*, 1 April 1928, 2; "Trabajos de Arocagua," *El Republicano*, 21 May 1928, 2; "La captación de aguas" (editorial), 10 October 1928, 3; "Captación de Aguas" (editorial), *El Comercio*, 9 October 1928, 2; "Captación de aguas," *El Comercio*, 14 October 1928, 2.

147. "El poema," *El Comercial*, 16 October 1928, 2.

148. "¡Agua!," *El Republicano*, 1 October 1929, 3.

149. "Aguas de Arocagua," *El Comercio*, 19 October 1928, 2.

150. "Inspección a Lagunmayu," *El Comercio*, 18 October 1929, 2.

151. "El problema del agua potable," *El Republicano*, 18 October 1929, 1; Bolivia, "Aguas potables," Resolución Suprema, 13 May 1930, *Gaceta Oficial*; "Sesión ordinaria de 16 September 1930," *Gaceta Municipal*, AHMC; "Aguas potables de Cochabamba," Bolivia, Resolución Suprema, 25 February 1931, *Gaceta Oficial*.

152. "Las aguas de Quintanilla," *El Imparcial*, 17 October 1931, 4.

153. Klein, *Concise History of Bolivia*, 72–73; Shesko, *Conscript Nation*, 88.

154. Gustafson, *bolivia in the age of gas*, 35; Cote, *Oil and Nation*, 70.

155. Klein, *Concise History of Bolivia*, 182.

156. Klein, "David Toro," 27–28; Cote, "War for Oil in the Chaco," 749.

157. Klein, *Concise History of Bolivia*, 170.

158. "El problema de la captación de aguas" (editorial), *El Imparcial*, 3 August 1934, 4; "Se inician los trabajos de perforación de pozos," *El Imparcial*, 7 October 1934, 2.

159. Averanga Mollinedo, *Aspectos generales de la población boliviana*, 58.

160. On community closures, see Jackson, *Regional Markets and Agrarian Transformation*; Larson, *Cochabamba, 1550–1900*; Larson, *Trials of Nation Making*; Rodríguez Ostria, "Entre reformas y contrareformas."

CHAPTER 2. ENGINEERING WATER REFORM

1. Shesko, *Conscript Nation*, 89, 112.

2. Zavaleta Mercado, *Lo nacional-popular en Bolivia*, 262. See also Zavaleta Mercado, "Consideraciones generales," 81–82.

3. Klein, "David Toro," 25, 34.

4. Young, *Blood of the Earth*, 24.

5. Klein, "David Toro," 36–37.

6. Buckley, *Technocrats and the Politics of Drought*, 4, 9.

7. Sanjinés Gonzales, *La reforma agraria en Bolivia* (1945), 149.

8. Soliz, *Fields of Revolution*; Gildner, "Indomestizo Modernism"; Gotkowitz, *Revolution for Our Rights*; Gordillo Claure, *Campesinos revolucionarios en Bolivia*.

9. Barragán, *Asambleas Constituyentes*, 100; Gotkowitz, *Revolution for Our Rights*, 117, 127, 219–224; Klein, *Parties and Political Change*, 8.

10. Bolivia, Constitución Política de 1938, Article 17.

11. Kiddle, *Mexico's Relations with Latin America*.

12. Despite advances, Vitz concludes that "Mexico City's housing and sanitary infrastructure were not a major priority for [the Cárdenas] administration." Vitz, *City on a Lake*, 175–176.

13. While dam projects increased irrigation water supply and made access more equal in Mexico, inadequate supply and inequalities endured. Wolfe, *Watering the Revolution*, 4, 184, 190, 226.

14. Bolivia, Constitución Política de 1938, Article 107.

15. Klein, *Concise History of Bolivia*, 192. For discussion of food imports, see Gotkowitz, *Revolution for Our Rights*, 143–144.

16. Sanjinés Gonzales, *La reforma agraria en Bolivia* (1932), 4.

17. Quoted in Sanjinés Gonzales, *La reforma agraria en Bolivia* (1945), 5. I was unable to find this quote in the 1932 edition.

18. Sanjinés Gonzales, *La reforma agraria en Bolivia* (1945), 139; Sanjinés Gonzales, *La reforma agraria en Bolivia* (1932), 258.

19. Kiddle, *Mexico's Relations with Latin America*, 144; Wolfe, *Watering the Revolution*, 4, 15.

20. Buckley, *Technocrats and the Politics of Drought*; Rogers, *Deepest Wounds*, 187.

21. Sanjinés Gonzales, *La reforma agraria en Bolivia* (1945), 148–164; Kiddle, *Mexico's Relations with Latin America*, 143–149. It is worth noting that Sanjinés referred to Indians as "savages" repeatedly and as "individualistic, egocentric, and exclusionary" in an interview he conducted with Leon Trotsky. Sanjinés Gonzales , *La reforma agraria en Bolivia* (1945), 30.

22. Saavedra Antezana, "Ideas generales sobre obras de irrigación en Bolivia," 16. Saavedra's was a much more optimistic view than those of many Bolivian intellectuals of his day. See especially Mendoza, *El factor geográfico en la nacionalidad boliviana* (1925) and *El Macizo Boliviano* (1935) for pessimistic and racist geographical determinist appraisals of Bolivia's natural and human resources.

23. Sanjinés Gonzales, *La reforma agraria en Bolivia* (1945), 166.

24. Additional research on the design, construction, and reception of the project planned for 2019 was not possible due to the COVID–19 pandemic.

25. Soliz, *Fields of Revolution*, chapter 2.

26. Saavedra Antezana, "Ideas generales sobre obras de irrigación en Bolivia," 11.

27. *Tierra*, 11 August 1942. Quoted in Soliz, *Fields of Revolution*, 58.

28. Sanjinés Gonzales, *La reforma agraria en Bolivia*, 167.

29. Nobbs-Thiessen, *Landscape of Migration*, 17.

30. Bohan, *Plan Bohan*, 76, 78, 80.

31. Bolivia, Decreto Supremo, 30 August 1939, *Gaceta Oficial.*

32. Bolivia, Decreto Supremo, 20 June 1940, *Gaceta Oficial.*

33. "Expropiación Vaso de la Angostura," October 1942, AHDGC, Exp. Rep., 1942.

34. Bolivia, Decreto Supremo, 31 July 1941, *Gaceta Oficial.*

35. León Rocha quoted in "Expropiación Vaso de la Angostura," 150.

36. On the role of such intermediaries, see Burns, *Into the Archive*, 39.

37. Dandler Hanhart, *El sindicalismo campesino en Bolivia*, 68.

38. "Expropiación Vaso de la Angostura."

39. Villarroel was a member of the clandestine military lodge Razón del Patria (RADE-PA) that along with the Movimiento Nacionalista Revolucionario (MNR) Party overthrew Peñaranda in 1943. The Villarroel administration aligned itself with the masses, sponsoring the 1945 Indigenous Congress in La Paz whose organizers called for ending obligatory non-agricultural labor in the countryside, building schools on rural properties, and an agrarian labor code. Gotkowitz, *Revolution for Our Rights*, 219–223.

40. Vitz, *City on a Lake*, 54.

41. Buckley, *Technocrats and the Politics of Drought.*

42. Jose Gordillo Claure, personal communication with author, June 2020.

43. Sanjinés Gonzales, *La reforma agrarian en Bolivia* (1945), 165.

44. See Wolfe, *Watering the Revolution*, chapter 2.

45. Buckley, *Technocrats and the Politics of Drought*, 85, 142.

46. Thornton, "'Mexico Has the Theories.'"

47. Sanjinés Gonzales, *La reforma agrarian en Bolivia* (1945), 159, 163.

48. Kiddle, *Mexico's Relations with Latin America*, 145.

49. Inter-American Conference on Indian Life, "Final Act," Pátzcuaro, Mexico, 14–24 April 1940 (Washington, DC: Bureau of Indian Affairs, 1941), 13–14.

50. Kiddle, *Mexico's Relations with Latin America*, 148–149.

51. Saavedra Antezana, "Ideas generales sobre obras de irrigación en Bolivia," 15–16.

52. Saavedra Antezana, "Ideas generales sobre obras de irrigación en Bolivia," 17.

53. Mexican president Plutarco Calles took such an approach in postrevolutionary Mexico in the 1920s, which Luis Aboites has termed "revolutionary irrigation." Aboites, *El agua de la nación.* In historian Michael Wolfe's words, Calles's approach was a "socially transformative federal policy that would nonetheless bypass more radical approaches to agrarian reform, such as redistributing prime hacienda land." Wolfe, *Watering the Revolution*, 72.

54. Sanjinés Gonzales, *La reforma agrarian en Bolivia* (1945), 152.

55. Sanjinés Gonzales, *La reforma agrarian en Bolivia* (1945), 149.

56. "Partido Obrero Revolucionario," in *Programas politicos de Bolivia*, ed. Cornejo Solis, 368, 370–371, 377–378.

57. Federación Sindical de Trabajadores Mineros de Bolivia, *Tesis de Pulacayo* (1946).

58. Anaya, *Unidos venceremos*, 38, 42.

59. "Principios y acción del 'Movimiento Nacionalista Revolucionario,'" in *Programas politicos de Bolivia*, ed. Cornejo Solis, 149–150, 164, 172.

60. Rama, *Lettered City*, 69.

61. Blasier, *Hovering Giant*, 128–129.

62. Gotkowitz, *Revolution for Our Rights*, chapter 8; Klein, *Concise History of Bolivia*, 205–206; Universidad Mayor de San Simón, *Cuestiones de derecho agrario*, 30.

63. Quoted in Soliz, "La modernidad esquiva," 45.

64. Solares Serrano, *Historia, espacio y sociedad*, 309.

65. Goldstein, *Spectacular City*, 61.

66. Solares Serrano, *Historia, espacio y sociedad*, 366–367; Solares Serrano, *La larga marcha*, 111.

67. The city's population in 1945 was approximately 76,500. Averanga Mollinedo, *Aspectos generales de la población boliviana*, 58.

68. Solares Serrano, *La larga marcha*, 370; *El País*, 19 July 1943, quoted in Solares Serrano, *Historia, espacio y sociedad*, 371.

69. "Obras indispensables," *El País*, 24 April 1937, 2; "Es inútil construir," *El País*, 3 August 1937, 2.

70. There are thousands of these petitions in the Archivo Histórico Departamental de la Gobernación de Cochabamba's Expedientes Republicanos from 1936 through 1949.

71. "Consecuencias," *El País*, 2 July 1936, 3; "Agua potable," *El País*, 8 December 1939, 4.

72. Lauderdale Graham, "Writing from the Margins," 613.

73. "Necesidades primordiales," *El País*, 23 July 1937, 2; "Sindicato de ingenieros," *El País*, 1 August 1937, 2.

74. "Aguas Potables," *El País*, 9 August 1938, 4; Damian Pariente, "Solicitud," 22 June 1939, AHDGC, Exp. Rep., 1939, vol. 271.

75. Ing. Ricardo Urquidi, "Aguas Potables de Cbba," *El País*, 6 August 1938, 9; Ing. Ricardo Urquidi, "Aguas Potables de Cbba," *El País*, 10 August 1938, 2; Hardin, "Tragedy of the Commons," 1243–1248.

76. "Aguas Potables," *El País*, 9 April 1938, 5.

77. "Compra de medidores de agua," AHDGC, Exp. Rep., 1938, vol. 260; "Propuestas," *El País*, 4 June 1938, 7; "Medidores," *El País*, 19 July 1938, 2; "Aviso," *El País*, 29 October 1938, 5.

78. "Medidores," *El País*, 2 October 1938, 2; Decreto del Ministerio de Obras Públicas, 2 February 1940.

79. "Medidores," AHDGC, Exp. Rep., 1942, vol. 311.

80. Rodríguez Ostria and Solares Serrano, *Maíz, chicha y modernidad*, 144–155.

81. "Captación," *El País*, 3 July 1938, 4.

82. "Futura prosperidad," *El País*, 19 July 1936, 5.

83. Bolivia, Decreto Supremo, 20 June 1936, *Gaceta Oficial*; *Gaceta Municipal* no. 28, 19 May 1936, AHMC; Bolivia, Resolución Suprema, 2 November 1936, *Gaceta Oficial*. See daily press coverage in *El País*, 1936–1939.

84. *Gaceta Municipal*, Cochabamba, 1 September 1939, AHMC.

85. "Problem," *El País*, 26 November 1936, 6.

86. "Aguas potables" *El País*, 27 November 1936, 2.

87. "Propuestas conduccion Arocagua," AHDGC, Exp. Rep., 1936, vol. 242; "Captación Wara Wara y Chungara," AHDGC, Exp. Rep., 1937, 25; "Quebrada Chungara-Huarahuara," AHDGC, Exp. Rep., 1938, vol. 261. See daily press coverage in *El País*, 1936–1938, especially Ricardo Urquidi, "Aguas Potables," *El País*, 6 August 1938, 9, and Eduardo Prudencio, "Agua es la vida de Cochabamba," *El País*, 29 August 1949, 2.

88. The Arocagua project affected some smallholders but mostly impacted large land-owners. For examples of the project's effects on smallholders and their protests, see "Acequia 'Las Tercias,'" AHDGC, Exp. Rep., 1937, vol. 254, and "Huarahuara y Chungara," *El País*, 25 January 1939, 7.

89. Bolivia, Decreto Supremo, 16 April 1937, *Gaceta Oficial*. See daily press coverage in *El País*, 1937–1938, especially Julio Knaudt, "Nueva captación," *El País*, 29 July 1937, 2.

90. Carlos Saavedra, "Estudios de provisión de aguas potables," AHDGC, Exp. Rep., 1940, vol. 286.

91. "Entrega," *El País*, 2 July 1938, 4; "Aguas Potables," *El País*, 6 August 1938, 9.

92. "¡Cochabamba se morirá de sed!," *El País*, 27 April 1940, 5.

93. See daily press coverage in *El Imparcial*, 1939–1940, for instance, "Carestía de agua," *El Imparcial*, 11 July 1939, 2.

94. "Falta de agua al sud de la ciudad," *El Imparcial*, 2 April 1940, 7; "Empeora el estado sanitario," *El Imparcial*, 27 July 1940, 2.

95. See daily press coverage in *El Imparcial*, 1939–1940, for instance, "Multa por conexión clandestina," *El Imparcial*, 29 March 1940, 3.

96. "Captación," *El Imparcial*, 10 December 1939, 4.

97. See, for example, "Propietarios de Wara Wara," *El Imparcial*, 2 August 1940, 2.

98. "Obras," *El Imparcial*, 16 August 1940, 6.

99. "Laguna Alalay," *El Imparcial*, 13 July 1940, 4.

100. "Obras," *El Imparcial*, 16 August 1940, 6.

101. "Expropiación Chocaya, Montesillo y Taquiña," AHDGC, Exp. Rep. 1940, vol. 286; Saavedra, "Estudios, transcritos," AHDGC, Exp. Rep. 1940, vol. 286.

102. Besides Rafael, affected landowners included at least four other members of the Salamanca family.

103. "Personas representativas," *El País*, 23 July 1940, 5; "Captación Montesillo," *El Imparcial*, 30 July 1940, 5; "Expropiación Chocaya, Montesillo y Taquiña."

104. "Respuesta de Policarpo Vargas," 21 July 1940, "Expropiación Chocaya, Montesillo y Taquiña."

105. "Respuesta de piqueros," 22 July 1940, "Expropiación Chocaya, Montesillo y Taquiña."

106. "Respuesta de piqueros," 22 July 1940, "Expropiación Chocaya, Montesillo y Taquiña."

107. Cultivators and the beer factory in Taquiña also protested the expropriation; their responses are included in the case record.

108. Antonio Zimmerman, "Propuesta," AHDGC, Exp. Rep. 1941, vol. 292.

109. Mavrich and Company, "Propuesta," 10 August 1940, AHDGC, Exp. Rep. 1940, vol. 286.

110. Antonio Zimmerman, "Propuesta"; Mavrich and Company, "Propuesta."

111. Julio Arauco Prado, Decree, 30 June 1941, "Expropiación de las lagunas de Chapisirca" (hereafter "Expropiación Chapisirca"), AHDGC, Exp. Rep. 1941, vol. 299, 32.

112. Ing. Eligio Esquivel Mendez, Memo to the prefect, 26 June 1941, "Expropiación Chapisirca."

113. "Partición de bienes hermanos Salamanca," 12 April 1928, AHDGC, Exp. Rep. 1942, vol. 306; "Expropiación Chapisirca."

114. "Partición de bienes hermanos Salamanca."

115. The Chapisirca hacienda was left to Raquel. "Expropiación Chapisirca," 35.

116. "Amparo administrativo impuesto por Alfonzo Z. y Raquel Salamanca de Gumucio contra Antonio Zimmerman," 4 October 1939, AHDGC, Exp. Rep. 1939, vol. 276, 2.

117. "Informe del perito fiscal," 2 September 1941, "Expropiación Chapisirca."

118. "Respuesta de los herederos del Dr. Salamanca al perito fiscal," 22 September 1941, "Expropiación Chapisirca."

119. The final price was calculated as follows:

Water sales	Bs. 793,333.00
Depreciation	Bs. 1,937,000.00
Infrastructure and land expropriation	Bs. 165,200.00
TOTAL	Bs. 2,895,533.00

120. Solares Serrano, *Historia, espacio y sociedad*, 346, 350–351.

121. "Conducción de Aguas de Chapisirca," AHDGC, Exp. Rep., 1942, vol. 311; "Captación," *El País*, 27 February 1948, 2; "Testimonio de venta," 24 December 1946, Tirani Community Documents.

122. "Títulos de las propiedades de Cala-Cala, Temporal, Tirani e Incahuacasca y las Lagunas de San Juan," AHDGC, Exp. Rep., 1946, vol. 344.

123. "Testimonio de venta."

124. "Devolución de las Lagunas de San Juan y San Pablito," AHDGC, Exp. Rep., 1947, vol. 354.

125. "Expropiación cañería Calacala," AHDGC, Exp. Rep., 1948, vol. 357.

126. Jose Gordillo Claure, personal communication with author, June 2020.

127. Alfredo Marrón y Carlos Saavedra, "Memoria y presupuesto, Proyecto de captación de aguas potables en Chapisirca," 28 October 1949 (hereafter "Memoria y presupuesto"), SEMAPA.

128. "Agua limpia," *El País*, 26 February 1948, 2.

129. Quoted in Hall, *Cities of Tomorrow*, 222.

130. "Proyecto," *El País*, 18 September 1946, 3.

131. Urquidi Zambrana, *La urbanización de la ciudad*, 28.

132. Hall, *Cities of Tomorrow*; Solares Serrano, *Historia, espacio, y sociedad*, 389.

133. Solares Serrano, *Historia, espacio, y sociedad*, 403–406.

134. Solares Serrano, *Historia, espacio, y sociedad*, 350.

135. Hall, *Cities of Tomorrow*, 88–187.

136. Solares Serrano, *Historia, espacio y sociedad*, 415–416.

137. Le Corbusier, *The Athens Charter*, 43–44.

138. Solares Serrano, *Historia, espacio y sociedad*, 403–406; Hall, *Cities of Tomorrow*, chapter 4.

139. Solares Serrano, *Historia, espacio y sociedad*, 389.

140. "Urbanización," *El País*, 5 December 1946, 3; "Problema del agua," *El País*, 18 September 1946, 3.

141. Jorge Urquidi Z., "Informe," 3 November 1948, Municipalización de los Servicios Públicos de Pavimentación, Aguas Potables y Alcantarillado, AHMC, Fs. 42.

142. "Chapisirca," *El País*, 20 February 1948, 2.

143. Juan R. Torres, "Carta a La Paz," 14 October 1948, Municipalización de los Servicios Públicos, AHMC, Fs. 42.

144. "Obras públicas," *El País*, 22 January 1948, 5; "Falta agua," *El País*, 26 July 1949, 4.

145. "Agua Potable," *El País*, 14 September 1948, 6; "Multa Enrique Beha," AHDGC, Exp. Rep., 1946, vol. 344.

146. "Comité Pro-Cochabamba," *El País*, 30 October 1943, 5.

147. Bolivia, Decreto Supremo 2661, 16 May 1951, *Gaceta Oficial*.

148. Bolivia, Ley, 6 December 1948, *Gaceta Oficial*; "Acta de entrega," *Gaceta Municipal*, 19 January 1950, AHMC.

149. "Derrumbe," *El País*, 17 February 1949, 5; "Crédito," *El País*, 5 March 1949, 2.

150. "Falta de agua potable," *El País*, 24 July 1949, 5.

151. "Problema del agua" (editorial), *El País*, 25 July 1936, 4.

152. Wolfe, *Watering the Revolution*; Nelson, "Fifty Years of Hydroelectric Development in Chile," 196–197.

153. Ferguson, *Anti-Politics Machine*; Li, *Will to Improve*.

154. Buckley, *Technocrats and the Politics of Drought*.

CHAPTER 3. WATER FOR THOSE WHO USE IT

1. Walter Guevara Arze as quoted in Bolivia, *El libro blanco de la reforma agraria*, 160.

2. Dunkerley, *Rebellion in the Veins*, 38–39.

3. On earlier violent changes of power, see Klein, *Parties and Political Change in Bolivia*.

4. On urban reform in La Paz, see Calderón and Szmukler, *La política en las calles*. On urban reform in Cochabamba, see Solares Serrano, *Historia, espacio y ciudad*, and Solares Serrano, *La larga marcha*.

5. Early scholarship on the Bolivian revolution, like MNR leaders, focused on the MNR and celebrated its achievements. See Alexander, *Bolivian National Revolution*. Revisionist scholars in the 1960s, 1970s, and 1980s took a more skeptical view, calling the revolution "incomplete" or even authoritarian, mirroring the MNR-centrism of their predecessors while faulting the MNR for not being revolutionary enough. See Antezana Ergueta, *De la reforma a la contra reforma agraria*; Dunkerley, *Rebellion in the Veins*; Klein, *Parties and Political Change*; Malloy, "Revolutionary Politics." Like MNR leaders, these scholars usually overlooked the long history of organizing by supposedly "apolitical" peasants and Indians and deemed peasant mobilization during the revolution spontaneous, if they acknowledged it at all. Quote from Goodrich, "Bolivia in Time of Revolution," 5.

6. *Indianista* scholarship in the 1980s also critiqued the revolution but, rather than emphasizing its limits, condemned the revolutionary nationalist project for erecting yet another authoritarian and exploitative state. These scholars highlighted popular mobilization but downplayed its effectiveness, portraying popular groups as either passive beneficiaries or victims of the clientelist MNR. Albó, "Achacachi: Medio siglo de luchas campesinas"; Albó, "From MNRistas to Kataristas to Katari"; Harris and Albó, *Monteros y guardatojos*; Platt, *Estado boliviano y ayllu andino*; Rivera Cusicanqui, *Democracia liberal y democracia del ayllu*, 144; Rivera Cusicanqui, *Oprimidos pero no vencidos*, esp. 149–150. These scholars drew

a stark distinction between Cochabamba where the revolution produced smallholders with land titles and the Altiplano where, they claimed, the MNR imposed top-down and oppressive unions and pushed for hacienda division rather than community restoration. Silvia Rivera Cusicanqui distinguished between the highland Aymara indigenous movement rooted in "the long memory" of eighteenth-century anticolonial struggles and Cochabamba's Quechua peasantry whose intellectual horizon was informed by "the short memory" of revolutionary nationalism and mestizo peasant union organizing. Rivera Cusicanqui, *Oprimidos*, 78. Indeed, Cochabamba experienced a more rapid process of peasantization whereas ayllus remained strong in the highlands. But as Brooke Larson has observed, these ostensibly regional contrasts masked ideological differences over whether class or ethnicity was the key to understanding—and fighting—oppression. Larson, *Cochabamba*, 338. In the 1980s, some scholars credited popular classes with making the revolution revolutionary. Dandler, *El sindicalismo campesino en Bolivia*; Zavaleta Mercado, "Consideraciones generales."

7. A new generation of historians has shifted focus away from the MNR to the bases that pushed the MNR to deal with their long-standing grievances. Cote, *Oil and Nation*; Gildner, "Indomestizo Modernism"; Gordillo Claure, *Arando en la historia*; Gordillo Claure, *Campesinos revolucionarios en Bolivia*; Gotkowitz, *Revolution for Our Rights*; McGrath, "Devil's Bargains"; Nobbs-Thiessen, *Landscape of Migration*; Pacino, "Constructing a New Bolivian Society"; Pacino, "Creating Madres Campesinas"; Pacino, "Stimulating a Cooperative Spirit?"; Pacino, "Bringing the Revolution to the Countryside"; Shesko, *Conscript Nation*; Soliz, *Fields of Revolution*; Soliz, "'Land to the Original Owners'"; Young, *Blood of the Earth*. Rather than a victory for or a betrayal of the popular classes, these histories depict the revolution as a contested process negotiated by a diversity of actors that produced mixed results. To riff on Gilbert Joseph and Daniel Nugent's assessment of scholarship on the Mexican revolution, these scholars have brought the people back in without leaving the state out. Joseph and Nugent, "Popular Culture and State Formation," 12.

8. Some scholars maintain the Indianista view that the MNR did more to strengthen internal colonialism than to dismantle it. Ari Chachaki, *Earth Politics*; Sanjinés C., *Embers of the Past*; Sanjinés C., *Mestizaje Upside-Down*.

9. Grieshaber, "Fluctuaciones en la definición del indio," 59.

10. Carlos Flores Rodríguez, "Del Seminario de Educación Fundamental," *Gaceta Campesina*, April 1953, 38.

11. Nobbs-Thiessen, *Landscape of Migration*, 44, emphasis in original.

12. On agrarian reform debates, see Antezana Ergueta, *De la reforma a la contrareforma agraria*; Gordillo Claure, *Arando en la historia*, 139–143; Gordillo Claure, *Campesinos revolucionarios en Bolivia*, 29, 36–46.

13. Dunkerley, *Rebellion in the Veins*, 98–102, 65–66.

14. Klein, *Concise History of Bolivia*, 209–210.

15. Dunkerley, *Rebellion in the Veins*, 65.

16. Rivas Antezana and Gordillo Claure, *Los hombres de la revolución*, 71–80.

17. In 1954 the MNR specifically recognized highland indigenous communities' land claims with Decreto Ley no. 3732, 19 May 1954. On indigenous community mobilization leading to this decree, see Soliz, "'Land to the Original Owners,'" and Soliz, *Fields of Revolution*.

18. Siekmeier, *Bolivian Revolution and the United States*, 43.

19. Goodrich, "Bolivia in the Time of Revolution," 20.

20. Antezana Ergueta and Romero Bedregal, *Origen, desarrollo y situación actual*; Dandler Hanhart, *El sindicalismo campesino en Bolivia*; Gordillo Claure, *Campesinos revolucionarios en Bolivia*; Gotkowitz, *Revolution for Our Rights*, 114, 132, 270; Rivera Cusicanqui, *Oprimidos pero no vencidos*, 112–113.

21. Richard Patch, "The Progress of Land Reform in Bolivia: Land Tenure Center Discussion Paper 2" (Madison, WI: Land Tenure Center, May 1963), LTC, Bolivia Files.

22. Ñuflo Chávez Ortiz, "Discurso prenunciado en la 'Semana de la Siembra,'" *Gaceta Campesina*, April 1953, 30.

23. "Ponencias a exponer en el congreso indigenal," undated petition, ABNB, Exp. Pres. Rep. 765. Other scholars have noted popular groups' use of pro-MNR revolutionary nationalist rhetoric to frame and justify their claims. Soliz, *Fields of Revolution*; Pacino, "Bringing Revolution to the Countryside."

24. Petition dated 3 July 1952, ABNB, Exp. Pres. Rep. 765; Petition dated 30 June 1952, ABNB, Exp. Pres. Rep. 759.

25. Young, *Blood of the Earth*, 7. See also Cote, *Oil and Nation*; Gotkowitz, *Revolution for Our Rights*; Soliz, *Fields of Revolution*.

26. Wolfe, *Watering the Revolution*, 12–14.

27. Ñuflo Chávez, Ministro de Asuntos Campesinos, speech published in *Gaceta Campesina*, August 1952. President Germán Busch had declared August 2 the national "día del indio" in 1937 to commemorate the founding of the country's first indigenous school in Warisata (La Paz Department) on that day in 1931.

28. Nobbs-Thiessen, *Landscape of Migration*, 3–4.

29. Bolivia, Decreto Básico de la Reforma Agraria, No. 3301, 20 January 1953, *Gaceta Oficial*.

30. Dunkerley, *Rebellion in the Veins*, 72.

31. On the MNR's program to improve peasants' health, see Pacino, "Constructing a New Bolivian Society."

32. Félix Eguino Zaballa y Zenón Barrientos Mamani, "Ponencia sobre la reforma agraria ante la 6a. convención del MNR," *Gaceta Campesina*, April 1953. See also Victor Paz Estenssoro's supreme decree creating the Ministerio de Asuntos Campesinos, *Gaceta Campesina*, August 1952, and "Bolivia define su doctrina en materia de educación fundamental," *Gaceta Campesina*, August 1954. On revolutionary-era public health reform, see Pacino, "Bringing the Revolution to the Countryside"; Pacino, "Constructing a New Bolivian Society"; Pacino, "Stimulating a Cooperative Spirit?"

33. Eguino Zaballa and Barrientos Mamani, "Ponencia."

34. Bolivia, Decreto Supremo 3185, 15 April 1952, *Gaceta Oficial*; Jorge Muller Barragán, "Transformación de la Socio-Economía del Altiplano de La Paz," *Gaceta Campesina*, August 1954.

35. Felix Eguino Zaballa, "Una contribución al planteamiento de la reforma agrarian," *Gaceta Campesina*, August 1952.

36. "Plan General para el Estudio de la Reforma Agraria," 7 April 1953, published in *Gaceta Campesina*, August 1953, 83–118.

37. Goodrich, "Bolivia in Time of Revolution," 21; Dandler, *El sindicalismo campesino*, 37.

38. A *decreto ley*, or decree law, has the power of a law but has not been passed by congress. As Carmen Soliz explains, they are usually "signed by a de facto president or in a revolutionary context." Soliz, *Fields of Revolution*, 183–184. Because Congress dissolved after the April 1952 insurrection, MNR President Victor Paz Estenssoro implemented revolutionary reform through a series of decree laws. The 2 August 1953 Agrarian Reform Decree Law 3464 was passed into law by the new congress on 29 October 1956. Bolivia, Ley de 29 October 1956, *Gaceta Oficial*.

39. Bolivia, Decreto Ley 3464, 2 August 1953, *Gaceta Oficial*.

40. Bolivia, Decreto Ley 3464, 2 August 1953, Article 154, *Gaceta Oficial*.

41. Bolivia, Decreto Ley 3464, 2 August 1953, Articles 151 and 102, *Gaceta Oficial*, my emphasis.

42. Zimmerer, "Spatial-Geographic Models of Water Scarcity," 175.

43. "Propietarios de Aguas" (editorial), *El Pueblo*, 5 September 1953, 4.

44. *Gamonalismo* comes from the word *gamonal*, meaning "a large landowner" and refers to the exploitation of the indigenous population.

45. "Juntas de Propietarios de Agua," *El Pueblo*, 10 November 1954, 5.

46. Luis Soria Lens, "La ciencia agrícola de los antiguos Aymaras," *Gaceta Campesina*, August 1953.

47. Juan Flores y Oblitas and Luis Aliaga Moller, "Analisis del problema agrario y del indígena en Bolivia," *Gaceta Campesina*, August 1953.

48. Bolivia, Decreto Ley 3464, 2 August 1953, Articles 152 and 155, *Gaceta Oficial*.

49. Bolivia, Decreto Supremo 03471, 27 August 1953, *Gaceta Oficial*.

50. Gordillo Claure, *Campesinos revolucionarios en Bolivia*, 170–171.

51. The law set out four categories of agricultural land: small properties (*propiedades pequeñas*), medium-sized properties (*propiedades medianas*), large estates (*latifundios*), and agricultural enterprises (*empresas agrícolas*). See the appendix for maximum holdings under the 1953 agrarian reform law.

52. Caso agrario "Chullpas Quinto Suyo," Cantón Toco, Provincia Germán Jordán, INRA-C, Exp. 1798, Número de control 5513.

53. Quoted in Gordillo Claure, *Arando en la historia*, 111.

54. Tinsman, *Partners in Conflict*, 171.

55. *Arrimantes* were peasants who farmed *colonos'* land, often in exchange for assistance in carrying out obligations for the *patrón*. They were often referred to as the *colonos* of the *colonos*. Dandler, *El sindicalismo campesino en Bolivia*, 160.

56. Ingeniería Global, "Solicitud de préstamo, Vol. I," 11 December 1962, 43, ADPGC, HC-294 v. 1.

57. "Aprovisionamiento," *El País*, 6 December 1952, 4; "Poco caudal", *El País*, 25 January 1953, 4.

58. "Lagunas," *El Pueblo*, 5 September 1953, 5.

59. On urban *mnrista* hostility toward peasant unionists, see Gordillo Claure, *Campesinos revolucionarios en Bolivia*, 129–135, 151–163.

60. Solares Serrano, *La larga marcha*, 178–179.

61. "Reforma Urbana," *El Pueblo*, 13 July 1955, 3; Bolivia, Decreto Supremo 3482, 2 September 1953, *Gaceta Oficial*; Bolivia, Decreto Supremo 3819, 26 August 1954, *Gaceta Oficial*.

62. On urban reform in Cochabamba, see Solares Serrano, *La larga marcha*, 148–189.

63. The municipality's solution was to require that developers (*loteadores*) provide drinking water and other services, but the municipality rarely enforced these regulations.

64. "Falta de agua en la ciudad" *El Pueblo*, 10 January 1956, 5.

65. "El Temporal sin agua potable," *El País*, 11 October 1952, 5; "Agua potable para Mayorazgo," *El Pueblo*, 26 May 1954, 3; "Aguas potables" *El Pueblo*, 15 December 1955, 3; "Piden instalación de piletas" *El Pueblo*, 3 January 1956, 5; "Falta agua potable en Aranjuez," *El Pueblo*, 22 September 1956, 3; "Síntesis de las Labores," *Anuario Municipal 1956*.

66. "Informativo municipal," *Los Tiempos*, 5 December 1952, 5; "Barrio Periodista sufre escasez de agua," *Prensa Libre*, 28 September 1961, 4; "Las Cuadras," *El Pueblo*, 23 March 1958, 5; "Barrio Periodista," *El Pueblo*, 28 April 1959, 1; "Barrio Periodista," *Prensa Libre*, 28 September 1961, 4; "Piden provision de agua potable en Barrio Gráfico," *Prensa Libre*, 4 December 1962, 4; "Zona sud-este privada de agua potable," *Prensa Libre*, 1 September 1963, 5.

67. "Alarmante escasez," *El País*, 10 October 1952, 5; "Escasez de agua," *Los Tiempos*, 18 October 1953, 5; "Carencia de agua," *El Pueblo*, 25 March 1954, 5; "Vecinos de Villa Galindo," *El Pueblo*, 4 September 1955, 4; "Villa Galindo," *El Pueblo*, 14 September 1955, 5; "Zonas urbanas" *El Pueblo*, 14 December 1955, 4; "Aguas potables," *El Pueblo*, 15 December 1955, 3.

68. "Patéticas situaciones," *El Pueblo*, 24 December 1954, 5.

69. "Vecinos reclaman provisión de agua," *El País*, 19 June 1952, 4; "Obras municipales," *Los Tiempos*, 29 August 1952, 4; "Informativo Municipal," *Los Tiempos*, 18 September 1952, 2; "Ampliación," *El País*, 2 October 1952, 4.

70. "Resguardo y vigilancia," *El País*, 10 May 1952, 2.

71. "Desperdicio de aguas potables," *El Pueblo*, 11 July 1954, 5.

72. "Inspección de aguas potables," *El Pueblo*, 10 December 1956, 3; "Inspección a Chapisirca," *El Pueblo*, 28 March 1957, 2; "Inspección a las Lagunas del Tunari," *El Pueblo*, 17 January 1958, 4.

73. "Escasez," *El Pueblo*, 23 December 1958, 5.

74. "Uso discrecional," *El Pueblo*, 3 October 1954, 4; "Desperdicio de agua," *El Pueblo*, 4 April 1956, 3; "Desperdician agua," *El Pueblo*, 6 July 1956, 2; "Escasez de agua," *El Pueblo*, 10 July 1956, 5; "Escasez de agua," *El Pueblo*, 17 August 1956, 2; "Pozos de Arocagua," *El Pueblo*, 14 July 1956, 3.

75. "Aprovechamiento de varias lagunas," *El Pueblo*, 5 September 1953, 5.

76. "Tabla de turnos de riego de la[s] mitas de los propietarios de terrenos de Tirani de Inca Huarkasga del río Tirani y las Lagunas de San Juan y San Pablito," 2 June 1946, Tirani Community Documents.

77. Gordillo Claure, "Peasant Wars in Bolivia," 107.

78. Dunkerley, *Rebellion in the Veins*, 67–72.

79. Butrón Mendoza, *Eran solo unos indios*, 65–66.

80. Butrón Mendoza, *Eran solo unos indios*, 69.

81. Dandler, *El sindicalismo campesino*, 45.

82. Gordillo Claure, *Campesinos revolucionarios en Bolivia*, 43.

83. This overview draws on Jose Gordillo's pathbreaking study of Cochabamba's peas-

ant unions that reveals diverse and competing agrarian projects among Cochabamba peasants, the extent and limits of their power, and the ways that peasant politics shaped and were shaped by relationships with national political leaders and processes. Gordillo Claure, *Campesinos revolucionarios en Bolivia*.

84. Gordillo Claure, *Campesinos revolucionarios en Bolivia*, 82.

85. Gordillo Claure, *Campesinos revolucionarios en Bolivia*, 103, 151.

86. Gordillo Claure, *Campesinos revolucionarios en Bolivia*, 94.

87. Gordillo Claure, *Campesinos revolucionarios en Bolivia*, 156.

88. Gordillo Claure, personal communication with author, 16 July 2020; Bolivia, Decreto Supremo 3699, 8 April 1954, *Gaceta Oficial*.

89. Gordillo Claure, *Campesinos revolucionarios en Bolivia*, 78.

90. Gordillo Claure, personal communication with author, 16 July 2020.

91. Rivas Antezana and Gordillo Claure, *Los hombres de la revolución*, 74.

92. "Títulos de las propiedades de Cala-Cala, Temporal, Tirani e Incahuacasca y las Lagunas de San Juan," AHPC, Exp. Rep., 1946, vol. 344; "Testimonio de la escritura de venta de los fundos del Temporal, Incahuarakaska, Tirani, así como de la mitad de las aguas de La Laguna San Juan," 24 December 1946, 2, Tirani Community Documents.

93. Dionisio Hurtado, author interview, Tirani, 15 June 2011. *Pongueaje* was the system of unpaid services by *colonos* for the hacienda owner either on the hacienda or in his residence in the city. See Dandler Hanhart, *El sindicalismo revolucionario*, 167.

94. Josué Arias, author interview, Tirani, 14 August 2011.

95. Joaquín Arias discussing conversations with his father, interview with Jorge Camacho, Tirani, 21 November 2020.

96. Josué Arias, author interview, Tirani, 14 August 2011.

97. Author interviews, Tirani, June–August 2011.

98. Caso agrario de la propiedad Tirani, Testimony of Juan Rocha, Severino Pacheco García, Eusebio Valencia Sanchez, and others, INRA–C, Caja 01-42, Expediente (Exp.) No. 54617, Cuerpo II, 392–400.

99. Claudia Vargas de Portillo, author interview, Tirani, 26 July 2011.

100. Joaquín Arias, interview with Jorge Camacho, Tirani, 13 December 2020.

101. Bolivia, Resolución Suprema 75422, 13 November 1957, "Caso agrario Tirani," INRA–C, Exp. No. 54617 (Exp. No. 1551-1 acumulado), Cuerpo I, Caja 01-42, 260–263.

102. According to Cochabamba's 1965 loan application to the Inter-American Development Bank, 50 percent of the lake's waters belonged to (*pertenecía a*) the municipality. República de Bolivia, Ministerio de Economía Nacional, Deutsche Projekt Union, and GMBH Ingenieria Global, "Solicitud de préstamo para el abastecimiento de agua potable para la ciudad de Cochabamba," Cochabamba, 15 May 1965, SEMAPA.

103. Hans-G. Kracht, "Informe sobre abastecimiento de agua potable en la ciudad de Cochabamba," Cochabamba, 10 June 1963, ADPGC.

104. República de Bolivia, Ministerio de Economía, and Nacional Deutsche Projekt Unión GMBH Ingeniería Global, "Solicitud de préstamo para el abastecimiento de agua potable para la ciudad de Cochabamba–Bolivia, Primera etapa de la solución definitiva plan maestro, Volumen I de III tomos: Informe, Contrato del 11.12.1962 (hereafter "Solicitud de préstamo 1962, Vol. I"), HC-294 v. 1, ADPGC.

105. Wara Wara is alternatively spelled Huara Huara. To distinguish Lake Wara Wara from the smaller Lake Huara Huara in the Chusequeri system, I have used Wara Wara throughout and changed the spelling in quotations where necessary.

106. "Caso agrario de la propiedad Pacata Alta," INRA–C, Exp. No. 12422 (Exp. No. 27869 acumulado), Caja 10-22.

107. "Caso agrario Pacata Alta."

108. "Caso agrario Pacata Alta."

109. Hendriks, "Negociación de intereses locales," 30.

110. "Caso agrario de la afectación y expropiación del fundo Montesillo," INRA–C; Exp. No. 7701, Caja 09-21; "Caso agrario de la propiedad Chilimarca," INRA–C, Exp. No. 5962. See also Fernández Quiroga, "La relación tierra-agua," 39.

111. "Caso agrario de la dotación de la propiedad Linde," INRA–C, Exp. No. 9379, Caja 09-22. See also Fernández Quiroga, "La relación tierra-agua," 40–41.

112. "Caso agrario Chilimarca," *Sentencia*, 30 June 1959.

113. "Caso agrario de la propiedad San Vicente de Coña Coña," INRA–C, Exp. 10775, Caja 01-13. See also Salazar Ortuño, "Autoridades de agua," 110.

114. Winchell, "After Servitude," 458.

115. Fredy Omar Fernández Quiroga, author interview, 27 February 2014.

116. The Chilimarca case was decided in 1963, the Montesillo and Coña Coña cases in 1964, and the Linde case in 1966.

117. "Más agua" *El Pueblo*, 14 October 1955, 2.

118. "Mitas," *El Pueblo*, 7 October 1958, 5.

119. Fredy Omar Fernández Quiroga, author interview, 27 February 2014.

120. "Sequía," *El Pueblo*, 9 October 1956, 2; Ordenanza Municipal, 8 November 1956, *Anuario Municipal 1956*, AHMC.

121. "Comité progresista," *El Pueblo*, 7 October 1958, 4; "Fundamentales planteamientos," *El Pueblo*, 7 October 1958, 5.

122. "Oligarcas," *El Pueblo*, 30 December 1958, 4.

123. "Nueva directiva," *El Pueblo*, 23 January 1959, 4.

124. "Nuevo embalse," *El Pueblo*, 15 July 1959, 2; "Alcalde," *El Pueblo*, 16 July 1960, 3.

125. "Ampliación," *El Pueblo*, 26 September 1959, 5.

126. In 1964 the municipality received 600,000 cubic meters from Saytukocha's owners alone. "Solicitud de préstamo 1962, Vol. I."

127. Gordillo Claure, *Arando en la historia*, 111–113.

128. Jose Gordillo Claure, personal communication with author, 15 September 2019.

129. Boyer, *Becoming Campesinos*, 2.

130. Gordillo Claure, "Peasant Wars in Bolivia," 261. See also Silvia Rivera Cusicanqui's discussion of mestizo culture, what she calls *ch'ixi*. Rivera Cusicanqui, *Ch'ixinakax utxiwa*, 105. On *campesino* identity formation in Mexico, see Boyer, *Becoming Campesinos*.

131. Soliz, "'Land to the Original Owners'"; Soliz, *Fields of Revolution*.

132. "Agua potable," *Prensa Libre*, 20 October 1961, 5; "Servicios públicos" (editorial), *Prensa Libre*, 13 January 1962, 4; "Desarrollo," *Prensa Libre*, 23 February 1962, 4.

133. "Periferia urbana," *El Pueblo*, 16 October 1960, 5; "Perforaciones de pozos," *El Pueblo*, 15 June 1960, 5.

134. "Barrios populares," *Prensa Libre*, 7 May 1963, 5.

135. "Zona Sur," *Prensa Libre*, 15 October 1961, 5.

136. "Cooperativa," *Prensa Libre*, 21 January 1964, 5.

137. "Tupuraya," *Prensa Libre*, 16 August 1964, 4.

138. "Zona Sur," *El Pueblo*, 5 December 1959, 5.

139. "Problemas," *El Pueblo*, 9 December 1959, 1; "Zona Sur-este," *Prensa Libre*, 1 September 1963, 5; "Esfuerzos comunales," *Prensa Libre*, 2 December 1962, 5.

140. Knudson, *Bolivia: Press and Revolution*, 196.

141. "Barrio Obrero," *El Pueblo*, 12 September 1958, 5; "Servicios urbanos" (editorial), *El Pueblo*, 5 October 1958, 4.

142. Marrón and Saavedra, "Memoria y presupuesto."

143. "Solicitud de préstamo 1962, Vol. I," 37.

144. See daily coverage in *El Pueblo* and *Prensa Libre* from 1959 to 1961, especially, "Escasez de agua," *Prensa Libre*, 19 October 1961, 4.

145. Lehman, *Bolivia and the United States*, 134.

146. Gill, *School of the Americas*.

147. DeWitt, "Policy Directions in International Lending"; Krasner, "Power Structures and Regional Development Banks"; Thornton, *Revolution in Development*, 153.

148. Field, *From Development to Dictatorship*, 61; Lehman, *Bolivia and the United States*, 91–179, especially 109–113; Siekmeier, *Bolivian Revolution and the United States*, 38–102.

149. Siekmeier, *Bolivian Revolution and the United States*, 91.

150. Blasier, *Hovering Giant*, 144; Siekmeier, *Bolivian Revolution and the United States*, 48.

151. "Solicitud de préstamo 1962, Vol. I."

152. "Ministro de OO.PP.," *El Pueblo*, 15 October 1960, 5.

153. "Chapisirca," *Prensa Libre*, 5 December 1962, 4.

154. "Alarma," *Prensa Libre*, 6 December 1962, 4.

155. "Preocupación constante," *Prensa Libre*, 6 December 1962, 4.

156. "Inversiones," *Prensa Libre*, 25 December 1962, 5.

157. "B.I.D.," *Prensa Libre*, 17 January 1962, 4; "Consultoras," *Prensa Libre*, 26 January 1962, 5.

158. "Solicitud de préstamo 1962, Vol. I," 57–59; "Síntesis de Labores," *Anuario Municipal 1963*, AHMC; Ingeniería Global, "Estudio del agua subterránea," 15 April 1964, SEMAPA; daily press coverage in *Prensa Libre*, July 1963.

159. "Solicitud de préstamo 1962, Vol. I," 63.

160. "Estudios preliminares" *El Pueblo*, 23 February 1960, 1.

161. "Misicuni," *Prensa Libre*, 23 September 1966, 1.

162. "Agua potable" (editorial), *Prensa Libre*, 7 November 1963, 4; "Dotación," *Prensa Libre*, 7 December 1963, 3.

163. "Problema," *Prensa Libre*, 19 July 1964, 4.

164. "Villa Busch," *Prensa Libre*, 29 July 1964, 4.

165. Saul Hansell, "George Jackson Eder" (obituary), *New York Times*, 4 January 1998.

166. Quoted in Lehman, *Bolivia and the United States*, 123.

167. Dunkerley, *Rebellion in the Veins*, 83–119; Lehman, *Bolivia and the United States*,

91–146; Shesko, *Conscript Nation*, 163–169; Siekmeier, *Bolivian Revolution and the United States*, 73–102; Young, *Blood of the Earth*, 59–89.

168. Field, *From Development to Dictatorship*, 22, 25, 51–61, 87–130.

169. Field, *From Development to Dictatorship*, 96–97.

170. Gordillo Claure, *Campesinos revolucionarios en Bolivia*, 231.

171. Field, *From Development to Dictatorship*, 148.

172. Quoted in Shesko, *Conscript Nation*, 158.

173. Gordillo Claure, *Campesinos revolucionarios en Bolivia*, 121–128; Shesko, *Conscript Nation*, 168.

174. Field, *From Development to Dictatorship*, 79–87; Gordillo Claure, *Campesinos revolucionarios en Bolivia*, 135; Shesko, *Conscript Nation*, 170–171; Siekmeier, *Bolivian Revolution and the United States*, 82.

175. Geidel, *Peace Corps Fantasies*, 190.

176. Shesko, *Conscript Nation*, 171–172.

177. Dunkerley, *Rebellion in the Veins*, 118.

178. Quoted in Lehman, *Bolivia and the United States*, 144.

179. García, *Diez años de reforma agraria*, 76.

180. García, *Diez años de reforma agraria*, 34.

181. Heath, Buechler, and Erasmus, *Land Reform and Social Revolution in Bolivia*, 373–374.

182. Bolivia, *Bolivia: 10 años de revolución*.

CHAPTER 4. POPULAR ENGINEERING

1. Dunkerley, *Rebellion in the Veins*, 211–212, 218.

2. Nobbs-Thiessen, *Landscape of Migration*, 143.

3. Klein, *Concise History of Bolivia*, 222, 223; Dunkerley, *Rebellion in the Veins*, 121; Malloy, "Revolutionary Politics," 145. Indianista scholarship also emphasized continuities in MNR and dictatorship land policy. Albó, "From MNRistas to Kataristas to Katari," 385–386; Rivera Cusicanqui, *Oprimidos pero no vencidos*, 170.

4. Fields, *From Development to Dictatorship*; McGrath et al., "'Restorative' Dictatorship, Contentious Clientelism, and Problematic Intermediaries."

5. On similar dynamics in Brazil, see Blanc, *Before the Flood*.

6. Review of the IDB projects in Bolivia, https://www.iadb.org/en/projects-search?country=BO&sector=&status=Closed&query=, accessed 19 August 2020; review of World Bank projects in Bolivia, https://projects.worldbank.org/en/projects-operations/projects-list?lang=en&countrycode_exact=BO&os=0, accessed 19 August 2020.

7. Goldman, *Imperial Nature*, 67–71; Woods, *Globalizers*, 44–47.

8. Offner, *Sorting Out the Mixed Economy*. See also Siekmeier, *Bolivian Revolution and the United States*, 155; McGrath, "(Un)Cooperative Labor?"

9. World Commission on Dams, *Dams and Development*.

10. An average of 54 percent of its population was living in cities of twenty thousand or more in 1970. Borsdorf, "Population Growth and Urbanization in Latin America."

11. Castells, *Urban Question*; Castells, *City and the Grassroots*; Quijano, *Dependencia,*

urbanizacion y cambio social; Singer, *Economía política de la urbanización*; Germani, "La ciudad como mecanismo integrador."

12. Solares Serrano, *La larga marcha*, 231.

13. The term *loteador* connotes the illegal methods of developers and their dual role as representatives and exploiters of their clients.

14. Solares Serrano, *La larga marcha*, 234; "Determinaciones del Plan Regulador," *Prensa Libre*, 14 February 1965, 1.

15. SEMAPA, "Solicitud de préstamo presentada a consideración del Banco Interamericano de Desarrollo, Proyecto Agua Potable para la Cuidad de Cochabamba, Republica de Bolivia, 1974 (hereafter "Solicitud de préstamo 1974"), SEMAPA, 18–19; IDB, "Loan to the Republic of Bolivia for Water Supply and Sewerage," 15 November 1967 (hereafter "1967 Loan Project Report"), Anexo II, IDB, 2.

16. IDB, "Project Report, Bolivia: Second Stage of the Water Supply Program for Cochabamba," 17 September 1974 (hereafter "1974 Loan Project Report"), IDB, 5; SEMAPA, "Solicitud de préstamo 1974," 25.

17. "Necesidades," *Prensa Libre*, 21 August 1965, 4.

18. "Venta de agua," *Los Tiempos*, 10 August 1973; IDB, "1974 Loan Project Report," 5.

19. "Servicio de agua potable," *Prensa Libre*, 8 January 1971, 5; "Solución," *Prensa Libre*, 25 March 1971, 5.

20. Solares Serrano, *Historia, espacio y sociedad*; IDB, "1967 Loan Project Report," 9; IDB, "1974 Loan Project Report," 2, 7.

21. For instances of housewives' protests, see "Falta agua a zona este," *Prensa Libre*, 9 August 1967, 3; "Agua en abundancia," *Prensa Libre*, 4 October 1967, 5; "Incremento de agua," *Prensa Libre*, 8 November 1969, 4; "Preocupación general," *Prensa Libre*, 13 December 1972, 5; "Escasez," *Los Tiempos*, 14 November 1983; "Anuncio previo," *Los Tiempos*, 1 January 1984.

22. "Pedimos agua," *Prensa Libre*, 25 October 1968, 4.

23. "Zona Este," *Los Tiempos*, 16 October 1968, 6.

24. "Barrio del Magisterio," *Prensa Libre*, 6 March 1972, 4.

25. Jacobo Cardoso, author interview, 11 July 2014.

26. Solares Serrano, *La larga marcha*, 204.

27. JUNCO was a new cross-class civic organization comprised of the neighborhood federation, urban labor unions, peasant unions, university students and professors' federations, professional organizations, business associations, and women's groups.

28. "Necesidades inmediatas," *Los Tiempos*, July 1967, 5.

29. "Marcada escasez," *Prensa Libre*, 25 April 1969, 5; "Suministro," *Prensa Libre*, 2 September 1969, 4; "Uso del agua," *Prensa Libre*, 28 August 1975, 5.

30. "Uso racional," *Prensa Libre*, 16 May 1969, 4.

31. The Chusequeri project involved building a 12-meter dam that would store a million cubic meters of water that would then be transported via a 12-kilometer canal to the Chapisirca system. Marrón and Saavedra, "Memoria y presupuesto."

32. "Síntesis Informativa de las Labores," *Anuario Municipal 1967*.

33. IDB, "1967 Loan Project Report," 4.

34. "Agua potable," *Prensa Libre*, 17 January 1968, 4.

35. Offner, *Sorting Out the Mixed Economy*.

36. On contested views of social citizenship, see Grandin, *Last Colonial Massacre*.

37. Offner, *Sorting Out the Mixed Economy*, 79.

38. SEMAPA did not fully take over operation of the drinking water system until 1974. "Prerrogativas de SEMAPA," *Prensa Libre*, 7 May 1967, 5; Bolivia, Ley, 12 July 1967, *Gaceta Oficial*; Bolivia, Ley, 11 November 1971, *Gaceta Oficial*.

39. "Problema de agua potable," *Prensa Libre*, 14 January 1968, 4.

40. IDB, "1967 Loan Project Report."

41. IDB, "1967 Loan Project Report," PRA-3; Boyle Engineering, "Ampliación y mejoras del sistema de agua potable de Cochabamba, Informe de factibilidad," Cochabamba, February 1967 (hereafter "1967 Feasibility Study"), BUMSS, VI-1 to VI-2, VI-16, VI-20 to VI-22.

42. IDB, "1967 Loan Project Report," PRA-29.

43. "Tasa agua potable," *Prensa Libre*, 13 April 1967, 4.

44. Boyle, "1967 Feasibility Study," VI-1 to VI-2, VI-16, VI-20 to VI-22.

45. "Agua potable" (editorial), *Prensa Libre*, 17 August 1967, 5.

46. "El problema del agua" (editorial), *Prensa Libre*, 7 October 1967, 5.

47. "Falta explicar" (editorial), *Prensa Libre*, 24 August 1967, 5.

48. Dunkerley, *Rebellion in the Veins*, 178–200; Klein, *Concise History of Bolivia*, 226–228; Lehman, *Bolivia and the United States*, 164–165.

49. Klein, *Concise History of Bolivia*, 230.

50. Dunkerley, *Rebellion in the Veins*, 219–220.

51. Lehman, *Bolivia and the United States*, 165. See also Dunkerley, *Rebellion in the Veins*, 205.

52. "Junta de Comunidad," *Prensa Libre*, 27 August 1972, 5.

53. "Agua potable," *Prensa Libre*, 2 November 1972, 3.

54. "¿SEMAPA autónoma?" (editorial), *Prensa Libre*, 22 January 1973, 5.

55. "JUNCO y SEMAPA," *Prensa Libre*, 22 January 1973, 5; "Memorial de JUNCO," *Prensa Libre*, 8–12 February 1973, 3.

56. IDB, "1974 Loan Project Report," 5–7, 59–64; IDB, Authorizing Memorandums 10/72 and 5/74, IDB; SEMAPA, "1974 Informe final," 11–12.

57. "Agua potable" (editorial), *Prensa Libre*, 4 October 1973, 5; "Préstamo," *Prensa Libre*, 18 November 1973, 4; "Oficinas del BID," *Prensa Libre*, 19 November 1973, 5.

58. Severo Vega, author interview, 24 May 2011.

59. IDB, "1974 Loan Project Report," 1, 59–61.

60. Dunkerley, *Rebellion in the Veins*, 209–210.

61. Klein, *Concise History of Bolivia*, 229–230.

62. Dunkerley, *Rebellion in the Veins*, 211–212.

63. SEMAPA, "1974 Solicitud de préstamo," 92; Bolivia, Decreto Supremo 11968, 14 November 1974, *Gaceta Oficial*; IDB, "1974 Loan Project Report," 9, 19, 34.

64. IDB and Bolivia, "Contrato de préstamo," 26 March 1975, clauses 8, 11, 13, 14.

65. IDB, "1974 Loan Project Report," 49–51.

66. PAHO, "Informe asesoría desarrollo institucional, Vol. II," September 1972; SEMAPA, "1974 Informe final," 23.

67. IDB, "1974 Loan Project Report," 12, 29, 30, 38.

68. See, for instance, "Pueblo debe aportar," *Prensa Libre*, 26 March 1975, 4.

69. "Tarifas racionales," *Prensa Libre*, 13 June 1974, 4.

70. SOFRELEC Ingenieurs Conseils, "Estudio de Prefactibilidad del Proyecto de Aprovechamiento Múltiple de Misicuni – Síntesis" (Cochabamba: Asociáción Misicuni, February 1975) (hereafter "SOFRELEC síntesis"), ADPGC, HC-247 síntesis.

71. "Corte de agua," *Prensa Libre*, 11 April 1975, 5.

72. "Corte de servicio" (editorial), *Prensa Libre*, 9 April 1975, 4.

73. On USAID efforts to strengthen self-help measures in Bolivia, see Comptroller General of the United States, "Report to Congress: Bolivia," 30 January 1975, 12, LTC, Bolivia files.

74. "JUNCO pedirá informe," *Prensa Libre*, 27 June 1974, 4.

75. "Cartas de lectores," *Prensa Libre*, 7 March 1975, 4.

76. "Junta vecinales," *Prensa Libre*, 15 April 1975, 5.

77. See daily press coverage in *Prensa Libre* from March through July 1975, for instance, "JUNCO definió su posición," *Prensa Libre*, 9 April 1975, 5.

78. "Oposición a tarifas," *Prensa Libre*, 13 March 1975, 5.

79. "La realidad" (editorial), *Prensa Libre*, 4 April 1975, 5.

80. "Junta vecinales," *Prensa Libre*, 15 April 1975, 5.

81. "Tarifas," *Prensa Libre*, 6 August 1975, 5; "SEMAPA conexiones," *Prensa Libre*, 19 December 1975, 5; "Consumo de agua," *Prensa Libre*, 31 December 1975, 4; "Reglamentación," *Prensa Libre*, 1 January 1976, 5; "SEMAPA tomará medidas," *Prensa Libre*, 16 May 1976, 5; IDB, "Préstamo 414/SF-BO para la segunda etapa del proyecto de agua potable de la ciudad de Cochabamba," IDB.

82. "El problema del agua," *Prensa Libre*, 10 November 1976, 4.

83. "Usarios no cancelan," *Prensa Libre*, 21 May 1977, 5.

84. "Consumo de agua," *Prensa Libre*, 3 November 1976, 4.

85. "Trabajos de renovación," *Prensa Libre*, 11 June 1977, 4.

86. "Misión del alcalde," *Prensa Libre*, 18 October 1966, 1; "Medidores de agua," *Prensa Libre*, 31 January 1969, 4.

87. Global Engineering, "Solicitud de préstamo para el abastecimiento de agua potable para la ciudad de Cochabamba," vol. 2 (Cochabamba, 15 May 1965), article 324, SEMAPA.

88. According to Boyle Engineering's 1967 feasibility study, 13 percent of the city's homes (223 households) had their own wells. Although a luxury, the wells' quality was often quite poor. Boyle, "1967 Feasibility Study," IV-7-8, VI-22; IDB, "1967 Loan Project Report," Anexo II, 2.

89. "Alerta propietarios de pozos," *Prensa Libre*, 10 December 1966, 5.

90. "Las aguas subterráneas," *Prensa Libre*, 23 November 1966, 3.

91. Rafael Peredo A., "Escasez de aguas potable y de riego," *Los Tiempos*, 25 January 1970, 4; Lauro Morales Navia, "Agua potable para Cochabamba," *Prensa Libre*, 26 February 1970, 5.

92. "El problema del agua potable," *Prensa Libre*, 3 July 1969, 3.

93. "Carta," *Prensa Libre*, 28 January 1967, 1; "Chusequeri," *Prensa Libre*, 29 January 1967, 1.

94. Guillermo Canedo C., "Aguas potables" (editorial), *Los Tiempos*, 23 July 1969, 4.

95. "Agricultores de Tiquipaya," *El Pueblo*, 12 March 1960, 5.

96. See daily coverage in *Los Tiempos* and *Prensa Libre* from 1969 to 1975.

97. *Los Tiempos*, 9 July 1973.

98. SOFRELEC síntesis.

99. CORDECO, "Decreto de su creación," 6 November 1970, ADPGC; CORDECO, "Climatología e ecología" (Cochabamba, 1971), ADPGC, HC-029. See daily coverage in *Los Tiempos* and *Prensa Libre* from November 1970 to March 1971.

100. SEMAPA, "1974 Solicitud de préstamo," 18–19.

101. See daily coverage in *Los Tiempos* and *Prensa Libre* from 1972 to 1974.

102. "Fabriles respaldan al proyecto Misicuni," *Prensa Libre*, 4 April 1975, 5.

103. See daily coverage in *Prensa Libre* from 1974 to 1975.

104. Lamarre Valois International, "Proyecto Múltiple Misicuni, estudio de factabilidad: Síntesis general," December 1979, ADPGC, 2–3, (this document has not yet been catalogued by the archive). See daily coverage in *Prensa Libre* for 1975.

105. Mayor Humberto Coronel Rivas, cited in "Alcaldía propicia visita a la región de Misicuni," *Prensa Libre*, 7 September 1975, 5.

106. "JUNCO prepará caravana," *Prensa Libre*, 17 September 1975, 5; "SEMAPA participará en la caravana," *Prensa Libre*, 21 September 1975, 5.

107. "Caravana a Misicuni," *Prensa Libre*, 29 September 1975, 4.

108. "CAF acordó crédito," *Los Tiempos*, 10 November 1975.

109. "Apoyo a CORDECO," *Prensa Libre*, 3 January 1976, 4.

110. Bolivia, Decreto Supremo 13212, 18 December 1975, *Gaceta Oficial*. See daily coverage in *Los Tiempos* and *Prensa Libre* October 1975–January 1976.

111. See daily coverage in *Los Tiempos* and *Prensa Libre* July 1976–September 1977, for instance, "Decidida acción del Gral. Banzer," *Los Tiempos*, 18 July 1976.

112. "Ante crisis registrada," *Los Tiempos*, 22 October 1976; "Caudal de agua potable," *Prensa Libre*, 22 December 1976, 5; "Canal aductor," *Los Tiempos*, 18 January 1977.

113. "Campesinos pedirán indemnización," *Los Tiempos*, 27 December 1976; "Escasez," *Los Tiempos*, 15 January 1977.

114. "San Miguel," *Prensa Libre*, 1 February 1977, 4.

115. "CPC censura a SEMAPA," *Prensa Libre*, 19 February 1977, 4.

116. "Pronunciamiento de JUNCO," *Prensa Libre*, 26 February 1977, 5.

117. "Uso indebido," *Los Tiempos*, 4 February 1977.

118. "Pdte Banzer," *Prensa Libre*, 18 July 1976, 5.

119. "Recursos hídricos," *Prensa Libre*, 3 September 1977, 4.

120. "Medidas," *Prensa Libre*, 5 March 1977, 4.

121. Bolivia, Decreto Supremo 14470, 5 April 1977, *Gaceta Oficial*. See daily press coverage in *Prensa Libre* and *Los Tiempos*, March–August 1977, especially, "YPFB solucionará el problema de agua," *Los Tiempos*, 6 May 1977, and "Trabajos de SEMAPA," *Prensa Libre*, 19 June 1977, 4.

122. Comité Técnico Inter-Institucional Cochabamba, "Abastecimiento de agua potable de la ciudad de Cochabamba: Estudio de alternativas de emergencia," February 1977, SEMAPA.

123. "Perforación de pozos," *Prensa Libre*, 7 April 1977, 4.

124. "YPFB considerará denuncias," *Prensa Libre*, 26 August 1977, 4.

125. See daily coverage in *Prensa Libre* in August 1977 and correspondence and agreements between SEMAPA and Vinto communities in SEMAPA's Legal Department files.

126. Agenda of the cabildo abierto en Vinto, 17 September 1977, SEMAPA Legal Department files; Letter from the Comité Pro-Vinto to SEMAPA, 22 November 1977, SEMAPA Legal Department files; "Construcción del acueducto Vinto – Cala Cala," *Los Tiempos*, 3 September 1977.

127. "Captación de agua," *Los Tiempos*, 27 August 1977.

128. "Perforación de pozos," *Prensa Libre*, 8 April 1977, 5.

129. "Denuncias," *Prensa Libre*, 26 August 1977, 4.

130. "Trabajos de captación," *Los Tiempos*, 27 August 1977.

131. Letter from the Comité Pro-Vinto to SEMAPA, 22 November 1977; "Construcción," *Los Tiempos*, 3 September 1977.

132. Letter from the Comité Pro-Vinto to SEMAPA, 22 November 1977.

133. A 1978 United Nations Development Program (UNDP) and GEOBOL study of hydraulic resources in Cochabamba's four valleys, for instance, determined that "future exploitation will affect the hydrodynamic situation and interfere with existing wells, and this interference will need to be compensated." GEOBOL and UNDP, "Proyecto integrado de recursos hídricos Cochabamba, investigaciones de aguas subterráneas," 1978, SEMAPA, 224.

134. "Convenio suscrito entre autoridades de gobierno con entidades y representantes de Vinto," 1 December 1977, SEMAPA Legal Department files.

135. Dangl, *Five Hundred Year Rebellion*, 68–69.

136. "Gerente de SEMAPA informó sobre proyecto planteados," *Prensa Libre*, 22 October 1977, 5.

137. "Captación en Vinto," *Los Tiempos*, 24 November 1977; Dunkerley, *Rebellion in the Veins*, 240–248; Lavaud, *La dictadura minada*; Dangl, *Five Hundred Year Rebellion*, 56.

138. Lehman, *Bolivia and the United States*, 186.

139. Dunkerley, *Rebellion in the Veins*, 226.

140. Klein, *Concise History of Bolivia*, 233; Dunkerley, *Rebellion in the Veins*, 231–241.

141. Woods, *Globalizers*, 49.

142. Lehman, *Bolivia and the United States*, 191.

143. Dunkerley, *Rebellion in the Veins*, 326–327. On peasant protest against austerity, see Dangl, *Five Hundred Year Rebellion*, 75–78.

144. Lehman, *Bolivia and the United States*, 192.

145. Lehman, "Completing the Revolution?," 15.

146. Lehman, *Bolivia and the United States*, 193; Siekmeier, *Bolivian Revolution and the United States*, 156.

147. "Labor de SEMAPA," *Prensa Libre*, 10 November 1977, 3.

148. SEMAPA, "Informe final, Préstamo 414/SF/BO," 1983 (hereafter "1983 Informe final"), 34.

149. See daily press coverage May 1978–January 1979, especially "Subcontratistas paralizarán trabajo," *Los Tiempos*, 30 September 1978. See also SEMAPA, "1983 Informe final," 35.

150. "JUNCO pedirá juicio," *Los Tiempos*, 4 October 1978; quotation from "Vecinos bloquean calles," *Los Tiempos*, 10 October 1978.

151. "La situación de SEMAPA," *Los Tiempos*, 17 December 1978; "Nuevo gerente," *Los*

Tiempos, 17 December 1978; "Mayor control," *Los Tiempos*, 7 January 1979; "Juicio por irregularidades," *Presencia*, 7 April 1979; SEMAPA, "1983 Informe final," 22.

152. See daily press coverage in *Los Tiempos* and *El Diario*, November 1983–June 1984, for instance, "Censuran actitud de SEMAPA," *Los Tiempos*, 21 June 1984. See also SEMAPA, "1983 Informe final," 48–50, 58–61.

153. "SEMAPA 10° aniversario," *Los Tiempos*, 12 July 1983.

154. SEMAPA, "1983 Informe final," 34–35, 62.

155. See daily press coverage in *Los Tiempos*, November 1980–March 1981; "Incrementan caudal," *Los Tiempos*, 17 June 1982.

156. Convenio entre SEMAPA y los propiertarios y usuarios de la Laguna de "Saytu Ckocha," 11 May 1982; Convenio entre SEMAPA y los propiertarios y usuarios de la Laguna de "Saytu Ckocha," 17 May 1982; Convenio entre SEMAPA y la comunidad de propiertarios y usuarios de Lagun Mayu y Machu Mita, 30 August 1983; Convenio entre SEMAPA y la comunidad de propiertarios y usuarios de Lagun Mayu, 30 August 1983. All are from SEMAPA's Legal Department files.

157. "Corte del servicio de agua," *Los Tiempos*, 7 June 1985.

158. Lehman, *Bolivia and the United States*, 169.

159. As Greg Grandin has written, "the history of how democracy came to be defined downward, from entailing both liberty and some degree of social equality to meaning just individual freedom, is *the* story of the twentieth century." Grandin, *Last Colonial Massacre*, xiv.

160. "Proyecto Misicuni," *Prensa Libre*, 29 October 1975, 4.

161. See, for example, "Ejecucion del proyecto Misicuni," *Los Tiempos*, 23 October 1983.

162. "Aprobación oficial," *Los Tiempos*, 2 March 1982.

163. Laurie and Marvin, "Globalisation, Neoliberalism, and Negotiated Development," 1409.

CHAPTER 5. THE WATER IS OURS

1. Klein, *Concise History of Bolivia*, 241.

2. On Mexican officials' similar enthusiasm for neoliberal reforms, see Thornton, *Revolution in Development*, 194.

3. Klein, *Concise History of Bolivia*, 254–260; Lehman, *Bolivia and the United States*, 196–210.

4. Lehman, "Completing the Revolution?," 17.

5. Goldstein, *Spectacular City*, 88; Postero, *Now We Are Citizens*, 125.

6. Bolivia, Instituto Nacional de Estadística, 1992 Census; Ledo García, *Ubanisation and Poverty*, 127–129.

7. SEMAPA, "Programa de Emergencia 1989"; Comité de Emergencia Sequía Cochabamba, "Plan para afrontar los efectos de la sequía," 1990, 14–15; SEMAPA, "Plan Operativo Gestión 1989," 2–3, CORDECO HC-313.1; SEMAPA, "Plan maestro de abastecimiento de agua potable 1994," CORDECO P1-0237.

8. García Orellana, García Yapur, and Quitón Herbas, "La crisis política," 18.

9. Marvin and Laurie, "An Emerging Logic of Urban Water Management," 343.

10. JICA, "Informe del estudio básico del proyecto de rehabilitación y extensión de fuentes de rehabilitación y extensión de fuentes de agua subterránea en el área de Cochabamba" (May 1991) (hereafter JICA, "Informe"), CORDECO P1-0239.

11. International Development Association and Republic of Bolivia, "Development Credit Agreement (Major Cities Water Supply and Sewerage Rehabilitation Project)," 17 December 1990, 23–24.

12. World Bank, "Memorandum and Recommendation on Proposed Credit to the Republic of Bolivia for the Major Cities Water and Sewerage Rehabilitation Project," 6 November 1990 (hereafter World Bank, "1990 Memorandum"), 14, www-wds.worldbank.org/external/default/WDSContentServer/WDSP/IB/1990/11/06/000009265_3960929124939/Rendered/INDEX/multi_page.txt, accessed 19 June 2015.

13. Klein, *Concise History of Bolivia*, 258.

14. Klein, *Concise History of Bolivia*, 254–261.

15. Albro, *Roosters at Midnight*; Goldstein, *Spectacular City*; Lazar, *El Alto, Rebel City*.

16. Postero, *Now We Are Citizens*, 15. See also Hylton and Thomson, *Revolutionary Horizons*, 99.

17. Goldman, *Imperial Nature*, 100–150; Postero, *Now We Are Citizens*, 131.

18. Goldman, *Imperial Nature*, 232.

19. Marvin and Laurie, "An Emerging Logic of Urban Water Management," 346.

20. Assies, "David versus Goliath," 16; García Orellana, García Yapur, and Quitón Herbas, "La crisis política," 24–25.

21. Carlos Saavedra, "Exposición de motivos y propuesta para la creación de la Dirección Departamental de Recursos Hidráulicos (DIDERHI)" (Cochabamba: CORDECO, 1987), 3.1.4.

22. CORDECO, "Informe de Actividades 1988" (Cochabamba: CORDECO, 1988), annex, 20, 13.

23. CORDECO, "Inventario de pozos," 1988–1991; BRGM–SEURECA, "Evaluación de los recursos de agua y abastecimiento en agua potable de la ciudad de Cochabamba, Bolivia," 1990; Stimson et al., "Isotopic and Geochemical Evidence of Regional-Scale Anisotropy" (study carried out in 1991); Organismo Internacional de la Energía Atómica–Instituto Boliviano de Tecnología y Energía Nuclear, "Investigación de aguas subterráneas en la cuenca de Cochabamba-Quillacollo," 1991; L. Jordan D., GRNMA, CORDECO, "Sobre la explotación y procesos de contaminación en los acuíferos de la cuenca de Cochabamba por efectos de sequía," 1992; GEOBOL–CABAS, "Inventario de pozos," 1992; SEURECA, "Estudio de recursos subterráneos," 1994.

24. CORDECO, "Aguas subterráneas en el Valle de Cochabamba-Bolivia," circa 1987, 8; SEURECA, "Estudio de recursos subterráneos," 1, 32

25. BRGM–SEURECA, "Evaluación de los recursos de agua"; SEURECA, "Estudio de recursos subterráneos."

26. World Bank, "1990 Memorandum," 16.

27. "Cochabamba amenaza con paro general," *El Mundo*, 8 December 1992.

28. "Informe sobre proyecto Misicuni," *Opinión*, 13 December 1992.

29. "Juntas vecinales," *Los Tiempos*, 14 December 1992.

30. "Incremento de tarifas," *Opinión*, 1 April 1993.

31. Carlos Canelas, "Condición Irracional," *Los Tiempos*, 7 July 1993.

32. "Tarifas de agua," *Opinión*, 26 August 1993.

33. See daily press coverage in *Opinión* and *Los Tiempos*, June–September 1993.

34. Bolivia, Ley 1544, 21 March 1994, *Gaceta Oficial*.

35. Postero, *Now We Are Citizens*, 125.

36. "Desde lunes," *Opinión*, 6 March 1994.

37. Luján as quoted in "SEMAPA aumentó la tarifa de agua potable," *Presencia*, 30 March 1994.

38. "Subió el precio del agua," *Opinión*, 21 March 1996.

39. "Fortalecimiento de SEMAPA," *Los Tiempos*, 23 March 1996.

40. "SEMAPA y turrileros," *Presencia*, 19 May 1996.

41. "Tarifas de agua," *Última Hora*, 26 April 1996.

42. Goldman, *Imperial Nature*, 188.

43. Achi and Kirchheimer, "Innovar para alcanzar," 212.

44. Goldstein, *Spectacular City*, 72–79.

45. SEMAPA, Centro de Investigación, Promoción y Desarrollo de la Cuidad (CIPRO-DEC), and el Comité de Agua Potable de Puntiti, Convenio, 15 July 1994, SEMAPA Legal Department files.

46. "Tanque de agua en Puntiti," *Los Tiempos*, 27 February 1995; "SEMAPA," *Los Tiempos*, 21 July 1996; "Agua potable," *Opinión*, 29 September 1996.

47. "Agua," *La Razón*, 22 July 1998.

48. Jesús Salazár, author interview, Quintanilla, 15 June 2011; "Quintanilla," *Opinión*, 28 January 1991.

49. Author interviews with Chilimarca residents, February–May 2007.

50. Guadalupe Yacupaico, author interview, 24 March 2007.

51. Santiago Torrez, author interview, 12 April 2007.

52. Goldstein, *Spectacular City*, 88.

53. Achi and Kirchheimer, "Innovar para alcanzar," 212. See also Ledo García, *Agua potable a nivel de hogares*.

54. Cited in Achi and Kirchheimer, "Innovar para alcanzar," 214.

55. Goldstein, *Spectacular City*, 99–100, 108.

56. Esteban Yanez, author interview, 6 March 2007.

57. Hipólito Condori, author interview, 26 January 2007.

58. Goldstein, *Spectacular City*, 119–121.

59. Antonio Heredia, author interview, 27 April 2007.

60. Abraham Grandydier, author interview, 23 March 2007.

61. Albro, *Roosters at Midnight*, 98.

62. Miguel Palma Chambi, author interview, 15 March 2007.

63. Goldstein, *Spectacular City*.

64. Albro, *Roosters at Midnight*, 79.

65. Goldstein, *Spectacular City*, 93, 108, 114, 119–121, 192.

66. "Pozos," *Primera Plana*, 4 July 1996.

67. Achi and Kirchheimer, "Innovar para alcanzar," 215; Ledo García, "Agua potable a nivel de hogares," 137.

68. "Sin agua," *Presencia*, 16 March 1997; "Barrios pagan," *La Razón*, 19 April 1996.

69. Cited in Achi and Kirchheimer, "Innovar para alcanzar," 214.

70. Achi and Kirchheimer, "Innovar para alcanzar," 214.

71. "Precio de oro," *Hoy*, 25 July 1998; "Facturas," *Opinión*, 9 October 1996.

72. "Aguda escasez," *Opinión*, 30 September 1994; "Agua potable gratis," *Opinión*, 4 October 1994; "SEMAPA cumplirá," *Opinión*, 5 October 1994.

73. Goldstein, *Spectacular City*, 4–5. See also Tate, "Aspirational State"; Frazier, *Desired States*.

74. Assies, "David versus Goliath," 19.

75. "Perforación de pozos," *Opinión*, 30 April 1987; "Campo de pozos," *Los Tiempos*, 8 June 1988; "Estudio técnico," *Opinión*, 30 October 1988.

76. "Campesinos se oponen a proyecto de pozos," *Opinión*, 20 October 1988.

77. "Perforación de pozos," *Los Tiempos*, 7 April 1989, 5.

78. "Prefecto busca solución," *Opinión*, 12 May 1989, 9.

79. "Agua de Tiquipaya," *Opinión*, 31 March 1989, 8.

80. "Principio de autoridad," *Los Tiempos*, 20 April 1989, 6.

81. "Problema con campesinos," *Los Tiempos*, 6 May 1989, 7.

82. "Campesinos se oponen," *Opinión*, 20 October 1988.

83. "Proyecto de pozos," *Opinión*, 21 January 1989, 7.

84. "Prefecto busca solución," *Opinión*, 12 May 1989, 9; "Perforación de pozos," *Los Tiempos*, 13 May 1989.

85. "Acuíferos en El Paso," *Los Tiempos*, 17 April 1989, 7; "Proyecto en El Paso," *Opinión*, 17 April 1989.

86. SEMAPA and El Paso, Convenio and anexo, 16 May 1989, SEMAPA Legal Department files.

87. "Última reunión," *Los Tiempos*, 16 May 1989, 7.

88. "Perforación de pozos en El Paso," *Los Tiempos*, 24 June 1989.

89. "Frenan bombeo de agua," *Opinión*, 10 November 1989; "Campesinos permitirán bombear agua," *VA*, 15 November 1989.

90. Goldman, *Imperial Nature*, 183.

91. Healy, *Llamas, Weavings, and Organic Chocolate*, 361–395.

92. Bolivia, Decreto Supremo 22710, 18 January 1991, *Gaceta Oficial*.

93. Bolivia, Ley 1493, 17 September 1993, Article 20, *Gaceta Oficial*.

94. Shallow wells were less than 100 meters deep by definition and on average 60 meters deep. "Irracional explotación de recursos hídricos," *Primera Plana*, 9 December 1994; "Perforación de pozos profundos," *Opinión*, 28 January 1995.

95. "Vinto se opone," *Opinión*, 18 December 1994.

96. "Pobladores del valle bajo," *Los Tiempos*, 30 September 1994.

97. "Perforación de pozos," *Los Tiempos*, 24 October 1994.

98. "Resistirán intervención militar," *Los Tiempos*, 16 February 1995.

99. Marcelo Delgadillo, personal communication with author, October 2020.

100. "Provincia Quillacollo solidaria con los pobladores de Sipe Sipe," *Los Tiempos*, no date.

101. "Resistirán intervención militar," *Los Tiempos*, 16 February 1995.

102. "Pobladores del Valle Bajo marcharon," *Los Tiempos*, 8 October 1994.

103. "Marcha," *Opinión*, 6 October 1994.

104. "Marcha de protesta," *Opinión*, 8 October 1994.

105. Marcelo Delgadillo, personal communication with author, October 2020.

106. "Sabotaje," *La Razón*, 26 October 1994.

107. "SEMAPA," *Los Tiempos*, 30 November 1994.

108. "Rechazo a perforación de pozos," *Opinión*, 24 December 1994.

109. "Perforación de pozos profundos," *Opinión*, 28 January 1995.

110. "Perforación de pozos," *Opinión*, 4 February 1995.

111. "Ejército garantizará perforación," *Los Tiempos*, 15 February 1995.

112. "Provincia Quillacollo solidaria con los pobladores de Sipe Sipe," *Los Tiempos*, no date.

113. Fernando Salazar, "Gestión de agua en el municipio de Sipe Sipe," in *Aguas y municipios*, ed. Hoogendam, 61.

114. CORDECO, El Paso, Cochabamba Prefecture, and SEMAPA, "Convenio de Intercambio Agua por Agua," 10 April 1996, SEMAPA Legal Department files. See also Crespo Flores, "Bolivia: La guerra de los pozos en Vinto y Sipe Sipe."

115. World Bank, "Implementation Completion Report, Bolivia Major Cities Water and Sewerage Rehabilitation Project," 12 June 1998, www-wds.worldbank.org/external/default/WDSContentServer/WDSP/IB/1998/06/12/000009265_3980728143441/Rendered/PDF/multi_page.pdf, accessed 19 June 2015.

116. Goldstein, *Spectacular City*, 214.

117. "El problema del agua" (editorial), *Los Tiempos*, 29 September 1994,

118. "Intolerable actitud," *Opinión*, 7 October 1994.

119. Fredy Omar Fernández Quiroga, "Federación Departamental Cochabambina de Regantes," in Ceceña, *La guerra por el agua*, 64–67.

120. Perreault, "Custom and Contradiction," 842.

121. Fernández Quiroga, "Federación Departamental," 68.

122. Crespo Flores, Fernández Quiroga, and Peredo, *Los regantes de Cochabamba*, 61.

123. Crespo Flores, Fernández Quiroga, and Peredo, *Los regantes de Cochabamba*, 70.

124. Fredy Omar Fernández Quiroga, personal communication with author, November 2020.

125. Perreault, "Custom and Contradiction," 834–854. See also Carlos Crespo Flores, "El movimiento nacional del agua boliviano," in *Modelos de gestion del agua en los Andes*, ed. Poupeau and González.

126. Albro, *Roosters at Midnight*, 198.

127. Fredy Omar Fernández Quiroga, personal communication with author, October 2020.

128. Marcelo Delgadillo, personal communication with author, October 2020.

129. For a similar argument about ethnic and Black identity in coastal Colombia, see Escobar, *Territories of Difference*, 10, 210. On ethnic identity in nineteenth- and twentieth-century Bolivia, see Ari Chachaki, *Earth Politics*; Gordillo Claure, *Campesinos revolucionarios en Bolivia*; Gotkowitz, *Revolution for Our Rights*; Larson, "Redeemed Indians, Barbarized Cholos."

130. Bjork-James, *Sovereign Street*, 165.

131. Gill, *Teetering on the Rim*; Postero, *Now We Are Citizens*.

132. Bolivia, Ley 1715 ("Ley INRA"), 18 October 1996, *Gaceta Oficial*.

133. Albro, *Roosters at Midnight*, 126.

134. "Reorganización de SEMAPA," *Los Tiempos*, 14 August 1996.

135. "SEMAPA es municipal," *Opinión*, 11 March 1997.

136. "¿De quién es SEMAPA?," *La Razón*, 21 August 1996.

137. "Ingenieros se oponen a la privatización de SEMAPA," *Primera Plana*, 12 September 1996.

138. "Estado de emergencia," *Hoy*, 26 July 1996.

139. "Reorganización de SEMAPA," *Los Tiempos*, 19 October 1996.

140. "Trabajadores y vecinos resistirán," *Presencia*, 20 October 1996.

141. "FEJUVE rechaza privatización," *Opinión*, 17 August 1996; "Pronunciamiento de Cochabamba," *Los Tiempos*, 20 August 1996.

142. Luján as quoted in "FEJUVE espera decisión cívica," *Opinión*, 23 October 1996.

143. "Provincias," *Los Tiempos*, 23 February 1997.

144. See press coverage in *Opinión*, *Los Tiempos*, and *Presencia*, March 1997.

145. Laserna, "Cochabamba: La guerra contra el agua," 17.

146. "Convocatoria," *Opinión*, 12 March 1997.

147. "Cochabambinos marcharán hoy," *Presencia*, 13 March 1997.

148. "Marcha de la cochabambinidad," *Los Tiempos*, 13 March 1997.

149. "Cochabambinos marcharon," *La Razón*, 14 March 1997.

150. "Una multitudinaria marcha," *Los Tiempos*, 14 March 1997.

151. "Cochabambinos en emergencia," *Presencia*, 14 March 1997.

152. See daily coverage in *Opinión*, *Los Tiempos*, *El Deber*, and *Presencia*, March–April 1997.

153. "Licitación de SEMAPA," *Presencia*, 22 May 1997.

154. "Licitación de SEMAPA," *Opinión*, 13 June 1997

155. "Concesión de SEMAPA," *Presencia*, 15 June 1997.

156. "Fortalecimiento de SEMAPA," *Los Tiempos*, 17 June 1997.

157. "Cochabamba confía en fallo," *Opinión*, 16 June 1997.

158. Bolivia, Decreto Supremo 24828, 25 August 1997, *Gaceta Oficial*.

159. World Bank, "Completion Report," ii, iv–vii, 6, 17–18, 20–23, 28, 30–32.

160. "Apoyo a la licitación," *Los Tiempos*, 16 May 1998.

161. "Cívicos rechazan tarifazo," *Hoy*, 23 July 1998.

162. "No todo es tan bueno como parece," *Presencia*, 27 August 1998.

163. Uzín as quoted in "Los Cochabambinos deben sacrificarse," *Los Tiempos*, 30 August 1998.

164. "La otra cara," *Presencia*, 21 March 1998; "Millonaria inversión," *El Diario*, 19 April 1998.

165. "Sociedad de Ingenieros," *La Razón*, 19 March 1998; "A la opinión pública," *Los Tiempos*, 24 April 1998.

166. "Manifiesto," *Opinión*, 15 January 1998.

167. "Guerra por el agua," *Los Tiempos*, 18 March 1998.

168. "FEJUVE apoya perforación," *Opinión*, 20 March 1998.

169. "Los campesinos piden respeto," *Los Tiempos*, 24 June 1998.

170. Crespo Flores, Fernández Quiroga, and Peredo, *Los regantes de Cochabamba*, 66–67.

171. Fernández Quiroga, "Federación Departamental," 68–69; Crespo Flores, Fernández Quiroga, and Peredo, *Los regantes de Cochabamba*, 121.

172. Crespo Flores, Fernández Quiroga, and Peredo, *Los regantes de Cochabamba*, 121.

173. "Licitación," *El Diario*, 25 August 1998;

174. Assies, "David versus Goliath," 22; García Orellana, García Yapur, and Quitón Herbas, "La crisis política," 40.

175. Finnegan, "Leasing the Rain," *The New Yorker*, 1 April 2002; Bollaín, *También la lluvia.*

176. Assies, "David versus Goliath," 21.

177. Kruse, "La Guerra del Agua en Cochabamba, Bolivia," 99.

178. Bolivia, Ley 2029, 29 October 1999, Articles 19 and 34, *Gaceta Oficial.*

179. Bolivia, Ley 2029, 29 October 1999, Article 70, *Gaceta Oficial.*

180. Bolivia, Ley 2029, 29 October 1999, Articles 23 and 49, *Gaceta Oficial.*

181. Nickson and Vargas, "Limitations of Water Regulation," 112.

182. Crespo Flores, Fernández Quiroga, and Peredo, *Los regantes de Cochabamba*, 92.

183. Fernández Quiroga, "Federación Departamental," 70.

184. Fernández Quiroga, "Federación Departamental," 70.

185. Crespo Flores, Fernández Quiroga, and Peredo, *Los regantes de Cochabamba*, 90.

186. Crespo Flores, Fernández Quiroga, and Peredo, *Los regantes de Cochabamba*, 109–110.

187. Crespo Flores, Fernández Quiroga, and Peredo, *Los regantes de Cochabamba*, 111.

188. Quoted in Crespo Flores, Fernández Quiroga, and Peredo, *Los regantes de Cochabamba*, 113.

189. Crespo Flores, Fernández Quiroga, and Peredo, *Los regantes de Cochabamba*, 128.

190. Crespo Flores, Fernández Quiroga, and Peredo, *Los regantes de Cochabamba*, 134.

191. Crespo Flores, Fernández Quiroga, and Peredo, *Los regantes de Cochabamba*, 204.

192. Quoted in García Orellana, García Yapur, and Quitón Herbas, "La crisis política," 78.

193. García Orellana, García Yapur, and Quitón Herbas, "La crisis política," 86–87.

194. Olivera and Lewis, *¡Cochabamba!*, 30.

195. Orellana Aillón, "El proceso insurrecional de abril," 501. See also Assies, "David versus Goliath," 31.

196. Crespo Flores, Fernández Quiroga, and Peredo, *Los regantes de Cochabamba*, 96.

197. Albro, "'The Water Is Ours, Carajo!'" 255; Simmons, *Meaningful Resistance*, 46. For a sympathetic take, see Bjork-James, *Sovereign Street*, 164–165.

198. Fernández Quiroga, "Federación Departamental," 69–77.

199. Crespo Flores, Fernández Quiroga, and Peredo, *Los regantes de Cochabamba*, 138.

200. Angelo Paredes and Rodrigo Cruz, author interview, 7 March 2007.

201. Esteban Yanez, author interview, 6 March 2007.

202. Antonio Heredia, author interview, 27 April 2007.

203. Isadora Alemán, author interview, 10 May 2007.

204. Abraham Grandydier, author interview, 23 March 2007.

205. Joaquín Arias, interview with Jorge Camacho, Tirani, 21 November 2020.

206. Teodoro García Hinojosa, author interview, 11 April 2007.

207. Miguel Palma Chambi, author interview, 15 March 2007.

208. Guadalupe Yacupaico, author interview, 24 March 2007.

209. Agustín Rojas, author interview, 30 January 2007.

210. Marcela Olivera, personal communication with author, 20 October 2020.

211. Bechtel Corporation, "Bechtel Perspective on the Aguas del Tunari water concession in Cochabamba, Bolivia," December 2005, www.bechtel.com/files/perspective-aguas-del-tunari-water-concession/, accessed 27 July 2015.

212. Olivera and Lewis, ¡Cochabamba!, 30.

213. Juan Sánchez Ayala, author interview, 20 March 2007.

214. Kruse and Vargas, "Las victorias de abril," 11.

215. Orellana Aillón, "El proceso insurrecional de abril," 510, 525.

216. Los Tiempos, 8 December 1999.

217. Spronk, "Roots of Resistance to Urban Water Privatization," 18.

218. Assies, "David versus Goliath," 24; Kruse, "La Guerra del Agua en Cochabamba, Bolivia," 154–155.

219. Oscar Olivera, "Federación de Trabajadores Fabriles," in Ceceña, La guerra por el agua, 84–93.

220. Olivera, "Federación de Trabajadores Fabriles," 84–93.

221. Crespo Flores, "Continuidad y ruptura," 26.

222. Gabriel Herbas Camacho, "El Foro Cochabambino de Medio Ambiente," in Ceceña, La guerra por el agua, 57.

223. Quoted in Ceceña, La guerra por el agua, 33.

224. Quoted in Albro, Roosters at Midnight, 10.

225. Albro, Roosters at Midnight, 4, 57.

226. Orellana Aillón, "El proceso insurrecional de abril," 509–511.

227. Olivera and Lewis, ¡Cochabamba!, 32.

228. Crespo Flores, Fernández Quiroga, and Peredo, Los regantes de Cochabamba, 134.

229. Crespo Flores, Fernández Quiroga, and Peredo, Los regantes de Cochabamba, 135.

230. Fernández Quiroga, "Federación Departamental," 75; Crespo Flores, Fernández Quiroga, and Peredo, Los regantes de Cochabamba, 136.

231. Olivera and Lewis, ¡Cochabamba!, 36.

232. Juan Sánchez Ayala, author interview, 20 March 2007.

233. Webber, Red October, 160.

234. Bjork-James, Sovereign Street, 77.

235. García Orellana, García Yapur, and Quitón Herbas, "La crisis política," 103.

236. Crespo Flores, Fernández Quiroga, and Peredo, Los regantes de Cochabamba, 192; García Orellana, La crisis de la política, 55l; Orellana Aillón, "El proceso insurrecional de abril," 520.

237. Laurie, "Establishing Development Orthodoxy," 537.

238. Perreault, "From the Guerra del Agua to the Guerra del Gas," 164.

CHAPTER 6. AFTER THE WAR

1. Bolivia, Ley 2066, Article 5, *Gaceta Oficial.*

2. Bolivia, Ley 2066, Article 8, *Gaceta Oficial.*

3. Bolivia, Ley 2066, Article 24, *Gaceta Oficial.*

4. René Orellana Halkyer, "Agua, Saneamiento y Riego," in *Modelos de gestion*, ed. Poupeau and González.

5. Bolivia, Ley 2066, Articles 28–35, *Gaceta Oficial.*

6. Bolivia, Ley 2066, Article 28, *Gaceta Oficial.*

7. Bolivia, Ley 2066, Article 49, *Gaceta Oficial.*

8. Seemann, *Water Security, Justice and the Politics of Water Rights*, 163–165.

9. Fernández Quiroga, "Federación Departamental," 77. See also Luis Sánchez Gómez and Philipp Terhorst, "Cochabamba, Bolivia: Public-Collective Partnership after the Water War," in *Reclaiming Public Water*, ed. Brennan et al., 121.

10. Gutiérrez Aguilar, *Rhythms of the Pachakuti*, 26.

11. Olivera and Lewis, *¡Cochabamba!*, 45.

12. Coordinadora Departamental de Defensa del Agua y de la Vida, "Apuntes de clausura del Seminario de Propuestas para la gestion del agua en Cochabamba," in Ceceña, *La guerra por el agua y por la vida*, 181.

13. Razavi, "'Social Control' and the Politics of Participation," 9.

14. Fernández Quiroga, "Federación Departamental," 78; Gutiérrez Aguilar, "The Coordinadora," in Olivera and Lewis, *¡Cochabamba!*, 58.

15. Fernández Quiroga, "Federación Departamental," 79.

16. Olivera and Lewis, *¡Cochabamba!*, 89.

17. Olivera and Lewis, *¡Cochabamba!*, 89–90.

18. Spronk, "Roots of Resistance," 21; Luis Sánchez Gómez and Phillip Terhorst, "Asociaciones públicas," in *Por un modelo público de agua*, ed. Brennan et al., 135.

19. Razavi, "'Social Control' and the Politics of Participation," 10–12.

20. Simón Gomez, author interview, SEMAPA, 16 May 2011.

21. International Centre for Settlement of Investment Disputes (ICSID), "Aguas del Tunari versus Bolivia (Netherlands-Bolivia BIT)," http://iiapp.org/media/uploads/aguas_del_tunari_v_bolivia.rev.pdf, accessed 27 July 2015.

22. ICSID, "Aguas del Tunari S.A. versus Republic of Bolivia (ICSID Case No. ARB/03/2)," https://icsid.worldbank.org/ICSID/FrontServlet?requestType=CasesRH&actionVal=showDoc&docId=DC628&caseId=C210, accessed 30 July 2015.

23. Coordinadora de Defensa del Agua y de la Vida, Federación Departamental Cochabambina de Organizaciones Regantes, SEMAPA Sur, Friends of the Earth Netherlands, Oscar Olivera, Omar Fernández Quiroga, Father Luis Sánchez Gómez, and Congressman Jorge Alvarado, "Petition," 29 August 2002, Case No. ARB/02/3, Aguas del Tunari, S.A., Claimant/Investor and Republic of Bolivia, Respondent/Party, www.italaw.com/sites/default/files/case-documents/ita0018.pdf, accessed 30 July 2015. See also Carlos Crespo Flores, "Agua, soberanía national y resistencia social," in Crespo Flores and Spronk, *Después de las guerras del agua*, 133.

24. Jim Shultz, "Cochabamba Water Revolt," in Shultz and Draper, *Dignity and Defi-*

ance, 30–32; Albro, "'The Water Is Ours, Carajo!,'" 257–259; Crespo Flores, "Agua, soberanía national y resistencia social," 119; Kohl and Farthing, *Impasse in Bolivia*, 188–190.

25. "Bechtel Drops Claim," *Environmental News Service*, 19 January 2006.

26. Olivera and Lewis, *¡Cochabamba!*.

27. Christian Molinari, "Bolivia: Government Reaches Agreement with Aguas del Tunari," *BN Americas*, 2 January 2006.

28. Shultz, "Cochabamba Water Revolt," 32.

29. Bechtel Corporation, "Bechtel Perspective on the Aguas del Tunari Water Concession in Cochabamba, Bolivia," December 2005, www.bechtel.com/files/perspective-aguas-del-tunari-water-concession/.

30. World Bank Operations Evaluation Department, "Bolivia Water Management: A Tale of Two Cities," *Précis* 222 (Spring 2002).

31. Clark, Kosec, and Wallsten, "Has Private Participation in Water and Sewerage Improved Coverage?," 329, 335, 348.

32. Botton, Hardy, and Poupeau, "Water from the Heights."

33. Olivera and Lewis, *¡Cochabamba!*, i.

34. Bakker, *Privatizing Water*, 173–176; Barlow, *Blue Covenant*, 103–104; De Angelis, *Omnia Sunt Communia*, 91–97; Dwinell and Olivera, "Water Is Ours Damn It!"; Linsalata, *Cuando manda la asamblea*; Linsalata, "Ni público, ni privado: común"; Shiva, *Water Wars*, 102–103.

35. Shiva's preface to Olivera and Lewis, *¡Cochabamba!*, xi.

36. Olivera and Lewis, *¡Cochabamba!*, 126–127.

37. Zibechi, *La mirada horizontal*, 69.

38. Zibechi, *Dispersing Power*, 16.

39. Hardt and Negri, *Multitude*, xiii–xiv.

40. Holloway, *Change the World without Taking Power*; Katz, "Los problemas de autonomismo."

41. Kohl, "Challenges to Neoliberal Hegemony in Bolivia," 318; Kohl and Farthing, *Impasse in Bolivia*, 167–169; Mamani, *El rugir de las multitudes*, 77; Webber, *Red October*, 168–169.

42. Olivera and Lewis, *¡Cochabamba!*, 129–139.

43. Coordinadora de Defensa del Agua y de la Vida, "Propuesa de Asamblea Constituyente," October 2000.

44. Bjork-James, *Sovereign Street*, 80.

45. Crespo Flores, "El movimiento nacional de agua boliviano: De la resistencia a la cooptación (2000-2007)," in *Modelos de gestión*; Fredy Omar Fernández Quiroga, personal communication with author, October 2020.

46. Oscar Olivera, "Comunicado de prensa," 20 September 2002; Fundación Abril, "Quiénes somos," www.fundacionabril.org/quienes-somos/, accessed 21 October 2020.

47. Abraham Grandydier, author interview, 23 March 2007.

48. Kohl and Farthing, *Impasse in Bolivia*, 171.

49. Webber, *Red October*, 181.

50. Kohl, "Challenges to Neoliberal Hegemony in Bolivia," 319.

51. Kohl, "Challenges to Neoliberal Hegemony in Bolivia," 319.

52. Ellison, *Domesticating Democracy*, 31–35, 178; Perreault, "From the Guerra del Agua to the Guerra del Gas," 159.

53. Kohl and Farthing, *Impasse in Bolivia*, 173–175; Olivera and Lewis, ¡*Cochabamba!*, 177; Perreault, "From the Guerra del Agua to the Guerra del Gas," 161–163.

54. Ramos Andrade, *Agonía y rebellion social*, 349–362.

55. Ellison, *Domesticating Democracy*, 50; Webber, "Carlos Mesa, Evo Morales, and a Divided Bolivia."

56. Komives, "Designing Pro-Poor Water and Sewer Concessions," 29–30; Spronk, "Roots of Resistance," 18–20.

57. Hailu, Osorio, and Tsukada, "Privatization and Renationalization," 2565.

58. Botton, Hardy, and Poupeau, "Water from the Heights," 5.

59. Crespo Flores, "Agua, soberanía national y resistencia social," 109–146; Spronk and Webber, "Struggles against Accumulation by Dispossession in Bolivia," 39, 41.

60. Julián Perez, "Avances de la Comisión Interinstitucional en la elaboración de un nuevo modelo de gestion para la entidad prestadora de servicio de agua en las ciudades de La Paz y El Alto," in *Modelos de gestión*, ed. Poupeau and González.

61. Botton, Hardy, and Poupeau, "Water from the Heights," 7.

62. Fabricant and Hicks, "Bolivia's Next Water War," 139.

63. Gustafson, *bolivia in the age of gas*, 114–118.

64. Webber, "Carlos Mesa, Evo Morales, and a Divided Bolivia."

65. Herbas, "Foro Cochabambino del Medio Ambiente," 60–61.

66. These organizations included the Confederación Sindical Única de Trabajadores Campesinos de Bolivia (CSUTCB), the Confederación Sindical de Comunidades Interculturales de Bolivia (CSCIB), the Confederación Nacional de Mujeres Campesina Indígena Originarias de Bolivia "Bartolina Sisa" (CNMCIOB-BS), the Confederación de Pueblos Indígenas del Oriente Boliviano (CIDOB), and the Consejo Nacional de Ayllus y Markas del Qullasuyu (CONAMAQ).

67. Articles 2 and 15, quoted in Garcés, *El Pacto de Unidad*, 37.

68. Chapon, *Abuela Grillo*.

69. Escobar, "Latin America at a Crossroads," 4.

70. Coodinadora, "Propuesta de Asamblea Constituyente"; Prada, *Subversiones indígenas*, 133; Garcés, *El Pacto de Unidad*; Tapia, *La conyuntura de la autonomía relativa del estado*, 66–68; Postero, *Indigenous State*, chapter 2; Bjork-James, *Sovereign Street*, 172–173.

71. Bjork-James, *Sovereign Street*, 184.

72. Fredy Omar Fernández Quiroga, personal communication with author, October 2020.

73. "Propuesta del Pacto de Unidad hacia la Asamblea Constituyente (primera version)," Sucre, 5 August 2006, chapters III and IV.

74. "Propuesta consensuada del Pacto de Unidad, Constitución Política del Estado," Sucre, 23 May 2007, Articles 32 and 166–172.

75. Bolivia, Constitución Política del Estado, 2009, Preamble.

76. Bolivia, Constitución Política del Estado, 2009, Articles 16 and 20.

77. Bolivia, Constitución Política del Estado, 2009, Articles 304, 373, and 374.

78. Fredy Omar Fernández Quiroga, personal communication with author, October 2020.

79. Fredy Omar Fernández Quiroga, personal communication with author, November 2020.

80. Olivera, "Palabras contra el olvido," in Gutiérrez Aguilar et al., *Palabras para tejernos, resistir y transformer*, 17, 22, 28.

81. Estado Plurinacional de Bolivia, Ley de la Madre Tierra, 2012, Articles 4, 13, 14, 19, and 27, *Gaceta Oficial*.

82. The 2008–2015 Plan Nacional de Saneamiento Básico also avowed the human right to water, state obligations to fulfill it, and respect for *usos y costumbres*. Estado Plurinacional de Bolivia, Ministerio de Medio Ambiente y Agua, "Plan Nacional de Saneamiento Básico 2008–2015" (La Paz, 2009).

83. Baer, "From Water Wars to Water Rights," 358; Fredy Omar Fernández Quiroga, personal communication with author, October 2020.

84. UN General Assembly, Resolution 64/292, 28 July 2010, Articles 2–3.

85. Ballestero, *Future History of Water*, 34, quotation p. 58.

86. Ballestero, *Future History of Water*, 18.

87. Bakker, *Privatizing Water*, 147–152.

88. Bolivia, Plan Nacional de Desarrollo, 2006, 30, 74–80, 123–127.

89. Estado Plurinacional de Bolivia, Ministerio de Medio Ambiente y Agua, "Rendición pública de cuentas, Audiencia Inicial 2019," www.mmaya.gob.bo/transparencia/rendicion-de-cuentas/, accessed 23 October 2019; Baer, "From Water Wars to Water Rights," 359.

90. Razavi, "'Social Control' and the Politics of Participation," 14; Orellana Halkyer, "Agua, saneamiento y riego," in *Modelos de gestion*, ed. Poupeau and González.

91. Baer, "From Water Wars to Water Rights," 367.

92. Olivera, "Palabras contra el olvido," 23.

93. Olivera, interview with Kontext TV, 2 July 2012, www.kontext-tv.de/en/broadcasts/oscar-olivera-water-war-cochabamba-and-rights-nature, accessed 21 October 2020.

94. Crespo Flores, "El derecho humano al agua en la práctica," 2.

95. Fredy Omar Fernández Quiroga, personal communication with author, October and November 2020.

96. Kelly, *Sovereign Emergencies*, 8–9.

97. Stites Mor, *Human Rights and Transnational Solidarities*, 7. See also Moyn, *Not Enough*.

98. On alternative ontologies, see Escobar, "Latin America at a Crossroads," 9, 39–44; Escobar, *Territories of Difference*; De la Cadena, *Earth Beings*.

99. Bustamante, Crespo Flores, and Walnycki, "Seeing through the Concept of Water as a Human Right in Bolivia."

100. Goodale, *Revolution in Fragments*, 181.

101. Farthing and Kohl, *Evo's Bolivia*, 150; Goodale, *Revolution in Fragments*, 59; Gustafson, *bolivia in the age of gas*, 16, 155, 174; Postero, *Indigenous State*, 4; Webber, "Evo Morales," 331–332; Webber and Carr, *New Latin American Left*, 5.

102. Author observation, 12 September 2011.

103. Rendición Pública de Cuentas Gestión 2010, author observation, SEMAPA, 14 January 2011.

104. Luis Camargo, author interview, SEMAPA, 31 May 2011.

105. Abraham Grandydier, author interview, Cochabamba, 22 June 2011; Baer, "From Water Wars to Water Rights," 365.

106. Razani, "'Social Control' and the Politics of Participation," 15.

107. Fabiola Fernandez and Oscar Zelada Jaldin, author interview, EMAPAS, 24 May 2011.

108. Author interviews with cooperative leaders, June 2011.

109. Sebastián Chambi, author interview, Cochabamba, 1 September 2011.

110. Juan José Paz, author interviews, Arocagua, 26 June and 8 July 2011.

111. Sebastián Chambi, author interview, Arocagua, 26 June 2011.

112. Ricardo Fortún Medina, author interview, SEMAPA, 6 May 2011.

113. Fabiola Fernandez and Oscar D. Zelada Jaldin, author interview, EMAPAS, 24 May 2011.

114. Armando Leygue, author interview, 25 April 2011.

115. Armando Leygue, presentation at that Sociedad de Ingenieros Bolivianos, Cochabamba, 20 May 2011; Julio Vargas, author interview, SEMAPA, 31 May 2011.

116. Roberto Fuentes, author interview, EMAPAQ, 30 May 2011.

117. Rafael Farfán, author interview, SEMAPA, 18 May 2011.

118. Author observations and conversations, El Paso, 31 August 2011.

119. Pasqual Mendoza, author interview, El Paso, 31 August 2011.

120. Rendición Pública de Cuentas Gestión 2010, author observation, SEMAPA, 14 January 2011.

121. Julio Vargas, author interview, SEMAPA, 31 May 2011.

122. Juan Carlos Cabrerizo, author interview, Empresa Misicuni, 18 January 2011.

123. Armando Leygue, author interview, Cochabamba, 1 March 2011.

124. Armando Leygue, author interview, Cochabamba, 2 March 2011.

125. Francisco Cáceres, author interview, Cochabamba, 4 May 2011.

126. Simón Gomez, author interview, SEMAPA, 27 April 2011.

127. Luís Camargo, author interview, SEMAPA, 31 May 2011.

128. Rafael Farfán, author interviews, SEMAPA, 18 May and 27 May 2011.

129. Sebastián Chambi, author interview, Arocagua, 26 June 2011.

130. Javier Molina, author interview, Tirani, 27 May 2011.

131. Benicio Portillo, author interview, Tirani, 6 July 2011.

132. Fernanda Guzmán, author interview, Tirani, 27 July 2011.

133. Sergio Portillo, author interview, Tirani, 25 July 2011.

134. Daniel Molina, author interview, Tirani, 11 September 2011.

135. Cesar Suarez Velarde, interview with Jorge Camacho, Tirani, 21 November 2020.

136. Daniel Molina, author interview, Tirani, 11 September 2011.

137. Zacarías Arteaga, author interview, Tirani, 6 July 2011; community meeting, author observation, Tirani, 3 July 2011.

138. Fredy Omar Fernández Quiroga, author interview, Cochabamba, 27 February 2014.

139. Fredy Omar Fernández Quiroga, author interview, Cochabamba, 27 February 2014.

140. Dionisio Hurtado, author interview, Tirani, 15 June 2011.

141. Bonifacio Posada, author interview, Taquiña, 27 May 2011.

142. Canessa, *Natives Making Nation*; Postero and Tockman, "Self-Governance"; Tockman and Cameron, "Indigenous Autonomy."

143. Rocio Bustamante et al., "Supporting Local Organisations in Peri-urban Cochabamba, Bolivia," in *Peri-Urban Water Conflicts*, ed. Butterworth, 25.

144. "Sindicatos no ceden," *Opinión*, 4 October 2012.

145. "Batalla campal por agua," *La Razón* (La Paz), 6 March 2013.

146. "Disputa por agua," *El Diario* (La Paz), 5 March 2013.

147. "Cinco Salidas marcha," *Los Tiempos*, 28 August 2014.

148. Fabricant and Hicks, "Bolivia's Next Water War," 142.

149. Hines, "The Power and Ethics of Vernacular Modernism."

150. "Cargo de riego," *Los Tiempos*, 30 September 2019.

151. "Promesas de Evo," *Los Tiempos*," 16 October 2019.

152. "Comunarios toman Misicuni," *Los Tiempos*, 9 November 2019.

153. "Misicuni descarta atentado," *Los Tiempos*, 12 November 2019; "Militares resguardan instalaciones," *Los Tiempos*, 14 November 2019.

154. Gustafson, *bolivia in the age of gas*; Jeffery Webber, "From Left-Indigenous Insurrection," in Webber and Carr, *New American Left*, 171.

155. Escobar, "Latin America at a Crossroads," 4; Postero, *Indigenous State*, 57–58, 114.

156. Olivera, "Palabras contra el olvido," 14.

CONCLUSION

1. Fredy Omar Fernández Quiroga, personal communication with author, November 2020.

2. Aboites, *El agua de la nación*; Boyer, *Political Landscapes*; Olsson, *Agrarian Crossings*; Santiago, *Ecology of Oil*; Vitz, *City on a Lake*; Wakild, *Revolutionary Parks*; Wolfe, *Watering the Revolution*.

3. Funes Monzote, *Nuestro viaje a la luna*; Funes Monzote, "Geotransformación"; Wolfe, "'Revolution Is a Force More Powerful Than Nature.'"

4. Scott, *Art of Not Being Governed*, 330.

5. "Todos somos coordinadora del agua y la vida," www.somossur.net/sociedad/1837-todos-somos-coordinadora-del-agua-y-la-vida.html, accessed 11 November 2019.

6. Bjork-James, *Sovereign Street*, 113.

7. "The really critical thing isn't who's sitting in the White House, but who is sitting in—in the streets, in the cafeterias, in the halls of government, in the factories." Howard Zinn as quoted in Street and DiMaggio, *Crashing the Tea Party*, 165.

REFERENCES

ARCHIVAL AND INSTITUTIONAL SOURCES

Cochabamba, Bolivia

Archivo y Biblioteca de la Empresa Misicuni

Archivo del Departamento de Planificación de la Gobernación de Cochabamba ("Ex-COR-DECO") (ADPGC)

Archivo de la Federación Departamental Cochabambina de Organizaciones Regantes (FEDECOR)

Archivo Histórico Departamental de la Gobernación de Cochabamba (AHDGC)

Archivo Histórico y Hemeroteca Municipal de Cochabamba (AHMC)

Archivo del Instituto Nacional de la Reforma Agraria–Cochabamba (INRA–C)

Archivo del Servicio Municipal de Agua Potable y Alcantarillado (SEMAPA)

Biblioteca del Colegio de Arquitectos, Cochabamba (BCAC)

Biblioteca de la Universidad Mayor de San Simón (BUMSS)

Centro de Documentación e Información Bolivia (CEDIB)

Fundación Simón Patiño (FSP)

Personal files of residents of the community of Tirani (Tirani Community Documents)

SEMAPA Legal Department files

La Paz, Bolivia

Archivo Histórico del Honorable Congreso Nacional de Bolivia (AHHCN)

Biblioteca Arturo Costa de la Torre (BACT)

Gaceta Oficial del Estado Plurinacional de Bolivia (*Gaceta Oficial*), online data base

German Technical Cooperation Agency (GTZ)

Hemeroteca de la Universidad Mayor de San Andrés (HUMSA)

Ministerio de Medio Ambiente y Agua (MMAA)

Servicio Nacional de Meteorología e Hidrología (SENAMHI)

Sucre, Bolivia

Archivo y Biblioteca Nacionales de Bolivia (ABNB)

United States

Inter-American Development Bank (IDB)
Land Tenure Center, University of Wisconsin–Madison (LTC)
World Bank Archive

Amsterdam, The Netherlands

Movimiento Nacionalista Revolucionario Collection, International Institute for Social History (IISH)

PERIODICALS

Clippings Collection, Archivo y Biblioteca de la Empresa Misicuni, Cochabamba, Various, 1985–2000
Clippings Collection, Centro de Documentación e Información Bolivia, Cochabamba, Various, 1970–2000
El Comercio, Cochabamba
El Ferrocarril, Cochabamba
El Heraldo, Cochabamba
El Imparcial, Cochabamba
El País, Cochabamba
El Pueblo, Cochabamba
El Republicano, Cochabamba
14 de Septiembre, Cochabamba
Opinión, Cochabamba
Prensa Libre, Cochabamba
Los Tiempos, Cochabamba

INTERVIEWS (*INDICATES PSEUDONYM)

*Alemán, Isadora. Primero de Mayo, 10 May 2007.
*Arias, Joaquín. Interviewed by Jorge Camacho, Tirani, 21 November 2020 and 13 December 2020.
*Arias, Josué. Tirani, 14 August 2011.
*Arteaga, Zacarías. Tirani, 6 July 2011.
Cabrerizo, Juan Carlos. Empresa Misicuni, 18 January 2011.
*Cáceres, Francisco. Cochabamba, 4 May 2011.
Camargo, Luis. SEMAPA, 31 May 2011.
*Cardoso, Jacobo. Cochabamba, 11 July 2014.
*Chambi, Sebastián. Arocagua, 26 June 2011 and 1 September 2011.
*Condori, Hipólito. Cochabamba, 26 January 2007.
*Cruz, Rodrigo. Quillacollo, 7 March 2007.
Delgadillo, Marcelo. Email correspondence, October 2020.

*Farfán, Rafael. SEMAPA, 18 May and 27 May 2011.

Fernández Quiroga, Fredy Omar. Cochabamba, 27 February 2014; email correspondence October and November 2020.

Fernandez, Fabiola. EMAPAS, 24 May 2011.

*Fortún Medina, Ricardo. SEMAPA, 6 May 2011.

*Fuentes, Roberto. EMAPAQ, 30 May 2011.

*García Hinojosa, Teodoro. Chilimarca, 11 April 2007.

*Gomez, Simón. SEMAPA, 27 April 2011 and 16 May 2011.

Grandydier, Abraham. Zona Sud, 23 March 2007; Cochabamba, 22 June 2011.

*Guzmán, Fernanda. Tirani, 27 July 2011.

*Heredia, Antonio. Primero de Mayo, 27 April 2007.

*Hurtado, Dionisio. Tirani, 15 June 2011.

Leygue, Armando. Cochabamba, 1 March, 2 March, and 25 April 2011.

*Mendoza, Pasqual. El Paso, 31 August 2011.

*Molina, Daniel. Tirani, 11 September 2011.

*Molina, Javier. Tirani, 27 May 2011.

Olivera, Marcela. Email correspondence, 20 October 2020.

*Ortiz Flores, Osvaldo. Cochabamba, 20 March 2007.

*Palma Chambi, Miguel. Cochabamba, 15 March 2007.

*Paredes, Angelo. Quillacollo, 7 March 2007.

*Paz, Juan José. Arocagua, 26 June and 8 July 2011.

*Portillo, Benicio. Tirani, 6 July 2011.

*Portillo, Sergio. Tirani, 25 July 2011.

*Posada, Bonifacio. Taquiña, 27 May 2011.

*Rojas, Agustín. Cochabamba, 30 January 2007.

Salazár, Jesús. Quintanilla, 15 June 2011.

*Sánchez Ayala, Juan. Cochabamba, 20 March 2007.

*Suarez Velarde, Cesar. Interviewed by Jorge Camacho, Tirani, 21 November 2020.

*Torrez, Santiago. Chilimarca, 12 April 2007.

Vargas, Julio. SEMAPA, 31 May 2011.

*Vargas de Portillo, Claudia. Tirani, 26 July 2011.

Vega, Severo. Cochabamba, 24 May 2011.

*Yacupaico, Guadalupe. Chilimarca, 24 March 2007.

*Yanez, Esteban. Cochabamba, 6 March 2007.

Zelada Jaldin, Oscar. EMAPAS, 24 May 2011.

PUBLISHED SOURCES

Aboites Aguilar, Luis. *El agua de la nación de México, 1888–1946*. Mexico City: CIESAS, 1998.

———. *La decadencia del agua de la nación: Estudio sobre desigualdad social y cambio político en México (segunda mitad del siglo XX)*. Mexico City: El Colegio de México, Centro de Estudios Históricos, 2009.

Aceituno, Patricio, Maríadel del Rosario Prieto, María Eugenia Solari, Alejandra Martínez,

Germán Poveda, and Mark Falvey. "The 1877–1878 El Niño Episode: Associated Impacts in South America." *Climatic Change Climatic Change* 92, no. 3–4 (2009): 389–416.

Achi, Amonah, and Rebecca Kirchheimer. "Innovar para alcanzar el derecho humano al agua de la zona sur de Cochabamba: La experiencia de apoyo a los comités de agua potable de la Fundación Pro Hábitat." In *Apoyo a la gestión de Comités de Agua Potable: Experiencias de fortalecimiento a Comités de Agua Potable Comunitarios en Bolivia y Colombia*, edited by Franz Quiroz, Nicolá Faysse, and Raúl Ampuero, 209–238. Cochabamba, Bolivia: Universidad Mayor de San Simón, Centro AGUA, 2006.

Agrawal, Arun. "Dismantling the Divide between Indigenous and Scientific Knowledge." *Development and Change* 26, no. 3 (1995): 413–439.

———. *Environmentality: Technologies of Government and the Making of Subjects*. Durham, NC: Duke University Press, 2012.

Albó, Xavier. *Achacachi: Medio siglo de luchas campesinas*. La Paz: CIPCA, 1979.

———. "From MNRistas to Kataristas to Katari." In *Resistance, Rebellion, and Consciousness in the Andean Peasant World, 18th to 20th Centuries*, edited by Steve J. Stern, 379–419. Madison: University of Wisconsin, 1987.

Albro, Robert. *Roosters at Midnight: Indigenous Signs and Stigma in Local Bolivian Politics*. Santa Fe, NM: School for Advanced Research, 2010.

———. "'The Water Is Ours, Carajo!': Deep Citizenship in Bolivia's Water War." In *Social Movements: An Anthropological Reader*, edited by June Nash, 249–271. Malden, MA: Blackwell, 2005.

Alexander, Robert J. *The Bolivian National Revolution*. Westport, CT: Greenwood Press, 1974.

Amann, Edmund, and Werner Baer. "Neoliberalism and Its Consequences in Brazil." *Journal of Latin American Studies* 34, no. 4 (2002): 945–959.

Anand, Nikhil. *Hydraulic City: Water and the Infrastructures of Citizenship in Mumbai*. Durham, NC: Duke University Press, 2017.

———. "Pressure: The Politechnics of Water Supply in Mumbai." *Cultural Anthropology* 26, no. 4 (2011): 542–564.

Anand, Nikhil, Akhil Gupta, and Hannah Appel, eds. *The Promise of Infrastructure*. Durham, NC: Duke University Press, 2018.

Anaya, Ricardo. *Unidos venceremos: PIR, mensaje al pueblo boliviano*. Santiago de Chile: publisher unknown, 1945.

Antezana Ergueta, Luis. *De la reforma a la contrareforma agraria*. La Paz: La Juventud, 1992.

Antezana Ergueta, Luis, and Hugo Romero Bedregal. *Origen, desarrollo y situación actual del sindicalismo campesino en Bolivia*. La Paz: LTC/CIDA, 1968.

Appadurai, Arjun. "Deep Democracy: Urban Governmentality and the Horizon of Politics." *Environment and Urbanization*. 13, no. 2 (2001): 23–43.

———. *Modernity at Large: Cultural Dimensions of Globalization*. Minneapolis: University of Minnesota Press, 1996.

Ari Chachaki, Waskar. *Earth Politics: Religion, Decolonization, and Bolivia's Indigenous Intellectuals*. Durham, NC: Duke University Press, 2014.

Assies, Willem. "David versus Goliath in Cochabamba: Water Rights, Neoliberalism, and the Revival of Social Protest in Bolivia." *Latin American Perspectives* 30, no. 3 (2003): 14–36.

Auyero, Javier, and Debora Alejandra Swistun. *Flammable: Environmental Suffering in an Argentine Shantytown*. New York: Oxford University Press, 2009.

Averanga Mollinedo, Asthenio. *Aspectos generales de la población boliviana*. La Paz: Librería Ed. Juventud, 1998.

Baer, Madeline. "From Water Wars to Water Rights: Implementing the Human Right to Water in Bolivia." *Journal of Human Rights* 14, no. 3 (2015): 353–76.

Bakker, Karen J. *Privatizing Water: Governance Failure and the World's Urban Water Crisis*. Ithaca, NY: Cornell University Press, 2010.

Ballestero, Andrea. *A Future History of Water*. Durham, NC: Duke University Press, 2019.

Barandiarán, Javiera. *Science and Environment in Chile: The Politics of Expert Advice in a Neoliberal Democracy*. Cambridge, MA: MIT Press, 2018.

Barlow, Maude. *Blue Covenant: The Global Water Crisis and the Coming Battle for the Right to Water*. New York: The New Press, 2007.

Barragán, Rossana. *Asambleas constituyentes: Ciudadanía y elecciones, convenciones y debates (1825–1971)*. La Paz: Muela del Diablo, 2006.

———. "Bridges and Chasms." In *A Companion to Latin American Anthropology*, edited by Deborah Poole, 32–55. Malden, MA: Blackwell, 2008.

———. "The Census and the Making of a Social 'Order' in Nineteenth-Century Bolivia." In *Histories of Race and Racism: The Andes and Mesoamerica from Colonial Times to the Present*, edited by Laura Gotkowitz, 113–133. Durham, NC: Duke University Press, 2011.

Basadre, Jorge. *Historia de la República del Perú*. Volume 8. Lima: Historia, 1963.

Bjork-James, Carwil. *The Sovereign Street: Making Revolution in Urban Bolivia*. Tucson: University of Arizona Press, 2020.

Blanc, Jacob. *Before the Flood: The Itaipu Dam and the Visibility of Rural Brazil*. Durham, NC: Duke University Press, 2019.

Blasier, Cole. *The Hovering Giant: U.S. Responses to Revolutionary Change in Latin America*. Pittsburgh: University of Pittsburgh Press, 1989.

Boelens, Rutgerd. *Water, Power, and Identity: The Cultural Politics of Water in the Andes*. New York: Routledge, 2015.

Boelens, Rutgerd, Rocio Bustamante, and Hugo de Vos. "Legal Pluralism and the Politics of Inclusion: Recognition and Contestation of Local Water Rights in the Andes." In *Community-Based Water Law and Water Resource Management Reform in Developing Countries*, edited by Barbara van Koppen, Mark Giordano, and John Butterworth, 96–113. Cambridge, MA: CBI, 2007.

Boelens, Rutgerd, Jaime Hoogesteger, Erik Swyngedouw, Jeroen Vos, and Philippus Wester. "Hydrosocial Territories: A Political Ecology Perspective." *Water International* 41, no. 1 (2016): 1–14.

Boelens, Rutgerd, Thomas Perreault, and Jeroen Vos, eds. *Water Justice*. New York: Cambridge University Press, 2018.

Bohan, Merwin L. *Plan Bohan: Informe de la Misión Económica de los Estados Unidos a Bolivia (1942)*. Translated by G. V. Bilbao la Vieja. La Paz: Editorial Carmach, 1988.

Bolivia, Dirección Nacional de Informaciones. *Bolivia: 10 años de revolución (1952–1962)*. La Paz: Empresa Industrial Gráfica E. Burillo, 1962.

Bolivia, Government of. *El libro blanco de la reforma agraria*. La Paz: Subsecretaria de Prensa, Informaciones, y Cultura, 1953.

———. "Disentailment and Its Discontents." In *The Bolivia Reader*, edited by Sinclair Thomson, Rossana Barragán, Xavier Albó, Seemin Qayum, and Mark Goodale, 184–187. Durham, NC: Duke University Press, 2018.

———. "The Slow and Gradual Disappearance of the Indigeneous Race." In *The Bolivia Reader*, edited by Sinclair Thomson, Rossana Barragon, Xavier Albó, Seemin Qayum, and Mark Goodale, 251–255. Durham NC: Duke University Press, 2018.

Bollaín, Icíar. *Tambien al lluvia*. Madrid: Morena Films, 2011.

Borsdorf, Axel. "Population Growth and Urbanization in Latin America." *GeoJournal* 2, no. 1 (1978): 47–60.

Borsdorf, Axel, and Christoph Stadel. *The Andes: A Geographical Portrait*. New York: Springer, 2015.

Botton, Sarah, Sabastien Hardy, and Franck Poupeau. "Water from the Heights, Water from the Grassroots: The Governance of Common Dynamics and Public Services in La Paz-El Alto." Washington, DC: World Bank, 2017.

Boyer, Christopher R. *Becoming Campesinos: Politics, Identity, and Agrarian Struggle in Postrevolutionary Michoacán, 1920–1935*. Stanford, CA: Stanford University Press, 2003.

———. *Political Landscapes: Forests, Conservation, and Community in Mexico*. Durham, NC: Duke University Press, 2015.

Bray, Tamara L. "Water, Ritual, and Power in the Inca Empire." *Latin American Antiquity* 24, no. 2 (2013): 164–190.

Brennan, Brid, Olivier Hoedeman, Philipp Terhorst, Satoko Kishimoto, and Belén Balanyá. *Por un model público de agua: Triunfos, luchas y sueños*. Amsterdam: Transnational Institute and Corporate Europe Observatory, 2007.

———. *Reclaiming Public Water: Achievements, Struggles and Visions from Around the World*. Amsterdam: Transnational Institute and Corporate Europe Observatory, 2005.

Buckley, Eve E. *Technocrats and the Politics of Drought and Development in Twentieth-Century Brazil*. Chapel Hill: University of North Carolina Press, 2017.

Burns, Kathryn. *Into the Archive: Writing and Power in Colonial Peru*. Durham, NC: Duke University Press, 2010.

Bustamante, Rocio. "De las 'permanencias' y los 'cambios' en las organizaciones de riego y el 'modelo Boliviano de descentralizacion': Estudio de caso en la Municipalidad de Tiquipaya, Bolivia." Master's thesis, Wageningen University, 1997.

Bustamante, Rocio, Carlos Crespo, and Anna Walnycki. "Seeing through the Concept of Water as a Human Right in Bolivia. In *The Right to Water: Politics, Governance and Social Struggles*, edited by Farhana Sultana and Alex Loftus, 223–240. New York: Earthscan, 2012.

Butrón Mendoza, Julio. *Eran solo unos indios: Pasajes de la cara india de una revolución*. Bolivia: Weinberg, 1992.

Butterworth, John. *Peri-Urban Water Conflicts: Supporting Dialogue and Negotiation*. Delft, Netherlands: International Water and Sanitation Centre, 2007.

Buytaert, W., et al. "Citizen Science in Hydrology and Water Resources: Opportunities for Knowledge Generation, Ecosystem Service Management, and Sustainable Development." *Frontiers in Earth Science* 2 (2014): 1–21.

Calderón G., Fernando, and Alicia M. Szmukler. *La política en las calles: Política, urbanización y desarrollo*. La Paz: Plural, 2000.

Canessa, Andrew. *Natives Making Nation: Gender, Indigeneity, and the State in the Andes.* Tucson: University of Arizona Press, 2011.

Cárdenas, Victor Hugo. "'La lucha de un pueblo.'" In *Raíces de América: El Mundo Aymara*, compiled by Xavier Albó, 495–534. Madrid: Alianza Editorial, 1988.

Carey, Mark. *In the Shadow of Melting Glaciers: Climate Change and Andean Society.* New York: Oxford University Press, 2010.

Carney, Judith A. *Black Rice: The African Origins of Rice Cultivation in the Americas.* Cambridge, MA: Harvard University Press, 2009.

Carse, Ashley. *Beyond the Big Ditch: Politics, Ecology, and Infrastructure at the Panama Canal.* Cambridge, MA: MIT Press, 2014.

Castells, Manuel. *The City and the Grassroots: A Cross-Cultural Theory of Urban Social Movements.* Berkeley: University of California Press, 1983.

———. *The Urban Question: A Marxist Approach.* Cambridge, MA: MIT Press, 1977.

Ceceña, Ana Esther. *La guerra por el agua y por la vida.* Buenos Aires: Madres de Plaza de Mayo, 2005.

Chapon, Denis, director. *Abuela Grillo.* Viborg, Denmark: The Animation Workshop, 2009.

Chastain, Andra, and Timothy Lorek, eds. *Itineraries of Expertise: Science, Technology, and the Environment in Latin America.* Pittsburgh: University of Pittsburgh Press, 2020.

Choque Canqui, Roberto. *Sublevación y masacre de Jesús de Machaqa de 1921.* La Paz: Fundación Diálogo, 1998.

Clarke, George, Katrina Kosec, and Scott Wallsten. "Has Private Participation in Water and Sewerage Improved Coverage? Empirical Evidence from Latin America." *Journal of International Development* 21 (2009): 327–61.

Cochabamba Departamento de Cultura. *Repartimiento de tierras por el Inca Huayna Capac.* Cochabamba, Bolivia: Universidad Mayor de San Simón, Departamento de Arqueología, 1977.

Colloredo-Mansfeld, Rudi. *Fighting Like a Community: Andean Civil Society in an Era of Indian Uprisings.* Chicago: University of Chicago Press, 2009.

Inter-American Conference on Indian Life, and US Bureau of Indian Affairs. *Final Act of the First Inter-American Conference on Indian Life.* Washington, DC: US Office of Indian Affairs, 1941.

Le Corbusier. *The Athens Charter.* New York: Grossman Publishers, 1973.

Cornejo Solis, Alberto, ed. *Programas politicos de Bolivia.* Cochabamba, Bolivia: Imprenta Universitaria, 1949.

Cote, Stephen C. *Oil and Nation: A History of Bolivia's Petroleum Sector.* Morgantown: West Virginia University Press, 2016.

———. "A War for Oil in the Chaco, 1932–1935." *Environmental History* 18, no. 4 (2013): 738–758.

Crespo Flores, Carlos. "Bolivia: La guerra de los pozos en Vinto y Sipe Sipe." In *Comunidades y conflictos socioambientales: Experiencias y desafíos en America Latina*, edited by Pablo Ortiz, 293–328. Quito: Abya-Yala, 1999.

———. "Continuidad y ruptura: La 'Guerra del Agua' y los nuevos movimientos sociales en Bolivia." *OSAL* 2 (2000).

———. "El derecho humano al agua en la práctica: La política de agua y recursos naturales del gobierno de Evo Morales." Cochabamba, Bolivia: Universidad Mayor de San Simón, Centro de Estudios Superiores/Centro de Investigaciones Sociales, 2010.

Crespo Flores, Carlos, Omar Fernández Quiroga, and Carmen Peredo. *Los regantes de Cochabamba en la guerra del agua: Presión social y negociación.* Cochabamba, Bolivia: Universidad Mayor de San Simón, Centro de Estudios Superiores, 2004.

Crespo Flores, Carlos, and Susan Spronk. *Después de las guerras del agua.* La Paz: Plural, 2007.

Cushman, Gregory T. *Guano and the Opening of the Pacific World: A Global Ecological History.* New York: Cambridge University Press, 2013.

Dandler Hanhart, Jorge. *El sindicalismo campesino en Bolivia: Los cambios estructurales en Ucurena.* Mexico City: Instituto Indigenista Inter-Americano, 1969.

Dangl, Benjamin. *The Five Hundred Year Rebellion: Indigenous Movements and the Decolonization of History in Bolivia.* Chico, GA: AK Press, 2019.

Davis, Mike. *Late Victorian Holocausts: El Niño Famines and the Making of the Third World.* New York: Verso, 2001.

De Angelis, Massimo. *Omnia Sunt Communia: On the Commons and the Transformation to Postcapitalism.* London: Zed Books, 2017.

De la Cadena, Marisol. *Earth Beings: Ecologies of Practice across Andean Worlds.* Durham, NC: Duke University Press, 2015.

De la Torre, Oscar. *The People of the River: Nature and Identity in Black Amazonia, 1835–1945.* Chapel Hill: University of North Carolina Press, 2018.

DeWitt, R. Peter. "Policy Directions in International Lending, 1961–1984: The Case of the Inter-American Development Bank." *Journal of Developing Areas* 21, no. 3 (1987): 277–284.

Dunkerley, James. *Rebellion in the Veins: Political Struggle in Bolivia, 1952–82.* London: Verso, 1984.

Dwinell, Alexander, and Marcela Olivera. "The Water Is Ours Damn It! Water Commoning in Bolivia." *Community Development Journal* 49 (2014): i44–i52.

Ellison, Susan H. *Domesticating Democracy: The Politics of Conflict Resolution in Bolivia.* Durham, NC: Duke University Press, 2018.

Escobar, Arturo. *Encountering Development: The Making and Unmaking of the Third World.* Princeton, NJ: Princeton University Press, 1994.

———. "Latin America at a Crossroads." *Cultural Studies* 24 (2010): 1–65.

———. *Territories of Difference: Place, Movements, Life, Redes.* Durham, NC: Duke University Press, 2008.

Eyferth, Jacob. *Eating Rice from Bamboo Roots: The Social History of a Community of Handicraft Papermakers in Rural Sichuan, 1920–2000.* Cambridge, MA: Harvard University Press, 2009.

Fabricant, Nicole, and Kathryn Hicks. "Bolivia's Next Water War: Historicizing the Struggles over Access to Water Resources in the Twenty-First Century." *Radical History Review* 116 (2013): 130–145.

Farthing, Linda C., and Benjamin H. Kohl. *Evo's Bolivia: Continuity and Change.* Austin: University of Texas Press, 2014.

Federación Sindical de Trabajadores Mineros de Bolivia. *Tesis de Pulacayo.* La Paz: Masas, 1980.

Ferguson, James. *The Anti-Politics Machine: Development, Depoliticization, and Bureaucratic Power in Lesotho*. Minneapolis: University of Minnesota Press, 1994.

Fernandes, Sujatha. *Who Can Stop the Drums?: Urban Social Movements in Chávez's Venezuela*. Durham, NC: Duke University Press, 2010.

Fernández Quiroga, Fredy Omar. "La relación tierra-agua en la economía campesina de Tiquipaya." Undergraduate thesis, Universidad Mayor de San Simón, 1996.

Fiege, Mark. *Irrigated Eden: The Making of an Agricultural Landscape in the American West*. Seattle: University of Washington Press, 2015.

Field, Thomas C. *From Development to Dictatorship: Bolivia and the Alliance for Progress in the Kennedy Era*. Ithaca, NY: Cornell University Press, 2014.

Finnegan, William. "Leasing the Rain." *The New Yorker*, 1 April 2002.

Fischer, Brodwyn. *A Poverty of Rights: Citizenship and Inequality in Twentieth-Century Rio de Janeiro*. Stanford, CA: Stanford University Press, 2010.

Fischer, Brodwyn, Bryan McCann, and Javier Auyero, eds. *Cities from Scratch: Poverty and Informality in Urban Latin America*. Durham, NC: Duke University Press, 2014.

Foss, Sarah. "On Our Own Terms: Development and Indigeneity in Cold War Guatemala." Unpublished manuscript. Under contract with the University of North Carolina Press.

Foster, John Bellamy. *Marx's Ecology: Materialism and Nature*. New York: Monthly Review Press, 2000.

Francovich, Guillermo. *El pensamiento boliviano en el siglo XX*. La Paz: Los Amigos del Libro, 1985.

Frazier, Lessie Jo. *Desired States: Sex, Gender, and Political Culture in Chile*. New Brunswick, NJ: Rutgers University Press, 2020.

Funes Monzote, Reinaldo. "*Geotransformación*: Geography and Revolution in Cuba from the 1950s to the 1960s." In *The Revolution from Within: Cuba, 1959–1980*, edited by Michael Bustamante and Jennifer Lambe, 117–145. Durham, NC: Duke University Press, 2019.

———. *Nuestro viaje a la luna: La idea de la transformación de la naturaleza en Cuba durante la Guerra Fría*. Havana: Casa de las Américas, 2019.

Gandy, Matthew. *Concrete and Clay: Reworking Nature in New York City*. Cambridge, MA: MIT Press, 2002.

———. *The Fabric of Space: Water, Modernity, and the Urban Imagination*. Cambridge, MA: MIT Press, 2014.

———. "Landscapes of Disaster: Water, Modernity, and Urban Fragmentation in Mumbai." *Environment and Planning A* 40, no. 1 (2008): 108–130.

———. "The Paris Sewers and the Rationalization of Urban Space." *Transactions of the Institute of British Geographers* 24, no. 1 (1999): 23–44.

———. "Rethinking Urban Metabolism: Water, Space and the Modern City." *City* 8, no. 3 (2004): 363–379.

Garcés, Fernando. *El Pacto de Unidad y el proceso de construcción de una propuesta de constitución política del estado: Sistematización de la experiencia*. La Paz: Preview Gráfica, 2010.

García, Raúl Alfonso. *Diez años de reforma agraria en Bolivia: 1953–1963*. La Paz: Dirección Nacional de Informaciones, 1963.

García Orellana, Luis Alberto, Fernando García Yapur, and Luz Quitón Herbas, "La crisis política. La 'Guerra del Agua' en Cochabamba." La Paz: PIEB, Aug. 2003.

Geidel, Molly. *Peace Corps Fantasies: How Development Shaped the Global Sixties*. Minneapolis: University of Minnesota Press, 2015.

Germani, Gino. "La ciudad como mecanismo integrador." *Revista Mexicana de Sociología* 29, no. 3 (1967): 387–406.

Gilbert, Jess. "Low Modernism and the Agrarian New Deal: A Different Kind of State." In *Fighting for the Farm: Rural America Transformed*, edited by Jane Adams, 129–146. Philadelphia: University of Pennsylvania Press, 2003.

Gildner, R. Matthew. "Indomestizo Modernism: National Development and Indigenous Integration in Postrevolutionary Bolivia, 1952–1964." PhD dissertation, University of Texas–Austin, 2013.

Gill, Leslie. *The School of the Americas: Military Training and Political Violence in the Americas*. Durham, NC: Duke University Press, 2004.

———. *Teetering on the Rim: Global Restructuring, Daily Life, and the Armed Retreat of the Bolivian State*. New York: Columbia University Press, 2000.

Giraudo, Laura, and Juan Martín-Sánchez. *La ambivalente historia del indigenismo: Campo interamericano y trayectorias nacionales 1940–1970*. Lima: IEP, 2012.

Gaonkar, Dilip Parameshwar. "On Alternative Modernities." In *Alternative Modernities*, edited by Dilip Parameshwar Gaonkar, 1–23. Durham, NC: Duke University Press, 2001.

Goldman, Michael. *Imperial Nature: The World Bank and Struggles for Social Justice in the Age of Globalization*. New Haven, CT: Yale University Press, 2008.

Goldstein, Daniel M. *Owners of the Sidewalk: Security and Survival in the Informal City*. Durham, NC: Duke University Press, 2016.

———. *The Spectacular City: Violence and Performance in Urban Bolivia*. Durham, NC: Duke University Press, 2004.

González, Roberto J. *Zapotec Science: Farming and Food in the Northern Sierra of Oaxaca*. Austin: University of Texas Press, 2001.

Goodale, Mark. *Dilemmas of Modernity: Bolivian Encounters with Law and Liberalism*. Stanford, CA: Stanford University Press, 2009.

———. *A Revolution in Fragments: Traversing Scales of Justice, Ideology, and Practice in Bolivia*. Durham, NC: Duke University Press, 2019.

Goodrich, Carter. "Bolivia in Time of Revolution." In *Beyond the Revolution: Bolivia Since 1952*, edited by James Malloy and Richard Thorn, 3–24. Pittsburgh: University of Pittsburgh Press, 1971.

Gordillo Claure, Jose M. *Arando en la historia: La experiencia política campesina en Cochabamba*. La Paz: Plural, 1998.

———. *Campesinos revolucionarios en Bolivia: Identidad, territorio y sexualidad en el Valle Alto de Cochabamba, 1952–1964*. La Paz: Plural, 2000.

———. "Peasant Wars in Bolivia: Making, Thinking, and Living the Revolution in Cochabamba (1952–64)." Unpublished manuscript.

Gordillo Claure, Jose M., and Robert H. Jackson, "Mestizaje y proceso de parcelización en la estructura agrarian de Cochabamba, (El caso de Sipe-Spie en los Siglos XVIII–XIX)." *HISLA* 10 (1987): 15–37.

Gotkowitz, Laura, ed. *Histories of Race and Racism: The Andes and Mesoamerica from Colonial Times to the Present*. Durham, NC: Duke University Press, 2012.

———. *A Revolution for Our Rights: Indigenous Struggles for Land and Justice in Bolivia, 1880–1952*. Durham, NC: Duke University Press, 2008.

Goubert, Jean-Pierre. *The Conquest of Water: The Advent of Health in the Industrial Age*. Translated by Andrew Wilson. Princeton, NC: Princeton University Press, 1989.

Gould, Jeffrey L. *To Lead as Equals: Rural Protest and Political Consciousness in Chinandega, Nicaragua, 1912–1979*. Chapel Hill: University of North Carolina Press, 1990.

Grandin, Greg. *The Last Colonial Massacre: Latin America in the Cold War*. Second edition. 2004; Chicago: University of Chicago Press, 2011.

Grieshaber, Erwin P. "Fluctuaciones en la definición del indio: Comparación de los censos de 1900 y 1950." *Historia Boliviana* 5, nos. 1–2 (1985): 45–65.

Gross, Miriam. "Between Party, People, and Profession: The Many Faces of the 'Doctor' during the Cultural Revolution." *Medical History* 62, no. 3 (2018): 333–359.

———. *Farewell to the God of Plague: Chairman Mao's Campaign to Deworm China*. Oakland: University of California Press, 2016.

Guevara Arze, Walter. *Plan inmediato de politica economica del gobierno de la revolución nacional*. La Paz: Ministerio de Relaciones Exteriores, 1955.

Gustafson, Bret. *bolivia in the age of gas*. Durham, NC: Duke University Press, 2020.

Gutiérrez Aguilar, Raquel. *Rhythms of the Pachakuti: Indigenous Uprising and State Power in Bolivia*. Translated by Stacey Alba D. Skar. Durham, NC: Duke University Press, 2014.

Gutiérrez Aguilar, Raquel, Raúl Zibechi, Natalia Sierra, Héctor Mondragón, Pablo Dávalos, Vilma Almendra, Pablo Mamani, and Emmanuel Rozental. *Palabras para tejernos, resistir y transformar en la época que estamos viviendo*. Cochabamba, Bolivia: Textos Rebeldes, 2011.

Hailu, Degol, Rafael Guerreiro Osorio, and Raquel Tsukada. "Privatization and Renationalization: What Went Wrong in Bolivia's Water Sector?" *World Development* 40, no. 12 (2012): 2564–2577.

Hall, Peter. *Cities of Tomorrow: An Intellectual History of Urban Planning and Design in the Twentieth Century*. Malden, MA: Blackwell Publishers, 2002.

Hardin, Garrett. "The Tragedy of the Commons." *Science* 162, no. 3859 (13 December 1968): 1243–1248.

Hardt, Michael, and Antonio Negri. *Multitude: War and Democracy in the Age of Empire*. New York: Penguin, 2005.

Harris, Olivia. "Ethnic Identity and Market Relations: Indians and Mestizos in the Andes." In *Ethnicity, Markets, and Migration in the Andes*, edited by Brooke Larson and Olivia Harris, 351–390. Durham, NC: Duke University Press, 1995.

Harris, Olivia, and Xavier Albó. *Monteros y guardatojos: Campesinos y mineros en el Norte de Potosí*. La Paz: CIPCA, 1976.

Healy, Kevin. *Llamas, Weavings, and Organic Chocolate: Multicultural Grassroots Development in the Andes and Amazon of Bolivia*. Notre Dame, IN: University of Notre Dame Press, 2001.

Heath, Dwight B., Hans C. Buechler, and Charles J. Erasmus. *Land Reform and Social Revolution in Bolivia*. New York: Praeger, 1970.

Hecht, Gabrielle, ed. *Entangled Geographies: Empire and Technopolitics in the Global Cold War*. Cambridge, MA: MIT Press, 2011

———. *The Radiance of France: Nuclear Power and National Identity after World War II*. Cambridge, MA: MIT Press, 2009.

Hendriks, Jan. "Negociación de intereses locales en el manejo de cuenca: El caso de Tiquipaya, Bolivia." Cochabamba, Bolivia: Universidad Mayor de San Simón, Centro AGUA, 2003.

Henriques, Rosario. "Análisis de los niveles de vida y desigualdad en la ciudad de Cochabamba durante el primer siglo republicano, 1825–1925." PhD dissertation, Universidad Nacional de Educación a Distancia (Spain), 2016.

Hines, Sarah. "The Power and Ethics of Vernacular Modernism: The Misicuni Dam Project in Cochabamba, Bolivia, 1944–2017." *Hispanic American Historical Review* 98, no. 2 (2018): 223–256.

Holloway, John. *Change the World without Taking Power: The Meaning of Revolution Today*. London: Pluto Press, 2002.

Holston, James. *Insurgent Citizenship: Disjunctions of Democracy and Modernity in Brazil*. Princeton, NJ: Princeton University Press, 2009.

Hoogendam, Paul, ed. *Aguas y municipios: Retos para la gestión municipal de agua*. Cochabamba, Bolivia: Plural, 1999.

Horowitz, Leah S., and Michael J. Watts, eds. *Grassroots Environmental Governance: Community Engagements with Industry*. New York: Routledge, 2019.

Hylton, Forrest. "Reverberations of Insurgency: Indian Communities, the Federal War of 1899, and the Regeneration of Bolivia." PhD dissertation, New York University, 2011.

Hylton, Forrest, and Sinclair Thomson. *Revolutionary Horizons: Past and Present in Bolivian Politics*. New York: Verso, 2007.

Jackson, Robert H. "The Decline of the Hacienda in Cochabamba, Bolivia: The Case of the Sacaba Valley, 1870–1929." *Hispanic American Historical Review* 69, no. 2 (1989): 259–281.

———. *Regional Markets and Agrarian Transformation in Bolivia Cochabamba, 1539–1960*. Albuquerque: University of New Mexico Press, 1994.

Jackson, Robert H., and Jose M. Gordillo Claure. "Formación, crisis y transformación de la estructura agraria de Cochabamba: El caso de la hacienda de Paucarpata y de la comunidad del Passo, 1538–1645 y 1872–1929." *Revista de Indias* 53, no. 199 (1993): 723–760.

James, Daniel. *Doña María's Story: Life History, Memory, and Political Identity*. Durham, NC: Duke University Press, 2007.

Jiménez, Christina Marie. *Making an Urban Public: Popular Claims to the City in Mexico, 1879–1932*. Pittsburgh: University of Pittsburgh Press, 2019.

Jørgensen, Dolly, Finn Arne Jørgensen, and Sara B. Pritchard. *New Natures: Joining Environmental History with Science and Technology Studies*. Pittsburgh: University of Pittsburgh Press, 2013.

Joseph, Gilbert M., and Daniel Nugent. "Popular Culture and State Formation in Revolutionary Mexico." In *Everyday Forms of State Formation: Revolution and the Negotiation of Rule in Modern Mexico*, edited by Gilbert M. Joseph and Daniel Nugent, 3–23. Durham, NC: Duke University Press, 2012.

Kaika, Maria. *City of Flows: Modernity, Nature, and the City*. New York: Routledge, 2005.

Kaika, Maria, and Erik Swyngedouw. "Fetishizing the Modern City: The Phantasmagoria of

Urban Technological Networks." *International Journal of Urban and Regional Research* 24, no. 1 (2000): 120–138.

Katz, Claudio. "Los problemas de autonomismo." 10 May 2005. www.lahaine.org/b2-img/katz_aut.pdf.

Kelly, Patrick William. *Sovereign Emergencies: Latin America and the Making of Global Human Rights Politics.* New York: Cambridge University Press, 2018.

Kiddle, Amelia M. *Mexico's Relations with Latin America during the Cárdenas Era.* Albuquerque: University of New Mexico Press, 2016.

Klein, Herbert S. *A Concise History of Bolivia.* Second edition. 2003; New York: Cambridge University Press, 2011.

———. "David Toro and the Establishment of 'Military Socialism' in Bolivia." *Hispanic American Historical Review* 45, no. 1 (1965): 25–52.

———. *Parties and Political Change in Bolivia, 1880–1952.* New York: Cambridge University Press, 1969.

Knudson, Jerry W. *Bolivia: Press and Revolution, 1932–1964.* New York: University Press of America, 1986.

Kohl, Benjamin. "Challenges to Neoliberal Hegemony in Bolivia." *Antipode* 38, no. 2 (2006): 304–326.

Kohl, Benjamin, and Linda C. Farthing. *Impasse in Bolivia: Neoliberal Hegemony and Popular Resistance.* New York: Zed Books, 2006.

Komives, Kristin. "Designing Pro-Poor Water and Sewer Concessions: Early Lessons from Bolivia." Washington, DC: World Bank, 1999.

Krasner, Stephen D. "Power Structures and Regional Development Banks." *International Organization* 35, no. 2 (1981): 303–328.

Kruse, Thomas. "La Guerra del Agua en Cochabamba, Bolivia: Terrenos complejos, convergencias nuevas." In *Sindicatos y nuevos movimientos sociales en América Latina,* edited by Enrique de la Garza Toledo, 121–161. Buenos Aires: CLACSO, 2005.

Kruse, Thomas, and Humberto Vargas. "Las victorias de abril: Una historia que aún no concluye." *Observatorio Social de America Latina* 2 (September 2000).

Kuenzli, E. Gabrielle. *Acting Inca: Identity and National Belonging in Early Twentieth-Century Bolivia.* Pittsburgh: University of Pittsburgh Press, 2013.

Langer, Erick. *Economic Change and Rural Resistance in Southern Bolivia 1880–1930.* Stanford, CA: Stanford University Press, 1989.

Larkin, Brian. "The Politics and Poetics of Infrastructure." *Annual Review of Anthropology* 42 (2013): 327–343.

Laserna, Roberto. "Cochabamba: La guerra contra el agua." *OSAL* (September 2001): 15–20.

Larson, Brooke. *Cochabamba, 1550–1900: Colonialism and Agrarian Transformation in Bolivia.* Durham, NC: Duke University Press, 1998.

———. "Redeemed Indians, Barbarized Cholos: Crafting Neocolonial Modernity in Liberal Bolivia, 1900–1910." In *Political Cultures in the Andes, 1750–1950,* edited by Nils Jacobsen and Cristóbal Aljovín de Losada, 230–252. Durham, NC: Duke University Press, 2005.

———. *Trials of Nation Making: Liberalism, Race, and Ethnicity in the Andes, 1810–1910.* New York: Cambridge University Press, 2004.

Lauderdale Graham, Sandra. "Writing from the Margins: Brazilian Slaves and Written Culture." *Comparative Studies in Society and History* 49, no. 3 (2007): 611–636.

Laurie, Nina. "Establishing Development Orthodoxy: Negotiating Masculinities in the Water Sector." *Development and Change* 36, no. 3 (2005): 525–549.

Laurie, Nina, and Simon Marvin. "Globalisation, Neoliberalism, and Negotiated Development in the Andes: Water Projects and Regional Identity in Cochabamba, Bolivia." *Environment and Planning A* 31 (1999): 1401–1415.

Lavaud, Jean-Pierre. *La dictadura minada: La huelga de hambre de las mujeres mineras. Bolivia 1977–1978.* Lima: Institut français d'études andines, 2015.

Lazar, Sian. *El Alto, Rebel City: Self and Citizenship in Andean Bolivia.* Durham, NC: Duke University Press, 2008.

Ledo García, M. del Carmen. *Agua potable a nivel de hogares con una dimensión de género: Derecho de las mujeres al agua en las ciudades de El Alto, La Paz y Cochabamba.* Cochabamba, Bolivia: CEPLAG, 2005.

———. *Urbanisation and Poverty in the Cities of the National Economic Corridor in Bolivia: Case Study: Cochabamba.* Delft, Netherlands: Delft University Press, 2002.

Lehman, Kenneth. *Bolivia and the United States: A Limited Partnership.* Athens: University of Georgia Press, 1999.

———. "Completing the Revolution? The United States and Bolivia's Long Revolution." *Bolivian Studies Journal* 22 (2016): 4–35.

Li, Tania Murray. *The Will to Improve: Governmentality, Development, and the Practice of Politics.* Durham, NC: Duke University Press, 2007.

Linsalata, Lucía. *Cuando manda la asamblea: Lo comunitario-popular en Bolivia: Una mirada desde los sistemas comunitarios de agua de Cochabamba.* Cochabamba, Bolivia: Sociedad Comunitaria de Estudios Estratégicos, 2015.

———. "Ni público, ni privado: común. Prácticas y sentidos de la gestión comunitaria del agua en la zona sur de Cochabamba en Bolivia." In *Territorios en disputa: Despojo capitalista, luchas en defensa de los bienes comunes naturales y alternativas emancipatorias para América Latina,* edited by Claudia Composto, Mina Lorena Navarro, and Alberto Acosta, 249–266. Mexico City: Bajo Tierra, 2014.

Lipsett-Rivera, Sonya. *To Defend Our Water with the Blood of Our Veins: The Struggle for Resources in Colonial Puebla.* Albuquerque: University of New Mexico Press, 1999.

Loreto López, Rosalva, ed. *Agua, poder urbano y metabolismo social.* Puebla, México: Instituto de Ciencias Sociales y Humanidades, Benemérita Universidad Autónoma de Puebla, 2009.

Maita Morales, Juan Carlos. "Estudio de las características de gestión del sistema de riego Lagum Mayu administrado por usuarios en la zona de Tiquipaya." Cochabamba, Bolivia: Universidad Mayor de San Simón, 1994.

Mallon, Florencia E. *The Defense of Community in Peru's Central Highlands: Peasant Struggle and Capitalist Transition, 1860–1940.* Princeton, NJ: Princeton University Press, 1983.

———. "The Promise and Dilemma of Subaltern Studies: Perspectives from Latin American History." *American Historical Review* 99, no. 5 (1994): 1491–1515.

Malloy, James. "Revolutionary Politics." In *Beyond the Revolution: Bolivia since 1952,* edited by James Malloy and Richard Thorn, 111–156. Pittsburgh: University of Pittsburgh Press, 1971.

Mamani Condori, Carlos B. *Taraqu: 1866–1935: Masacre, guerra y "renovación" en la biografía de Eduardo L. Nina Qhispi.* La Paz: Aruwiyiri, 1991.

Mamani Ramírez, Pablo. *El rugir de las multitudes: La fuerza de los levantamientos indígenas en Bolivia/Qullasuyu*. La Paz: Aruwiyiri, 2004.

Marvin, Simon, and Nina Laurie. "An Emerging Logic of Urban Water Management, Cochabamba, Bolivia." *Urban Studies* 36, no. 2 (1999): 341–357.

Marx, Karl. *The Eighteenth Brumaire of Louis Bonaparte*. 1852; New York: International Publishers, 1963.

Marx, Karl, and Friedrich Engels. *The German Ideology: Parts I & III*. 1932; New York: International Publishers, 1967.

Mathews, Andrew S. *Instituting Nature: Authority, Expertise, and Power in Mexican Forests*. Cambridge, MA: MIT Press, 2011.

Mavhunga, Clapperton Chakanetsa. *Transient Workspaces: Technologies of Everyday Innovation in Zimbabwe*. Cambridge, MA: MIT Press, 2014.

McCook, Stuart George. *States of Nature: Science, Agriculture, and Environment in the Spanish Caribbean, 1760–1940*. Austin: University of Texas Press, 2002.

McDowell, Julia, and Jeremy Hess. "Accessing Adaptation: Multiple Stressors on Livelihoods in the Bolivian Highlands under a Changing Climate." *Global Environmental Change* 22, no. 2 (2012): 342–352.

McGrath, Elena. "Devil's Bargains: The Limits of Worker Citizenship and Resource Nationalism in Bolivia." Manuscript in progress.

———. "(Un)Cooperative Labor? Women's Work, Cooperatives, and the Foundations of Austerity in Bolivia." Paper presented at the 2018 American Historical Association annual meeting, held in Washington, DC.

McGrath, Elena, Elizabeth Shesko, Bridgette Werner, and Kevin Young. "'Restorative' Dictatorship, Contentious Clientelism, and Problematic Intermediaries: Legacies of Revolution in Post-1964 Bolivia." Panel at the 2019 annual meeting of the Latin American Studies Association, held in Boston, MA.

McKibben, Bill. *The End of Nature*. New York: Random House, 1989.

Medina, Eden. *Cybernetic Revolutionaries: Technology and Politics in Allende's Chile*. Cambridge, MA: MIT Press, 2014.

Medina, Eden, Ivan da Costa Marques, and Christina Holmes. *Beyond Imported Magic: Essays on Science, Technology, and Society in Latin America*. Cambridge, MA: MIT Press, 2014.

Mehos, Donna C., and Suzanne M. Moon. "The Uses of Portability: Circulating Experts in the Technopolitics of Cold War and Decolonization." In *Entangled Geographies: Empire and Technopolitics in the Global Cold War*, edited by Gabrielle Hecht, 43–74. Cambridge, MA: MIT Press, 2011.

Melosi, Martin V. *Precious Commodity: Providing Water for America's Cities*. Pittsburgh: University of Pittsburgh Press, 2011.

———. *The Sanitary City: Urban Infrastructure in America from Colonial Times to the Present*. Baltimore, MD: Johns Hopkins University Press, 2000.

Méndez, Cecilia. *The Plebeian Republic: The Huanta Rebellion and the Making of the Peruvian State, 1820–1850*. Durham, NC: Duke University Press, 2005.

Mendoza, Jaime. *El Macizo Boliviano* [1935]; *El factor geográfico en la nacionalidad boliviana* [1925]. La Paz: Presidencia de la Asamblea Legislativa Plurinacional, Vicepresidencia del Estado, 2016.

Meyer, Michael C. *Water in the Hispanic Southwest: A Social and Legal History, 1550–1850*. Tucson: University of Arizona Press, 1996.

Mikhail, Alan. *Nature and Empire in Ottoman Egypt: An Environmental History*. New York: Cambridge University Press, 2011.

Mitchell, Timothy. *Rule of Experts: Egypt, Techno-Politics, Modernity*. Berkeley: University of California Press, 2002.

Moyn, Samuel. *Not Enough: Human Rights in an Unequal World*. Cambridge, MA: Belknap Press, 2019.

Mukerji, Chandra. *Impossible Engineering: Technology and Territoriality on the Canal Du Midi*. Princeton, NJ: Princeton University Press, 2009.

Mumford, Jeremy Ravi. *Vertical Empire: The General Resettlement of Indians in the Colonial Andes*. Durham, NC: Duke University Press, 2012.

Murphy, Edward. *For a Proper Home: Housing Rights in the Margins of Urban Chile, 1960–2010*. Pittsburgh: University of Pittsburgh Press, 2015.

Murra, John V. *Formaciones económicas y políticas del mundo andino*. Lima: Instituto de Estudios Peruanos, 1975.

Navarro, Gonzalo, and Mabel Maldonado. *Geografía ecológica de Bolivia: Vegetación y ambientes acuáticos*. Cochabamba, Bolivia: Centro de Ecología Simón I. Patiño, 2002.

Nelson, Michael. "Fifty Years of Hydroelectric Development in Chile: A History of Unlearned Lessons." *Water Alternatives* 6, no. 2 (2013): 195–206.

Nickson, Andrew, and Claudia Vargas. "The Limitations of Water Regulation: The Failure of the Cochabamba Concession in Bolivia." *Bulletin of Latin American Research* 21, no. 1 (2002): 99–120.

Nobbs-Thiessen, Ben. *Landscape of Migration: Mobility and Environmental Change on Bolivia's Tropical Frontier, 1952 to the Present*. Chapel Hill: University of North Carolina Press, 2020.

Nugent, David. *Modernity at the Edge of Empire: State, Individual, and Nation in the Northern Peruvian Andes, 1885–1935*. Stanford, CA: Stanford University Press, 1997.

Nugent, David, and Christopher Krupa, eds. *State Theory and Andean Politics: New Approaches to the Study of Rule*. Philadelphia: University of Pennsylvania Press, 2015.

Offner, Amy C. *Sorting Out the Mixed Economy. The Rise and Fall of Welfare and Developmental States in the Americas*. Princeton, NJ: Princeton University Press, 2019.

Olivera, Oscar, and Tom Lewis. *¡Cochabamba! Water War in Bolivia*. Cambridge, MA: South End Press, 2004.

Olsson, Tore C. *Agrarian Crossings: Reformers and the Remaking of the US and Mexican Countryside*. Princeton, NJ: Princeton University Press, 2017.

Orellana Aillón, Lorgio. "El proceso insurrecional de abril: Estructuras materiales y superestructuras organizativas de los campesinos regantes en el Valle Central Cochabambino." In *Ruralidades Latinomaericanas: Identidades y luchas sociales*, edited by Norma Giarracca and Betina Levy, 477–550. Buenos Aires: CLACSO, 2004.

Orlove, Benjamin S., John C. H. Chiang, and Mark A. Cane. "Forecasting Andean Rainfall and Crop Yield from the Influence of El Niño on Pleiades Visibility." *Nature* 403 (2000): 68–71.

Ostrom, Elinor. *Governing the Commons: The Evolution of Institutions for Collective Action*. New York: Cambridge University Press, 1990.

Pacino, Nicole L. "Bringing the Revolution to the Countryside: Rural Health Programmes as State-Building in Post-1952 Bolivia." *Bulletin of Latin American Research* 38, no. 1 (2019): 50–65.

———. "Constructing a New Bolivian Society: Public Health Reforms and the Consolidation of the Bolivian National Revolution." *The Latin Americanist* 57, no. 4 (2013): 25–56.

———. "Creating Madres Campesinas: Revolutionary Motherhood and the Gendered Politics of Nation Building in 1950s Bolivia." *Journal of Women's History* 27, no. 1 (2015): 62–87.

———. "Stimulating a Cooperative Spirit? Public Health and U.S.-Bolivia Relations in the 1950s." *Diplomatic History* 41, no. 2 (2017): 305–335.

Palerm Viqueira, Jacinta, and Tomás Martínez Saldaña. *Antología sobre pequeño riego*. Volumes 1–3. Mexico City: Plaza y Valdés, 1997, 2000, 2006.

Pentimalli de Navarro, Michela, and Gustavo Rodríguez Ostria, "Las razones de la multitud (Hambruna, motines y subsistencia: 1878–79)." *Estado y Sociedad* 5 (1988): 15–33.

Perreault, Thomas. "Custom and Contradiction: Rural Water Governance and the Politics of Usos y Costumbres in Bolivia's Irrigators' Movement." *Annals of the Association of American Geographers* 98, no. 4 (2008): 834–854.

———. "From the Guerra del Agua to the Guerra del Gas." *Antipode* 38, no. 1 (2006): 150–172.

Pisani, Donald J. *Water and American Government: The Reclamation Bureau, National Water Policy, and the West, 1902–1935*. Berkeley: University of California Press, 2002.

Platt, Tristan. *Estado boliviano y ayllu andino: Tierra y tributo en el norte de Potosí*. Lima: Instituto de Estudios Peruanos, 1982.

Poole, Deborah. *Vision, Race, and Modernity: A Visual Economy of the Andean Image World*. Princeton, NJ: Princeton University Press, 1997.

Postero, Nancy Grey. *The Indigenous State: Race, Politics, and Performance in Plurinational Bolivia*. Oakland: University of California Press, 2017.

———. *Now We Are Citizens: Indigenous Politics in Postmulticultural Bolivia*. Stanford, CA: Stanford University Press, 2007.

Postero, Nancy Grey, and Jason Tockman. "Self-Governance in Bolivia's First Indigenous Autonomy: Charagua." *Latin American Research Review* 55, no. 1 (2020): 1–15.

Poupeau, Franck, and Claudia González. *Modelos de gestión del agua en los Andes*. La Paz: PIEB, 2010.

Prada Alcoreza, Raúl. *Subversiones indígenas*. La Paz: Muela del Diablo, 2008.

Pritchard, Sara B. *Confluence: The Nature of Technology and the Remaking of the Rhône*. Cambridge, MA: Harvard University Press, 2011.

Querejazu Calvo, Roberto. *Guano, salitre, sangre: Historia de la Guerra del Pacífico*. La Paz: Los Amigos del Libro, 1979.

Quijano, Aníbal. *Dependencia, urbanización y cambio social en Latinoamérica*. Lima: Mosca Azul, 1977.

Quiroga, B. "Una sentencia injusta: Pleito civil entre el Directorio de Propietarios de Lagum Mayu y el señor Jesús Aguayo." Cochabamba, Bolivia: López-Santivañez, 1927.

Raffles, Hugh. *In Amazonia: A Natural History*. Princeton, NJ: Princeton University Press, 2002.

Rama, Angel. *The Lettered City*. Durham, NC: Duke University Press, 1996.

Ramos Andrade, Edgar. *Agonía y rebellion social: 543 motivos de justicia urgente.* La Paz: Editora Presencia, 2004.

Razavi, Nasya. "'Social Control' and the Politics of Public Participation in Water Remunicipalization, Cochabamba, Bolivia." *Water* 11, no. 7, 1455 (2019): 1–19.

Reisner, Marc. *Cadillac Desert: The American West and Its Disappearing Water.* New York: Viking, 1986.

"Rethinking Indigenismo on the American Continent." *Latin American Perspectives* 39, no. 5 (September 2012): Special Issue.

Rivas Antezana, Sinforoso, and Jose M. Gordillo Claure. *Los hombres de la revolución: Memorias de un líder campesino.* La Paz: Plural, 2000.

Rivera Cusicanqui, Silvia. *Ch'ixinakax Utxiwa: Una reflexión sobre prácticas y discursos descolonizadores.* Buenos Aires: Tinta Limón, 2010.

———. *Oprimidos pero no vencidos: Luchas del campesinado aymara y qhechwa de Bolivia, 1900–1980.* La Paz: Hisbol–CSUTCB, 1984.

———. *Violencias (re)encubiertas en Bolivia.* Santander, Spain: Otramérica, 2012.

Rodríguez, Ileana. "Reading Subalterns Across Texts, Disciplines, and Theories: From Representation to Recognition." In *The Latin American Subaltern Studies Reader,* edited by Ileana Rodríguez, 1–32. Durham, NC: Duke University Press, 2001.

Rodríguez Ostria, Gustavo. "Entre reformas y contrareformas: Las comunidades indígenas en el Valle Bajo cochabambino (1825–1900)." In *Los Andes en la encrucijada: Indios, comunidades y estado en el Siglo XIX,* edited by Heraclio Bonilla, 277–334. Quito: Libri Mundi, 1991.

Rodríguez Ostria, Gustavo, and Humberto Solares Serrano. *Maíz, chicha y modernidad: Telones y entretelones del desarrollo urbano de Cochabamba: (siglos XIX y XX).* Santa Cruz de la Sierra, Bolivia: El País, 2011.

Rogers, Thomas D. *The Deepest Wounds: A Labor and Environmental History of Sugar in Northeast Brazil.* Chapel Hill: University of North Carolina Press, 2010.

Roseberry, William. "Hegemony and the Language of Contention." In *Everyday Forms of State Formation: Revolution and the Negotiation of Rule in Modern Mexico,* edited by Gilbert M. Joseph and Daniel Nugent, 355–356. Durham, NC: Duke University Press, 2012.

Rosemblatt, Karin Alejandra. *The Science and Politics of Race in Mexico and the United States, 1910–1950.* Chapel Hill: University of North Carolina Press, 2018.

Saavedra Antezana, Carlos. "Ideas generales sobre obras de irrigación en Bolivia." *Irrigación en México* 27, no. 1 (1946): 10–18.

Salazar Ortuño, Fernando. "Autoridades de agua en organizaciones locales de Riego: Estudio de caso del sistema de riego Sayt'u Khocha en Cochabamba, Bolivia." Master's thesis, Wageningen University, 1997.

———. "Gestión del agua en el municipio de Sipe Sipe." In *Aguas y municipios: Retos para la gestión municipal de agua,* edited by Paul Hoogendam, 51–86. La Paz: Plural, 1999.

Sanjinés C., Javier. *Embers of the Past: Essays in Times of Decolonization.* Durham, NC: Duke University Press, 2013.

———. *Mestizaje Upside-Down: Aesthetic Politics in Modern Bolivia.* Pittsburgh: University of Pittsburgh Press, 2004.

Sanjinés Gonzales, Alfredo. *La reforma agraria en Bolivia.* First edition. La Paz: Renacimiento, 1932.

————. *La reforma agraria en Bolivia*. Second edition. La Paz: Universo, 1945.

Santiago, Myrna I. *The Ecology of Oil: Environment, Labor, and the Mexican Revolution, 1900–1938*. New York: Cambridge University Press, 2009.

Sater, William F. *Andean Tragedy: Fighting the War of the Pacific, 1879–1884*. Lincoln: University of Nebraska Press, 2009.

Schmalzer, Sigrid. *Red Revolution, Green Revolution: Scientific Farming in Socialist China*. Chicago: University of Chicago Press, 2016.

Schwartz, Diana Lynn. "Transforming the Tropics: Development, Displacement, and Anthropology in the Papaloapan, Mexico, 1940s–1970s." PhD dissertation, University of Chicago, 2016.

Scott, Colin. "Science for the West, Myth for the Rest?: The Case of James Bay Cree Knowledge Construction." In *Naked Science: Anthropological Inquiry into Boundaries, Power, and Knowledge*, edited by Laura Nader, 69–86. New York: Routledge, 1996.

Scott, James C. *The Art of Not Being Governed: An Anarchist History of Upland Southeast Asia*. New Haven, CT: Yale University Press, 2009.

————. "High Modernist Social Engineering: The Case of the Tennessee Valley Authority." In *Experiencing the State*, edited by Lloyd I. Rudolph and John Kurt Jacobsen, 3–52. New York: Oxford University Press, 2010.

————. *The Moral Economy of the Peasant: Rebellion and Subsistence in Southeast Asia*. New Haven, CT: Yale University Press, 1976.

————. *Seeing Like a State: How Certain Schemes to Improve the Human Condition Have Failed*. New Haven, CT: Yale University Press, 1998.

Seemann, Miriam. *Water Security, Justice and the Politics of Water Rights in Peru and Bolivia*. New York: Palgrave Macmillan, 2016.

Sen, Amartya. *Poverty and Famines: An Essay on Entitlement and Deprivation*. New York: Oxford University Press, 1981.

Sherbondy, Jeanette. "Water Ideology in Inca Ethnogenesis." In *Andean Cosmologies through Time: Persistence and Emergence*, edited by Robert Dover, Katharine Seibold, and John McDowell, 46–66. Bloomington: Indiana University Press, 1992.

————. "Water and Power: The Role of Irrigation Districts in the Transition from Inca to Spanish Cuzco." In *Irrigation at High Altitudes: The Social Organization of Water Control Systems in the Andes*, edited by William P. Mitchell and David Guillet, 69–97. Arlington, VA: American Anthropological Association, 1993.

Shesko, Elizabeth. *Conscript Nation: Coercion and Citizenship in the Bolivian Barracks*. Pittsburgh: University of Pittsburgh Press, 2020.

Shiva, Vandana. *Water Wars: Privatization, Pollution and Profit*. Cambridge, MA: South End Press, 2002.

Shultz, Jim, and Melissa Draper. *Dignity and Defiance: Stories from Bolivia's Challenge to Globalization*. Berkeley: University of California Press, 2008.

Siekmeier, James F. *The Bolivian Revolution and the United States, 1952 to the Present*. University Park: Pennsylvania State University Press, 2011.

Simmons, Erica S. *Meaningful Resistance: Market Reforms and the Roots of Social Protest in Latin America*. New York: Cambridge University Press, 2016.

Simpson, Hugh, Rob de Loë, and Jean Andrey. "Vernacular Knowledge and Water Management—Towards the Integration of Expert Science and Local Knowledge in Ontario, Canada." *Water Alternatives* 8, no. 3 (2015): 352–372.

Singer, Paul Israel. *Economía política de la urbanización.* Mexico City: Siglo Veintiuno, 1975.

Smith, Neil. *Uneven Development: Nature, Capital, and the Production of Space.* Third edition. 1984; Athens: University of Georgia Press, 2008.

Solares Serrano, Humberto. *Historia, espacio y sociedad: Cochabamba, 1550–1950: Formación, crisis y desarrollo de su proceso urbano.* Cochabamba, Bolivia: CIDRE, 1990.

———. *La larga marcha de los cochabambinos: De la villa de Oropesa a la metropolización.* Cochabamba, Bolivia: Grafisol, 2011.

Soliz, Carmen. *Fields of Revolution: Agrarian Reform and Rural State Formation in Bolivia, 1935–1964.* Pittsburgh: University of Pittsburgh Press, 2021.

———. "'Land to the Original Owners': Rethinking the Indigenous Politics of the Bolivian Agrarian Reform." *Hispanic American Historical Review* 97, no. 2 (2017): 259–296.

———. "La modernidad esquiva: Debates políticos e intelectuales sobre la reforma agraria en Bolivia (1935–1952)." *Revista Ciencia y Cultura* 16, no. 29 (2012): 23–47.

Soluri, John. *Banana Cultures: Agriculture, Consumption, and Environmental Change in Honduras and the United States.* Austin: University of Texas Press, 2005.

Soto Laveaga, Gabriela. *Jungle Laboratories: Mexican Peasants, National Projects, and the Making of the Pill.* Durham, NC: Duke University Press, 2009.

Spain and Consejo de Indias. *Recopilación de leyes de los reynos de las Indias.* 1791; Madrid: Boletín Oficial del Estado, 1998.

Spaulding, Karen. *Huarochirí: An Andean Society under Inca and Spanish Rule.* Palo Alto, CA: Stanford University Press, 1984.

Spronk, Susan. "Roots of Resistance to Urban Water Privatization in Bolivia: The 'New Working Class,' the Crisis of Neoliberalism, and Public Services." *International Labor and Working-Class History* 71, no. 1 (2007): 8–28.

Spronk, Susan, and Jeffery Webber. "Struggles against Accumulation by Dispossession in Bolivia." *Latin American Perspectives* 34, no. 2 (2007): 31–47.

Stepan, Nancy Leys. *"The Hour of Eugenics": Race, Gender, and Nation in Latin America.* Ithaca, NY: Cornell University Press, 1991.

Stimson, J., Shaun K. Frape, Robert J. Drimmie, and David Rudolph. "Isotopic and Geochemical Evidence of Regional-Scale Anisotropy and Interconnectivity of an Alluvial Fan System, Cochabamba Valley, Bolivia." *Applied Geochemistry* 16, no. 9 (2001): 1097–1114.

Stites Mor, Jessica, ed. *Human Rights and Transnational Solidarity in Cold War Latin America.* Madison: University of Wisconsin Press, 2013.

Storey, William Kelleher. *Guns, Race, and Power in Colonial South Africa.* New York: Cambridge University Press, 2008.

Street, Paul, and Anthony DiMaggio. *Crashing the Tea Party: Mass Media and the Campaign to Remake American Politics.* New York: Routledge, 2011.

Sutter, Paul S. "Nature's Agents or Agents of Empire? Entomological Workers and Environmental Change during the Construction of the Panama Canal." *Isis* 98, no. 4 (2007): 724–754.

Swyngedouw, Erik. *Social Power and the Urbanization of Water: Flows of Power.* New York: Oxford University Press, 2004.

Tapia, Luis. *La conyuntura de la autonomía relativa del estado.* La Paz: CLASCO/Mucla del Diablo/Comuna, 2009.

Tate, Winifred. "The Aspirational State: State Effects in Putumayo." In *State Theory and Andean Politics: New Approaches to the Study of Rule,* edited by Christopher Krupa and David Nugent, 234–253. Philadelphia: University of Pennsylvania Press, 2015.

Thomson, Sinclair. "Was There Race in Colonial Latin America? Identifying Selves and Others in the Insurgent Andes." In *Histories of Race and Racism: The Andes and Mesoamerica from Colonial Times to the Present,* edited by Laura Gotkowitz, 72–91. Durham, NC: Duke University Press, 2011.

Thomson, Sinclair, Rossana Barragán, Xavier Albó, Seemin Qayum, and Mark Goodale. *The Bolivia Reader: History, Culture, Politics.* Durham, NC: Duke University Press, 2018.

Thornton, Christy. "'Mexico Has the Theories': Latin America and the Invention of Development in the 1930s." In *The Development Century: A Global History,* edited by Stephen J. Macekura and Erez Manela, 263–282. New York: Cambridge University Press, 2018.

———. *Revolution in Development: Mexico and the Governance of the Global Economy.* Oakland: University of California Press, 2021.

Tinsman, Heidi. *Partners in Conflict: The Politics of Gender, Sexuality, and Labor in the Chilean Agrarian Reform, 1950–1973.* Durham, NC: Duke University Press, 2002.

Tockman, Jason, and John Cameron. "Indigenous Autonomy and the Contradictions of Plurinationalism in Bolivia." *Latin American Politics and Society* 56, no. 3 (2014): 46–69.

Trawick, Paul. "Against the Privatization of Water: An Indigenous Model for Improving Existing Laws and Successfully Governing the Commons." *World Development* 31, no. 6 (2003): 977–996.

Two Lawyers from La Paz. "Transforming the Property Regime." In *The Bolivia Reader,* edited by Sinclair Thomson, Rossana Barragán, Xavier Albó, Seemin Qayum, and Mark Goodale, 181—183. Durham, NC: Duke University Press, 2018.

Universidad Mayor de San Simón, and Facultad de Derecho. *Cuestiones de derecho agrario en torno al proyecto de creación del Instituto de Reforma Agraria.* Cochabamba, Bolivia: Imprenta Universitaria, 1949.

Urquidi Zambrana, Jorge. *La urbanización de la ciudad de Cochabamba y el desarrollo regional y urbano (1950–1980): Examen Crítico.* Cochabamba, Bolivia: Colegio de Arquitectos de Bolivia, 1986.

Velasco, Alejandro. *Barrio Rising: Urban Popular Politics and the Making of Modern Venezuela.* Oakland: University of California Press, 2015.

Viedma, Francisco de. *Descripción geográfica y estadística de la provincia de Santa Cruz de la Sierra.* Third edition. 1836; Cochabamba, Bolivia: Los Amigos del Libro, 1969.

Vitz, Matthew. *A City on a Lake: Urban Political Ecology and the Growth of Mexico City.* Durham, NC: Duke University Press, 2018.

von Hardenberg, Wilko Graf, Matthew Kelly, Claudia Leal, and Emily Wakild, eds. *The Nature State: Rethinking the History of Conservation.* New York: Routledge, 2017.

von Schnitzler, Antina. "Citizenship Prepaid: Water, Calculability, and Techno-Politics in South Africa." *Journal of Southern African Studies* 34, no. 4 (2008): 899–917.

———. *Democracy's Infrastructure: Techno-Politics and Protest after Apartheid.* Princeton, NJ: Princeton University Press, 2016.

————. "Traveling Technologies: Infrastructure, Ethical Regimes, and the Materiality of Politics in South Africa." *Cultural Anthropology* 28, no. 4 (2013): 670–693.

Wachtel, Nathan. "The Mitimas of the Cochabamba Valley: The Colonization Policy of Huayna Capac." In *Inca and Aztec States, 1400–1800: Anthropology and History*, edited by George Collier, Renato I. Rosaldo, and John D. Wirth, 199–235. New York: Academic Press, 1982.

Wakild, Emily. *Revolutionary Parks: Conservation, Social Justice, and Mexico's National Parks, 1910–1940.* Tucson: University of Arizona Press, 2011.

Webber, Jeffery R. "Carlos Mesa, Evo Morales, and a Divided Bolivia (2003–2005)." *Latin American Perspectives* 37, no. 3 (2010): 51–70.

————. "Evo Morales, 'transformismo' y consolidación del capitalismo agrario en Bolivia." *Cuestión Agraria* 3 (2017): 157–186.

————. *From Rebellion to Reform in Bolivia: Class Struggle, Indigenous Liberation, and the Politics of Evo Morales.* Chicago: Haymarket Books, 2011.

————. *Red October: Left-Indigenous Struggles in Modern Bolivia.* Chicago: Haymarket Books, 2012.

Webber, Jeffery R., and Barry Carr. *The New Latin American Left: Cracks in the Empire.* New York: Rowman and Littlefield, 2013.

White, Richard. "'Are You an Environmentalist or Do You Work for a Living?': Work and Nature." In *Uncommon Ground: Rethinking the Human Place in Nature*, edited by William Cronon, 171–185. New York: Norton, 1995.

Winchell, Mareike. "After Servitude: Bonded Histories and the Encumbrances of Exchange in Indigenizing Bolivia." *Journal of Peasant Studies* 45, no. 2 (2018): 453–473.

Wittfogel, Karl August. *Oriental Despotism: A Comparative Study of Total Power.* New Haven, CT: Yale University Press, 1957.

Wolfe, Mikael D. "The Climate of Conflict: Politico-Environmental Press Coverage and the Eruption of the Mexican Revolution, 1907–1911." *Hispanic American Historical Review* 99, no. 3 (2019): 467–499.

————. "'A Revolution Is a Force More Powerful Than Nature': Extreme Weather and the Cuban Revolution, 1959–64." *Environmental History* 25, no. 3 (2020): 469–491.

————. *Watering the Revolution: An Environmental and Technological History of Agrarian Reform in Mexico.* Durham, NC: Duke University Press, 2017.

Woods, Ngaire. *The Globalizers: The IMF, the World Bank, and Their Borrowers.* Ithaca, NY: Cornell University Press, 2014.

World Commission on Dams. *Dams and Development: A New Framework for Decision-Making.* New York: Earthscan, 2000.

Worster, Donald. *Rivers of Empire: Water, Aridity, and the Growth of the American West.* New York: Oxford University Press, 1992.

Young, Kevin A. *Blood of the Earth: Resource Nationalism, Revolution, and Empire in Bolivia.* Austin: University of Texas Press, 2017.

Zavaleta Mercado, René. "Consideraciones generales sobre la historia de Bolivia (1932–1971)." In *América Latina: Historia de Medio Siglo*, edited by Pablo González Casanova, Volume 1, 74–178. Mexico City: Siglo XXI, 1977.

————. *Lo nacional-popular en Bolivia.* Madrid: Siglo Ventiuno, 1986.

Zhang, Ling. *The River, the Plain, and the State: An Environmental Drama in Northern Song China, 1048–1128*. New York: Cambridge University Press, 2016.

Zibechi, Raúl. *Dispersing Power: Social Movements as Anti-State Forces*. Oakland, CA: AK Press, 2010.

———. *La mirada horizontal: Movimientos sociales y emancipación*. Quito: Abya-Yala, 2000.

Zimmerer, Karl S. "The Origins of Andean Irrigation." *Nature* 378 (1995): 481–483.

———. "Rescaling Irrigation in Latin America: The Cultural Images and Political Ecology of Water Resources." *Ecumene* 7, no. 2 (2000): 150–175.

———. "Spatial-Geographic Models of Water Scarcity and Supply in Irrigation Engineering and Management: Bolivia, 1952–2009." In *Knowing Nature: Conversations at the Intersection of Political Ecology and Science Studies*, edited by Mara J. Goldman, Paul Nadasdy, and Matthew D. Turner, 167–185. Chicago: University of Chicago Press, 2011.

Zulawski, Ann. *Unequal Cures: Public Health and Political Change in Bolivia, 1900–1950*. Durham, NC: Duke University Press, 2007.

INDEX

Note: page numbers followed by *f* refer to figures and those followed by *m* refer to maps. Those followed by *n* refer to notes, with note number.

Abengoa (Spanish construction company), 182, 200

Aboites, Luis, 245*n*53

Abuela Grillo (Grandmother Cricket) (2009 animated short), 205–6

access to water: agrarian reforms and, 226; collective labor and, 2; inequality of, 227; water rationalization and, 153–59, 226

Acción Democrática Nacionalista (ADN) party, 152, 160, 176, 180

acquifers, 8, 186

ADN (Acción Democrática Nacionalista) party, 152, 160, 176, 180. *See also* Banzer, Hugo

Agrarian Reform Commission, 86

Agrarian Reform Council, 84

Agrarian Reform Decree Law of 1953, 87–88, 229–30

agrarian reforms, 1–2; in 1940s, 51, 61; in 1950s, 81–83, 106–8; Chapisirca project, 108–15; distribution of water during, 17; evaluation of revolutionary, 117–20; expropriation and, 91–96; hydraulic development and, 59–60, 96–98; Lagunmayu Lake, 102–6; Lake Wara Wara and, 100–102; Ley INRA of 1996, 155; under military socialism, 53; MNR and, 83–91, 110–17; San Juan Lakes and, 98–100; Saytukocha Lake, 102–6; United States and, 54; water access gains and, 226

Agrawal, Arun, 235*n*54

Agua para Todos policy, 209

Aguas de Arocagua, 35–36

Aguas del Illimani South America (AISA), 204

Aguas del Tunari: 1999 government contract with, 3; contracting of, 180–85; contract termination, 197, 199–200; contract with, 182; mobilization against, 186, 187, 188

Aguas de Quintanilla project, 44

aguateros (water vendors), 12, 124, 125, 153, 164, 165, 195, 212

Aguayo, Jesus, 76

Aguirre, Nataniel, 28

Ahenke, Encarnación, 68

airline industry, 3

AISA (Aguas del Illimani South America), 204

Alalay Lake, 33*f*2, 63*m*6, 66, 71

Alalay neighborhood, 63*m*6, 93*m*8

Albro, Robert, 163, 176, 190

Alemán, Isadora, 162, 187

Alliance for Progress, 111

Almaraz Paz, Sergio, 116

Altiplano Zone, 5–10; haciendas expansion in, 28, 30; indigenous communities of, 36, 59, 107–8; maximum holdings in, 229, 230; *mestizaje* process, 25; precolonial Aymara and, 6; resistance to disentailment in, 46; Spanish conquest and, 7; tin miners from, 97

Anaya, Franklin, 73, 74

Anaya, Ricardo, 60

Andean Development Corporation, 140

Andes Mountains, 5, 5–10, 6, 7

Anglo-Chilean Nitrate and Railway Company, 28
Angostura canal system, 86
Angostura dam, 53, 56, 56f4, 57, 59, 86, 107, 138m10
Angostura irrigation system, 49, 86, 230. See also
    Angostura project
Angostura Lake, 9m2, 33f2
Angostura project, 53–59, 73, 77, 78, 79
Angostura reservoir, 66, 138m10
anti-indigenous racism, 29–30
antiplano punas, in precolonial Aymara, 6
anti-privatization activists, 3
Apote, Bolivia, 93m8, 103m9
Arani, Bolivia, 27, 230
Aranjuez neighborhood, 93m8
Arauco Prado, Julio, 65, 69, 70
Arbenz, Jacobo, 112
Arce, Aniceto, 36
architect-planners: legal actions by, 147; munici-
    palization plans and, 72–78
Argentina, xixm1, 6f1; Cornejo, Favio, 110; min-
    ing in, 60; neoliberal economic restructuring
    in, 3; Pink Tide and, 4, 195; POR party, 60;
    sugar plantations of, 30
Arias, Joaquín, 187
Arocagua, Bolivia, 20, 33f2, 40–44, 67m7, 73,
    93m8
Arocagua project, 65, 247n88
Arocagua Springs, 35–38, 41–42, 43, 45, 100, 108
Arque River, 9m2
arrendatarios (renters), 30, 31, 32
arrimantes (landless rural laborers), defined,
    xvii, 91, 252n51
artesian wells: in peripheral neighborhoods, 93;
    use of, 10, 125; water access structure and, 38
Asamblea por la Soberanía de los Pueblos (ASP),
    154
ASICA-Sur (Asociación de Sistemas Comuni-
    tarios de Agua del Sur), 163, 187
Asociación de Sistemas Comunitarios de Agua
    del Sur (ASICA-Sur), 163, 187
ASP (Asamblea por la Soberanía de los Pueblos),
    155
Association of Irrigation Systems of Tiquipaya-
    Colcapirhua, 168, 172
autonomous collective control, 1, 4, 14, 15–16
Avenida Blanco Galindo, 103m9
ayllus (kin groups): in altiplano communities, 25;
    of precolonial Aymara, 6–7
Aymara people: ayllus (kin groups), 6–7, 250n6;
    Aymara-speaking migrants, 159, 162, 164;
    community mobilizations of, 190, 250n6;

Federal War of 1899 and, 40; hydraulic engi-
    neers of, 89; identifying as, 89, 190; mitimaes
    (groups of settlers), 6–7, 23; precolonial, 6–7

Baldi, Francisco, 126, 128, 129, 129f8, 133
Ballestero, Andrea, 208
Banzer, Hugo, 3, 122, 130, 151–52, 160, 181, 182,
    191, 203
Banzer administration, 121, 130–32, 137, 139–45,
    146, 148–49, 170, 176, 180
Baptista, Mariano, 36
Barragán, Rossana, 30
Barrientos Ortuño, René, 114, 114–15, 116, 117, 121,
    122, 126, 130
Barrio del Magisterio, 125
Barrio Gráfico neighborhood, 94
Barrio Militar neighborhood, 95, 98
Barrio Petrolero neighborhood, 135
Basadre, Jorge, 28
Bechtel, 3, 182, 188, 200
Bechtel, Riley, 200
Bella Vista hacienda, 31
Beni, Bolivia, 6f1
Beni province, 170, 230
BIT (Netherlands-Bolivia Bilateral Trade Agree-
    ment), 199
Bjork-James, Carwil, 16, 174
Blanco, Cleómede, 243n143
Blasier, Cole, 61
blockades, 184, 187
Bohan, Merwin L., 54
Bohan Report, 84
Bolivia, xixm1; Bolivian Congress, 3; Netherlands-
    Bolivia Bilateral Trade Agreement (BIT), 199;
    Plurinational State of Bolivia, 196, 207, 222;
    political map, xixm1; topography of, 6f1, 6–7
Bolivia: 10 años de revolución (1952–62), 119f7
Bolivian Civil War (Federal War of 1899), 36–37,
    40
Bolivian Development Corporation, 111
Bolivian Geological Service (GEOBOL), 142–43,
    169
Bolivian Miners' Federation, 60
Bolivian revolution of 1952: limits and reach of
    water reform, 16; MNR and, 249n5; mobiliza-
    tion after, 82; monopoly dismantling and, 16,
    225; peasants' conquest of water during, 14;
    popular hydraulic society, 13; terminology,
    233n2; Tirani colonos after, 1; as watershed
    moment, 2; wealth redistribution after, 81.
    See also agrarian reforms

Borsdorf, Axel, 5
Boyer, Christopher, 107
Boyle Engineering, 128, 260n88
Bray, Tamara, 7, 34
Brazil, xixm1, 6f1; International Seminar in Support of SEMAPA, 198; Pink Tide and, 4, 195; technocratic projects in, 50, 57, 79
Buckley, Eve, 19–20, 50, 79
Busch, Germán, 49, 51–54, 65, 251n27
Bustos, Daniel, 73
Butrón Mendoza, Julio, 96

cabildos, 192–93
Caine River, 9m2
Caja de Agua, 37m5
Cala Cala, Bolivia, 31, 63m6, 93m8, 98, 187
Calles, Plutarco, 52, 245n53
Calvo Soux, Luis, 114, 137, 138, 139
Camino Chapisirca, 103m9
campesino (peasant/cultivators of land): deep well opposition by, 127; defined, xvii; identifying with indigenous ancestry, 107–8, 108, 190; indio status and, 40; treatment of, 162; urban fear and, 222
Canal Norte Sistema Nacional de Riego No. 1, 103m9
canals: Angostura system, 86; Chapisirca Lakes and, 73; maintenance of, 1; open-air canals, 10; use of, 8
Canata, Bolivia, 22m3
Canelas, Carlos, 157
Canelas family, 138
Capacachi, Bolivia, 93m8, 103m9
Capacachi Lake, 68
Capinota, Bolivia, 23m4
Capitalization Law of 1994, 157
Caraza Valley, 230
Cárdenas, Lázaro, 51, 52, 57–58, 244n12
cardenista model of reform, 53
Carse, Ashley, 15
Casco Viejo, 154m11
Catavi mine, 97, 125, 145
CBF (Corporación Boliviana de Fomento), 111, 113
CDM (Comando Departamental del MNR), 97
Central Obrera Boliviana (COB), 97, 130, 146
Central Obrera Departamental (COD), 111, 112, 125, 157, 158, 166, 177, 185
Central Valley, Cochabamba, Bolivia, 8, 9m2, 184, 191; 1950s agrarian reforms and, 96, 97; in 2011, 217f15; about, 1; agricultural settlements in, 23; disentailment in, 29; hacienda fragmentation in, 31; Incas colonization of, 21; indigenous communities in, 31; mobilization of irrigators from, 186. See also Angostura project
Cerro San Pedro, Bolivia, 33f2, 63m6
Céspedes, Augusto, 44
Chacaltaya glacier, 10
chácaras (small and medium-sized agricultural properties), 23
chacareros (owners of small and medium-sized properties), 23
Chacnacollo hacienda, 31
Chaco War, 31, 44–45, 45, 47, 48, 70, 78
Chambi, Sebastián, 218
Ch'ampa Guerra conflict, 116
chancas system, 103m9
Chapisirca, Bolivia, 67m7
Chapisirca dam, 106
Chapisirca hacienda, 31, 70, 248n115
Chapisirca Lakes, 48, 68; 1950s agrarian reforms and, 105, 108; engineers, 76; expropriation of, 49, 61–72, 77, 78, 79; improvements to, 73; project delays, 73; trading water of, 73. See also Escalerani Lake; Toralaguna Lake
Chapisirca system, 111, 113, 258n31
Chávez, Ñuflo, 83, 85
chicha (corn beer) production, prohibition of, 27, 64, 247n107
Chile, xixm1, 6f1; copper mines, 8; Cornejo, Favio, 110; coups in, 121; grain imports from, 30; Hartley scandal, 147; Herrera, Felipe, 126; irrigation access promotion in, 58; neoliberal economic restructuring in, 3; nitrate fields, 8, 30, 47; Pink Tide and, 4, 195; War of the Pacific, 28, 30, 45
Chilimarca, Bolivia, 93m8, 102, 103m9, 160, 160–61, 162, 163, 187–88
Chilimarca hacienda, 102, 104
Chimba neighborhood, 93m8
Chiquicollo neighborhood, 93m8
Chocaya, Bolivia, 33f2, 67–68
Chocaya-Montesillo-Taquiña proposal, 67–69, 72
cholos, 25
Chorrillos Springs, 243n143
Chullpakaka Springs, 42
Chullpas Quinto Suyo, 90–91
Chuquisaca, Bolivia, 6f1, 139
Chusequeri Lake, 33f2, 67m7
Chusequeri project, 126, 258n31

Chutacahua River, 103*m*9

Chutakjawa, 161

Chuyes people, 21

Cinco Salidas, Bolivia, 93*m*8, 221

citizenship: exclusionary policies for, 34–35; insurgent citizenship, 14; modernization and, 12–13; social citizenship models, 227

city residents. *See* urban residents

Civic Committee (Cochabamba), 62, 62–63, 157, 171, 175, 176–77, 179, 180, 182, 185, 189, 191, 192

Claure Paz, Edgar, 143, 144, 147

climate: changes in, 10; El Niño, 19, 148, 181, 237*n*2

Cliza, Bolivia, 27, 74

CNI (Comisión Nacional de Irrigación), 50, 52, 53, 57–58

CNRA (National Agrarian Reform Council), 90, 100–101, 117

COB (Central Obrera Boliviana), 97, 130, 146

coca, 7, 98; coca eradication, 4, 202, 203–4; cocaine trafficking, 98

Cocabamba, Bolivia, 33*f*2, 138*m*10

cocaleros union, 155, 181, 188, 202, 203–4. *See also* Morales Ayma, Evo

coca union, 155, 181, 188, 202, 203–4. *See also* MAS (Movimiento al Socialismo) party; Morales Ayma, Evo

Coca War, 205

Cochabamba Engineers Association, 62–63, 109, 176

Cochabamba Society of Engineers, 183

cochalos, 162, 163, 164

COD (Central Obrera Departamental), 111, 112, 125, 157, 158, 166, 177, 185

CODAEP (Comité de Defensa del Agua y la Economía Popular), 182–83, 185

Colcapirhua, Bolivia, 33*f*2, 67*m*7, 103*m*9, 169

collective control: of infrastructure, 13; of planning, 13; of provision of water, 13; of water sources, 13

collective knowledge, 33

collective labor, 33; maintaining access and rights by, 2; *suyus* (agricultural land) and, 21; water access and, 7; water rights and, 21

collective practices of water users, extended to periurban and municipal water systems, 13

collective water management practices, 13–14; during 1880s to 1920s, 20; continuation of, 33–34; regional mestizo culture, 20. *See also* governance of water access; vernacular environmental governance

Collpapampa hacienda, 31

Colón beer factory, 70

colonial era: dispossession in, 21–26; protections in, 24–25; *pueblos reales de indios*, 23*m*4

colonos (estate workers): 1950s agrarian reforms and, 105–6; after revolution, 82; *arrimantes* and, 252*n*51; building of lakes' dams and canals by, 1, 102; defined, xvii; during drought, 26; indigenous members as, 29; labor of, 1, 33; loyalty to *patrones*, 78; *pongueaje* labor system, 254*n*93; purchase of community land by, 30–31; purchase of hacienda land, 54; redistribution issues and, 90–91; usufruct rights of, 1; water source needs of, 2; water sources and infrastructure control by, 32, 47. *See also* estate tenants (*colonos*); peasants

Colquiri mine, 97, 160

Coluyo Grande, Bolivia, 67*m*7

Comando Departamental del MNR (CDM), 97

COMIBOL (Corporación Minera de Bolivia), 97

Comisión Nacional de Irrigación (CNI), 50, 52, 53, 57–58

Comité de Agricultores Progresistas, 105

Comité de Defensa Ambiental de Cochabamba, 169

Comité de Defensa Ambiental de Vinto y Sipe Sipe, 169, 170–71. *See also* Olivera, Amador

Comité de Defensa del Agua y la Economía Popular (CODAEP), 182–83, 185

Comité de Defensa de los Recursos Hídricos, 168

Comité Pro-Captación de Aguas, 44

Comité Pro-Cochabamba (CPC), 63, 76–77, 97, 105, 125, 133, 134, 136, 137, 138

Committee for the Defense of Water and the Popular Economy (CODAEP), 182–83, 185

communal labor: as basis for property claims, 2, 34, 98, 101*f*6, 174, 219; Bray on, 34; building and managing water infrastructure, 14; of *colonos*, 32–33; dams and, 99, 101, 160, 174, 219, 220; influencing state policy, 14; organizing distribution, 14; refashioning of, 33; Spanish water law, 24; water distribution and, 39; water property rights and, 5, 13; Water War of 2000 and, 187; water worship and, 7

communal land: defense of ownership of, 36; practices of, 10; of *pueblos reales de indios*, 25, 28

community dispossession, in 1870s, 16

community governance, 13–14. *See also* governance of water access community land: leasing and selling of, 24, 30; privatization of, 28–29; water allocations to, 24

community management of natural resources, 13–14. *See also* governance of water access; vernacular environmental governance

community-popular *pachakuti*, 4

community property: claims on irrigation infrastructure as, 2; claims on San Juan Lakes as, 2

comunarios (rural community members), defined, xvii

Coña Coña, Bolivia, 93*m*8, 102, 103*m*9, 104, 145

Condebamba neighborhood, 93*m*8

CONDEPA (Consciousness of the Fatherland), 154, 171, 180

Condori, Hipólito, 162

Confederación Sindical Única de Trabajadores Campesinos de Bolivia (CSUTCB), 145

conquest, 7

Consciousness of the Fatherland (CONDEPA), 154, 171, 180

Conservative Party: in 1870s, 26; during 1880s to 1920s, 28, 36; Bolivian Civil War and, 36; *El Heraldo* and, 38, 43

Constitution of 1938, 50–52, 55, 56, 197

Constitution of 2009, 196, 208, 211

Coordinadora de Defensa del Agua y de la Vida (Coordinating Committee for the Defense of Water and Life), 4, 185, 188, 189–93, 197–98, 199–202, 206, 227; social mobilizations and, 205. *See also* Olivera, Oscar

Coordinadora Nacional por la Defensa y Recuperación del Gas, 204

Coordinating Committee for the Defense of Water and Life (Coordinadora de Defensa del Agua y de la Vida), 4, 185, 188, 189–93, 197–98, 199–202, 206, 227

Corani Lake, 9*m*2, 76, 78, 138*m*10

Corani project, 78, 177

Corani reservoir, 177

CORDECO (Corporación de Desarrollo de Cochabamba), 139–40, 142, 155–56, 166, 171

Cordillera Occidental, 5, 70

Cornejo, Alberto, 42

Cornejo, Favio, 110–11, 112

Coronel Rivas, Humberto, 140, 144, 147

Corporación Boliviana de Fomento (CBF), 111, 113

Corporación de Desarrollo de Cochabamba (CORDECO), 139–40, 142, 155–56, 166, 171

Corporación Minera de Bolivia (COMIBOL), 97

Cossio Salinas, Héctor, 111, 112

Cotapachi, Bolivia, 22*m*3

Cotas people, 21

CPC (Comité Pro-Cochabamba), 63, 76–77, 97, 106, 125, 133, 134, 136, 137, 138

creoles: anti-indigenous racism of, 29–30; defined, xvii; disproportionate water rights, 23, 24, 25; land and labor reforms and, 53; land appropriation by, 25; MNR and, 82; as newspaper owners, 17

Crespo, Carlos, 190

crops: 1877–1878 failure of, 19, 26–27; effects of irrigation rights on, 26; grain imports and, 30; irrigation water for, 1, 165; of precolonial Aymara, 6–7; water rationing and, 94–95; water table and, 180–81

Cruz, Rodrigo, 186

CSUTCB (Confederación Sindical Única de Trabajadores Campesinos de Bolivia), 145

Cuba: dams and reservoir construction in, 226; revolution in, 82; water management and distribution in, 226

dams: access and, 226; Angostura dam, 50, 53, 56*f*4, 57, 59, 107, 138*m*10; as basic means of water systems, 10; Chapisirca dam, 106; Chusequeri project, 258*n*31; communal labor and, 99, 101, 160, 174, 219, 220; Coordinadora de Defensa del Agua y de la Vida and, 193; in Cuba, 226; demands for, 120, 121, 123, 127, 136, 137; Escalerani dam, 222; IDB funding and, 123, 136, 137, 141, 149; irrigation authority, 58–59; Lagunmayu dam, 106; Lake Escalerani dam, 71, 73; Lake Wara Wara dam, 214*f*13; Langumayu irrigation system, 32; maintenance of, 1; in Mexico, 50, 52, 52–53, 244*m*3; Misicuni dam, 114, 121, 142, 149, 177, 182, 188, 195, 222, 224; MNR and, 86, 87, 118; Tirani *colonos* and, 98; use of, 8; vernacular hydraulic expertise and, 15; World Bank and, 122–23, 177

Davis, Mike, 19

Daza, Hilarion, 27, 28

Daza, Victor Hugo, 192

Daza administration, 27

debt crisis, 146

decentralization, 11–12

decision-making power, 227

decreto ley (decree law), 252*n*38

Delgadillo, Marcelo, 169, 174

democratization of engineering, 13

democratization of governance, 2, 13, 78
democratization of modernity, 15, 39, 149, 171,
    193, 224
democratization of water access, 2, 13; future role
    of, 227; municipalization and, 78; social mo-
    bilizations and, 16; social movements and, 5
dictatorships, 3, 16, 226; hydraulic governance
    and, 121–50. *See also* Banzer, Hugo
Diez años de reforma agraria en Bolivia,
    1953–1963, 117
Dirección General de Riegos, 58
disease: in 1870s, 19, 20, 26, 27, 28, 29, 30, 237*n*2;
    during 1880s to 1920s, 34, 43; in 1940s, 69; in
    1970s, 131, 133; in 1990s, 164–65
disentailment, 20, 29, 46
Dispersing Power (Zibechi), 202
dispossession: in 1870s, 20, 21, 26–34; colonial
    dipossession, 21–26; *hacendados'* control of
    water supply, 27, 30–34; indigenous com-
    munities and, 46; water privatization, 27–30,
    33–34
distribution: communal labor organizing, 14, 33;
    inequality of, 14, 38–39, 47, 68–69; renova-
    tions of system of, 38; rotation system during
    Inca Empire, 21
drinking water: creation of modern supply, 21;
    distribution system, 21; IDB funding and,
    112; independent water systems, 3; Liberal
    Party and, 36–37; redistribution issues and,
    49; from San Juan Lake, 1; from San Pablito
    Lake, 1; shortages of, 45; social struggles over,
    10; springs systems, 35–36; water sources
    needed for, 2; water source treatment for, 66
Drinking Water and Sanitation Law, 175, 196
droughts: in 1870s, 16, 19, 21, 26–34, 46, 225,
    237*n*2; challenges of, 10; disentailment and,
    29; effects on urban water system, 34; migra-
    tions and, 8; taking advantage of, 26, 225
Dunkerley, James, 84, 86, 116, 130, 145

early Republican era, 21–22
economic diversification, 54
economic issues, popular economy, 127–36
economic liberalism: *hacendados* and, 46; indig-
    enous communities and, 28; influence of, 27
Economic Stabilization Plan, 115
Ecuador: Monolitica, 147; Pink Tide and, 4, 195
Eder, George Jackson, 115
Edison, 182
Eguino Zaballa, Felix, 86
El ayllu (Saavedra), 40
El Comercio (periodical), 46

electricity: redistribution issues and, 227; rights
    of urban poor to, 14
El Ferrocarril (periodical), 38
El Heraldo (periodical), 38, 42, 43, 44
El Imparcial (periodical), 45, 66
elites: 1870s mobilization by, 21; concept of
    Indian, 30; domination by, 20; fear of the
    masses, 16; hydraulic infrastructure and, 50;
    industrial expansion and, 124; progressive,
    35; purchase of community land by, 31, 46;
    purchase of hacienda land, 31, 46
El Molino, Bolivia, 33*f*2
El Niño, 19, 148, 181, 237*n*2
El País (periodical), 62, 64, 66, 77
El Paso, Bolivia, 22, 22*m*3, 23*m*4, 30–31, 67*m*7,
    145, 156, 166–67, 169, 170–72, 180, 215*f*14
El Pueblo (periodical), 88, 110
El Republicano (periodical), 42, 44
EMAPAQ (Empresa Municipal de Agua Potable
    y Alcantarillado de Quillacollo), 215*f*14, 216
EMAPAS (Empresa Municipal de Agua Potable
    y Alcantarillado de Sacaba), 212–13
Empresa Misicuni, 169, 177, 217
Empresa Municipal de Agua Potable y Alcan-
    tarillado de Quillacollo (EMAPAQ), 215*f*14,
    216
Empresa Municipal de Agua Potable y Alcanta-
    rillado de Sacaba (EMAPAS), 212–13
ENDE (national electric company), 142, 152
engineering, 14
engineering techniques, 86; democratization of,
    13; evolution of, 10; of Mexico, 53
engineers: Calvo Soux, Luis, 114; Cochabamba
    Engineers Association, 62–63, 109; hydraulic
    expertise and, 15, 79; Knaudt, Julio, 65–66;
    legal actions by, 147; municipalization plans
    and, 72–78, 73; perspectives of, 17; Rivero,
    Ramón, 65; rural water monopoly chal-
    lenges and, 69, 78; Sánchez de Lozada, 65;
    water source study, 65
ENTEL (Empresa Nacional de Telecomunica-
    ciones), 152
Entidades Prestadoras de Servicios de Agua
    Potable y Alcantarillado Sanitario (EPSAs),
    196–97, 205
environmental contamination, 62
environmental governance, 13–14. *See also* gover-
    nance of water access
EPSAs (Entidades Prestadoras de Servicios de
    Agua Potable y Alcantarillado Sanitario),
    196–97, 205
Escalerani dam, 70, 71, 73, 222

Escalerani Lake, 33*f*2, 67*m*7, 70, 71, 73, 76, 78, 91, 214
Escobar, Arturo, 206
Estancia Titiri, 103*m*9
Estancia Totora, 103*m*9
estate tenants (*colonos*): during 1880s to 1920s, 20; collective water management practices, 2; labor of, 1; popular hydraulic society and, 225; usufruct rights of, 1; water source needs of, 2
ex-*colono* communities: in 1930s, 33; assertion of rights by, 2; communal labor of, 34; labor of, 33; *piqueros* (independent smallholders) communities and, 2; popular hydraulic society and, 225. *See also* Tirani community
expropriation: Angostura project and, 54–59, 79; Angostura reservoir and, 50; of Chapisirca Lakes, 49, 61–72; Chapisirca project and, 79; of private land, 50, 51, 52; of private water sources, 50, 102; protests over, 247*n*107

Fabricant, Nicole, 222
fabriles, 125, 166, 189–90
famine: in 1870s, 16, 19–20, 21, 26, 29, 30, 225; taking advantage of, 225
FEDECOR (Federación Departamental Cochabambina de Organizaciones Regantes), 172–73, 181–82, 183, 184–85, 186, 187, 190, 197, 199, 206, 210; social mobilizations and, 205
Federación de Juntas Vecinales (FEJUVE), 125–26, 128, 134, 135, 147, 157, 158, 165, 169, 176–77, 178, 180–81, 182, 185, 189, 204
Federación Departamental Cochabambina de Organizaciones Regantes (FEDECOR), 172–73, 181–82, 183, 184–85, 186, 187, 190, 197, 199, 206, 210
Federación Rural de Cochabamba (FRC), 57, 61, 97
Federación Sindical de Trabajadores Campesinos de Cochabamba (FSTCC), 97
Federación Sindical de Trabajadores Mineros de Bolivia (FSTMB), 97, 130
Federación Sindical Única de Trabajadores Campesinos de Cochabamba (FSUTCC), 172–73, 185
Federal War of 1899 (Bolivian Civil War), 36–37, 40
FEJUVE (Federación de Juntas Vecinales), 125–26, 128, 134, 135, 147, 157, 158, 165, 169–70, 176–77, 178, 180–81, 182, 185, 189, 204
Ferguson, James, 79
Fernández, Max, 154, 160

Fernández, Omar, 104, 168, 172–74, 184, 186, 198, 199, 206, 207–8, 210, 220, 225
Ferrufino, Hugo, 73
Finnegan, William, 182
First Inter-American Indigenista Congress, 58
floodwater irrigation, 8
Fondo Nacional de Inversión Social, 161
foreign engineers, perspectives of, 17
foreign influence: disputes over, 5; international trade dependence, 39
Fourth World Water Forum, 209
FRC (Federación Rural de Cochabamba), 57, 61, 97
free market exchange, in 1870s, 27, 28, 46
free trade policies, 30
Friends of the Earth, 199
FSTCC (Federación Sindical de Trabajadores Campesinos de Cochabamba), 98
FSTMB (Federación Sindical de Trabajadores Mineros de Bolivia), 98, 130
FSUTCC (Federación Sindical Única de Trabajadores Campesinos de Cochabamba), 172–73, 185
Fuentes family, 173
Fundación Abril, 203, 206, 221–22

Gaceta Campesina (periodical), 83, 86, 89
gamonalismo, 252*n*44
García, Raul Alfonso, 117
García Hinojosa, Teodoro, 187–88
García Meza Tejada, Luis, 146, 151
Garden City movement, 64, 74, 75, 77
Gas War, 205
Geddes, Patrick, 74, 75
Geidel, Molly, 116
General Resettlement, 7, 22–23, 239*n*54
GEOBOL (Servicio Geólogico de Bolivia), 142–43, 169, 262*n*133
German Development Agency (GTZ), 169
Gilbert, Jess, 12
glaciers, 10
Global Engineering, 113, 122
Global South, 12
Goldman, Michael, 155, 158–59, 167
Goldstein, Daniel, 161, 165, 171
Gómez García, Alfredo, 182
Goodale, Mark, 211
Good Neighbor Policy, 54
Gordillo, Jose, 23, 24, 30, 57, 95, 97, 107, 115, 253*n*83
Gotkowitz, Laura, 29, 35
Goubert, Jean-Pierre, 34

governance of water access, 2, 13–14; democratization of, 13; future role of, 227
grain: 1870s crop destruction, 26; Chilean grain imports, 30; hoarding of, 27, 46
Gran Chaco, 44
Grandin, Greg, 263n59
Grandydier, Abraham, 163, 187, 203
Great Depression, 45
Grieshaber, Erwin, 83
GTZ (German Development Agency), 169
Guatemala, 112, 117, 121
Guevara Arze, Walter, 60, 81, 83, 84, 87, 106, 108, 120
Gumucio, Rafael, 68, 104
Gumucio, Vicente, 32
Gustafson, Bret, 45
Gutiérrez, Raquel, 4, 233n9
Guzmán, Fernanda, 219

hacendados (owners): 1950s agrarian reforms and, 105–6; Angostura project and, 54; benefits from droughts, 20, 26, 46; community conflicts with, 23; community land appropriation by, 23, 24, 25, 46; control over water sources and infrastructure by, 17; damming of lakes, 40; defined, xvii; dispossession of communities' water sources, 24; expropriation and, 66–67, 78; hacienda water monopolists, 16; irrigation rights appropriation, 46; irrigation systems and, 32; negotiations with, 17, 70–72; power of, 51; protests by, 48; purchase of water from, 31; selling of land, 31; shift from, 2; under Spanish Empire, 23–24; water access gains and, 24, 25; water dispossession by, 21, 23–24; water monopolies, 47; water provision control and, 23; water source hoarding, 2, 21; water sources and, 32–33, 33f2, 46; water sources and systems, 34, 79–80
haciendas: community land sales and, 46; in early 20th century, 33f2; emergence of, 23; expropriation of water sources of, 78; fragmentation of, 31; grain exports and, 25; maximum holdings, 230; patrones as owners of, 1; purchase of hacienda land, 54, 72–73; Salamanca family's, 31, 32; tenants during 1880s to 1920s, 16; Tirani colonos' rights to, 1
Haras Nacional, 73
Hardt, Michael, 202
Harris, Olivia, 30, 190
Hartley scandal, 147

Heredia, Antonio, 163, 187
Herrera, Felipe, 126
Hicks, Kathryn, 222
highland communities: grain exports of, 25; in Spanish colonial era, 23; tin mines, 47
high modernism, 15
hinterlands, 14
Hipódromo, Bolivia, 63m6, 93m8
historic labor and maintenance, 32–33. See also communal labor
hoarding: of grain, 27; of water sources, 2, 21, 27
Holloway, John, 202
Holston, James, 14
housing: complaints in press, 62; hoarding, 92; military housing, 73; redistribution issues and, 227; rights of urban poor to, 14; segregated systems of, 92
Howard, Ebenezer, 74, 75
Huara Huara Lake, 111
Huayculí River, 90
Huayna Capac, Emperor of the Incas, 21, 22m3
Hurtado, Dionisio, 220
hydraulic development, 10–11; alternative history of, 13; approaches to, 226–27; democratization of, 13; land dispossession and, 21; local debates about, 17; in Mexico, 50, 51, 52; military socialism and, 48–80; modernity and, 15, 34, 59; municipalization and, 77; national debates about, 17; nature and, 11; popular groups pressing for, 47; SEMAPA and, 17; state-led, 15; technocratic approach, 50, 57–58
hydraulic engineering, of reform era, 50, 78
hydraulic expertise: collective labor and, 33; development of, 13; water infrastructure control and, 15, 79
hydraulic governance: during 1960s, 121–23; in 1970s, 138–45, 149; democracy and, 145–48; democratization of, 13; expertise under dictatorship and, 121–50; Misicuni project, 136–41, 149; national hydraulic service, 71; urban growth and, 123–27; War of the Wells of 1977, 141–45; water rates, 127–36
hydraulic infrastructure: colonos maintenance of, 1; democratization of, 13
hydraulic infrastructure projects: for irrigation, 16; irrigation water and, 50; for urban supply, 16; urban water access and, 49–50
hydraulic justice, 17
hydraulic labor, of San Juan Lakes, 32–33
hydraulic society theory, 11
hydroelectric projects, 177

hygiene: modernity and, 34; poor sanitary conditions, 62; water scarcity and, 66; water treatment, 98, 188

ICSID (International Center for Settlement of Investment Disputes), 199–200
IDB (Inter-American Development Bank), 4, 111–13, 122–23, 126–37, 141, 143, 145, 146–49, 153, 158, 175–76, 193, 212, 254n102
ILO (International Labor Organization), 174
imperial labor drafts, 7
Inca Empire: colonization by the, 21–22; communal labor and rituals, 7, 34; land distribution by, 22m3; rulers of, 22m3; Spanish property claims and, 25; Tirani community and, 219; water tenure relations under, 16; water use history of, 87. See also Huayna Capac, Emperor of the Incas
independent water systems: Aguas del Tunari and, 3; as free from state and international institutions, 15; periurban neighborhood residents and, 2; in periurban neighborhoods, 3
Indian (term), xvii, xviii
indigenismo ideology, 39–40, 89
indigenistas, 53, 249n6, 250n8
indigenous (term), xvii
indigenous communities: after Chaco War, 48–49; after revolution, 82; disentailment's effects on, 46; dissolution of, 16, 20, 21, 25, 28, 29, 46, 225; First Inter-American Indigenista Congress, 58; in foothills, 23; gamonalismo, 252n44; General Resettlement of, 7, 22–23, 239n54; heritage of, 163–64; in highlands and tropics, 4; Indigenous Congress, 85, 245n39; land and water dispossession and, 21, 26–34, 46; MAS party and, 4; under military socialism, 53; Plurinational State of Bolivia and, 196; protections for, 24, 25; Quispe, Rafael, 203; social movements by, 4; taking advantage of, 21, 46, 225. See also Aymara people; Morales Ayma, Evo
indio status, 29–30, 39–40
inequalities: in 1870s, 16, 46; protests against, 49; results of, 227; in water access, 20
infant mortality rates, 62
infrastructure: collective control of, 13, 16; communal labor building and managing of, 14; community control of, 13; dispossession of, 20; distribution improvements to, 20; historic labor and maintenance of, 5; increas-

ing control of, 227; integration of national territory through, 34; land dispossession and, 21; popular control of, 5; water users' ownership claims of, 13. See also irrigation infrastructure
inherited water rights, 24
INRA (Instituto Nacional de la Reforms Agraria), 17
insecurity, 20, 38, 124
Instituto Nacional de la Reforms Agraria (INRA), 17
Inter-American Development Bank (IDB). See IDB (Inter-American Development Bank)
inter-Andean valleys, 5, 6f1
International Center for Settlement of Investment Disputes (ICSID), 199–200
international development agencies, 13
international financial organizations, 3, 15
International Labor Organization (ILO), 174
International Monetary Fund, 3
International Telephone and Telegraph Company, 115
International Waters, 200
irrigation: maximum holdings, 229, 230; water sources needed for, 2
irrigation infrastructure: as community property, 2; hydraulic society theory and, 11–12; in Spanish colonial era, 21; Tirani colonos' rights to, 1; Tirani community members claims on, 2
Irrigation Law of 2004, 197
irrigation rights: haciendas appropriation of, 46; irrigation turn rights, 31, 33; leasing and selling of, 24
irrigation systems: Aguas del Tunari and, 3; Langumayu irrigation system, 32; in Mexico, 50–51, 52. See also collective water management practices
irrigation systems in rural areas: building and management of, 13; during Inca Empire, 21; rotation system under Spanish Empire, 24
irrigation turn rights, 31, 33
irrigation water: fights over, 8; hydraulic infrastructure projects and, 50; inequal access to, 79; municipalization of, 213f12; national authority, 58; rights to, 24, 55–56; from San Juan Lake, 1; from San Pablito Lake, 1; social struggles over, 10; value of, 71. See also Angostura project
irrigator unions, MAS party and, 4
Iturralde province, 230

Jackson, Robert, 23, 24, 30, 239n67
Jakarta, 3
James, Daniel, 17
Japanese International Cooperation Agency
    (JICA), 153
Jayhuayco, Bolivia, 63m6, 93m8
JICA (Japanese International Cooperation
    Agency), 153
Jiménez, Christina, 39
Johannesburg, 3
Juan XXIII neighborhood, 125
JUNCO (Junta de la Comunidad), 125, 130, 134,
    136, 139–40, 147, 258n27
Junta de la Comunidad (JUNCO), 125, 130, 134,
    136, 139–40, 147, 258n27

Katz, Claudio, 202
Kelly, Patrick William, 210
Kennedy, John F., 111
Khora River, 103m9
kin groups (ayllus), 6
Klein, Herbert, 40, 45, 52, 54, 132
Knaudt, Gustavo, 73
Knaudt, Julio, 65–66
knowledge, labor-produced, 5, 47, 235n59
Kohl, Benjamin, 203
Kruse, Tom, 189

LAB (national airline), 152
labor: migration to escape labor drafts, 24;
    pongueaje labor system, 50; reforms, 53;
    withholding, 16; work rotation, 10
Labuna Rebalses, 103m9
La Cancha, 154m11
La Chimba, Bolivia, 63m6
Lacma neighborhood, 93m8
Laguna Alalay. See Alalay Lake
Laguna de la Angostura. See Angostura Lake
Laguna Lagunmayu. See Lagunmayu Lake
Laguna San Ignacio. See San Ignacio Lake
Laguna Saytukhocha. See Saytukocha Lake
Laguna Taquiña. See Taquiña Lake
Laguna Totora. See Totora Lake
Laguna Wara Wara. See Lake Wara Wara
Lagunmayu dam, 106
Lagunmayu irrigation system, 32, 225
Lagunmayu Lake, 33f2, 67m7, 68, 92, 103m9, 138k
    239n71; 1950s agrarian reforms and, 95, 108,
    112–13
Lagunmayu system, 103m9, 148
La Isla property, 243n143
Lake Alalay. See Alalay Lake

Lake Escalerani. See Escalerani Lake
Lake Escalerani Dam. See Escalerani Dam
Lake Huara Huara. See Huara Huara Lake
Lake Titikaka, 84, 229, 230
Lake Wara Wara, 33f2, 67m7, 91, 92, 213–14, 218;
    in 1920s, 101f6; 1950s agrarian reforms and,
    95, 100–102, 104; in 2011, 214f13, 217f15; Aguas
    de Arocagua and, 35–36; dam at, 214f13;
    rebuilding dam of, 102, 141, 213, 214f13
La Maica, Bolivia, 63m6, 67m7
land claims, 17
land dispossession: in 1870s, 20; General Re-
    settlement, 7, 22–23, 239n54; in Inca Empire,
    21; in Spanish colonial era, 21–24
land distribution, by Huayna Capac, 22m3
landlords: in 1870s, 16, 20, 30; in colonial era,
    25–26; in early national era, 25–26; opposi-
    tion to, 48; sobras (excess water rights) and,
    25–26
land ownership: smallholders (piqueros) of, 31;
    tripartite division, 23; water rights and, 21
land reform: creole reformists and, 53; mestizo
    reformists and, 53; in Mexico, 51, 52; water
    reform and, 49
land rights, hacienda colonos winning of, 2
land scarcity, coping with, 10
land seizures, 1, 16
La Paz, Bolivia, 6f1, 81, 84, 160, 171, 191, 230;
    climate change in, 10; drinking water proj-
    ects in, 112; uprisings in, 28; "Water for All"
    challenge, 10
"La política de irrigación en beneficio del indio"
    ("Irrigation Policy to Benefit the Indian"), 58
La reforma agraria en Bolivia (Sanjinés), 52
Larson, Brooke, 250n6
Las Cuadras, Bolivia, 63m6, 93m8, 94, 125
Laurie, Nina, 149
Law for the Rights of Mother Earth of 2012, 208,
    209
laws: Agrarian Reform Decree Law of 1953,
    87–88; agricultural land categories, 252n51;
    Capitalization Law of 1994, 157; colonial-era
    legal challenges, 25; on community land
    tenure, 28; decree law (decreto ley), 252n38;
    Drinking Water and Sanitation Law, 175, 196;
    on indigenous communities, 28; Irrigation
    Law of 2004, 197; Law for the Rights of
    Mother Earth of 2012, 208; Ley 2029 de Agua
    Potable y Alcantarillado Sanitario, 183, 184,
    185, 191, 193, 196; Ley 2066, 196, 197; Ley de
    Exvinculación of 1874, 28, 30; Ley de Partici-
    pación Popular (LPP), 176; Ley de Reform

Educativa of 1994, 155; Ley INRA of 1996, 155, 174, 190, 202; Municipalities Law of 1999, 175, 176; municipalization of public services law of 1948, 77; Popular Participation Law of 1994, 174; riparian water property rights, 30; Spanish water laws, 24–25, 30, 32; water law of 1906, 52, 70; water law of November 1999, 3; water regulation of 1879, 31–32, 46

"Leasing the Rain" (Finnegan), 182

Lechín, Juan, 83

Le Corbusier, 74–75

Ledo, Carmen, 164

Lehman, Kenneth, 112, 148

letrados, 35

Ley 2029 de Agua Potable y Alcantarillado Sanitario, 183, 184, 185, 191, 193, 196

Ley 2066, 196, 197

Ley de Decentralización, 154

Ley de Exvinculación of 1874, 28, 30

Ley de Participación Popular (LPP), 154, 176

Ley de Reform Educativa of 1994, 155

Leygue, Armando, 215, 216

Ley INRA of 1996, 155, 174, 190, 202

Li, Tania Murray, 79

liberal era: dispossession in, 19–47; drought in, 19–47; economics of, 27, 46; exclusionary policies of, 34–35; modernization in, 19–47; political reforms, 46; urban water supply, 34–39. *See also* Liberal Party

liberalism, classical, contradictions of, 46, 240n87

Liberal Party: in 1870s, 26; during 1880s to 1920s, 28; after Bolivian Civil War, 36–39; after Chaco War, 48; Republican Party and, 31, 39, 40

liberal policies: in 1870s, 26; elites mobilization for early, 21; oppositions to early, 21; taking advantage of, 46, 225

limited markets, 10

Linde, Bolivia, 103m9

Linde hacienda, 102, 104

Lipsett-Rivera, Sonia, 34

literacy, 51

Litoral province, 28

local officials, 47

loteador (term), 258n13

Los Tiempos (periodical), 97, 138

lowland indigenous groups, 4

LPP (Ley de Participación Popular), 154, 176

Luján, Eloy, 158, 169, 177

Machu Mita irrigation system, 68, 103m9, 225

management rights, 15

MAP International, 161

Marcha por el Agua y la Vida of 1992, 157

Marcha por el Agua y la Vida of 1994, 169–170

Marcha por el Agua y la Vida of 1997, 177

March for Territory and Dignity of 1990, 167

marginalized populations: after the revolution, 82, 106; effects of climate on, 19–20; housing and, 92; Leygue on, 215–16; MNR on, 60; water access disparity and, 124, 135

Marquina Lakes, 70

Marrón, Alfredo, 73, 76, 78, 110, 126

Marvin, Simon, 149

Marx, Karl, 11

MAS (Movimiento al Socialismo) party, 4, 155; indigenous communities and, 4; irrigator unions and, 4; peasant unions and, 4; periurban neighborhoods and, 4; popular groups and, 196; urban peripheral neighborhoods and, 4; water rights and, 226; water sources and, 4; water systems and, 4. *See also* Morales administration; Morales Ayma, Evo

Massacre of the Valley, 132

mass layoff, privatization and, 3

Matilde Mine, 130

Mavrich & Company, 69

Mayerski, Boleslao, 35–36

Mayerski Commission, 35–36

Mayorazgo, Bolivia, 63m6

Mayorazgo neighborhood, 93, 93m8

McNamara, Robert, 123

Méndez, Coronel, 65

Mendez, Gustavo, 158, 168, 170

Mendoza, Pasqual, 216

Mercado, Zenón, 188

Mesa, Carlos, 28, 204, 205

Mesadilla, Bolivia, 22m3, 93m8

mestizaje process, 25, 29–30, 237n27

mestizo (term), xvii, 25

mestizo culture, 107–8; during 1880s to 1920s, 20, 29–30; during colonial era, 25; of water, 34

mestizo peasantry: consolidation of, 31; land and labor reforms and, 53; MNR and, 82

Mexico: *campesino* identity in, 107; Constitution of 1917, 51, 52, 87–88; dams projects in, 244n13; engineering techniques, 53, 59; First Inter-American Indigenista Congress, 58; irrigation systems in, 50–51, 57–58, 235n55, 244n13, 245n53; popular hydraulic society, 88; postrevolutionary era, 85; revolution in, 82, 84; water management and distribution in, 226. *See also* Cárdenas, Lázaro migrations: in 1960s and 1970s, 123–24; droughts and, 8; to escape tribute levies and labor drafts, 24; forced migrations, 7; militant class conflict and, 47; urban migration, 10, 23–24, 47, 123; voluntary migrations, 7

militarist nationalism: militant class conflict, 47; oil and gas industries and, 45. *See also* Tupac Katari Guerilla Army

Military-Peasant Pact (Pacto Militar Campesino), 116, 132, 144, 148

military socialist era: beginning of, 49; *hacendados* (owners) and, 70; hydraulic development and, 48–80; irrigation programs of, 54; Mexico and, 50–51; prefecture officials in, 78; water limitations, 63–65

Milner, Wilfredo, 71

miners: after Chaco War, 48–49; after revolution, 82; migrations of, 102; MNR and, 82; mobilization of, 82; peasant/miner solidarity, 163; Quillacollo Federation of Retired Miners, 186; Triangular Plan, 115

mining, 139; Catavi mine, 97, 125, 145; Colquiri mine, 97, 160; COMIBOL, 97; copper mines, 8; migration from, 10; POR party and, 60; Potosí silver mines, 22, 25, 125, 139; Siglo XX mine, 97, 125, 145; silver mines, 8, 28, 36, 60, 139; state-supported management of, 175. *See also* tin mines

MIP (Movimiento Indígena Pachakuti), 155

MIR (Movimiento de la Izquierda Revolucionaria) 152, 171, 180

Misicuni dam, 67*m*7, 114, 121, 138*m*10, 142, 149, 177, 182, 188, 195, 222, 224

Misicuni project, 114, 121, 136–41, 149, 169, 177, 179, 180–81, 184, 222

Misicuni reservoir, 67*m*7, 138*m*10

Misicuni River, 9*m*2, 114, 121, 138*m*10, 222

mita rights, 31

mitas, 21, 68, 69

mitimaes (groups of settlers), 6–7, 23

mixed ancestry/cultural (mestizo) traditions, xvii

MNR (Movimiento Nacionalista Revolucionario), 46, 60–61, 177, 245*n*39, 250*n*7, 250*nn*7–8; agrarian reforms and, 81–82; water rights and, 226

mobilizations, after Chaco War, 48–49

modernity: alternative vision of, 15; democratization of, 15, 38; high modernism, 15; hydraulic development and, 15; vernacular modernism, 15; water users and, 15

modernization: in 1870s, 20; of cities and infra-

structure, 34; citizen participation and, 12–13; in liberal era, 19–47; planned inequality in, 35; rural modernization, 59; vernacular modernizers, 35

Molina, Javier, 1–3, 5, 13, 218

Molle Molle hacienda, 31

monopolies: over water sources, 5, 20; by rural elites, 20

Montenegro, Armando, 92, 95, 96, 98, 102, 105, 106, 108

Montesillo, Bolivia, 33*f*2, 67*m*7, 93*m*8, 102, 103*m*9, 106, 173; expropriation in, 67–68

Montesillo hacienda, 31, 70, 72, 102, 104

Morales administration, 4, 196, 203, 209, 211–23, 224. *See also* MAS (Movimiento al Socialismo); Morales Ayma, Evo

Morales Ayma, Evo, 222; 2005 election of, 4, 195, 206; *cocaleros* union, 181; SEMAPA and, 211; water politics of, 17; Water War of 2000 and, 188, 203, 223. *See also* MAS (Movimiento al Socialismo) party; Morales administration

Movimiento al Socialismo (MAS) party, 4, 155. *See also* MAS (Movimiento al Socialismo) party

Movimiento de la Izquierda Revolucionaria (MIR), 152, 171, 180

Movimiento Indígena Pachakuti (MIP), 154

Movimiento Nacionalista Revolucionario (MNR), 60–61, 177; agrarian reforms and, 81–82. *See also* MNR (Movimiento Nacionalista Revolucionario)

municipal customers: popular hydraulic society and, 225; shift to, 2; water rates for, 3, 12

Municipalities Law of 1999, 175, 176

municipalization: in 1940s, 72–78; architect-planners and, 72–78; of irrigators' water sources, 213*f*12; of neighborhood cooperatives, 213*f*12; shift to, 2

municipal officials: in 1870s, 27; during 1880s to 1920s, 16; in 1920s, 66, 78; in 1940s, 66, 69, 78; agrarian reforms and, 95

municipal system: growth by incorporation of independent neighborhoods' water sources and systems, 14, 17; in peripheral neighborhoods, 94

municipal water companies, water rights of, 2

municipal water coverage, 1910 and 1940, 63*m*6

municipal water system: development of, 45; peripheral neighborhoods and, 62. *See also* SEMAPA (Servicio Municipal de Aqua Potable y Alcantarillado)

Murra, John, 7
Muyurina, Bolivia, 63*m*6, 148

National Agrarian Reform Council (CNRA), 90,
    100–101, 117
national government: attacks on *pueblos'* com-
    munal land and water, 28; drinking water
    provisions, 36; irrigation programs of, 54;
    moderization by, 34; national hydraulic
    service, 71; negotiations with private water
    owners, 42–44; negotiations with rural water
    owners, 47; perspectives of, 17; Rivero con-
    troversy, 41–43; water project petitions, 63
National Indigenous Congress of 1945, 51
national political transformation, 10–11; in 1870s,
    16; power to access water under, 16
native (term), xvii
nature: human society and, 11; metabolic interac-
    tion and, 11; role of, 11
negotiations with rural water owners, 14, 17,
    70–72
Negri, Antonio, 202
neighborhood cooperatives, municipalization
    of, 213*f*12
neighborhood systems: purchased water by, 14;
    water sources of, 14
neighborhood water cooperatives, collective
    labor of, 2
neoliberal Bolivia: disputes over, 5; neoliberal
    privatization policies, 3; water privatization
    and war in, 151–94; water rights and, 226
NEP (New Economic Policy), 152
Netherlands-Bolivia Bilateral Trade Agreement
    (BIT), 199
New Economic Policy (NEP), 152
NFR (Nueva Fuerza Republicana), 160, 180, 185
nitrate fields, 8, 28, 30, 47
Nobbs-Thiessen, Ben, 7, 83, 85, 121
noninstitutionality, 4, 233*n*9
nonirrigation parcels, 24
Noreste neighborhood, 93*m*8, 154*m*11
Nueva Fuerza Republicana (NFR), 160, 180, 185

Offner, Amy, 123
oil and gas industries, 175; Coordinadora Nacio-
    nal por la Defensa y Recuperación del Gas,
    204; exports, 131; militarist nationalism and,
    45; privatization and, 3, 4. *See also* Yacimien-
    tos Petrolíferos Fiscales Bolivianos (YPFB)
Olivera, Amador, 170–71
Olivera, Marcela, 188

Olivera, Oscar, 185, 189–90, 199, 199–205,
    200–203, 204, 205, 208, 208–10, 224; as
    spokesperson, 3; on water access, 4, 233*n*10;
    World Bank and IMF protests, 3
open-air canals, use of, 10
Opinión (periodical), 172
Orellana, José, 185
Orellana Aillón, Lorgio, 186
Organizaciones Territoriales de Base (OTBs), 154
organizations for water access, 62–63; formation
    of, 14
originarios (indigenous community members),
    22
Oruro, Bolivia, 6*f*1, 65, 84, 112, 139, 170, 190
Ostrom, Elinor, 14
OTBs (Organizaciones Territoriales de Base), 154
Ovando Candia, Alfredo, 130
ownership rights, 2, 15. *See also* community/
    municipal ownership; democratization of
    governance; democratization of water access;
    under haciendas

Pacata Alta, Bolivia, 93*m*8, 108, 212
Pacata Alta hacienda, 33*f*2, 40–44, 91, 100
Pacata Peasant Union, 100
pachakuti (term), 4
Pachamama, 174, 187, 206
pact of reciprocity, 25
Pacto Militar Campesino (PMC), 116, 132, 144,
    148
PAHO (Pan American Health Organization), 132
Pairumani, Bolivia, 67*m*7
Palenque, Carlos, 154
Palma Chambi, Miguel, 163–64, 188
Panama Canal Zone, 111
Pan American Health Organization (PAHO), 132
Pando, Bolivia, 6*f*1
Pando, José Manuel, 37
Pando province, 230
Paraguay, xix*m*1, 4, 6*f*1, 45, 48
Paredes, Angelo, 186
parliamentary system of government, 28
participation, "right to interrupt" as, 227
Partido de la Izquierda Revolucionaria (PIR),
    60–61, 86
Partido Obrero Revolucionario (POR), 60, 86
Patch, Ricard, 84
Patiño, Simón, 73, 98
patrimony, water privatization and, 175–80
patrones, as beneficiaries of hydraulic infrastruc-
    ture, 1

Pauly, William, 113
payment withholding, 16, 134–35
Payrumani, Bolivia, 22*m*3
Paz Estenssoro, Victor, 60, 81–82, 83, 85, 87, 88*f*5, 111–12, 113, 115, 149–50, 151, 152
Paz Zamora, Jaime, 146, 152, 153, 157, 167
Peasant Affairs Ministry, 86
peasant communities: adaptations of, 10; organizing by, 53; peasant markets, 30; vernacular hydraulic expertise, 14–15
peasants: after Chaco War, 48–49; *arrimantes* (landless rural laborers), 91, 252*n*51; conquest of water during revolution, 14; control over water sources and infrastructure by, 17; democratization of water access and, 5; under military socialism, 51; peasant/miner solidarity, 163; purchase of community land by, 30–31
peasant unions: 1950s agrarian reforms and, 97, 104; attempts to end, 54; Ch'ampa Guerra conflict, 116; Gordillo on, 253*n*83; MAS party and, 4; Misicuni project, 181–82; threats from, 148; unionization of, 54
Peñaranda, Enrique, 54–55, 245*n*39
Pentimalli de Navarro, Michela, 27
Pequenas Lagunas Chankas, 33*f*2
Peredo, Carmen, 173, 186
peripheral neighborhoods: control over water sources and infrastructure by, 17; housing in, 92–93; negotiations of terms of inclusion/exclusion, 14; petitions from, 93; urban citizenship rights fight by, 62; vernacular engineering and, 159–65; water source trading and, 73
periurban neighborhood residents: independent water systems and, 2; popular hydraulic society and, 225; as water owners, 2
periurban neighborhoods: democratization of water access and, 5; independent water systems in, 3; inequalities and, 227; MAS party and, 4; regional water source control by, 13; water committees of, 190; water rates for, 12
Perreault, Thomas, 173
Peru, xix*m*1, 6*f*1, 28
Pinkas, Julio, 42
Pink Tide, 4, 195
piqueros (independent smallholders), 68–69; 1950s agrarian reforms and, 105–6; Angostura project and, 54; communal labor of, 34, 220; control of water sources by, 31; control over water sources and infrastructure by, 17;

defined, xvii; during drought, 26; ex-*colon* communities and, 2; free water project and, 57; *mestizaje* process, 29–30; in Montesillo, 68–69; popular hydraulic society and, 225; protests by, 48, 72, 78, 97; purchase of community land by, 30–31; water reforms and, 90; water rights of, 2; water sources and infrastructure control by, 32, 46–47. *See also* smallholders (*piqueros*)
PIR (Partido de la Izquierda Revolucionaria), 60–61, 86
planning, 13, 14, 15, 227
Plaza, Eduardo and Encarnación, 73, 98
Plaza family, 95
PMC (Pacto Militar Campesino), 116, 132, 144, 148
pongueaje labor system: 254*n*93; abolition of, 50; dams and, 98; manmade lakes and, 1
popular hydraulic society: about, 228; building of, 13, 150; inequality of, 227
Popular Participation Law of 1994, 174
POR (Partido Obrero Revolucionario), 60, 86
Portillo, Benicio, 218
Posada, Bonifacio, 220
Postero, Nancy, 155, 158
Potosí, Bolivia, 6*f*1, 28, 85
Potosí silver mines, 22, 25, 125, 139
Potrero, Bolivia, 22*m*3
power generation industry, 3
Pozo, Delfin, 143
Pozo, Erasmo, 100
Prada, Roberto, 157, 166
prefecture officials: in 1920s, 78; in 1940s, 78
Prensa Libre (periodical), 113, 130, 133, 135
Presa México, 86. *See also* Angostura dam
Presa Reguladora, 33*f*2
Presa Reguladora Lake, 67*m*7
press, 40, 41, 42; complaints in, 62; Rivero controversy, 44; on water treatment, 66. *See also* specific newspapers
Primero de Mayo, 162–64, 187
private firms: *aguateros* (water vendors), 12, 124, 125, 153, 164, 165, 195, 212; government contracts with, 3; water rates from, 12
private property rights: in 1870s, 27; during liberal era, 46
private water ownership: legitimacy of, 43–44, 47, 78; during liberal era, 46; SEMAPA and, 166–67; unequal access and, 79–80
privatization: collective water management and, 33; drought and, 239*n*55; effects on state

power, 47; implications of, 34; increasing of, 227; Morales on, 4; of oil and gas industries, 4; privatization protests, 3; SOEs and, 3; of water ownership, 52. *See also* neoliberal Bolivia; neoliberal privatization policies; water privatization; Water War of 2000

Progressive Cultivators Committee, 105, 106, 109

prohibitions on water use, 64

projects: project disruption, 16; project site occupations, 16; right to oversee and direct, 15

protests, 5; in 1870s, 27; organizing of, 4; over expropriation, 68–69; over privatization, 3; in peripheral neighborhoods, 62; political outcomes of, 4; pro-privatization activists, 3; protestors occupation by, 3. *See also* Water War of 2000

Pro-Vinto Committee, 144

provision of water: collective control of, 13; increasing control of, 227; water rationalization programs and, 226

Prudencio, Eduardo, 76, 111

public water utilities, 2

pueblos reales de indios (resettlement towns), 7, 22–23, 23*m*4, 239*n*54; communal land and water of, 25; during drought, 26; indigenous communities of, 25; liberal era opposition to, 46

Punata, Bolivia, 27

Punata Valley, maximum holdings, 230

Puntiti, Bolivia, 93*m*8

Putucuni River, 114, 138*m*10

Quechua language, 4, 81, 108, 116, 159, 164, 190, 205, 216; *qʼocha pampa* (lake plateau), 234*n*26

Quechua people: *campesino* identity and, 108; descendants of, 89; Quechua-speaking *cochalos*, 162, 163, 164; Quechua-speaking miners, 159, 164; regional indigenous congresses and, 54; social mobilizations of, 250*n*6

Queru Queru, Bolivia, 63*m*6, 93, 93*m*8

Queru Queru Alto neighborhood, 93*m*8, 243*n*143

Quillacollo, Bolivia, 22*m*3, 33*f*2, 67*m*7, 74, 138*m*10, 154*m*11, 166, 169, 184, 186, 190, 215*f*14, 216

Quillacollo Federation of Retired Miners, 186

Quintanilla, Bolivia, 44, 54, 93*m*8, 160, 162

Quiroga, Luis, 71

Quispe, Felipe, 154

Quispe, Rafael, 203

Raffles, Hugh, 33

railroad industry, xix*m*1, 3, 34

rainfall, 7, 8, 31, 46, 237*n*1

Rama, Angel, 60

rate hikes: increasing control of, 227; privatization and, 3; SEMAPA and, 149, 188–89

Rebalses Lake, 103*m*9

Recoleta neighborhood, 243*n*143

redistribution issues: in 1870s, 26; in 1930s, 52; in 1940s, 51, 57, 59, 60–61, 77; in 1950s, 104; access and, 226; resources, 5, 175, 227; wealth redistribution, 227. *See also* Angostura irrigation system

reducciones (resettlement towns), 7, 22–23, 239*n*54

regional policy, hydraulic expertise and, 15, 79

regional water sources: during 1880s to 1920s, 20; collective control of, 16, 20; community control of, 13

Republican Party: during 1880s to 1920s, 28; in 1920s, 39–40; *El Republicano* and, 42; founding of, 31, 39; *indigenismo* under, 39–45; Liberal Party and, 31, 39, 40; rural water monopoly challenges, 40–44

research methodology: organization, 16–17; pseudonym use, 18; sources, 17–18

Revollo, Alfonso, 178

revolutions: in Cuba, 226; language and promises of, 227; leaders of, 226; in Mexico, 226; as processes, 226. *See also* Bolivian Revolution of 1952

Reyes, Isabel, 55

Reyes Villa, Manfred, 158, 175, 176, 177, 179, 180, 185

Reza, José de la, 130

rights. *See* water rights

"right to interrupt," 227

Rio Chutacahua, 103*m*9

Río Khora, 103*m*9

Río Rocha, 9*m*2, 10, 22*m*3, 33*f*2, 54, 63*m*6, 65, 100

Rio Tamborada, 9*m*2, 33*f*2

Rio Taquiña, 103*m*9

Rio Tocayi, 103*m*9

riparian water property rights, 21, 30, 46

ritual practices, 7, 174, 187, 227. *See also* sacredness of water sources

Rivas Antezana, Sinforoso, 98

Rivera Cusicanqui, Silvia, 20, 22, 250*n*6

Rivero, Ramón, 40–44, 65, 66, 100

Rivero controversy, 41–43, 100–101

Rivero Torres, Ricardo, 100–101

Rivero Torres family, 40–44, 91, 100–101
rivers, 103*m*9
road blockades, 16
roads, xix*m*1, 103*m*9; integration of national territory through, 34
Rocha, Federico, 41
Rocha, León, 55
Rocha River, 9*m*2, 33*f*2, 63*m*6, 65, 100
Rodríguez Ostria, Gustavo, 27, 28, 239*n*54
Rojas, Agustin, 188
Roosevelt, Franklin D., 54
Roseberry, William, 15
rotational distribution system, 21
rural collectives, inequalities and, 227
rural communities: regional water source control by, 13; SEMAPA and water sources of, 17; state-led urban water development and, 14; water-sharing agreements, 17
rural elites, water source monopolies, 20
rural environments: state-led urban water development and, 14; urban hydraulic expansion and, 12
rural estate owners. See hacendados (owners)
rural history, about, 16
rural water monopoly: 1920s challenges to, 78; 1940s challenges to, 69, 78, 79; early challenges to, 21; as illegitimate, 66; Liberal challenges to, 40, 47; Republican challenges to, 40–44, 47; technocratic water reform, 79
rural water owners: challenging of, 47; forced negotiations with urban officials, 14
rural water supply, protest against inequality in, 49
rural water users, urban hydraulic expansion and, 12

Saavedra, Bautista, 39–40
Saavedra Antezana, Carlos, 53, 54, 59–60, 73, 76, 78, 110, 126, 244*n*22
Sacaba, Bolivia, 22*m*3, 74, 138*m*10, 154*m*11, 184
Sacaba Valley, Cochabamba, Bolivia, 8, 9*m*2, 90, 96, 97, 100, 191, 230
Sacaba water services, municipalization plan, 213*f*12
Sachs, Jeffrey, 152
sacredness of water sources, 4, 7, 79, 89, 187, 201, 233*n*10. See also ritual practices
safety: redistribution issues and, 20, 227; of wells, 148
Salamanca, Daniel, 31, 39, 45, 48, 68, 70
Salamanca, Hernán, 70
Salamanca, Jorge, 70

Salamanca, José Domingo, 31, 32
Salamanca, Laura, 70
Salamanca, Leonor, 70
Salamanca, Manuela, 70
Salamanca, Rafael, 68–69, 70, 104, 247*n*102
Salamanca, Raquel, 70, 248*n*115
Salamanca family, 31, 32, 69, 70–72, 78, 247*n*102
Salazár, Jesús, 160
Salinas Aramayo, Carlos, 53
San Antonio neighborhood, 39
Sánchez, Luis, 199
Sánchez Ayala, Juan, 188–89, 192
Sánchez Bustamante, Daniel, 29
Sánchez de Lozada, Gonzalo, 152, 155, 167, 170, 175–76, 177–78, 180, 203, 204
Sánchez de Lozada, Vicente, 65
Sánchez Gómez, Luis, 198
San Ignacio Lake, 67*m*7, 92, 103*m*9
sanitation: redistribution issues and, 227; rights of urban poor to, 14
Sanjinés, Alfredo, 50, 52–53, 57–58, 59–60, 244*n*21
Sanjinés, Oscar, 112
San Juan Lake: about, 1, 33*f*2, 67*m*7; dam and channeling waters from, 32; SEMAPA and, 214, 218. See also San Juan Lakes
San Juan Lakes: 1950s agrarian reforms and, 92, 95, 98–100; dam and channeling waters from, 32; ownership rights, 2, 32, 33, 73, 95, 102, 218, 225; problems after reforms, 108, 218, 219. See also San Pablito Lake
San Juan Lakes Water Users Society (Sociedad de Explotación de las Aguas de las Lagunas de San Juan), 32, 98
San Milán, Freddy, 221
San Pablito Lake: about, 1, 33*f*2, 67*m*7; dam and channeling waters from, 32; SEMAPA and, 214, 218. See also San Juan Lakes
San Pedro Hill, 162
San Pedro Tank, 37*m*5
San Sebastián neighborhood, 39, 41*f*3
Santa Cruz, Bolivia, 6*f*1, 54, 139, 171
Santa Vera Cruz, 164
Santiago del Passo, Bolivia, 22
Santiváñez, José María, 28
Sarco, Bolivia, 22*m*3, 63*m*6, 93*m*8
Sarcobamba neighborhood, 93*m*8
Saytukocha Lake, 32, 33*f*2, 67*m*7, 92, 103*m*9, 138; 1950s agrarian reforms and, 95, 108; damming of, 102
Saytukocha system, 103*m*9, 148

School of the Americas, 111

Scott, James, 12, 27

SEMAPA (Servicio Municipal de Aqua Potable y Alcantarillado): access to rural communities water sources, 17; conflicts with, 137, 142, 144–45; controls of, 126; deep well drilling, 141–42, 143, 156; democractic control of, 148; early operation of, 148; El Paso resident protest against, 215*f*14; FEJUVE and, 147; founding of, 102, 127, 148; Hartley scandal, 147; hydraulic development and, 17; hydraulic studies and project plans and, 17; ICSID and, 199; IDB funding and, 146, 148–49; Misicuni project, 140, 143, 145, 156–57; peripheral neighborhoods and, 159–65; rate hikes, 149, 188–89; reforms of, 197–99; refounding, 196–99, 223, 224; water privatization and, 175–80; water rates and, 127–36, 152; water rationing, 148; water rights of, 1; water-sharing agreements, 17; water source access by, 17; well-drilling program conflicts, 165–75; World Bank and, 156

Sen, Amartya, 19

SENARI (Servicio Nacional de Riego), 197

SERGEOMIN (Servicio Geológico Minero), 169

Servicio Geológico Minero (SERGEOMIN), 169

Servicio Nacional de Riego (SENARI), 197

SEURECA, 156

sewerage: access to, 35; improvement of, 34; municipalization of, 76–77; urban growth and, 62, 76

Sherbondy, Jeanette, 7, 21

Shesko, Elizabeth, 34, 116

Shipman, Harold, 128

Shiva, Vandana, 201

shortages: 1960s protests over, 124–25; in peripheral neighborhoods, 62

Siglo XX mine, 97, 125, 145

Siles Zuazo, Hernán, 60, 83, 115, 116, 146, 151

silver mines, 8, 28, 36, 60, 139

Sipe Sipe, Bolivia, 22*m*3, 67*m*7, 156, 168, 169, 170–72, 186; colonial-era *pueblos reales de indios*, 22, 23*m*4; protestors, 170*f*9; Soras people of, 21

Sirpita, Bolivia, 93*m*8, 103*m*9

SISAB (Superintendencia de Sanitación Básica), 155, 183, 197

smallholders (*piqueros*): during 1880s to 1920s, 16, 20; 1950s agrarian reforms and, 105–6;

collective water management practices, 20; communal labor of, 34; control of water sources by, 31; droughts and, 26; growth of, 25; negotiations with national government, 55, 56; popular hydraulic society and, 225; purchase of community land by, 31; purchase of hacienda land, 31; support of, 28; water rights of, 2; water source needs of, 2

smelting industry, 3

sobras (excess water rights), 24, 25–26

social justice: Cochabambinos and, 228; visions of hydraulic justice, 17; water rationalization programs and, 153–59, 226. *See also* hydraulic justice

social mobilizations, 10–11, 205; democratization of water access and, 16; factors contributing to, 4; Water War of 2000 and, 203–6, 223, 224. *See also* Coordinadora de Defensa del Agua y de la Vida (Coordinating Committee for the Defense of Water and Life); FEDECOR (Federación Departamental Cochabambina de Organizaciones Regantes)

social struggles, 14; legacy of, 17; militant class conflict, 47; nationalist feelings, 47; over drinking water, 10; over irrigation, 10; over local water policy, 16; over national water policy, 16; union organization, 47

social utility, 51–52

Sociedad de Explotación de las Aguas de las Lagunas de San Juan (San Juan Lakes Water Users Society), 32

SOFRELEC (Sté Fréjusienne d'Électricité), 139

Solares, Humberto, 75, 123–24

solidarity, 227

Soliz, Carmen, 107, 252*n*38

Solón, Pablo, 208

Soras people, 21

Soriano Badani, Eduardo, 114

Soruco, Alejandro, 41–42, 44

Southern Periphery, 154*m*11

Spaniards: disproportionate water rights, 23, 24, 25; land appropriation by, 25

Spanish ancestry: mestizo identity and, 29, 107. *See also* creoles

Spanish Empire: conquest and colonization by, 21–22, 107; General Resettlement, 7, 22–23, 239*n*54; irrigation projects, 8; water dispossession under, 23–25, 107; water laws of, 24–25, 30, 32; water tenure relations under, 16. *See also hacendados* (owners); Potosí silver mines

Spanish language, 190, 216, 218
Special Security Forces, 191
springs system(s), 103m9; in 1870s, 35–36; Aguas de Arocagua, 35–36; in peripheral neighborhoods, 93; use of, 8
Stadel, Christoph, 5
Sté Fréjusienne d'Électricité (SOFRELEC), 139
Stites Mor, Jessica, 210
subaltern communities, 15–16, 236n67
subsistence ethic, 27
Sucre, Bolivia, 27, 28, 36, 54, 70, 114
Sud Zud, 191
Suez (French water company), 204
Sulti River. See Tamborada River
Sumunpaya hacienda, 31
Superintendencia de Sanitación Básica (SISAB), 155, 183, 197
Sureste neighborhood, 93m8
Suroeste neighborhood, 93m8
suyus (agricultural land), 21, 25

También la lluvia (Even the Rain) (1999 film), 182
Tamborada, Bolivia, 67m7
Tamborada River, 9m2, 33f2, 53
tank storage, 10
Tapacarí, Bolivia, 23m4
Tapacari River, 9m2
Taquiña, Bolivia, 67m7, 67–68, 93m8, 161, 220, 247n107
Taquiña hacienda, 33f2
Taquiña Lake, 67m7
Taquiña River, 103m9, 161
Tarata, Bolivia, 27
Tardío family, 162
Tarija, Bolivia, 6f1, 85, 139
taxes: chicha taxes, 64; Tax War, 205
technocratic water reform: in 1940s, 12, 50, 57, 79, 132–33; in 1950s, 86
Tejada Sorzano, José, 45, 49
telecommunications industry, 3
Temporalpampa neighborhood, 93m8
Tennessee Valley Authority (TVA). See TVA (Tennessee Valley Authority)
Terceros, Gonzalo "Chaly," 160
Terceros, Oscar, 158
terminology, xvii–xviii
Terrazas, Ana María, 35–36, 37, 41–42, 43
Ticti neighborhood, 93m8
tin mines: decline in exports from, 39, 54; Liberal Party and, 36; migrants from, 47; miners

mobilization, 82, 97–98; Patiño, Simón, 98; price collapse and, 45; tin boom, 28, 131
Tiquipaya, Bolivia, 22m3, 33f2, 67m7, 93m8, 102, 169, 173–74, 174, 220–21; 1950s agrarian reforms and, 105, 112–13; colonial-era pueblos reales de indios, 22, 23m4; haciendas and irrigation systems, 103m9
Tirani, Bolivia, 93m8
Tirani community: 1950s agrarian reforms and, 98; communal labor of, 32–33, 218–19; maintenance by, 1–3; ongoing work of, 225; peasant unions, 1; Tirani colonos, 98; Water War of 2000 and, 2–3
Tirani hacienda, 33f2, 95
Tiwanaku, 83, 206
Tocayi River, 103m9
Tolata protest, 132
Toledo, Francisco de, Viceroy of Spain, 7, 22–23, 239n54
top-down approach, 11, 74, 198, 235n54, 250n6
topography of Bolivia, 6f1
Toro, David, 49, 65
Torolaguna Lake, 33f2, 67m7, 70
Torres, Juan de la Cruz, 37
Torres, Juan José, 130, 139, 161
Torrez, Santiago, 161
Torrico, Graciela, 100
Totora Lake, 103m9
trade, 7
transnational history, about, 16
transportation: redistribution issues and, 227; rights of urban poor to, 14
Triangular Plan, 115
tribute requirements, 7; hacendados benefit from, 24; mestizaje process, 25; migration to escape, 24
Trotsky, Leon, 244n21
Tunari Mountains, 1, 9m2, 15, 67m7, 138m10; 1950s agrarian reforms and, 109; Corani Lake, 76; glaciers of, 10; irrigation sources from, 57; lakes in, 45; Misicuni project, 114, 121, 136–41, 149; Salamanca's haciendas in, 32; water expansion projects in, 20. See also Chapisirca Lakes
Tupac Katari Guerilla Army, 4
Tupuraya, Bolivia, 63m6, 93, 93m8, 109
turn rights, 31
Turuni Lake, 33f2
TVA (Tennessee Valley Authority), 12–13

UCS (Unidad Cívica Solidaridad), 154, 160, 180

Ucureña, Bolivia, 81, 88f5
UDP (Unidad Democrática y Popular), 146
UMSS (Universidad Mayor de San Simón), 169
Unidad Cívica Solidaridad (UCS), 154, 160, 180
Unidad Democrática y Popular (UDP), 146
unionization. *See* peasant unions
United Nations, 167, 208, 262n133
United States: Alliance for Progress, 115; Banzer administration and, 130; Barrientos and, 117; Bolivian debt crisis and, 146; development aid, 115; Good Neighbor Policy, 54; International Seminar in Support of SEMAPA, 198; US Bureau of Indian Affairs, 58; US Latin America policy, 111–12; Washington Consensus, 123; "Water for All" challenge, 10
Unity Pact, 206–7
Universidad Mayor de San Simón (UMSS), 169
urban centers: migration to, 7; regional water source control by, 13
urban development: 1870s droughts and, 20, 35–36; *hacendados* purchases and, 72–73
urban expansions, 12, 61–63, 63m6
urban officials: 1870s mobilization by, 21; progressive, 35
urban peripheral neighborhoods: democratization of water access and, 5; MAS party and, 4; urban citizenship rights fight by, 14
urban residents: during 1880s to 1920s, 16, 20, 47; collective water management practices, 20; democratization of water access and, 5; landlords and, 26; occupations of, 16; progressive, 35; range of access to water of, 17; state-led urban water development and, 14; water access gains and, 226; water reforms and, 91; water scarcity and, 10; water source needs of, 2
urban water access, hydraulic infrastructure projects and, 49–50
urban water development: in liberal era, 34–39; private water owners and, 40–44; Rivero controversy, 40–44; threats to rural communities and environments, 14; threats to urban poor, 14
urban water supply: expansion of, 20, 40–42; improvement of, 34; municipalization plan for, 72–78; protest against inequality in, 49
urban water system, effects of drought on, 34
urban workers: after Chaco War, 48–49; after revolution, 82
Urquidi, Arturo, 86
Urquidi, Jorge, 73, 74, 75, 76, 78

Urquidi, Ricardo, 64
Uruguay, Pink Tide and, 4, 195
use-value approach, 79
usos y costumbres rights, 173, 181–82, 197, 274n82
Uspa Uspa neighborhood, 93m8, 103m9
U.S. Steel, 130
usufruct rights, 1, 29
Uzin, Luis, 189

Valdivieso, Antonio, 137
Valle Alto, 8, 9m2, 27, 53, 54, 81, 84, 90, 107, 116, 132, 138m10, 184, 191
Valle Bajo, 8, 9m2, 21, 23, 29, 31, 90, 96, 97, 156, 169, 171, 172, 180–81, 184, 186, 191, 239n54
Valle Hermoso, Bolivia, 74, 93m8, 162, 164
valley lands, 5, 6f1, 8, 230
Vargas, Humberto, 189
Vargas, Julio, 215, 216, 218
Vargas, Policarpo and Liboria, 68
Vázquez del Mercado, Francisco, 50, 53, 58
Vega, Severo, 131–34
Veizaga Guevara, Miguel, 107
Velarde, Cesar Suarez, 219
Velasco, Javier, 164
Venezuela, Pink Tide and, 4, 195
Vera, Ambrosio, 38
vernacular environmental governance, 13–14, 16, 235n52. *See also* collective water management practices; governance of water access
vernacular hydraulic expertise, 14–15, 235n58
vernacular modernism, 15, 35
verticality, 7, 10, 23
Viedma, Franciso de, 8, 10
Villa Busch neighborhood, 93m8, 114
Villa Galindo neighborhood, 94
Villa Pagador, 162, 164, 186
Villarroel Claure, Ramiro, 60, 112, 245n39
Villa Sebastián Pagador, 162
Viloma, Bolivia, 22m3
Vinteños, 144–45, 169
Vinto, Bolivia, 22m3, 67m7, 121, 138m10, 141–45, 148, 156, 165, 168, 169, 170–72, 170f9, 174, 180, 184, 186
Viscachas River, 114, 138m10
Vitz, Matthew, 57, 244n12
vivir bien principle, 206

Wara Wara Lake, 67m7, 92, 213–14, 218, 255n105; 1950s agrarian reforms and, 95, 100–102; rebuilding dam of, 102, 141, 213, 214f13
War of the Pacific, 28, 30, 36, 45

War of the Wells of 1977, 141–45
Washington Consensus, 123
water access: collective labor and, 7; demands for after Chaco War, 49; democratization of, 2, 38; equitable distribution of, 20; expansion of, 16; governance of, 2; *hacendados* gains in, 24; increasing demand for, 46; inequality in, 20, 40–42, 62, 124; rights of urban poor to, 14, 35; ritual practices and, 7; segregated systems of, 38–39. *See also* access to water
Water and Sanitation Service Providers (EPSAs), 196–97
Water and Sanitation Superintendency (SISAB), 155, 183, 197
"Water for All" challenge, 10, 79–80, 225–28
water holdings, of *pueblos reales de indios*, 25, 28
water management: experiments in, 225; Inca dual system of, 21; tensions over, 226
water meters, 64
water ownership: in 1870s, 16; associations, 89; growth after revolution, 2; inequality of, 79; privatization of, 52
water privatization: in 1980s, 153–59; Aguas del Illimani South America (AISA) and, 204; Aguas del Tunari, 180–85; global protests against, 3; in neoliberal era, 151–53; patrimony and, 175–80; vernacular engineering and, 159–65; water sector rationalization, 153–59, 226; Water War of 2000, 185–93
water provision: approaches to, 226–27; expansion of control over, 16. *See also* Aguas del Tunari
water rates: increasing control of, 227; negotiations for, 71; privatization and, 3; rate hikes, 149, 188–89; SEMAPA and, 127–36, 152
water rationalization, 153–59, 226
water rationing, 148
water reform: after Chaco War, 48–49; gains and limits of, 225; hydraulic infrastructure projects and, 50; Mexican model of, 50–51; technocratic approach, 12, 50, 57, 79, 86, 132–33. *See also* hydraulic development
water regulation of 1879, 31, 46
water rights: collective labor and, 2, 5, 21; competing and differing, 13; expropriation and, 68–69; flexibility and, 227; *hacendados* and, 20, 32; hacienda *colonos* winning of, 2; irrigation turn rights, 31; land ownership and, 21; private firms and, 3; reallocation of, 227; under Republican administrations, 39–45

water scarcity: Misicuni project and, 156–57; MNR and, 110; protest(s) over, 47, 61–64, 69, 78; technocratic approach to, 65; urban population increase and, 10
water-sharing agreements, 17, 98–99
water sources: control of, 5, 12, 13, 17, 20, 31, 227; democratization of, 227; in early 20th century, 33*f*2; efforts to increase urban, 34; equitable distribution of, 227; *hacendados* (owners) and, 21, 24, 32–33, 33*f*2, 40–44, 70; hoarding of, 2, 21, 47; land dispossession and, 21; managing of, 227; MAS party and, 4; municipal water system and, 45; peripheral neighborhoods and, 73; pressure increase on, 10; rights to, 1, 13, 227; rural elites and, 20; sacredness of, 4, 7, 79, 89, 187, 201, 233*n*10; in Spanish colonial era, 21, 23–24; trading of, 73; urban officials and, 14; water seizures, 16. *See also* Aguas del Tunari; water rights
water systems: building of, 227; control over, 17; labor-produced knowledge of, 5; managing of, 227; MAS party and, 4; planning of, 227; water sector rationalization, 153–59, 226. *See also* independent water systems
water tenure ownership: 1950s agrarian reforms and, 95; in early Bolivian republic, 16; in precolonial era, 16; reforms to, 78; under Spanish Empire, 16; transformation of, 5; water sector rationalization and, 153–59, 226
Water War of 2000, 5, 185–93, 192*f*10, 194*f*11, 227; aftermath of, 17, 195–96; global effects of, 3, 199–203; Morales administration, 211–23, 224; Morales and, 4, 17, 196, 203, 223; organizing of, 2–3; outcomes of, 3, 4; refounding SEMAPA, 196–99, 223, 224; social mobilization and, 203–6, 223, 224; water governance after, 206–11, 223, 224; water users' efforts and, 17
Webber, Jeffery, 3
wells: artesian wells, 10, 38, 93, 125; ecology of, 165–75; use of, 10
West Germany, 113, 122
White, Richard, 5
Willka, Zárate, 37
Winchell, Mareike, 104
Wittfogel, Karl, 11–12
Wolfe, Michael, 245*n*53
Wolfensohn, James, 200
Woods, Ngaire, 146
World Bank, 3, 4, 122–23, 128, 149, 153, 155–58,

162, 164, 166–67, 169, 171, 175–80, 183, 193, 199–201, 204

Worster, Donald, 11–12

Yacimientos Petrolíferos Fiscales Bolivianos (YPFB), 135, 142–43, 144, 145, 152

Yacupaico, Guadalupe, 160

Yanez, Esteban, 162, 187

Yankovic, Esteban, 55–56

Young, Kevin, 49, 85, 175

YPFB (Yacimientos Petrolíferos Fiscales Bolivianos), 135, 142–43, 144, 145, 152

yungas, 6f1

Yungas subzone, maximum holdings in, 229, 230

Yupanqui, Emperor of the Incas, 21

Zalles, Raul, 110

Zapkovic, Antonio, 55–56

Zavaleta Mercado, René, 48

Zibechi, Raúl, 201–2

Zimmerer, Karl, 25, 88, 234n29

Zimmerman, Antonio, 69, 70

Zinn, Howard, 228, 276n7

Zola River, 85

Zona Norte, Bolivia, 63m6, 95, 126, 136, 191

Zona Sud, Bolivia, 39, 62, 63m6, 92, 94, 109, 110, 124, 133, 135, 147, 158, 159, 161, 162, 164–65, 171, 175, 181, 185, 186, 198, 211–12, 216

Founded in 1893,
UNIVERSITY OF CALIFORNIA PRESS
publishes bold, progressive books and journals
on topics in the arts, humanities, social sciences,
and natural sciences—with a focus on social
justice issues—that inspire thought and action
among readers worldwide.

The UC PRESS FOUNDATION
raises funds to uphold the press's vital role
as an independent, nonprofit publisher, and
receives philanthropic support from a wide
range of individuals and institutions—and from
committed readers like you. To learn more, visit
ucpress.edu/supportus.

Made in the USA
Monee, IL
11 March 2023

29685206R00204